P9-AFD-373

BOWMAN LIBRARY
MENLO SCHOOL AND MENLO COLLEGE

c71

To write this significant reappraisal of the life and works of a great Elizabethan, who was in love with living and learning, the author personally examined every known original document bearing on Marlowe. Among the exciting new manuscript sources reported upon here for the first time are the Buttery Book of Corpus Christi, Cambridge, covering six years of Marlowe's university life, including the "lost" year; the last will of his murderer; his father's only known signature; and a series of documents throwing light on his university and home life, as well as on the social conditions of his time and the lives of his friends and associates. An extensive Bibliography, Appendices, Notes, and an Index are included.

ABOUT THE AUTHOR

John Bakeless is a distinguished American author, teacher, journalist, and lecturer. He holds a Harvard doctorate in English, a Harvard M.A., and a Williams B.A. in philosophy. He has been New York correspondent for the *Manchester Guardian,* editor of *The Living Age,* literary editor of *The Digest,* and assistant professor of journalism at New York University. A scholar in every sense of the word, Mr. Bakeless is also a magnificent writer.

CHRISTOPHER MARLOWE was originally published by William Morrow and Company.

Christopher MARLOWE

The Man in His Time

John Bakeless

WS P

WASHINGTON SQUARE PRESS, INC. • NEW YORK

CHRISTOPHER MARLOWE: The Man in His Time

William Morrow edition published November, 1937
A *Washington Square Press* edition
1st printing..........................July, 1964

A new edition of a distinguished literary work now made available in an inexpensive, well-designed format

L

Published by
Washington Square Press, Inc., 630 Fifth Avenue, New York, N.Y.

WASHINGTON SQUARE PRESS editions are distributed in the U.S. by Affiliated Publishers, a division of Pocket Books, Inc., 630 Fifth Avenue, New York 20, N.Y.

Copyright, ©, 1937, by John Bakeless. All rights reserved. This Washington Square Press edition is published by arrangement with William Morrow and Company, Inc. Printed in the U.S.A.

For

Katherine Little Bakeless

"You I must and will memorize more especially, for you recompence learning extraordinarilie. Pardon my presumption, lend patience to my prolixitie, and if anything at all please, thinke it was compiled to please you."

THOMAS NASHE

Acknowledgments

I owe a special debt of gratitude to Professor George Lyman Kittredge, of Harvard University, whom I have had the privilege of consulting personally at every stage of the research since it began seventeen years ago. Professor C. F. Tucker Brooke, of Yale University, has aided me in finding obscure material, has lent photostats and other material from his personal collections, and has responded cordially and promptly to innumerable appeals for aid. Professor John Livingston Lowes, of Harvard University, has not only been a constant source of encouragement but has guided me to materials which without his aid I should have missed entirely. The late Professor Beverly Sprague Allen, of New York University, suggested a great many critical ideas of which I have freely availed myself. Mr. Mark Eccles, of the University of Wisconsin, whose brilliant discoveries have recently added so much to our knowledge of Marlowe's London life, has read and criticized the entire manuscript. Professor John Tucker Murray, of Harvard University, aided materially by criticizing the new material relating to the sources of *Tamburlaine*.

Such a study as this naturally owes a great deal to librarians. Dr. T. F. Jones, Director of the General Library of New York University; the late Miss Elizabeth Haseltine and Mr. Mulford Martin, librarians of the Commerce Library, New York University; Miss Ermine Stone and Miss Frances Kemp of the Sarah Lawrence College Library have helped me constantly over a period of several years in gathering information from American, British, and European libraries.

At Corpus Christi College, Cambridge, every possible facility has been granted to me. The Master, Dr. Will Spens, personally aided in the search for documents. The Estates Bursar, Mr. T. R. B. Sanders, gave me free access to the college archives in the strongroom of the Estates Bursary and all the help and encouragement in the power of himself and his staff. The late Sir Edwyn Hoskyns, Bart., Librarian, permitted the use of the manuscript and other books of the Parker Bequest.

Dr. R. L. Ramsay, Master of Magdalene, kindly permitted examination of two rare Marlowes in the Pepysian Collection, one of which has not hitherto been listed. Mr. H. S. Bennett, Librarian of Emmanuel, allowed me to examine the copy of Marlowe's Ovid there preserved and volunteered to criticize my study of the sources of *The Massacre at Paris*. Mr. H. M. Adams, Librarian of Trinity, placed all the resources of his especially rich collections at my disposal. Mr. Donald Paige, of the Gonville and Caius Library, aided in establishing the provenance of an important book by means of his unique collection of binders' ornaments.

In the University Library, Cambridge, Mr. H. L. Pink, Mr. Criswick, Mr. D. G. Harrison, and Mr. H. R. Mallett took endless pains to meet every request; and in the University Registry, Mr. William J. Baker, Registrary's Clerk, and his staff searched the archives to find the documents needed.

Dr. J. A. Venn, President of Queen's, interrupted his vacation to aid me with a difficult problem in the records; deciphered a passage in the Buttery Book of Corpus Christi which had defied all other paleographers; and lent his exhaustive knowledge of Cambridge antiquities to clearing up one doubtful point after another.

At Oxford, Mr. E. Lobel deciphered correctly a manuscript which had defied all other paleographers; Mr. J. R. Liddell and Mr. Ian G. Philip, of the Bodleian Library, submitted to a running fire of questions with admirable grace; and Dr. M. R. Ridley, Fellow of Balliol, made a number of useful suggestions.

In London, officials of the British Museum, Public Record Office, and Somerset House did everything in their power to facilitate my work. I am especially indebted to Mr. Noel Blakiston and Mr. J. R. Crompton, of the Public Record Office, for assistance in untangling Elizabethan legal procedure and in deciphering and interpreting the more difficult documents. Mr. M. Minovi assisted me with Persian documents which I was unable to read for myself.

In Canterbury Mr. W. P. Blore, Librarian of the Cathedral Library, and Mr. Frank W. Tyler, Deputy Librarian, gave generously of their time and knowledge; the Rev. Canon F. J. Shirley, Headmaster of the King's School, lent every possible assistance; the Rev. Geoffrey Keable, Rector of the Church of St. George the Martyr, gave me free access to the parish records; Mrs. Dorothy Gardiner cleared up by her expert knowledge of Canterbury antiquities a number of puzzles; and Mr. H. T. Mead, Librarian of the Royal Museum and Public Library, gave me the privileges of honorary staff membership while working in the municipal archives now in his care.

It is a further pleasure to acknowledge assistance with various details of the investigation from scholars and librarians throughout the world, especially Dr. J. Q. Adams and Dr. Giles Dawson of the Folger Shakespeare Library, Washington; Mr. W. B. Briggs, Mr. George Parker Winship, and the staff of the Harvard College Library; Mr. C. K. Edmonds and the staff of the Huntington Library; Mr. Milton E. Lord and the staff of the Boston Public Library; Mr. Roger Howson and the staff of the Columbia University Library; Mr. Valta Parma, Mr. Linn R. Blanchard, and Miss Jessica L. Farnum, of the Library of Congress; the staff of the New York Public Library; Mr. Gilbert C. Troxell, of the Yale University Library; Miss Lilla Weed, of the Wellesley College Library; Miss Ruth Granniss, of the Grolier Club Library; Miss Lucy Eugenia Osborne, of the Chapin Library, Williams College; Miss Belle da Costa Greene, of the Pierpont Morgan Library; Mr. Cyril H. Wilkinson, of the Worcester College Library; Dr. O. Wilsengren and Mr. R. Ericksson, of the Kungliga Biblioteket, Stockholm; Dr. Menn, of the Greifswald University Library; Dr. Wilhelm Hopf, of the Kassel Landesbibliothek; Mr. George Dobbin Brown, of the Enoch Pratt Free Public Library, Baltimore; the authorities of the K. K. Realschule, Vienna; Dr. F. Herič, of the Public and University Library, Prague; Dr. Samuel A. Tannenbaum, of New York City; Professor J. L. Hotson, of Haverford College; Dr. A. S. W. Rosenbach, of New York and Philadelphia; Mr. A. Edward Newton, of Philadelphia; Professor T. W. Baldwin, of the University of Illinois; Professor T. M. Parrott, of Princeton University; Mr. G. H. W. Rylands, Fellow of King's College, Cambridge; the late Frank Brewer Bemis, of Boston, Mass.; Mr. Percy Simpson, of Oriel College, Oxford; Dr. Douglas Bush, of the University of Minnesota; Mr. Owen D. Young, of New York, and his librarian, Miss Sarah Dickson; Mr. Robert Garrett, of Baltimore; Mr. Henry Guppy, of the

John Rylands Library, Manchester; the Rt. Rev. Provost Michael J. Burns, Roman Catholic rector of Axminster, Devon; the Rev. Canon Edwin Henson, rector of the Colegio de Ingleses, Valladolid; Miss Henrietta C. Bartlett, of New Haven; Dr. G. B. Harrison, of King's College, London; Mr. F. C. Owlett, of London; Mr. W. Beattie, of the National Library of Scotland; Mr. P. J. Dobell, of Tunbridge Wells; Mr. H. M. Riley, of the Public Libraries, Leicester; Mr. Barnet J. Beyer, of New York; Professor A. V. Williams Jackson, of Columbia University; Mr. Charles Retz and Mr. Arthur Swann, of the American Art Galleries, New York; Mr. Naboth Hedin, of the American-Swedish News Exchange; Mr. A. Van de Put, former librarian, and Mr. Philip James, the present librarian of the Victoria and Albert Museum; Mr. William A. Jackson, of New York City; Miss Elizabeth K. Steele, of the Detroit Public Library; Dr. Wilhelm von Scholz, of Konstanz; Mrs. Bertha B. Bandler, of New York; Mr. George B. Arents, of New York, and his librarian, Mr. Jerome E. Brooks; Mr. John E. Hannigan, of Boston; Mrs. J. William Hebel, of Ithaca; Mr. B. H. Newdigate, of the Shakespeare Head Press, Oxford; Dr. B. A. P. Van Dam, of The Hague; Mr. Hiroshi Kawai and Mr. Masao Nagasawa, of the Tokyo Imperial Library; and the late T. J. Wise, veteran among British bibliographers.

Without their aid in finding obscure or rare volumes, checking bibliographical data, and photographing manuscripts and rare books, my own work would have been impossible.

J. B.

Foreword

Our knowledge of Christopher Marlowe's life has increased enormously in the last ten or twelve years, thanks to the researches of Professor C. F. Tucker Brooke, Professor J. L. Hotson, Mr. Mark Eccles, Miss Ethel Seaton, Miss Eugenie de Kalb, Miss U. M. Ellis-Fermor, Mr. Ford K. Brown, and others. But their results have hitherto been scattered in various special studies dealing only with isolated aspects of Marlowe's life and works; and, except for Professor Brooke's admirable but highly condensed introduction to Professor R. H. Case's edition of the *Works,* there has been no single definitive life of Marlowe. In fact, there has been no book at all dealing in detail with Marlowe's life and works as a whole, since John H. Ingram's study, published in 1904.

I have tried to bring together here all that is really important in three hundred and fifty years' discussion of Marlowe and his writings; to verify everything from original sources; and, where possible, to add new and previously undiscovered material of my own. The book is not, therefore, a mere compilation of the work of others. It reveals for the first time the existence of the Buttery Book of Corpus Christi College, which gives a week-by-week record of six years of Marlowe's life, including the unknown year for which the scholarship accounts are silent. It also reveals the actual document providing for Marlowe's scholarship at Corpus Christi, the conditions of which have hitherto been known only by the ingenious (and entirely correct) deductions of Mr. G. C. Moore Smith; attempts to trace the actual volumes which Marlowe read in preparation for his plays, many of which seem still to be on Cambridge shelves; provides six new documents relating to Marlowe's family life in Canterbury; reveals new evidence of Canterbury and Cambridge influence in the plays; suggests new source material for four of the plays; supplies the first exhaustive check list of extant copies of early editions of Marlowe's plays and poems; makes a more careful study of the social background of the three stages of his life in Canterbury, Cambridge, and London; and makes available for the first time a good deal of other new documentary material which it would be tedious to list here and which can readily be traced in the notes.

All of the manuscript discoveries and many of the other discoveries were made possible by the award of a fellowship by the John Simon Guggenheim Memorial Foundation, which enabled me to spend seven months in various British archives, checking known facts by the original documents and using them as a means to uncover entirely new facts.

Acknowledgments to the scholars who have lent of their time and learning in my aid are too numerous to be made here but are listed in a special section.

JOHN BAKELESS

New York, N. Y.
June 16, 1937

Contents

Acknowledgments	vii
Foreword	xi
1. *The Mind of Marlowe*	1
2. *A Shoemaker's Son*	9
3. *The King's Scholar*	21
4. *"Learning's Golden Gifts"*	35
5. *Archbishop's Bounty*	50
6. *"His Faithful Dealing"*	61
7. *London and Fame*	70
8. *A Young Career*	83
9. *"The Watch Strikes"*	103
10. *Bloody, Bold, and Resolute*	124
11. *A Great Play Botched*	138
12. *Maturity Achieved*	151
13. *Friends and Foes*	158
14. *"Stabd with a Dagger"*	179
15. *Poetic Interludes*	197
16. *"Marlowe's Mighty Line"*	210
17. *Marlowe's Influence*	235
18. *Marlowe and His Books*	251
Appendix A	267
Appendix B	281
Bibliography	285
Notes	295
Index	315

Christopher Marlowe:
The Man in His Time

1.

The Mind of Marlowe

> "And this the man that in his study sits."
> *Doctor Faustus*

Christopher Marlowe was a man of the Renaissance, in love with life and equally in love with the world in which he lived it. He loved beauty. He also loved learning; and being a true son of his time, he was wise enough to know that there is no conflict between them. He had the versatility of the Elizabethan. The foremost playwright of the day, he was also a valued secret agent of the Queen's government. The author of exquisite lyric verse, he was a ruffling bravo before whom the police quailed, skilled with sword and dagger and entirely willing to use them. A learned "scholler" of Cambridge University, he was also the most popular playwright of the hour.

It is conventional to say that we know little of the lives of Elizabethan playwrights and poets. Compared with the often superabundant detail in which it is possible to follow the lives of more recent literary figures, that is no doubt true. Yet we do not really lack much genuinely important knowledge that would help us to understand Christopher Marlowe. We have —granting some certain and other hypothetical losses—the main portion of his work. We know the social conditions under which he and his ancestors lived, the conditions, the very details of his education, and at least one biographical fact of importance for almost every twelvemonth of his brief but flaming career. We even have the record of his careless table talk, when wine was flowing, taken down by careful government spies.

Out of all the odds and ends of information about him that chance has preserved for us, there emerges a curiously consistent picture of a man. The plays, with their gorgeously ornamented, often over-ornamented, language and their quenchless yearning for the unattainable; the purely physical beauty of the verse, which to Marlowe's foes was a mere "drumming decasyllabon" and to his friends was the "mighty line"; the love of splendour that displays itself alike in Doctor Faustus's eagerness to "fill the publike schooles with silk," and in the very odd theology which holds that Roman Catholicism is the best religion "because the service of god is performed with more Cerimonies"[1]—everything reveals a richly sensuous nature, in love with all external beauty.

Marlowe's early friction with the University authorities; the duel with William Bradley; Thomas Kydd's loud complaints of his fiery temper;[2] the terrified appeal of the Shoreditch police for protection against the poet; the final quarrel in which he lost his life—all these display in Marlowe's personal life the same fiery, passionate mind that reveals itself in the plays and poems.

The bluntness which asserts that "all protestants ar hipocriticall Asses"[3] or the round condemnation of one unfortunate parson as "an asse,"[4] suggest an unwillingness to suffer fools gladly and a plainness of speech certain to make enemies, of whom Marlowe had an indubitable abundance.

Coupled with all this, however, is Marlowe's association with the foremost thinkers and writers of his age, the uniform praise of "kynde Kit Marlowe," Shakespeare's obvious affection for the man and admiration for the poet, Edward Blount's wistful regret for "the man, that hath beene deare vnto vs, liuing an after life in our memory," Thomas Thorpe's allusion to his "pure Elementall wit," and George Chapman's tribute to his "most strangely-intellectual fire"[5]—which suggest that, like so many hot-tempered, outspoken people, Marlowe was also a very brilliant and very lovable person.

It is usually difficult to read from his plays a dramatist's own real character; for he, above all other writers, is most completely concealed behind his work. There is a clearly marked strain of autobiography in most lyric poetry. In the epic as in the novel, the short-story, and the tale, the author speaks *in propria persona,* and is then very likely to voice personal opinions. But the dramatist, speaking only through his characters, is concealed by them. Even in the modern *drame à thèse,* the character whom the playwright invents to utter his own views must be opposed by others who contradict with equal vigour. Otherwise, there is no conflict and therefore no play.

But Marlowe, in this as in other respects, is an exceptional

(For all footnote references, see Appendix, pp. 295-313.

playwright. Dramatic technique in his England had not developed very far. His was an art that did not as yet conceal the artist, nor did his characterizations possess enough depth or subtlety to veil the mind from which they emerged. A poet rather than a playwright, Marlowe had, almost until the end, but one formula for his plays; and his unwavering persistence in it makes clear enough to the thoughtful reader the bent of his own mind.

According to that formula, his plays are built around a single Machiavellian superman—Tamburlaine, Faustus, Barabas, the Guise, even to some degree Young Mortimer. Each is surrounded by other figures who are not real characters at all, but only shadows of the hero. Of the true dramatic conflict, until he reaches *Edward the Second*, Marlowe knows very little. His heroes fall, indeed, as tragic heroes must; but they fall solely because they have sought the unattainable. Except in this one play, Marlowe neglects Aristotle's doctrine of ἁμαργία, that the ruin which overtakes the tragic hero must come from some flaw in his own character; and he anticipates the view—popular in our own day—that tragedy results simply enough when man comes into conflict with forces outside himself, forces too great for him, forces that grudge to poor humanity all that mere mortals never shall attain. For Marlowe, warlike conquest, metaphysical skill, vast wealth, political power all end in death because his heroes all reach for things that must elude the grasp even of extraordinary mortals. He is an early Hardy.

Even when the formula is varied at last in *Edward the Second*, it is too late for Marlowe to follow up his new ideas. Only in this play does he give us the sharp clash of wills—the king's and the barons'—and the struggle of Queen Isabel between two affections. Only here appears the kingly figure who falls from his doting fondness for unworthy favourites. It is worth observing that here too we have for the first time the real character of a genuine woman, instead of Marlowe's usual feminine lay figure.

It is notable that all Marlowe's plays deal with the upper levels of society, in accordance with the classic view which restricted tragedy to "the fine doings of fine people." Marlowe has no interest at all in the common folk from whom he and his Canterbury forebears sprang. The Stratford Burgess's son at least deigns to notice with ridicule Jack Cade's mob and the

Roman plebs and to see the humour in Bottom, Dogberry, and Launcelot Gobbo. But, except for the incidental exits and entrances of servants and a few clowns like Wagner and Robin (of dubious authenticity), Marlowe pays no heed to ordinary humankind.

In this obsession of the cobbler's son for the gloriously impossible, we have the true key to his character. Humbly bred in Canterbury and sent to the University to become an humble cleric, he revolts. A true son of the Renaissance, equally in love with life and with learning, he finds himself in a capital where wealth and rank—neither of which he possesses—are the passports to almost everything that he holds precious. Handicapped though he is, he forces his way up through the rigid stratification of Elizabethan society and becomes "Christopher Marlowe, Gentleman."

Wherever we find record of Marlowe in London, it is in contact with the upper classes or their hangers-on. Even when he goes to jail, it is in company with a gentleman. He is a friend of the Walsinghams, taking refuge at Thomas Walsingham's country seat in time of plague. Even before he leaves the University, the Privy Council itself intervenes to secure his degree. The murder charge against him is promptly and leniently handled. He becomes an associate of Raleigh and his group of social and intellectual aristocrats. Kydd's letter attacking Marlowe refers to his association with "my lord,"—otherwise unnamed. It is significant that we hear nothing more of Marlowe in humble Canterbury once he has left the King's School for the University.

Delighting in the brilliant and aristocratic circles in which he now moved, yet conscious still of his humble origin, it was natural for Marlowe to write about the shepherd who became a mighty conqueror, the quiet scholar who drew the devil himself to his command, the outcast Jew who by virtue of his wealth and cunning became ruler of a Christian island. It was equally natural for him to turn to Machiavellian "pollicie," in view of his overmastering ambition and the successful knavery that he saw about him; and natural also that he should invest all this with the splendour and strangeness which the mighty line and his own genius made possible.

Perhaps because of these preoccupations, Marlowe seems to have had little interest in romantic love. There is no trace of a romantic passion in his life, once we dismiss the canard that attributes his murder to a quarrel over a "lewd wench," who is now known to be the vainest of imaginations. Neither do we find it in his plays or poems. Zenocrate is merely one more of Tamburlaine's conquests, Helen a mere decoration. Nowhere in *Dido* does Marlowe advance one step beyond the *Aeneid,* so far as the love story is concerned, and even then he had Nashe's assistance. Henry of Navarre in *The Massacre at Paris* is the most prosaic of all bridegrooms. Hero and her Leander are immortal lovers without being really in love. The poem is a tissue of gorgeous embroidery and a pretty tale of physical passion but nothing more, told by a poet who was utterly unable to imagine a marriage of true minds. *The Passionate Shepherd* is at most an exquisite trifle. Only for a moment, in *Edward the Second,* does Marlowe seem to understand the love of woman—and then it is in the tale of a weakling's unhappy marriage and an unfaithful wife.

Yet in spite of this lack of romance, Marlowe was obviously a hot-blooded and impetuously emotional person, in whose mouth ginger was all too hot, and to whom the sensuous beauty of the world made a powerful appeal. One might deduce this from a hundred passages in the plays and poems, beginning with the fiery lines of Tamburlaine,[6]

> What daring God torments my body thus,
> And seeks to conquer mighty Tamburlaine

or the famous [7]

> If all the pens that euer poets held,

and ending with the passionate lines of *Hero and Leander.* Not for nothing did Marlowe pen his line about [8]

> Beauty, mother to the Muses.

But as a matter of fact, we are not constrained to fall back upon Marlowe's writings for this aspect of his character. There is abundant evidence in the events of his life.

It is easy to imagine what happened to the sensitive imagination of a lad from churchly Canterbury, reared in the pious atmosphere of an ecclesiastical school under the shadow of the cathedral when, in the University, he encountered the shock of philosophical doubt, metaphysics brought in from Germany and France, the political reasoning of Machiavelli, the conflict of Puritan and Catholic elements among the leaders of the colleges, the obvious worldliness of ecclesiastical and academic place-seeking, and all the youthful ferment of eager boys in the awakening process which goes with university study everywhere.

Association with the brilliant sceptics of the Raleigh circle a few years later inevitably helped on the process that made Marlowe pre-eminently a rationalist and led him to conclude that he might well [9]

> . . . count Religion but a childish Toy,
> And hold there is no sinne but Ignorance.

No wonder that Marlowe later is found perusing an heretical treatise and reading "the atheist lecture" to Raleigh's School of Night. Nor is it any less natural that this rationalist temper should make Marlowe the only Elizabethan dramatist in the entire series of whose plays there is not a single ghost—an omission all the more significant since he knew classical literature, with its abundant spectres, very well indeed.

With such a temperament as this there goes almost inevitably an impish, youthful delight in shocking the unco' guid, of whom there were many both in Puritan Corpus Christi and in Puritan London. That is perhaps half the secret of the wild mockery recorded in the various spies' reports.

With all this, too, there goes an inquiring mind, sensitive, alert, and curious—a poet's mind, no doubt, but also in very large measure the mind of a scholar. This aspect of Marlowe's mind appears in the images of his plays and poems. These are almost wholly drawn either from the starry heavens, the sun, the moon, and the planets; or else they come from books, mostly the Greek and Latin classics. If Pedro Mexia in telling the story of Tamburlaine gives a bibliography, Marlowe patiently follows it up. If Tamburlaine delivers an impromptu lecture on fortification to his sons, he does so only after Marlowe has attentively studied a recent treatise on the subject. If geographic names are needed, the poet examines the atlas of Ortelius. If there is a handy name for a blackamoor in an obscure manuscript in the library of Corpus Christi, it duly appears in *The Jew of Malta.* If Faustus contemplates his future life, he does so in terms of the traditional four university faculties. If he travels with a demon guide, he must at least follow an itinerary already laid down in print. If the philosopher Ramus is to die in *The Massacre at Paris,* he can die only after a short disquisition on his philosophy, as taught in Cambridge University.

Of the innumerable images that Marlowe drew from the skies, the most famous is the apostrophe to Helen,[10] but there are many others. Tamburlaine wishes to "chase the Stars from heauen,"[11] and would make meteors "run tilting round about the firmament."[12] Hero's heart is "like a planet, moouing seuerall waies."[13] The aspiring spirit of man is "alwaies moouing as the restles Spheares."[14] This is very different from Shakespeare, who finds his images in all nature, animate and inanimate, with no special preference for astronomy; in the life of the home and the street and countryside; in the body itself; and only very slightly in books, classical mythology, or anything that can be called learning.[15]

Again unlike Shakespeare, Marlowe, with all his brilliance and his power over words, has one fatal lack: his sense of humour is painfully limited. It is not true that Marlowe had no sense of humour at all (though many a critic has said so); but such humour as he had was of a grim and rather savage nature. One sees it in the answer of Mephastophilis when Faustus avers there is no hell:[16]

> I, thinke so still, till experience change thy minde.

Of the gentleness of Shakespeare's humour—that humour which, seeing folly and being diverted with it, yet keeps a certain tenderness and tolerance for the fool—Marlowe had none whatever. Humour for Marlowe did not represent a saving sense of proportion. Humour could never enable this fiery spirit to laugh at the evils and injustices surrounding it. That is why those evils and injustices galled and fretted this impassionate soul, drove it to wild, perilous freedom and forbidden speculation, to a philosophy of revolt against the state, against morals, against God himself.

Such a mind in such a period of the world's history could hardly hope for happiness, and one senses under all the sound and fury, tingeing all the beauty of Marlowe's verse, a constant unrest, unhappiness, a profound dissatisfaction with the scheme of things, at times an angry and bitter contempt. Marlowe may not have been a desperately unhappy man; it is certain that he never attained the calm detachment mingled with warm humanity that appear in Shakespeare's later plays, which give the reader the feeling of a mind at peace with itself, knowing humanity, knowing good, knowing evil, knowing joy and knowing sorrow, yet loving life and the world that all these things make.

Complicating Marlowe's unrest and unhappiness and helping it forward is a strange lack of moral sense. Other Elizabethans created brutes as violent as Tamburlaine; but they knew what they were doing; whereas Marlowe never suspects that his magnificent chieftain is at bottom a bloody and useless brute, his conquests tinsel that barely covers their misery. The whole of Marlowe's writings do not contain a single picture of benevolence and goodness like Shakespeare's Prospero or Friar Laurence. The best that Marlowe can produce is the passing figure of the Old Man or the Good Angel in *Doctor Faustus*, neither more than a morality play abstraction. The university-bred scholar never penetrated to the inner realities of life that the lad from the Stratford Grammar School thought out for himself.

Thus Marlowe the man emerges from the work of the dramatist. Brilliant, learned, eager, sceptical, passionate, none too scrupulous, delighted to shock his hearers, almost humourless, unable to laugh at himself or others or the world, bitter, quarrelsome—that was Marlowe. Of his personal character one can know little more, save that if there is no real evidence that Marlowe was very bad, there is even less evidence that he was very good. He would, at all events, have made a highly unsatisfactory clergyman, had he observed the original conditions of his scholarship.

That was the man, and the man is dead—stabbed and flung into an unmarked grave at Deptford.

His work is not dead. The "thousand ships" passage, the death scenes in *Doctor Faustus* and *Edward the Second*, the lament for Zenocrate, the passage on the poets in *Tamburlaine*, the jewelled verse of *Hero and Leander*, a single lyric, these are the Marlowe that mankind will know forever. In the mighty line—preserved and developed by other, greater poets, notably by Shakespeare, by many another Elizabethan, by that last, lost, strayed Elizabethan, John Keats—wherever beauty, the mother of the muses, is adored and the human spirit still climbs restlessly, there will be Marlowe.

2.

A Shoemaker's Son

"Now is he borne, his parents base of stocke."
Doctor Faustus

In the Year of Our Lord 1564, there was excitement in two households of Queen Bess's England. One was in the quiet country town of Stratford where nothing of much importance had ever happened. The other was in the Cathedral town of Canterbury, something over a hundred miles away, which since the year 597 had been the ecclesiastical centre of England and the seat of the Archbishop of Canterbury—head of the English Church and only less powerful in the realm's affairs than the great Queen herself.

In Stratford, Mistress Mary Shakespeare, the wife of John Shakespeare, was with child. In Canterbury, the wife of an obscure shoemaker, John Marlowe, was two months nearer to her time. Neither event seemed of any particular importance outside the families most concerned. Babies were not unusual in Elizabethan households. They were born and they died rather frequently.

The social position of the families was not dissimilar. Like Mary Arden, daughter of a "gentleman of worship" who married the Stratford tradesman, John Shakespeare, Katherine Arthur had married beneath her when she gave her hand to a mere Canterbury shoemaker, for there is every reason to believe that she was a clergyman's daughter. John Marlowe was, however, a shoemaker who prospered steadily in a mild way; who had at least four apprentices; and who was to end his life with two businesses of his own, one in shoes, hides, and leather; the other as a bondsman. He was also to alleviate the odour of the tannery with the odour of sanctity, for he rose to be a church warden and he died a parish clerk.

The name of Marlowe is pure English; but it is spelled in such a wild variety of ways—Marlowe, Marlow, Marloe, Marlo, Marlin, Marlen, Merlin, Marley, Marle, and even Morley—that it is quite impossible to discover the original meaning. It may be Anglo-Saxon and mean a dweller by the lake (from *mere,* lake, and *leah,* dweller); or it may come from *mere* and *hláew,* in which case it would mean a hill by the lake; or it may be an occupational name from the trade of the marler, a man who dug marle, an earth used for fertilizer, and spread it on the land. Or again, it may be none of these, but simply a place name taken from the village of Marlowe in Buckinghamshire.

Whatever its origin, Marlowe is an old Kentish name, found in Canterbury as early as 1414, when one William Morle, fuller—that is, a cleaner of cloth—becomes a freeman of the city by "emption" or "redemption," in other words, by paying ten shillings for the right to trade in the city and enjoy its privileges. He is followed by his son, Thomas Morle, also a fuller, who becomes a freeman of Canterbury in 1459, but who pays "nichil" for the privilege, "being the son of William Morle, freeman of the same." There is also a certain vintner, Simon Morle by name, who was admitted freeman "be redemption" in 1438. About the same time a certain Laurence Morley is mentioned in a will.[1]

Nobody knows whether these men were ancestors of Christopher Marlowe, the poet; but a few years later we are on slightly firmer ground. Christopher Marlowe, the poet, was probably the great-great-grandson of John Marle or Marley, tanner, who became a freeman of the city in 1467, not only paying the usual ten shillings for his freedom but making various special contributions as well. This John can hardly have been the son of Thomas Morle, since the sons of freemen became freemen without fee, but he may have been a collateral relative of some kind. He may also have been the son of John Marle, lockyer, who was one of the "intrantes"—Kentishmen dwelling near the city but outside its walls who, though not freemen, were permitted to enter the gates and do business on payment of a yearly "fine."

Richard Marle, the son of John Marle, tanner, follows the family trade, which persists for generation after generation, until at length the Marlowe family—more, doubtless, to its horror than its pride—produced a mad young genius, the first Marlowe in a century who had no interest whatever in leather. Outside the Canterbury walls to-day they will still show you the round flat stones, specially grooved, that ground the tanbark in ancient Canterbury, perhaps the very stones that ground the very stores of tanbark which the Marlowes are careful to mention in their wills, and from which Christopher Marlowe fled, first to the University, then to London and a career in letters.

Punctually in 1514, exactly one hundred years after the first recorded Marlowe, John Marley's son, Richard, appears in the city accounts among the admissions of freemen.[2] There is no doubt about his parentage, for the accounts describe him as "the sonne of John Marley tann*er** freman of the ſeid Citie byfore the ſeid Rychard Marley tann*er* was borne," the usual formula, which apparently indicates that only those sons born to a father who had already attained his freedom could inherit their own freedom without payment. The same rule, slightly varied, applied to daughters, who brought as a dower to their husbands special privileges in becoming freemen, as we shall see when Christopher Marlowe's sisters begin to marry.

Richard Marley's son was the first Christopher Marlowe, a tanner like his forebears. Richard Marley's will refers to "crystofer my son," but for some reason there is no record to show when this Christopher Marlowe became a freeman of Canterbury. His will appears in 1539/40,† however, as that of "christofer marley ta*n*ner of the p*ar*rissh of westgaytt dwellinge w*ith*in the wall*es* of the cetye of canterburye," clear evidence that he was a freeman.

At this point, however, an element of doubt enters the Marlowe genealogy. Christopher Marley's wife, Joan Marley, was with child when her husband made his will; and the dying man left "to the child that she goyth w*ith*all if hitt be a man child," two houses and various furnishings. John Marlowe, father of the poet, was born about 1540. It is probable, therefore, that the child Joan Marley was carrying at her husband's death *was* a man child, and that this man child grew up to be John Marlowe, shoemaker of Canterbury and father of the

* Mediæval and Elizabethan scribes lightened their labours—and increased those of modern scholars—by a complicated system of lines, twirls, and curlicues technically known as "cursive marks." As these defy type, it is usual to write them out in full, indicating the inserted letters by italics. The present work ignores the old-fashioned long "ſ" in most quotations.

† Until the latter part of the eighteenth century, the English New Year's Day was March 25 instead of January 1. The month of March belonged in two different years. In modern books, therefore, it is usual to give dates between January 1 and March 25 with two figures, the first representing the year according to the old reckoning and the second the year according to modern reckoning. In the ecclesiastical calendar, March 25 is the Feast of the Annunciation of the Blessed Virgin, usually called "Lady Day" in England.

poet. Unfortunately, no document to prove it has ever turned up. Christopher Marlowe's genealogy, therefore, depends wholly on assumption—a rather reasonable assumption, based on probability; on the sequence of dates; on the fact that all these Marleys were tanners, as if a family trade were being passed down from generation to generation; and on the further fact that the names Christopher and Joan reappear in John Marlowe's family, as if his children were being named for their grandparents.[3]

John Marlowe, father of the poet, appears in history for the first time when he is enrolled as the apprentice of Garrard Rychardsson, shoemaker of Canterbury, at the annual enrolment of Canterbury apprentices for the year 1559-1560. As only the children of freemen could become apprentices, this is one more reason for believing that he was actually the posthumous son of Christopher Marley. On May 22, 1561, as the Register of the Church of St. George the Martyr still shows, he married Katherine Arthur, who is supposed to have been the daughter of the Reverend Christopher Arthur, once rector of St. Peter's, Canterbury, though there is no real proof of her parentage. He had become an apprentice only a little more than a year earlier, and was not to become a freeman of the city for another three years; but he was at the beginning of a modest career in the shoe and leather business that seems to have grown steadily more prosperous throughout his life, though at the best never very successful.

The home that John and Katherine Marlowe established after their marriage in 1561 was the average Elizabethan tradesman's household. The house, which immemorial Canterbury tradition describes as "Marlowe's birthplace," still stands at the corner of St. George's Street and little St. George's Lane. There is some doubt whether all of the modern house belonged to John Marlowe, the tanner. According to tradition, there were once gardens in front of the house, which now abuts directly on the street; and one can see clearly that the front of the house was added to an even older rear structure, centuries ago. There is even a vague story that the Marlowes did not live in this particular house but in another, since destroyed, a few yards eastward, nearer to the city wall.[4]

At any rate the locale is right; the house is unquestionably of the period; and it is reasonable enough to suppose that the birthplace is authentic, for traditions linger firmly in Canterbury, and local interest in Marlowe's life had begun among Kentish antiquarians while the poet's father and mother were still alive. The house was probably already being pointed out to strangers, even while John and Katherine Marlowe still dwelt near it in the adjoining parish of St. Mary Bredman.[5]

St. George's Street is an important thoroughfare. St. George's Lane is so narrow that a tall man can almost span it with his arms—so narrow that the first cry of the infant poet must have echoed in ears next door and told the neighbours that a prospective freeman and heir to the shoemaking business had been born.

John Marlowe's was only a tradesman's dwelling in those spacious days, but by modern standards it was a fairly large house—large enough to accommodate half of an ambitious furniture store to-day—and its carved panelling was so beautiful that two of its rooms have been removed wholesale to provide a "Marlowe bedroom" for one of the modern Kentish gentry and a panelled dining-room for another, while the original old dining-room has been used to panel a display room for a Canterbury antique dealer. Round the upper part of the panelling of the various rooms ran friezes of intricate and beautiful carved patterns. One of the fireplaces had a huge carved mantel of red pine. As the centuries passed, later and unappreciative owners painted the carving over until it became almost a plane surface. One miscreant even stained and grained it to imitate mahogany!

Outside, the whole house must have been very like its one early Tudor wall, which still remains unchanged and unspoiled, facing on St. George's Lane. Heavy oaken timbers rose half-way up the first story. The second story overhung the lane, thriftily adding space for the numerous bedrooms of the shoemaker's rapidly growing family; and the overhang was supported by oaken braces, elaborately carved as heads and busts of grotesque creatures. To-day, blackened by the passing years, they seem more Mayan than Elizabethan.

Down St. George's Street the old house looked out on the Church of St. George the Martyr, which had already stood there for centuries. Like other old Canterbury churches, this was built of flint nodules, cracked to make them square on the outer edge and then plastered together. They were so hard that the passing centuries have altered them not a whit, though they were already ancient when the lad Marlowe passed them on his way up and down St. George's Street. To-day, their sharp flat surfaces remain as keen as arrow-heads, while the softer stone of carved windows and arches has weathered almost to nothing.

Up and down the streets that little Christopher paced toward the lacy towers of the Cathedral were other houses of timber and plaster, the wooden edges of their gables carved, the second stories overhanging the street a foot or so, like his own home, their wooden supports carved too, in many shapes and faces. Round about them all for more than a mile ran the chill grey walls of the city, dating from the Middle Ages, with their six towered gates with cells and guard-houses and crenellated walls above, while dotted here and there between them were twenty-odd "watching towers," above still older walls which the Romans had built, perhaps above earthworks older still, built by ancient Britons.

Small wonder that in later years *Tamburlaine* reveals the poet's keen interest in city walls and defensive works. When, in the play, the conqueror orders the unfortunate governor of Babylon hanged "vp in chaines vpon the citie walles," * he deals out the same fate that many a Kentish wretch had met, hanged from the walls of Westgate, almost in sight of the Marlowe house. And in the play, this very scene contains an allusion to "the westerne gate"! [6] Marlowe, writing his first successful tragedy, was re-living the scenes of his boyhood, though his subconscious mind probably never gave him time to know, as his goose-quill squeaked over the paper, whence its images came to him.

One by one Mistress Katherine Marlowe wrapped her children carefully against the raw Kentish air and carried them across the street to the Church of St. George the Martyr to be christened. Across that same street all too many of them were carried back to the church in tiny coffins a few years later, victims of the appalling sanitary conditions and perhaps also of the crude medical practice of the day.

Mary Marlowe, the first-born, disappears permanently from the records after her christening. She must have been the unnamed daughter of John Marlowe, buried August 28, 1568. The old Register Book of the Church of St. George the

* Quotations from Marlowe's works follow the Oxford (1910) edition by Tucker Brooke, which reproduces the original spelling. Elizabethan printers used "v" and "u," "i" and "j" almost interchangeably.

Martyr says only: "daughter of John Marlow."[7] Three other sons were born and died. One was christened in October, 1568, though his name is not recorded; and on November 5 we find again in the burial record, "The sonne of John Marle." Little Thomas Marlowe, christened July 26, 1570, was buried twelve days later; and when another son was born after a few years he, too, was christened Thomas, just as the Shakespeare family, in Stratford, named another daughter Joan in 1569 to replace the Joan Shakespeare who had died soon after her birth, eleven years before. The second Thomas Marlowe must have died early, for the wills of the parents, made in 1604, after the murder of their celebrated son, make no mention of any other, though they carefully list bequests to all the daughters of the house.

Christopher Marlowe had four sisters who lived to grow up: Margaret, born in 1565; Joan, born in 1569; "An," born in 1571; and "Daretye" [Dorothy], born in 1573. All of these girls were married to young Canterbury tradesmen—old maids were rare in Elizabethan days—and three of them by their marriages made their husbands freemen of the city.

This dignified and profitable station in life could be attained in four ways. One might be born the son of a freeman and be admitted to a freeman's rights and privileges without any payment at all; one might become an apprentice; one might become a freeman by "emption" or "redemption," that is, by paying a sum ranging from 6s. 8d. to 13s. 4d.; or one might marry the daughter of a freeman and pay only 11½d. To be a freeman was a matter of some importance, since only a freeman had the right to do business in Canterbury, the outsiders who came in as "intrantes" being merely on sufferance.[8]

The city belonged to its freemen, all of whom were "truely sworne uppon a boke"[9] to be loyal subjects of the Queen, and to maintain "the franchises customs and usages of the city." They received special privileges that gave them marked advantages in doing business. In John Marlowe's time these included provisos of which, says an ancient document, "On ys, that fremen may come to the counsell of the same cyte, and ther speke and be herd; wher other [men] shalbe voyde, and be put away." Of more importance to a rising young shoemaker was the provision that "freemen of the cyte may holde craft and opyn windowes, *with*out leve ther; other may nott, withowte agrement of the chamber." The freemen had many other privileges advantageous both in business and in personal life:

> Yeff a freman of Caunt'bery be condem*m*pnyd in eny dette, at sewte of eny man, he may have xv dayes of payement, under suerte.
>
> A Freman of Caunt'bery may ax and have part of vytyell and corn, and other that comyth to be sold yn the markett.
>
> Yeff a freman of Caunt'bery take aprentys to terme of yere, in the first yere, he may inroll him and pay 2s., and so be of record.

This last provision is to-day of great help in tracing the business careers of John Marlowe and his sons-in-law. Other privileges were of greater personal advantage:

> Ther schall be no freman of Caunt'bery be condempnyd, ne convyct be foryn men, nor eny trespass, but only by 'her concitezens.
>
> Yeff eny freman of Caunt'bery shuld be take*n* be his body, or arreynyd, wherfore he schuld suffre emprison*m*ent, he schall no where be imprisonyd, but only in the pr'son of Caunt'bery, ne no where be demyd [judged], but be concitezens of the same cite, be her charter.
>
> Fremen of Caunt'bery schall haue 'her huntyng and ther dysport, wythe-y*n* 'her boundys of 'her prevelege.

It was merry England, woods were plentiful about the town, and the freemen seem to have taken full advantage of this last privilege, even "at the sermon time." In 1569, a grand jury, considering the disturbance of religious services, "found that in this point there were very few or none within the City that were excusable and the cause thereof they thought to be the daily use of fowling." [10]

It is fairly easy to imagine the conditions under which young Christopher Marlowe grew up. His family's rank was humble, a fact occasionally flung in his teeth by envious rivals in the days of his theatrical success in London a few years later; but the life of a master craftsman's household, though unpretentious, was not uncomfortable. If John Marlowe was really the descendant of John, Richard, and Christopher Marley, he came of a prosperous family. His father, the elder Christopher Marlowe, had left the posthumous child two houses, in case it proved to be a boy; and to his wife he left £20 in money, twenty acres of land, a house, and a meadow. He also made bequests of money to relatives and friends, and his will mentions a servant, two assistants in the tannery, and apparently two apprentices besides. Hardly a poor man's last testament.

Old Richard Marley, dying in 1521, had had so many worldly goods to dispose of that his will occupies six pages. He took good care to direct "for my soule & all Cristen soul*es* at eu*ery* day of my fforthefare Monethys mynde and xij Monethys mynde a dyryge and a Trentall of massys," for which his executors were to pay, besides giving five shillings to the poor on each of these solemn occasions. Every house of friars in Canterbury received five shillings to pray for his soul for a year after his decease. In case of his son's death, he directed that "an honest secular p*re*ste shall syng for my soule my ffathers soule my ffrend*es* soul*es* that J am most bounden to p*ra*y for & all Cresten soul*es* in the seid Church of the holy Crosse [where he was buried] the space of oon holle yere."

Earlier than Richard Marley, the records are silent as to the worldly well-being of the Marlowe line. Beyond the fact that the first John Marley, freeman in 1467, was a tanner like the next three generations of Marlowes, we know nothing of him. Probably he was a good tanner and a godly man, who would have been just as much scandalized at having a genius in the family as all the other worthy folk of Canterbury.

The household of the second John Marlowe, father of the dramatist, Christopher Marlowe, was an ordinary tradesman's home, no better supplied with worldly goods than a hundred others, but certainly no worse. It was the house of a respectable freeman plying a respectable craft.

The tanners and shoemakers formed a single powerful guild, "the Brethren of the Assumption of Our Lady, of the Crafts and Mysteries of Shoe-Makers, Coriours and Cobbelers," co-operating in the control of the shoe and leather trade, and standing by each other in the great crises of the simple life of their little city.

In 1588, about the time that his brilliant son had gone up to London and taken the town by storm with his first plays, John Marlowe added to his shoe and leather business, practice as a professional bondsman. Elizabethan custom required that the officiating clergy be protected against matrimonial errors at every wedding they performed; and professional bondsmen were never far from the church door when a wedding was in prospect. John Marlowe was one of these. He appears as bondsman once in 1579. Then his name does not appear again until 1588, but thereafter he is bondsman nearly once a year until his death in 1604. In all, he gave bond at eighteen weddings. As early as 1579 he was rich enough to provide security for £100, no mean sum for the relatively humble folk, innkeepers, yeomen, and husbandmen, at whose marriages he appeared. The richest man in all Canterbury about this time had an income of but £531. If the ecclesiastical authorities thought John Marlowe was "good" for £100, he was presumably able to provide adequately if modestly for the family of five surviving children which was, by Elizabethan standards, not very large.

The shoemaker's shop, from first to last, did enough business to keep at least one apprentice pretty constantly employed. The Canterbury records show that in 1567/8, just after he had himself become a freeman, John Marlowe took his first apprentice, a certain Richard Umbarffeld, of whom nothing further is heard. In 1583, a certain Elias Martyn pays but 4s. 1d. on becoming a freeman, "because he was the aprentyce of John Marloe of the seid Cytie." In 1594 William Hewes, "late apprentice with John Marlowe," becomes a freeman; and his successor is Thomas Mychell, who is bound over by indenture for a full seven years' apprenticeship. John Marlowe may have had several other apprentices of whom no record survives. At least, he seems to have made a practice of taking a new one as soon as his old one had become a freeman with a shop of his own.[11]

His last will, made January 23, 1604, a few days before his death and nearly eleven years after his famous son had been stabbed at Deptford, gives very little information about his worldly goods. His marriage must have been happy, for he leaves everything that he owns to his wife: "As touching my temporall goods my debts and funeralls discharged & paid J give and bequeath wholy to my wife Katherine whome I make my sole executrix." Young Christopher's boyhood, then, was passed in the quiet of an harmoniously peaceful home. His mother was not one of those "curst shrews," of whom we hear so much among the Elizabethans, and for the amelioration of whose tongues and tempers ducking stools were invented.[12] The best that Ben Jonson could say of his wife was that she was "a shrew yet honest."

There was, however, occasional friction with relatives of

the Arthur family; for we catch definite echoes of it in the "will nuncupative" of Dorothy Arthur, Mistress Marlowe's sister. A will nuncupative is taken down in the presence of witnesses after questioning the maker of the will, who is supposed to be too weak to make ordinary testamentary arrangements. As her sister lay dying, shrewd old Mistress Marlowe "did aske her what she would give vnto her Aunte Barton (meaning the wife of Salomon Barton of Canterbury who was Aunte vnto the said dorothie by the mothers side)." In reply to which "the said dorothie said she would give her nothing: nor would not haue her sent for to come to her. Then being demaunded by the said Catherine Marley who should haue all her goods if it should please god to call her, the said dorothie said that she gave all she had vnto her said Aunte Catherine Marley." [13]

A queer little tragi-comedy, which shows that there was no lack of business acumen on the distaff side of the Marlowe household.

Mistress Katherine Marlowe lived only a little more than a year after her husband's death, and the length of her will and the minute detail in which she makes division of her worldly goods show that John Marlowe's widow had been well provided for. Her last wishes give an almost classic glimpse into the interior of a moderately prosperous tradesman's home in Elizabeth's reign.

The old woman who lay dying at Canterbury scarcely remembered any other monarch on the throne of England. Queen Bess had come to the throne in 1558, only four years before young Katherine Arthur married her shoemaker. She and the seven-year-old Christopher had seen the Queen—no one in Canterbury missed that gorgeous spectacle—when in 1573 Elizabeth and her Court visited the great Archbishop Parker in full state and regal splendour. She remembered the terrors of the Armada year, remembered her husband's drilling as an archer to help defeat the Spanish, remembered the victory of Queen Bess's sailors, which meant that one could sleep o'nights and there was no longer need for the shoemaker to turn soldier.

Christopher, her only son, had been slain in 1593, "within the verge" that surrounded the royal Court. Her Majesty's own coroner, instead of the ordinary official, had taken over the inquest.

Now Mistress Katherine lay dying, too. The old Queen had died three years before, no longer the brilliant young girl, so vain of her beautiful hands, who had come to the throne; but a woman ungracefully grown old, who held desperately to a youth long past, grimacing at the handsome young men of her Court, daubing herself with ridiculous colours, and at the end shutting herself alone in her room to face the death she did not dare to think about, while all England wondered what would come when the great Queen died and whether the King of Scots was really her legitimate successor.

The old Queen was dead at last; and the strange new King from Scotland was on the throne, surrounded by a horde of Scottish knights and nobles, whom England speedily made up its mind it did not very much like. New times, new ways. Mistress Katherine Marlowe quietly died too.

There is no record of her burial, but her will [14] is dated March 17, 1605/6. The inventory of her worldly goods is so detailed and elaborate that it extends even to her petticoats, which were respectably abundant and doubtless equally respectably voluminous. There are gold and silver rings, numerous silver spoons, six pairs of sheets for each of her four daughters, not to mention "a dosen of napkins to be diuided equallye beecause some are better then other." There is furniture and clothing and five pounds in cash. Since there were no banks and since stocks and bonds had not yet been invented to plague mankind, thrifty Elizabethans put their reserve wealth into gold coin or into articles of gold and silver, precious metal being of very stable value.

Mistress Marlowe has a maid, musically named Mary Maye, who is affectionately remembered in the will with "my red petticoate and a smocke." A certain Goodwife Morrice is given "one pillowecoate" and also "my petticoate that I doe weare daylye and a smocke and a wastcoate." Katherine Reve is given "one payre of pillowecoates." The nature of the bequests sounds as if all three of these women were servants—a stately household for a tanner's humble widow.

The widow's will was written by one Thomas Hudson and was witnessed by Goodwife Sarai Morrice and Mary Maye, who like their mistress signed only with their marks—a practice not uncommon in Canterbury testaments.

3.

The King's Scholar

"Settle thy studies Faustus, and beginne
To sound the deapth of that thou wilt professe."
Doctor Faustus

Outside his home, the bustling life of busy Canterbury gave the youthful Marlowe a life quite different from that of the youthful Shakespeare, dreaming beside the quiet Avon and among the Cotswold hills. Not large as the twentieth century judges cities, Canterbury had perhaps a few more than nine thousand inhabitants.[1] But it was the seat of the primate of all England, an ancient city whose arms bore the proud motto, "Ave mater Angliae"; and by decree of Edward IV in 1461, it was no mere part of the County of Kent, but an independent county in its own right—the city and county of Canterbury. It was already old when Julius Cæsar captured it. It was old when Chaucer and his pilgrims strolled curiously through the streets. To the Elizabethans it was already a city of dreams and stories in carven stone, even as it is to modern eyes.

Canterbury lay upon the high-road—the ancient Watling Street, built by the Romans—which led from London to Dover and the English Channel. Through the streets of the ancient town poured all of Elizabethan humanity—soldiers, full of strange oaths and bearded like the pard, men whose faces had been like the face of one of Marlowe's own characters, "a grind-stone for mens swords,"[2] bound for the Low Countries where the Spaniards fought the sturdy Dutch heretics, whom the equally heretical English frequently aided; sailors back from strange voyages to stranger lands only beginning to be discovered, and full of strange tales which later find their way into *Tamburlaine* and *Faustus;* scholars from the universities, come to see the learned Archbishop Parker and his library with its rare manuscripts; ecclesiastics of every rank from all over England, visiting the nation's religious capital; clergy from the Cathedral itself and the city's innumerable churches; gilded youth from the Court of the Great Queen, off for the Low Countries and a little adventure in the hope of glory like Sir Philip Sidney's; soldiers home from the wars, wounded in the Queen's service but neglected by the Queen's government, which permitted them only the privilege of begging at the town's end for the rest of their days, tragic figures, no doubt, but full of strange tales for wondering, imaginative cobbler's lads; sober citizens of Canterbury, well aware of their privileges as freemen; and their apprentices—far from sober—wild young lads, ready with their clubs, ready for a riot or a fight or a wench, and readier still to marry their master's daughters or their wealthy widows and become freemen themselves.

Along the high-road the players came wandering, too. Six times in Marlowe's life we have records of players in Canterbury: the Lord Warden's in 1569/70, Lord Morley's in 1581/2, the Earl of Hertford's men in 1582, Lord Leicester's men between 1585 and 1588. Last of all came Lord Strange's men, who are supposed to have produced some of Marlowe's own plays in London and who appeared in his native Canterbury in 1592, when he was at the height of his career as a dramatist. Old John and Katherine may have gone proudly to see their son's plays.[3] Probably there were many other visits from the actors, now unrecorded, for the players had been coming to the city with more or less regularity since 1473/4, when the accounts record the payment of five shillings to the players of the Duke of Clarence.[4]

A Canterbury lad did not have to depend upon strolling players, however, for initiation into the theatre. The King's School also engaged in "settynge forthe of Tragedyes, Comedyes, and interludes." It is vexing to find that there are no records of plays at the King's School while Marlowe was a scholar; but as there are plenty of records before and after, it is likely enough that the schoolboy Christopher played various parts upon the stage[5] long before he had ever left the shoemaker's household.

The city itself had once been proud of its theatrical pageant of Saint Thomas, and there seem to have been other religious dramas, given with the full approval of the Burghmote; but it is not by any means certain that these continued as late as Marlowe's boyhood.[6]

Most wonderful of all, in the eyes of the little boy who peered from the windows of the house on St. George's Lane, was the procession in which Queen Elizabeth passed down High Street to the Cathedral on her visit to Canterbury in 1573. It was the only visit of the Queen to his native city that Marlowe saw, for when she came again in 1582 he was a student at the University. In 1573, however, he saw the Mayor and aldermen go forth in their furred and scarlet gowns to meet their Sovereign, carrying a gift of £30 in a scented bag. Heralds, sergeants-at-arms, trumpeters, footmen, messengers, porters, the Black Guard, musicians, bedizened courtiers, and "Walter the Iester" accompanied the Queen; and to them all the munificent city gave presents.

At the West Door of the great cathedral, the Queen found the wealthy and learned Archbishop Parker, waiting with three other bishops to receive her, while a "grammarian"—a schoolboy from the King's School, which young Kit himself was to enter a few years later—made an oration in her honour. It was not the only speech-making of the visit, for the city "paid to Mr. Wyck for making the oration to the Queen," one pound.[7]

Elizabeth dwelt in Saint Augustine's Abbey, east of the city, but according to tradition she held her Court in a building just beyond the Marlowe house, where the "Queen Elizabeth room" is still shown. She attended service in the cathedral and celebrated her birthday in the episcopal palace. To the music of flute and drum all of this pageantry poured down St. George's Street, where the shoemaker's dwelling still stands—lords and soldiers, ecclesiastics, the guard, the ladies of the Court, the great Queen herself. Of this the young dramatist is thinking, when fifteen years later he writes in *Tamburlaine:* [8]

> Is it not passing braue to be a King,
> And ride in triumph through Persepolis?

Do these scenes from the boy's life again hover in the grown man's imagination when his verses make "the townes-men maske in silke and cloath of gold"?

When at length her royal but somewhat expensive majesty departed, the city gave her another £20. The Archbishop gave her an agate salt-cellar with a diamond inset, within which were six Portuguese gold pieces, worth some £200. It may be doubted whether the gallants of the Court were equally pleased with the learned Archbishop's gift of Latin treatises, which fell to their lot; or the gay ladies of the Court with the commentaries on Ecclesiastes or the Bibles given them, even though the Bibles were bound in leather nobly tooled.

The Archbishop was a bookworm and a book collector. He had been Master of Corpus Christi, Cambridge, the college where Marlowe was to study. He owned a magnificent collection of books and manuscripts, which is notable even to this day. And like every collector, he fancied that all men and women loved equally the treasures of piety and learning that he loved himself; but it is doubtful whether any Bibles were ever so little read as those bestowed upon the gay, light wenches, dazzlingly garbed and nobly born, but rather more than flirtatious, who attended upon the Virgin Eliza when she left at length the religious capital of her island kingdom.

The life of the Canterbury streets and public squares was exciting and stirring enough, even without this perpetual flow of strangers through the town. There was cock-fighting, dog-fighting, bull-baiting, and—a spectacle edifying to the godly and diverting to the unregenerate—the public execution of criminals. Cock-fighting then was about what it is now; but bull-baiting was a peculiarly Elizabethan pastime, which more sensitive later generations of Englishmen have permitted to die out. The bull—sometimes a bear—was chained to the stake and three or four savage dogs, especially bred for the purpose, were turned loose upon him. That is what Macbeth is thinking of in his speech at the end of Shakespeare's play—

> They have tied me to a stake; I cannot fly,
> But bear-like I must fight the course.

The dogs were mastiffs, or bull-dogs, from which the much smaller modern animals are descended. They took their own risks in the combat, along with the bull; but they were highly bred and valuable, and the managers of the fights tried to save them from destruction, whereas the bull was destined for ultimate translation into roast beef. The bull might gore the dogs, which could not be prevented if there was to be a fight worth seeing; but he might also toss them high in the air. When that happened, an attendant ran out with a leather-padded pole and eased the fall of the dog so as to save him for another fight.[9]

The pastime had the full approval of the city fathers of

Canterbury, who had passed a special decree of Burghmote that no beef might be marketed unless the animal had first been baited for the delectation of the populace, prior to slaughter. This, says one old Canterbury writer, with Puritanical primness, was "an ancient order and custom of the city used by the city butchers before their killing; not so much (if at all) for pleasure, as to make them man's meat and fit to be eaten." [10]

In spite of the brutality of the time, the city fathers were rigid moralists. A grand jury gravely reprove the throngs who chatter in the Cathedral's cloister and disturb the services. They order "that no Butcher should kill any Veal in the time of Lent." [11] When more serious delinquents are discovered, the City pays "for a Cart to carry three Harlots about the town 6d and to him that rang the bason 1d and to the painter for writing three Papers 6d." [12] These last were stuck up above the heads of the erring ladies when they were eventually set in the pillory to meditate upon their sins.

In 1562, the grand jury presents "the wife of Stephen Colyer for that she was not of good name nor Fame, but lived viciously; for the which she had been divers times banished out of one ward into another and in conclusion banished by all the Council of the Shire of Canterbury; and that notwithstanding she is abiding in the City viciously and idly using herself." [13] Evidently, the grand jurors concluded, there was very little you could do about the wife of Stephen Colyer. Stephen himself seems to have abandoned the effort from the start, for nothing whatever is heard of his views in the matter.

In spite of all this ardent morality, bulls for the stake were scarcely more plentiful than condemned felons for the gallows, who probably received little more sympathy from those who gathered to be entertained by the executions. The Elizabethans were a robust and far from squeamish race, and the freemen of Canterbury must have been hardier than usual. Their city had at least three gallows in the sixteenth century, all of which may have been in use at once; and as Canterbury was the ecclesiastical centre of England, heretics were often burned there. The town accounts for 1535 record the expenditure of 15s. 8d. for transporting an "Erytyk" from London. They casually add—as a mere matter of precise and careful bookkeeping—later expenditures of 2s. for a load and a half of wood, a pennyworth of gunpowder, and a six-penny stake with a two-penny staple.[14] The gunpowder was to put the victim out of his suffering quickly. As an heretic, he had to be burned, but to watch a man roasted alive was a little too much even for the sixteenth century. Hence a quick explosion to end matters. Fox's *Book of Martyrs* explains that the gunpowder "was not laid under the faggots, but only about their bodies to rid them out of their pains."

Such humanity was not invariable. There is one horrible story of a pregnant woman, condemned to be burned to death. In the agony of the moment, she gave premature birth to her child, which a bystander picked up and tossed back into the flames, so that even the seed of the heretic should perish.[15]

It is sometimes said that there were no burnings at all in Elizabeth's reign, but this is not strictly accurate. There were certainly no burnings at Canterbury—though legends of the dreadful fires of Martyrs' Green lingered then as they do today—but the heretic Francis Kett was burned in the castle moat at Norwich, not far away. Marlowe may have seen this spectacle, and certainly knew all about it, for Kett had been a fellow of Corpus Christi during his first year there. Their names still stand together upon the weekly accounts of the Buttery Book, payment day by day for bread and beer, with never a hint of what fate had in store for each of them.

Men were hanged—and for some hundreds of years continued to be hanged—in England for the most trivial crimes. One William Marlowe, perhaps a relative of the poet's, would have gone to the gallows in London in 1598 for stealing a black heifer, had he not been able to plead "benefit of clergy" and thereby save his life. Where the offence was too slight even for the brutal Elizabethan law to inflict a death penalty, there were other penalties almost as savage, slitting of nostrils, cutting off of hands or ears, branding—not even benefit of clergy saved a man from that. The City of Canterbury had "paid for the ingraving of one Iron to mark Murderers with—8d."[16]

In treason cases, even hanging was too mild a penalty. Traitors of high degree might be mercifully beheaded or hanged with a silken cord; but when the government wished to make an example, the traitor was first hanged, then cut down from the gallows while he was still alive, his living body opened, his entrails burnt before his face, after which his body, dead at last, was cut into quarters to be set up in various parts of the kingdom as an example to others.

This was the form of execution legally known as "hanging, drawing, and quartering." The traitor's head was often set up on a spike, and a hanged felon might be left dangling from the gallows in his chains till the weather and the birds or the need of the gallows for another execution ended the dreadful spectacle. In his later years, Marlowe must often have glanced up at the grim row of traitors' heads as he went back and forth across London Bridge, near which he lodged for at least part of his life in London. Goldsmith and Dr. Johnson saw the same grisly spectacle on Temple Bar three centuries later.

There was at least one execution of this sort in Canterbury during Henry VIII's attacks on the church; and though this was before Marlowe's birth, the grim story must have been told and retold in his hearing many a time, for it leaves a trace in his work. His villain-hero, Barabas, in *The Jew of Malta,* is boiled to death in a cauldron, exactly like the unfortunate Friar Stone of Canterbury—a grisly business recorded by the brisk, matter-of-fact city accounts, purely as a matter of book-keeping: [17]

Item paid for half a tonne of tymber to make a paire of gallowes for to hang ffryer Stone......	ii^s vj^d
Item paid to a Carpenter for makyng of the same Gallowes & the Dray..............................	xvj^d
Item to a laborer that dygged the holes............	iij^d
Item paid to iiij men to help Sett vp the gallowes	vij^d
Item paid for drynk for them..........................	j^d
Item paid for cariage of the same tymber from Stablegate to the Dongeon.............................	iiij^d
Item paid for a hardell..................................	vj^d
Item paid for a lode of wood & for a hors to drawe hym to the Dongeon..........................	ij^{s}iij^d
Item paid to ij men that set the ketill & *par*boyled hym..	xij^d
Item paid to iij men that caryed his quarters to the gates & set them vp................................	xij^d
Item paid for a Halter to hang hym.................	j^d
Item paid for ij ob [half-penny] Halters...........	j^d
Item paid for Sandwich cord............................	ix^d
Item paid for screwe..	j^d
Item paid to a woman that scowred the Ketyll	ij^d
Item paid to hym that did execucyon...............	iiij^s viij^d

During Marlowe's brief lifetime there were at least eight hangings in Canterbury,[18] six of them during his childhood, before he left the city for Cambridge. If the plays he was writing a few years later sometimes seem in their worst passages to have wild rant—savage, bombastious, bloody stuff—mingled with their beauty, we must remember some of these early impressions, forced upon the sensitive mind of an imaginative little boy—the deeds of the wisest, best, and greatest men of the kingdom.

Down in sleepy Stratford, John Shakespeare's lad was living the quieter life of a country boy. It was these days of calmer country life that helped to make the difference between the rounded humanity of Shakespeare's long career, and the fierce, turbulent, often unnaturally violent verse that Marlowe poured out in his few brief years. Not for the fiery Marlowe were daffodils that come before the swallows dare and take the winds of March with beauty, nor any sessions of sweet silent thought, nor meditative ponderings on to-morrow and to-morrow and to-morrow, nor even such commonplace, realistic, human types as Dogberry, Justice Shallow, Bully Bottom, Snout the Weaver, or those real men who actually lived in Warwickshire and whose existence can be demonstrated from the documents they have left behind them, "William Visor of Woncot," and "Clement Perkes o' the hill."[19]

Humorously sympathetic observation of human foibles and human frailties and the life of everyday was not for Marlowe. For him, the far-away, the terrible, the strange—devils, magicians, world-conquerors and kings who, as Ben Jonson thought, "fly from all humanity." Marlowe had plenty of first-hand experience with constables—but it was Shakespeare who created Verges, Dogberry, and the watch in *Much Ado*. Marlowe grew up in a shoemaker's household, but it was Thomas Dekker who wrote *The Shoe-Maker's Holiday*.

The country about Canterbury is almost as lovely as that about Stratford, and in the sixteenth century it was still thick with woods. The Stour is a clear river, winding gently through meadow land and low hills, overhung with willows and roses, with slow water weeds waving in its current, much like the Avon. The life of the Kentish countryside close about Canterbury differs little from that of Warwickshire. But there was a difference, some subtle and inexplicable distinction between the two boys. The lad Shakespeare saw and felt all this. The lad Marlowe could, if he wished, look past the towers of Westgate on his way to the King's School and see the distant hills, caught and framed there like a remote landscape in a Flemish picture; but for the most part it did not touch him.

Now and then he remembers [20]

> . . . shallow Riuers, to whose falls
> Melodious byrds sings Madrigalls,

or alludes casually to "Vallies, groues, hills and fieldes," or to "the Meads, the Orchards, and the Primrose lanes," among which his own Canterbury was set,

> Where painted Carpets o're the meads are hurl'd

and where the Stour was full of "Sedge and Reed." But these touches are few and far between and would, after all, fit almost any bit of English countryside.

It is when he thinks of his city and its life that Marlowe becomes specific, remembering his boyhood. Canterbury Cathedral has a "Dark Entry" near the Cloister. The lad Marlowe passed it every day on his way back and forth between the King's School and the Cathedral. Why, then, so too the nuns in his play, *The Jew of Malta,* must have a "darke entry" of their own as part of *their* cloister.[21]

When, in this same play, the Jew's wicked slave Ithamore refers to "Ierusalem, where the pilgrims kneel'd" upon "the Marble stones," Marlowe is thinking of the stones of Canterbury Cathedral, where pilgrims had knelt for centuries, and where in his own time the King's School boys trooped up and down. King Hal and his reformers had, to be sure, stopped the kneeling pilgrims before Marlowe's birth; but in that native city of all legends, such stories lingered on forever.[22]

When the fair Jewess Abigail is immured in a monastery, she is only duplicating the fate of the Maid of Kent, who had been immured in St. Sepulchre's Nunnery, in Canterbury. The real St. Augustine's Abbey at Canterbury stands just outside the town. That is why the Friars in *The Jew of Malta* live in

> the monastery
> Which standeth as an outhouse to the town.

And when, in *Edward the Second,* the hero threatens to make

The papall towers to kisse the lowlie ground,

Marlowe is thinking of the destruction of some of these friars' towers under Henry VIII—long before his birth but even longer remembered in Canterbury. And he remembers, too, Bell Harry, which then as now boomed from Bell Harry Tower in the Cathedral.

Shakespeare's verse is filled with images drawn from nature or from the everyday life of the country. Marlowe's verse has almost none of these. His images are from the classic myths he studied at the King's School and at Cambridge; from the glory of the heavens,[23]

the beauty of a thousand starres,

which his friend Thomas Harriot, most distinguished astronomer of the kingdom, knew so well; or from war and its alarms in which his friend Raleigh played a dashing part.

He was a freeman's son of a proud city. Though the countryside lay close about him, just beyond the walls, he scarcely saw it. Beauty, to reach his eyes, must be splendid, violent, wild, fierce, and close akin to passionate humankind. He could remember the legends of his city and violent death upon the old grey walls; but the peaceful fields beyond were not for him. In his plays as in his boyhood, Marlowe preferred to be[24] "Walking the backe lanes through the Gardens" which still spread in intricate profusion through the city; or coaxing a boat[25] along

the running streames And common channels

of the branching River Stour. Its channels for centuries have wound their way around the walls of Canterbury and also directly through its heart, straight across the way that the youthful Marlowe, with shining morning face newly scrubbed by Mistress Katherine Marlowe, trod somewhat unwillingly on his way to the King's School.

About the time when young Will Shakespeare was taken from the banks of the Avon and set to his tasks in Stratford Grammar School, the cobbler's child was probably learning his A.B.C.'s in "The Fyle," a shop near the Court Hall, where the corporation's clerk—"or one for him"—had been ordered to "do the duty of his office and instruct children."[26] The Fyle, where this municipal pedagogue held forth, was only a short distance from the Parish of St. George's, where the Marlowe family was living.

No one really knows where young Christopher Marlowe received his earliest education. His father, who later became a parish clerk and church-warden of St. Mary Bredman, may himself have taught the little boy to read and write. Wherever or however he secured it, the lad certainly had a fair grounding in the elements before entering the King's School, at the age of fourteen, an event with which the written record of his life begins again and runs steadily on, year by year, until his tragic death in 1593.

The Statutes of the Cathedral provided that no boys could be admitted to the King's School "before they have learned to read and write and are moderately versed in the first rudiments of grammar."

The King's School was one of the two most ancient in the kingdom—older by far than either university—when the fourteen-year-old Christopher entered; and since the day in 1580 when he left Canterbury it has gone placidly on sending generation after generation of Kentish schoolboys to Cambridge and to Oxford. Quite possibly the school was already nine centuries old when Marlowe entered it, for ancient tradition declares that it was founded by Archbishop Theodore in the year 600. However that may be, it was certainly ancient when it was re-established and given its royal title by King Henry VIII, who, having in 1541 driven the monks from Canterbury, set up a new collegiate body to administer the Cathedral and its enormous wealth. Among other things, these new authorities were to provide "two public teachers of the boys in grammar." These learned men were to devote their talents to "fifty poor boys, both destitute of the help of friends and endowed with minds apt for learning, who shall be called scholars of the grammar school, and shall be sustained out of the funds of our church conformable with the limitations of our statutes."

This sounds very much as if John Marlowe's family was very poor indeed. The term "poor boys" had, however, been so liberally interpreted that Archbishop Cranmer—the same who was later burned under Queen Mary—when he became the first visitor of the King's School, found a strong disposition to let none but sons of the gentry enter. Cranmer did not try to bar the gentry nor even to insist that they be impoverished gentry. All he said was: "If the gentleman's son be apt to learning let him be admitted; if not, let the poor man's child apt [sic] enter his room."

Even so, young Christopher was very nearly excluded from the King's School on account of his age. No boy, say the Statutes, can be elected "a poor scholar of our grammar school" who is less than nine years old or "who hath exceeded the fifteenth year of his age." As Marlowe had been born in February of 1564, he would have been fifteen some time in February of 1579. Furthermore, he could be admitted to the school only when a vacancy occurred. Luckily a vacancy did occur and he received his scholarship January 14, 1578/9, when he was barely under the age limit. A few weeks more, and Marlowe could never have entered the King's School.

There would have been no more learning beyond the bare rudiments taught at the Fyle or at his father's knee, no career at the University, no acquaintance with the great and powerful of the kingdom, able to further a young man's hopes and plans, no chance to read Archbishop Parker's books in the Library of Corpus Christi—and no *Tamburlaine,* no *Faustus,* no *Hero and Leander.* At best, he could have entered his father's shoe-shop and dreamed sometimes in the tan yard or at the cobbler's bench. The Elizabethan drama would have taken a different course. There would have been no Marlowe to guide the early work of the young Shakespeare, out of which the work of his maturity grew; and Shakespeare would have been something quite other than he was.

The schoolmasters who stretched a point to admit the boy probably took no special pride in his later career of secret politics, sceptical philosophy, poetry, and writing for the godless stage; but, for all that, they deserved better than they knew of their country and their country's literature, when they gave that eager, active, passionate mind its chance at the learning it was to use so well.

They were not, however, introducing him to a very easy life. School began at six in the morning with the responsive repetition of a psalm and ended with another psalm at five in the afternoon. Technically, Marlowe was part of the Cathedral's ecclesiastical organization; but he was "non-capitular," that is, not part of the chapter clergy. All such members of the Cathedral dined together at three tables, the third of which was occupied by the fifty King's Scholars and ten choir boys. Each was given cloth for a new gown at Christmas, two and a half yards to each boy, and free commons, which probably meant only the mid-day meal, besides an annual stipend of £1. 8s. 4d. Actually, the boys seem to have received £4 a year for cloth, commons, and stipend together.

The hours of study were no harder than those in Stratford Grammar School, which like the King's School still flourishes, or in any other school of the day. Discipline was severe, as in most Elizabethan schools, whose masters believed that "there is no other method of making a scholar than by beating him."

There is no record of just how submissive to the discipline of the King's School the fiery, rebellious spirit may have been that was later to terrorize the police of London. Amid the Cathedral's archives, however, a few of the accounts of the King's School for the year 1579, while Marlowe was a scholar, are still preserved. They show him drawing his stipend regularly; but he is not, alas! one of the schoolboys who signed their names when they drew their stipends, so that we have no scrap of his handwriting. The records for his second year are missing; but the Buttery Book of Corpus Christi College shows him arriving there in December, 1580. He obviously remained at school through all or most of the Michaelmas term of 1580 and was then, at the age of sixteen, ready for the University.

There is no hint that he was as yet in bad odour with the academic authorities; on the contrary, he is shown every favour, as if he were regarded as a youth of exceptional promise. He was given one of Archbishop Parker's scholarships at Cambridge, which would hardly have been possible unless the King's School was pretty well satisfied with him. Since these scholarships were intended for boys likely to become clergymen, the wild young scapegrace of the next decade must have been concealed beneath schoolboy decorum. Probably the lad himself had little idea enough whither his tastes and talents were to lead him, and was merely submissively following the course laid out for him by his schoolmasters and parents, who must at this stage of his career have been extremely proud of him.

The King's School begins Marlowe's life-long association with the great names of England. Among the family names, famous in English letters and in English history, which appear in the ancient records of the school are Shelley, Lewes, Lyly,

Sydney, Playfair, and Bentham. John Boyle, later Bishop of Cork, and his brother, Richard Boyle, later Earl of Cork, were schoolmates. By a curious irony, Stephen Gosson had left the King's School in 1572, a few years before Marlowe entered. Like Marlowe he, too, was to write for the theatre; but unlike Marlowe, he was to leave off these evil ways and write, in *The School of Abuse,* the most savage attack on the sinfulness of the stage and all its doings that had yet been written in England, "finding playes of the*m*selues, as filthy as the stables of Augia, impossible to bee cleansed before they be carried out of Englande wyth a styffe streame." [27]

4.

"Learning's Golden Gifts"

"Still climing after knowledge infinite."
I. Tamburlaine

One winter's day in 1580, young Kit Marlowe, soon to be seventeen years old, said good-bye to the cobbler and his wife, to Elias Martyn, the apprentice, to Anne, Margaret, Joan, and Dorothy, to the Reverend Nicholas Goldsborough, headmaster of the King's School, packed up such few belongings as he had, and set off for Cambridge. The road led west and north over the low hills, from which he caught a last glimpse of the Cathedral, whose towers dominate the landscape as far as eye can see the low-lying Kentish city. It was, perhaps, the last time he ever saw them, for there is no record that he ever returned to Canterbury. It is probable enough that he did come back during some of his long absences from the University; but whether or no he ever saw it again, Canterbury had left its indelible impress upon his mind, whence that impress was to emerge a few years later in some of the imperishable verse of English literature.

Cambridge was to leave other impressions that can be quite as clearly traced in his poetry. In *Tamburlaine,* in *The Jew of Malta,* in *The Massacre at Paris,* in *The Passionate Shepherd,* there are allusions to the Kentish scene that cannot be mistaken. In *Tamburlaine,* in *Doctor Faustus,* in *The Massacre at Paris,* in *The Jew of Malta,* and in *Edward the Second,* appear allusions to the dress of Cambridge students, to University buildings, and to University life, together with plain traces of the academic vocabulary characteristic of Cambridge. These mingle with allusions to the books in use at Cambridge in Marlowe's day, sometimes the very books and manuscripts that lay on the shelves of Archbishop Parker's Library, given to Corpus Christi five years before the poet entered the gateway of the Old Court.

Thanks to the bounty of the good and learned Archbishop —a bounty which for three centuries and a half has sent boys yearly from the King's School to Corpus—the shoemaker's son was on his way to a great and ancient seat of learning. The sons of the nobility and gentry, the clergy, the learned men of the kingdom, and sometimes learned men from afar, all mingled there with humbler lads from poorer families, for the yeomanry were beginning to make scholars of their sons, and the flame of the Renaissance was touching every level of society. When a "poor man's child apt," like Marlowe, appeared in certain fortunate cities, named in the wills of benefactors, he had the chance of winning a scholarship and being sent to the University for three years at least, and perhaps—if he did very well indeed—for two or three years more, until he attained the master's degree, one of the proudest academic distinctions in Elizabethan England.

The general terms of Marlowe's scholarship are outlined in the will of Archbishop Parker, who died in 1575, and are made more definite in a formal agreement of April 12, 1580, between the Archbishop's son, John Parker, and the dons of Corpus. The younger Parker reserves to himself the right to nominate the scholars and it was therefore his decision which gave Marlowe his education. The indenture provides that the Canterbury scholars "must at the time of their election be so entred into the skill of song as that they shall at the first syght solf [solve] and sing plaine song And that they shalbe of the best and aptest schollers well instructed in their gramer and if it may be such as can make a verse."

They were to occupy "that roome or chamber in the said Colledge late called a storehouse now repaired and finished for that purpose at the cost and charges of the said John Parker in accomplishment likewise of the will of the said most reverend father." The master and fellows of Corpus agreed to "give them reading in the hall within the said Colledge their barber and launder frely without any thing paying therfore" and to "use the said schollers in such convenient order and manner as other schollers."

It was further "provided that none of the said thre schollers thus last above founded shalbe absent out of the said Colledge for more than one moneth in any one yere except he be sent either vpon the Colledge busines or therto compelled thorough some notable sicknes during which time he shall not leese the comoditie of his Comons and allowaunces of xij^{d} the weke according to the Customes and statutes of the house." As the college Buttery Book shows, Marlowe greatly exceeded the permitted absence and he also spent a great deal more than a shilling a week.[1]

Founded, according to tradition, in the thirteenth century, Cambridge had grown to a university of fourteen colleges and eighteen hundred students. The religious note predominated, as it had at the King's School. Marlowe himself was probably already destined for holy orders—he certainly was when he received his B.A., four years later—and Cambridge University, according to a report made by the bishops to Parliament, included "an hundred preachers at the least, very worthy men, and not many less in the University of Oxford,"[2] for the sister university had grown at about the same pace. Cambridge was a smaller town than Canterbury, numbering about five thousand townsmen in addition to the University.

Corpus Christi College, of which Archbishop Parker had been Master and to which he directed that his scholars should be sent, was already old, though it was some two hundred years younger than the University of which it formed a part. Founded in the fourteenth century by Cambridge townsmen belonging to the Guild of Corpus Christi and to the Guild of St. Mary, it was officially the College of Corpus Christi and of the Blessed Virgin Mary, an origin which its sixteenth century arms still proclaim—the pelican and its brood for Corpus Christi, lilies for the Blessed Virgin.

More familiarly, Corpus was known as Benet Hall; for in Marlowe's time, having no chapel, the college used instead the Church of St. Benet [Benedict] immediately adjoining and connected with the Old Court by a special passage.

Originally established on the site of tenements owned by the brethren of the Guilds, the College had grown by lease and purchase until by the middle of the sixteenth century it occupied most of its present site, excepting the New Quadrangle, which was not erected until 1823-27. John Josselyn's history of Corpus Christi, written in 1569, describes the College buildings, "with walls of enclosure, chambers arranged about a quadrangle, Hall, Kitchen, and Master's Habitation,"[3] the latter once occupied by Archbishop Parker himself, when from 1544 to 1553 he had been Master of Corpus. Until the time of Henry VIII, the College had no glass in its windows. Then the Master and Fellows had their windows glazed; and gradually not only were all windows glazed but rooms and halls were panelled and plastered until in 1569, says Josselyn, the buildings of Corpus had attained "that elegance and beauty for which they are now conspicuous."[4]

Sixteenth century Cambridge had all its modern beauty. Paul Hentzner, the German traveller who wrote an account of his journey to England in 1598, only a few years after Marlowe left the University, says:[5] "All is splendid; the streets fine, the churches numerous, and those seats of the Muses, the Colleges, most beautiful; in these a great number of learned men are supported, and the studies of all polite sciences and languages flourish."

Free from the cares of practical life, in edifices ancient even then, surrounded by green lawns and spacious gardens filled with flowers, the company of scholars whom Marlowe came to join were—in theory at least—devoted wholly to the pursuit of learning. Gladly would they learn and gladly teach. So gracious was this cloistered yet eager life that in 1575 William Soone, Professor of Civil Law, observed as he renounced it for the sake of his Catholic faith: "The way of life in these colleges is the most pleasant and liberal; and if I might have my choice, and my principles would permit, I should prefer it to a kingdom."

Though pleasant, it was a restricted life. The English universities, like the King's School from which young Kit Marlowe came, were closely linked with the Established Church. Masters and Fellows were all in holy orders. The colleges existed mainly to provide an educated clergy for the future; and the scholarship on which Marlowe came to Corpus had been established by a famous prelate to train promising lads for the priesthood of the Church of England. Archbishop Parker's scholars were to hold their appointments for three years; and then, if they intended to become priests, they might continue for three years longer. Marlowe did remain for the additional three years—in fact he spent six and a half years in Cambridge—and must therefore have been regarded as a candidate for the Church. One can understand the horror of the Master and Fellows of Corpus as his later career unfolded.

Marlowe's religious views probably became tainted with unorthodoxy while he was still a student at Corpus. Francis Kett, later burned at the stake for his Unitarian views, had resigned his fellowship July 13, 1580, some months before Marlowe arrived. But weekly entries in the Buttery Book show that he continued in residence during the first part of the next year, long after Marlowe's arrival. Just before Marlowe left in 1587, there arrived one Thomas Fineux, another Kentishman, a great admirer of the poet, who presently also found himself in trouble because of his religious scepticism. It looks as if there was a continuous undercurrent of religious questioning beneath the strict orthodoxy of the College.[6]

In spite of its religious atmosphere, the titular head of Cambridge University was always a layman, a noble of high degree—in Marlowe's day no less a dignitary than Lord Cecil of Burghley, Lord Treasurer of the Kingdom and one of Elizabeth's most trusted advisers. The Vice-Chancellor was usually the head of one of the Colleges.

The University was actually governed by the "Caput," which consisted of three doctors of law, medicine, and divinity, respectively, and two others, usually including an M.A. of not more than three or four years' standing to represent the younger element in the University. This meant that he was very young indeed, rarely over twenty-five. Elizabeth's England was a land of young men, and the average age of the Caput was sometimes as low as thirty-one. Over their deliberations the Vice-Chancellor, acting head of the University, presided when—as was usually the case—Lord Burghley was absent. His Lordship, however, kept himself in close touch with University affairs.[7]

The authority of the Chancellor—which was usually exercised through the Vice-Chancellor—made him much more than a mere University head. He was an officer of the law, with cognizance of personal pleas, debts, accounts, contracts, and all breaches of the peace (except mayhem and felony) in which a member of the University or a University servant was a party. He had the right of arrest—and the town of Cambridge had to guard his prisoners for him. He had the right to seize bad foodstuffs. He could safeguard the morals of his youthful charges by driving daughters of joy from the vicinity. As the Charter put it,[8] he might search "pro omnibus et publicis mulieribus, pronubis, vacabundis, et aliis personis de malo suspectis," not only in Cambridge but also in towns and villages near it; for his authority extended one "English myle" around the city. He controlled the book trade in Cambridge, and all stationers gave bond to "provide sufficient store of all manner of books fit and requisite for the furnishing of all students continuing or abiding within the university, and the same books to be well bound, and to be sold at all and every time and times at reasonable prices." In return, the Chancellor protected the Cambridge dealers against their London rivals, who pirated Oxford and Cambridge editions impartially. No such pirated books could even be offered for sale in Cambridge; but a few years later some of these same piratical London publishers were to be among Marlowe's best friends. It is his quondam chamber-fellow, Thomas Kydd, who tells us that "some stationers in Paules churchyard" were "such as he conversd withall." [9]

The College of Corpus Christi and the Blessed Virgin Mary, when Marlowe entered, was governed by the Master and twenty Fellows. It chose as Fellows only "honestos, castos, humiles, pacificos & modestos graduatos." These paragons conversed wholly in Latin, save when the Master gave them special permission to use English. As a further precaution against academic indolence, they were required to proceed to the higher degrees within fixed periods. A half or a third had to be in priest's orders, and these received a somewhat larger payment than those in deacon's orders.[10]

An odder group of associates for the most turbulent and reckless spirit in all that turbulent and reckless day it would be hard to imagine. One may hope that he was "honestus" and "castus," though some of his reported conversation hardly bears it out; but "humilis," "pacificus," or "modestus" Christopher Marlowe certainly was not.

Life, studies, even the minute details of dress of the whole University, were strictly regulated; and the fiery spirit of the youthful Marlowe was already in rebellion against every restriction of any kind whatever. Elizabethans all, the Cambridge students had that love of finery typical of the great Queen's reign.

Eager and impetuous Elizabethan youth demanded linen shirts and ruffles, and the still more evil vanities of "long lockes of Hayre," the immense Elizabethan ruff, into which one might crowd as much as fifteen yards of cloth; "Barilled Hosen," adorned with "cut, welt, pincke or such-like,"—silk if possible; cut taffeta doublets; and as for gowns, if gowns they must wear, let them be as splendid as the imagination of their tailors might devise.[11]

Above all, they wanted hats instead of the round academic caps. And hats Lord Burghley, the Lord Treasurer of England, the great Queen's chief minister of state, who was also Chancellor of the University, was determined that they should not have. In May of 1588, the Armada Year, when all England was arming; when John Marlowe down in Canterbury is said to have been enrolled as a volunteer bowman; when Philip of Spain's armed might threatened England with the terrors of the rack, the block, the thumbscrew, and the stake; when the Duke of Parma's soldiery were gathering in the Low Countries ready for invasion; when the Armada was making ready to sail—a time, in short, when the Lord Treasurer of England might be supposed to have plenty to occupy his mind—My Lord Burghley was greatly worried about hats. He let the defence of the realm take care of itself while he scribbled endless directions about the clothes the boys and their dons were wearing in Cambridge, and sent from London stringent instructions "that no hatt be worne of any Graduate or Schollar." [12]

Matters had, indeed, reached a serious pass at Cambridge; for there was worse. It is painful to record that a year earlier the Lord Treasurer had discovered that even the College tutors were clad in "Satten Dublettes, silke and velvett overstockes, and facynge of gownes with velvett and satten to the grownde; and in fine great ruffs, contrarye to lawe and order."

It is true that the great Eliza and all her Court were even more vaingloriously arrayed; that half the nobles in her kingdom all but ruined themselves for the sake of their tailored splendour; and that the poorer gallants of London aped this finery as best they might. It was also true that they all went in daily and imminent danger of battle and peculiarly horrible death. Nevertheless, what worried the Lord Treasurer was that many Cambridge students had "left the ancient, grave, and comely apparell generally used of all scholars in both Universities." [13] And furthermore, His Lordship came back to that matter of hats, directing once again that "all Scholers being Graduats upon the charges of any Howse, do wear a square cap of clothe, and lykwise scholers of Howses that be no Graduats, and all other Scholers that have taken no degree of Scholers, and do lyve upon their own charges, do weare in the said University a round clothe cap."

Not that Lord Burghley was unwilling to make any reasonable concessions; for he added a magnanimous proviso: "Saving that it may be lawful for the sons of Noblemen, or the sons and heirs of Knights, to wear round caps of velvet."

"But," added My Lord Treasurer emphatically, "no hats!"

Who shall say what dire perils to the higher life of man the good Lord Burghley's efforts may have averted?

Just what constituted the "ancient, grave, and comely apparell generally used of all scholars" had been carefully defined in University Statutes of 1570, which were in force when Marlowe entered Corpus ten years later. No one was to "go forth from his college, except he be clad in a gown reaching down to his ankles and a hood befitting his degree, or at least having a sacerdotal distinction about his neck,—a fine of six shillings and eightpence shall be imposed on any one who disobeys in this respect."[14] Regulations of 1569 had already provided "that no scholler doe weare any long lockes of Hayre uppon his heade, but that he be polled, notted, or rounded after the accustomed manner of the gravest Schollers of the Universitie under payne of *6s. 8d.*"[15]

In 1585, just after Marlowe took his bachelor's degree, the dress of graduates, of whom he had just become one, was again minutely regulated. The University ordered "that no Graduate remayninge within any Colledge, Hostell, or Hall, or clayminge to enjoye the priviledge of a Scholler, do weare any stuffe in the outward part of his gowne, but woollen cloth of blacke, puke, London Browne, or other sad color." The hood was to be of "the same or like cloth and color." This was to prevent any possible excuse for wearing that dangerous fabric, silk; and there was a further proviso against "any stuffe in upon or about his doublett, coates, Jerkyn, jackett, cassock or hose, of velvett or silke." Nor was the graduate to wear any garment "that shal be embrodred, powdred, pynked, or welted, savinge at the handes, verge, showlder, or coller; or gathered, playted, garded, hacked, raced, laced or cutt, saving the cutt of the welt and button holes, nor of any other redde, grene, and such like other colour."

Further—for the Lord Treasurer's soul burned within him —"no hatt to be worne except for infirmities sake."

Against these restrictions, Marlowe's rebellious heart still rankled years later when he was writing his *Doctor Faustus* in London. Faustus, alone in his study, sits meditating what he will do when magic shall have placed all power in his hands; and one of his first thoughts is: [16]

> Ile haue them fill the publike schooles with silk,
> Wherewith the students shalbe brauely clad.

Marlowe is thinking of Cambridge and its costumes again when Tamburlaine bids his chieftains dress for his wedding in "scarlet roabes." [17] Cambridge doctors have always worn black silk on ordinary occasions, scarlet on great occasions.

University life, as Marlowe knew it, was not by any means completely care-free. A contemporary sermon describes a typical day in St. John's College, about Marlowe's time; and life in Corpus, which had Puritanical leanings, must have been nearly as severe.[18] Some students of St. John's rose at four or five, prayed and heard an exhortation from five to six; studied till dinner at ten—"whenas they be content with a penny piece of beef among four, having a pottage made of the same beef, with salt and oatmeal, and nothing else." Further intellectual pursuits till five; then supper, "not much better than their dinner. Immediately after which they go either to reasoning in problems or to some other study, until it be nine or ten of the clock; and then, being without fires, are fain to walk or run up and down half-an-hour to get a heat on their feet when they go to bed."

These earnest students were naturally chilly, for no fire could banish the cold that poured in through windows which were closed only by shutters, without glass. Academic dress had been designed for warmth, with flowing sleeves to wrap the hands, and mighty hoods to encompass the heads, but even this did not make for perfect comfort.

University life could be very severe in its simplicity. The inventory of all the worldly goods of a poor student in 1540/41 shows that he owned nothing but "a long Gowne with a Whood faced with Russels," a chest, two jackets, two doublets, one pair of hose, one cloak, three sheets, a coverlet, a blanket, a chair, a meat-knife, eight books, and—concession to the arts!—a lute.[19]

Marlowe probably owned a little more than this poor wretch; but even so, to his fiery spirit the contrast between his poverty as a pensioner and the luxury of the wealthier students, the "fellow-commoners," would be extremely galling. Just before Marlowe entered the University, the young Earl of Essex was able to spend more than seven pounds on furnishings alone, including extra glass for his windows, "new hangings in the study of painted cloth," and "a place makinge for the trindle bed to drawe through the waule."[20] Scholars slept on trundle beds, the larger beds being reserved for Bachelors of Arts who shared rooms with several juniors. Only Masters and Doctors could have rooms of their own. The unknown author of the Cambridge play, *The Return from Parnassus,* is thinking of these living arrangements when he alludes to the days "when I was in Cambridge and lay in a trundle-bed."[21]

The studies to which these students, rich and poor, applied themselves, were the result of two changes in curriculum. Royal Injunctions from Henry VIII had ended in 1535 the "frivolous questions and vain glosses," which were all that bluff and brutal King Hal saw in mediæval scholasticism. The University substituted for them classical and Biblical literature, together with a little science for graduates. Boys coming up from the schools could already read and write Latin; though some of the blunders in Marlowe's translation of Ovid leave one in doubt as to the perfection of their Latinity. A whole year was given to each subject—the first to rhetoric; the second and third to dialectics; the fourth to philosophy.

Chance has preserved[22] a list of all the students at Cambridge on October 29, 1581, together with the subjects of their studies. Marlowe, now in his second year, duly appears as "Merling" of Corpus Christi, among the students of "Mr. Johnes, professor lecturae dialecticae." It was probably under Mr. Johnes that Marlowe studied the modern and highly up-to-date *Logic* of Peter Ramus, which had recently replaced Aristotle's *Organon* as a Cambridge text.

At some time during his six years at Cambridge, Marlowe learned to know his Aristotle—probably during his last year of undergraduate study. "Quartus [annus] adjungat philosophiam," say the Cambridge Statutes;[23] and though modernistic and reforming dons might, in favour of Ramus, contemptuously reject the mighty "master of them that know" as a writer of textbooks on logic, they obviously could not teach philosophy without Aristotle. Marlowe knew the *Analytics* well enough.

> Sweete Analutikes tis thou hast rauisht me,

says Faustus,[24] dreaming in his lonely study of the endless power and endless knowledge that magic is to give him at the cost of his soul. Later, when Faustus abandons philosophy, he wishes to

Bid on cai me on farewell,

an allusion to the Aristotelean idea of ὂν καὶ μὴ ὄν—being and not being. The passage baffled the Elizabethan printers and it fared little better at the hands of Marlowe's later editors, appearing as mere gibberish, "oncaimeon," until at length a modern editor recognized it for what it really was.[25]

Though Marlowe's Faustus pretends to be a German, he is actually a Cambridge doctor through and through. Not only does he quote the books that Marlowe studied as a Cambridge scholar; his very speech bewrayeth him; for he uses the vocabulary peculiar to the University. Faustus is "grac't with Doctors name"; Cambridge degrees were granted by the passage of a "grace" and were recorded in a "Grace Book." Faustus says he has "commencde" in divinity; that is the Cambridge word for taking a new degree.

When, in 1584, Marlowe received his bachelor's degree, he passed to more advanced study. Candidates for the master's degree were to be "auditores assidui" at lectures upon philosophy, astronomy, perspective, and Greek. They were to make up "by their own industry" gaps in their earlier work; and they were to attend bareheaded *(aperto capite)* at the learned disputations of those who were already masters of the arts. "Nor," say the Statutes grimly, "will they depart thence without seeking permission from the proctor." Evidently, there were dull moments at these learned discourses, when even the charms of divine philosophy palled upon fledgling bachelors.

The classics and the astronomical studies of these later years seem especially to have interested Marlowe; for the images which appear in his poetry are drawn almost entirely from classical mythology or from the stars and planets, a fact perhaps not wholly unconnected with the presence in Archbishop Parker's library of a book on astronomy by that same Gemma Frisius whom Marlowe seems to have discussed with the astronomer Harriot in after life. He never tires of allusions to[26]

All things that mooue betweene the quiet poles

or to

The seuen planets, the firmament, and the imperiall heauen,

of which he had learned both at Cambridge and in conversation with his friend Thomas Harriot. We have the testimony of Harriot's own notes that he and his friend "Morly"[27] discussed scientific subjects together; and Marlowe's interest in them is plain enough in *Doctor Faustus*. There is a long scene in which Doctor Faustus and Mephastophilis do nothing but "argue of diuine Astrologie," discussing such matters as "coniunctions, oppositions, aspects, eclipsis." Strange to say, Marlowe like Milton usually adheres, for poetic purposes, to the Ptolemaic astronomy though he certainly knew all about the Copernican system.

Books filled with such lore were naturally plentiful in a University town. Not only did the Chancellor control booksellers; the University itself began printing again in 1584/5, while Marlowe was a student; and the neighbouring town of Sturbridge held an annual fair famous for its book-stalls.[28] Marlowe could pursue his studies in two of the finest libraries in England. Archbishop Parker's Library at Corpus Christi was rich in books and manuscripts, many of which show their influence in the plays. The University Library possessed "Globes, Astroglobes, and all other Instruments mathematicall." These were greatly valued and were kept "safly locked up in some convenient place within the Library with 2 severall locks and keys, whereof the one key to remaine with the Vice Chancellor, and the other to remain with the keeper of the Library."[29] To this day, the seal of Cambridge University is safeguarded in the same way.

The few hundred books in the library were almost equally priceless. There was a triple inventory. The Keeper gave £200 bond to "preserve safly all and every one of the Books not locked up." It was provided that "all masters of arte, batchelours of law or physick, or any other of the university above that degree, may have free accesse to the bookes of the saide librairie; so that at one time there be not more than tenne in the said librairie together (excepte the straungers that come only to see and not to tarry); and that none of them tarry above one houre at one booke at one tyme, if any other shall desire to use the sayd booke." [30]

Students did not have free access to the books, but as they paid fees for the use of the library on admission to degrees, they must certainly have used them under restrictions of some kind. Archbishop Parker provided that only dons might take books out of his library, a restriction which implies pretty plainly that others might at least use them in the library. The University's scale of library fees rose from the four pence paid by bachelors to sixteen pence for doctors. Many of the books were chained and the University accounts during Marlowe's student days contain payments for renewing the chains.

Thanks to the careful records of Richard Moodie and Henry Frogge, the librarians who dutifully gave their bonds of £200 and thankfully received their annual stipends of five marks a year while Marlowe was at the University, we know the titles of some of the books he had opportunity to read as a student; and it is no great surprise to find the contents appearing in his plays a year or two later.

Books that we know Marlowe used in writing his plays abounded in Cambridge. Graduates and friends of the University made frequent gifts. The generosity of these benefactors was piously recorded; later academic generations have with equal piety preserved the records; and so—although the great University and the Colleges which compose it have been piling up literary treasures through the intervening centuries—it is still often possible to look at individual volumes and name the very years when they reached the shelves which have been their home since the fifteen hundreds or even earlier.

That is why one can say positively that the undergraduate Marlowe found awaiting him within the University Library and in the Library of Corpus, copies of the *Theatrum Orbis Terrarum,* famous atlas of the German geographer Ortelius—plain Wortels in his native Germany. He also found in both libraries the works of the learned and long since forgotten Paulus Jovius, Bishop of Nocera. Marlowe took the very wild geography of *Tamburlaine,* mistakes and all, from the charts of Ortelius. He took parts of his story from Paulus Jovius. He may have added a detail or two from the writings of Pope Pius II, also known as Aeneas Sylvius Piccolomini, whose works were in the University Library and at Corpus, and from

Baptista Egnatius's *De Origine Turcarum Libellus* (1539), which was at Corpus.

Most of his *Edward the Second,* Marlowe took from Holinshed, that inexhaustible quarry from which Shakespeare was to dig so much material for *Macbeth* and his historical plays. And Holinshed was almost certainly in the Corpus Christi Library before Marlowe left the University. At least, one stout leather-bound volume to-day bears on the title page the donor's name and the date, 1587, the year of Marlowe's last degree.

Did Marlowe read the very copies of these books, which still stand upon Cambridge shelves? We do not know. He did not, alas! annotate the books if he ever read them. The modern University librarians who discourage undergraduates from scribbling in the books would be very glad if he had, for we should then possess a few lines of the poet's authentic handwriting. We might then even be able to make sure by comparison that the foolscap page of manuscript of *The Massacre at Paris,* now treasured at the Folger Shakespeare Library, or the "Dialogue in Verse" at Dulwich College, are actually in Marlowe's hand. All that we really know is that Marlowe shows a considerable knowledge of all these volumes; that Richard Harvey, who was leaving Cambridge just after Marlowe entered, seems familiar with many of the same books when he sits down to write his *Lamb of God;* that all of these books were in the Cambridge libraries and usually accessible to students.[31] Even the neo-Hellenic *Lexicon* of Suidas, with its articles on the legendary Musæus, whose *Hero and Leander* Marlowe was to make a dream for lovers in all lands and climes, lay there on the shelves to help set the young poet dreaming.

Over these old books Richard Moodie, the former "schoolkeeper," and Master Henry Frogge, of Trinity, kept a vigilant eye to make sure that there were "not more than tenne in the said librairie together," and that chance strangers, who came "only to see and not to tarry," deported themselves becomingly. They took good care of their books and even rebound Paulus Jovius, one of Marlowe's sources, while he was a student.[32]

The heavy covers that still protect its pages may be the very leather that he touched, new from the binder's hands, as he opened it to read of Tamburlaine and his barbarian hordes, or Persian nobles and raids and battles far away and long ago —all tucked between leather-covered boards, very old and scarred and cracked to-day, after the buffeting of the centuries. Leaning a-dream above the ranks of the chained books, his long black gown of "sad stuffe" reaching decorously to his heels, and the round cap, upon which Lord Burghley insisted so vehemently, decorously disposed above his brow, the shoemaker's son found the stuff of romance, forgot Canterbury, forgot Cambridge, forgot everything save shy romance—then hurried off to the old storehouse in a corner of the Old Court at Corpus, perhaps even then to pen the first draft of the verses that a few years later Edward Alleyn was to mouth upon the London stage.

These were the verses whose "drumming decasyllabons" caught the errant fancy of London, sent poor Robert Greene into venomous fits of envy, opened a new era on the English stage—and presently gave Shakespeare's Ancient Pistol an opening for a sly gibe.

5.

Archbishop's Bounty

"O what a world of profit and delight."
Doctor Faustus

Student life in Cambridge was not all serious, in spite of Lord Burghley's earnest efforts. The students "perhaps keep more dogs and greyhounds, that are so often seen in the streets, than they do books," observes the diary of a German nobleman who visited the University in 1602.[1] In 1581 a bear was "bayted in the sermon time, betwene one and two of the clock in the afternoon," and since Elizabeth's successor on the throne found it necessary to forbid "bear-baiting, bull-baiting, common plaies, public shewes, enterludes, comoedies or tragedies in the English language, games at loggats [bowling] and nine-holes," it seems likely that all these godless pastimes had long been popular. When Marlowe matriculated, students had just received permission to "play at the foot-ball, but only within the precincts of their several colleges."[2]

They were forbidden, however, to bathe or swim in any water in the county of Cambridge. "The Backs," where the River Cam flows through the smooth-shaven lawns of the Colleges, was evidently too tempting to resist on the hot summer days. This particularly beautiful part of the Cantabrigian landscape had attained its present beauty very early.

"Behind the colleges," says the diary of the Duke of Stettin-Pomerania, "flows a lovely river, with many bridges leading to a meadow pleasantly laid out with trees as a promenade for the students, who make pretty good use of the cheerful place."[3] Bathing does not appear to have been regarded as a "good use." For the first illicit plunge, undergraduates were punished with a public flogging; for a second, by expulsion. Bachelors of Arts were put in the stocks. The punishment of Masters of Arts who so far forgot their dignity as to cast silken robes aside in favour of the sixteenth century version of a bathing suit—which was only too probably nothing at all—

was left to the discretion and ingenuity of their Masters and Deans.

From Canterbury and the King's School, where the drama seems at least mildly to have flourished, Marlowe had come to a University where the classic drama was popular and where English plays were by no means unknown. James I may have frowned upon them but Queen Elizabeth was not so stern. The Queen's Players performed in Cambridge July 9, 1583, and Lord Rich's Players were there about 1587. Academic authorities encouraged student plays. A statute of 1560 at Queen's College directs the expulsion of any student refusing to take part; and the statutes of Trinity prescribe the performance of five plays at Christmas. Corpus Christi accounts refer to the performance of "the Comoedie" in 1581/2 and to "scenici ludi" in February, 1582/3, while Marlowe was in residence.

Gammer Gurton's Needle, the first English farce and the first university play in English, had been produced at Christ's College about 1553; and young Kit as a freshman probably saw Thomas Legge's *Richardus Tertius*, produced for three evenings at St. John's in 1580. He might also have seen *Meleager* at Christ's in 1581, or *Terminus et Non Terminus* at St. John's in 1586. Long, long afterward, his university mate and collaborator, Thomas Nashe, remembered "*Pedantius*, that exquisite Comedie in Trinitie Colledge," in 1580, when he was a freshman and Marlowe had probably not yet entered.[4] Half a century later, prim young John Milton, as a Cambridge student, viewed with cold disgust young academicians "upon the Stage writhing and unboning their Clergie limmes to all the antick and dishonest gestures of Trinculo's, Buffons, and Bawds."[5]

College theatricals were, as a matter of fact, amazingly lacking in decorum. Student "stage-keepers," appointed to maintain order, found it advisable to wear visors and steel caps and sometimes officiated "with a dager and sworde drawne." Uninvited guests assembled outside the college halls and indicated their displeasure by breaking the windows. Trinity College had to put in "lv foot of newe glasse in the hall after the playes" in 1582/3, and thereafter took the precaution of removing the windows entirely until the plays were over. St. John's College also preferred to make payments "to the glacer for taking downe and setting vpp the windowes."

Marlowe's years in Cambridge were enlivened by various diverting episodes. There was the alarming case of Dr. John Browning, who made the mistake of going to Oxford for his D.D., instead of proceeding as required by the statutes of Trinity College, Cambridge. Lost to all shame, this peccant divine returned to Trinity in 1584 and locked himself up in his room, whence he "would not depart, keeping his chamber door shut till some were sent to pull him out." Frustrated in these attempts, the college "made a decree, the next day by eight o'clock his doors should be broken open. And this was accordingly executed, and they carried him out by strong hand." It was one way of dealing with a doctor of divinity.[6]

At about the same time, the University was exercised over "unseemlye owtrages lately commytted by the yonge and unbridled heddes" at the expense of no less a person than Sir Walter Raleigh, then high in royal favour and either already a friend of Marlowe's or soon to become one. Queen Elizabeth, who delighted in royal gestures, liked to give her favourites magnificent rewards for their services. The only thing she delighted in still more was saving money. The penurious Queen was able to gratify all three tastes at once by patents granting royal monopolies to favoured courtiers. These gave exclusive right to trade in specified commodities anywhere in England. This was a royal gift by exercise of royal authority; it cost her miserly majesty exactly nothing; but it enabled the courtier who held the monopoly to charge his own prices for something or other that the long-suffering subjects of the Virgin Queen had to have—and they paid for it accordingly.

"It bringeth the general profit into private hand, and the end of all is beggary and bondage of the subject," said an indignant Member of Parliament, protesting against "the great grievances that the town and country which I serve suffereth by some of these monopolies." He was speaking in 1601, when there were monopolies on currants, iron, cards, ox shin-bones, train oil, blubber oil, transportation of leather (which must have annoyed John Marlowe), cloth, ashes, aniseeds, vinegar, sea-coal, salt-peter, lead, calamine stones, and pilchards.[7] Queen Bess's subjects could perhaps live happily without ox shin-bones, aniseeds, and calamine stones; but monopoly prices on iron, leather, coal, cloth, and fish were another matter. On one occasion Elizabeth gave her personal physician, that same

Doctor Lopez to whom Marlowe alludes and whom she later hanged, the sole right to sell sumac, an important medicine.

About this time, she had bestowed upon Sir Walter Raleigh the sole right to license vintners, and Sir Walter had issued one of his licenses to a certain Keymer, authorizing him to open a wine-shop in Cambridge. The University protested that it possessed special rights and that Sir Walter's protégé had no privilege within its jurisdiction. Whereupon the proctors tore down Keymer's sign—which the pugnacious vintner as promptly set up again.

The proctors received orders to tear it down once more, "which they indevored to doe, firste by themselves, the Beadall and their Servauntes only; but beinge purposely resisted with such provision as they litle looked for, as namely with skaldinge water myngled with lyme and aishes, and with stones and brickbattes they were forsed to send for the helpe of three or foure Masters of Arte moe."[8] Even a Master of Arts was robust and combative in the spacious days of great Elizabeth.

In 1587, the year when Marlowe received his own master's degree, town and gown fell foul of one another over the grievous matter of some five-and-thirty hogs belonging to William Hammond, bailiff and "berebruer" of Jesus College. In those days every college maintained a brewer to provide its own special brew. Hammond's swine had grazed on town lands. The borough of Cambridge promptly clapped them in the pound and then, to the scandal of the citizens, "Mr. Vicechauncelor made a replevin to delyver the hogges, which never any vicechauncellor dyd hertofore."

When this failed to bring home the bacon, students of Jesus College evidently took the matter into their own hands. The Mayor of Cambridge complained indignantly that "the pound in the night tyme hath bene twyse by great multitude of riotous persons with clubbes and other weapons sawne a sunder, and the hogges delyvered." The august head of the University primly denied that this could possibly be "the misdemeanour of any schollers."[9]

The bounty of Matthew Parker, Archbishop of Canterbury, who died in 1575, still keeps three lads from the King's School at Corpus Christi. Parker never lost his interest in Corpus, and a few years after he became archbishop was able to found a scholarship, partly with the money left by a certain John Mere, of whose will he had been named "supervisor," partly with gifts from others, and partly out of his own pocket.[10] Between 1567 and 1575, Parker founded thirteen scholarships, to be held by boys from the King's School, some to be chosen by the Dean and Chapter of Canterbury, others by the Mayor and Aldermen of Norwich.

Marlowe held one of the last three scholarships, founded for a boy at the King's School, by the will of the great Archbishop. We know this because the will is still preserved as well as the indenture, already described, which John Parker as executor made with the dons of Corpus; and also because, though the King's School records for Marlowe's last year are lost, the annual audits of Corpus Christi list a Canterbury lad, named Christopher Pashley, among the Canterbury scholars until the first quarter of 1580/81. Marlowe arrives at Corpus a little before Christmas in 1580. In the second quarter, Pashley's name disappears. He has gone to be ordained priest at Ely December 21, 1580, just about the time of his successor's arrival, and he soon becomes curate of St. Benet's (a living still in the gift of the College), rising later to be vicar of two parishes at once, until his death in 1612. Marlowe's name appears in the audits but is scored through and Pashley's name is substituted. Marlowe's name next appears in the audits for 1581, continuing in the scholarship accounts until he finally departs in 1587 with his M.A. and the blessing of Her Majesty's Privy Council, though without the blessing of either Corpus Christi or the University.

He has left a plain trail through the archives both of his college and of the University. When a new student entered Cambridge he was recorded in the books of his college. When he matriculated, he was recorded again in the Matriculation Book of the University. He also paid a fee to his college on entrance. When he got hungry, he paid a penny for something to eat or drink at the Buttery, a transaction immediately recorded in the Buttery Book. Such an entry is actually the earliest record that Corpus Christi has of its first and greatest dramatist.

Wealthy students and sons of noblemen entered as "fellow-commoners." The bulk of the students were, like Marlowe, "pensioners," who were entered on the "convictus secundus," or second list. The very poorest were sizars, the sons of parsons, yeomen, and tradesmen, who performed such menial services as rousing their masters in time for chapel, cleaning boots, dressing hair, and waiting at the high table. Even below them were the "quadrantarii," college servants who were permitted to study. As a tradesman's son, Marlowe was lucky to be a pensioner; but his luxury-loving nature must have resented taking second place, and yearned for the higher rank of fellow-commoner.

When a student was ready for his bachelor's degree, he handed in—or rather, the praelector of his college handed in for him—a "supplicat," in which he "prayed" the University to admit him to "answering the question," and thus proving his fitness for graduation. When, like Faustus, he was "grace't" with the degree, that fact was entered in the University Grace Book. Three years later, as a candidate for the master's degree, he went through the same formalities.

Archbishop Parker's scholars drew a regular stipend of one shilling for each week; and as these payments had to be recorded quarterly in the Bursar's Accounts of the College, one can trace the future dramatist's progress through six years of University life almost week by week except for one year, for which the annual audit is lost. For this year, fortunately, the Buttery Book of Corpus Christi, also kept weekly, is preserved. Interesting enough in themselves, the records of Marlowe's absences are of especial importance because he was obviously in bad odour with the academic authorities during his last year; and the irregular attendance during the three final years, which the accounts reveal, suggests one of the reasons. There were probably other reasons, numerous enough.

In Marlowe's case as in Shakespeare's, we can by good luck trace our author through almost every period of his active life. Shakespeare's boyhood is a blank; but thanks to the archives of the King's School, Marlowe's is not. We know what his early education was, what and where he studied for his University degrees. We even have the personal jottings of a friend and the intensely human record of his weekly buttery bills.

Scarcely has he left Cambridge in 1587, when he blazes into the official life of London, becomes a well-known if slightly scandalous figure—bitterly condemned by envious rivals and warmly praised by ardent friends—falls foul of the law at least three times, and so passes into legal archives; and ends at last in a coroner's inquest which in tedious legal Latin records the very last days of his life, hour by hour. Save for the Queen herself, no famous Elizabethan ever had a single day so minutely recorded, though scores of the humble and nameless —who, like the poet, fell foul of courts and constables—are reported with equal minuteness for a posterity that does not even care enough to look for them.

Marlowe arrived in Cambridge early in December, 1580. We know the date almost exactly because the fledgling poet was hungry—or more probably thirsty—and he spent one penny at the Buttery. The Bursar promptly charged it up to "Marlen," in the "ſeptimana 10a poſt Michael"; and that entry is the earliest recorded date in Marlowe's university career. The following week, with the fledgling freshman's usual abandon, he spends three shillings, one penny, ha'penny—almost exactly three times the amount of his scholarship! Thereafter he appears regularly in the Buttery Book, usually spending a good deal more than his shilling and sometimes several shillings, though there are some weeks when he lapses into economy and spends only a few pence.*

Unfortunately, the Bursar did not trouble to record exactly what articles of food Marlowe bought at the Buttery, though he sometimes placed a brief note, usually a single letter, above his entry of the amount. The frequent appearance of "b" suggests beer, for bread was supplied as part of the college commons; but there are at least three successive weeks when Marlowe must have bought both, for the Bursar's Latin notes are very specific about "bread" and "drink." Marlowe's expenditure is clearly marked "In pane In potu." The letters "g," "l," and "d" are more mysterious. "Co" probably means "commons," for the Bursar is very careful to mark Marlowe "non co"—"no commons"—during his frequent absences. Toward the end of his university career he is sometimes marked "se co"—"senior commons"—which probably means that there was a vacancy at the high table and, being already a graduate, Dominus Marlin was invited to occupy it.

Marlowe next appears in the Admission Book of Corpus Christi College, which carries the name of "Marlin" next to the last in the year 1580—that is, according to modern reckoning, some time in the winter of 1580/81 and not later than March 25.

There is always something just a little irregular about Mar-

* For the complete series of Marlowe entries, see Appendix A.

lowe's career. He enters the King's School when he is within the age limit by a few weeks only. He draws the stipend of a Canterbury scholar even before he is a regular member of his college or the University. He comes and goes more or less as he pleases, both the Buttery Book and the Scholarship Accounts showing absences of months at a time; and in the end he secures his master's degree only by the direct intervention of Her Majesty's Privy Council. He dies six years later by the assassin's dagger under circumstances which are, to say the least, peculiar, and at a time when vague charges which no one now understands are pending against him in that same Privy Council which six years before had been so friendly.

Marlowe's first appearance in the Corpus Christi scholarship accounts is in the second term, or trimester, at a time when he was not yet officially in Cambridge at all, though he had actually been living at Corpus for some months. The Bursar's Accounts for the "2a Trimestra," 1580/81, record a payment to "Marlin" of 12 shillings. Since his stipend was a shilling a week, he had by Lady Day been in residence officially for a full twelve weeks. The other two Canterbury scholars had presumably been there a week longer, for they each receive thirteen shillings. Indeed, the Bursar actually started to record a payment to Marlowe in the first trimester, and then crossed it off and substituted the name of Pashley, Marlowe's predecessor in the scholarship.

Thereafter the accounts record regular payments to Marlowe throughout his undergraduate career, except in the spring of 1583, when he defies the regulations which forbid any scholar to leave Cambridge for longer than a month, and is gone for seven weeks. We know this because he draws only six instead of the usual thirteen shillings.

In 1584, Marlowe is ready for his first degree. Though he had not entered the University formally until some time in 1581, he claims the completion of four years' study (*quadrennium completum*) under a decree of 1578/9. This permitted students to claim *quadrennium completum* if they had begun residence before the "sermon ad clerum," which "is or out to be made in the beginning of Easter term." They might then "proceed in the fourth Lent next following the sermon"; and this for Marlowe was the Lenten season of 1584, when he was "reputed and accounted to have wholly and fully satisfied the statute." [11]

To win his degree, an undergraduate had to keep two "Acts" or "Responsions," in the public schools. He announced three philosophical propositions which he was prepared to defend, and students from other colleges were then selected as his opponents. Marlowe is thinking of this public trial of wits when he makes the German but very Cantabrigian "First Scholar" in *Doctor Faustus* ask after "Faustus, that was wont to make our schooles ring with *sic probo*"—the Latin tag of the scholar engaged in a demonstration.[12] He even names the building in which the test took place, "The Schools," another local Cambridge name.

After these tests the same undergraduate had, in turn, to keep two "Opponencies," in which he publicly assailed the philosophy of two other students. The German university men of Faustus's Wittenberg are strangely familiar with Cambridge academic usage, just as the Roman heroes of Shakespeare are acquainted with firearms or Thomas Heywood's Romans in *Lucrece* with London street-cries.

These acts took place before an audience of graduates in a ceremony at which "All and singular bachelors and questionists" appeared "in their habits and hoods." A Master of Arts presided. One of the respondent's philosophical propositions having been selected, he defended it in a Latin thesis, after which he suffered the ordeal of three separate Latin refutations, each by a different opponent. Having given four demonstrations of his argumentative skill, twice as respondent and twice as opponent, he was "sent up" for the B.A., the granting of degrees being a matter for the University and not for the College.

The University's own examinations, lasting three days, were usually given just before Ash Wednesday. They were in the hands of the University Proctor and other officials. The successful questionists afterwards submitted "supplicats"—both of Marlowe's have survived—in which they humbly "prayed" that they might be admitted *ad respondendum quaestioni* before the Vice-Chancellor and the University Senate. The *quaestio* itself, an examination in Aristotle's *Prior Analytics*, does not seem to have daunted the budding dramatist in the least. A few years later, in writing *Doctor Faustus*, Marlowe makes his hero avow, in queer Latin and queerer Greek, a still queerer enthusiasm for this driest of philosophical treatises."[13]

The University Grace Book duly records in 1584 that

Chrōs. Marlyn ex coll. corp. chris.

was admitted to the question; and his supplicat is still preserved in the University Registry. In the usual formula, "Christopherus Marlin prayeth that twelve completed terms in which he hath heard the usual lectures (even though not wholly according to the form of the statute), together with all opponencies, responsions, and other exercises required by the royal statute may suffice for him to be admitted to the question." The clause, "even though not wholly according to the form of the statute," was a mere bit of legalistic caution, intended to cover any accidental irregularity. It occurs in all supplicats of the period, literally hundreds of which have survived.[14]

Having passed this appalling series of tests, the Canterbury shoemaker's son was at length a "determiner"—a student who had completed the requisite number of terms to the satisfaction of his college and the University. It is just about this time—the seventh week after Christmas, 1583/4—that he, who has been plain "Marlin" through four years of the Buttery Accounts, suddenly becomes "Dominus Marlin." He is made a Bachelor of Arts and thereby a "gentleman," no matter what his birth, on the following Palm Sunday.

At the same time, Thomas Nashe, who collaborated with Marlowe in writing *Dido Queene of Carthage*, also received a B.A. If, as many critics have believed, *Dido* is one of Marlowe's earliest plays, the two youngsters may have written it as undergraduates. Thomas Heywood, indefatigable play-hack of Elizabethan London, is said to have been a student at Peterhouse about this time and may perhaps have known both Marlowe and Nashe. It is pretty certainly he who later recasts Marlowe's *Jew of Malta*. Robert Greene, later Marlowe's bitterest enemy, had just left the University;[15] and Marlowe himself left Cambridge only a few years before John Fletcher—one of the famous Siamese twins of English letters, Beaumont and Fletcher—entered Corpus Christi in 1590. By that time, Marlowe was the most famous playwright of the day.

As an undergraduate, Marlowe was a satisfactory though hardly a brilliant student. Archbishop Parker's scholars were at least nominally in training for the Church; and the young firebrand who a few years later was shocking one half of London with religious radicalism while he dazzled the other half with some of the purest poetry—and also some of the purest rant—ever penned, was sufficiently sedate in the rôle of a candidate for holy orders to persuade the prim dons of Corpus Christi to send him up for his degree despite the fact that he had fulfilled the requirements by the very narrowest of margins, and had exceeded the absences permitted under the statute by a good three weeks. He even persuaded them to extend his scholarship to the longest period permitted under Parker's will—six years. Yet in the *Ordo Senioritatis* of the University's bachelors for his year, he ranks only 199th among 231 and he is eighth among the twelve from Corpus Christi.[16]

The renewed grant of the scholarship is even harder to understand because Corpus Christi was at this time administered by Robert Norgate, a Master with strong Puritan leanings who had gathered about him a group of dons with much the same views. Marlowe, on the other hand, was soon to become a religious sceptic who declared roundly that "all protestants ar hipocriticall Asses" and who held that "if there be any god or any true religion then it is the papists."[17]

6.

"His Faithful Dealing"

"Deserued to be rewarded for his faithfull dealinge."
Acts of the Privy Council, June 29, 1593

A change seems to have come over the shoemaker's son and over his life in the University, as soon as he has advanced to the rank of bachelor and has achieved the dignified title of "Dominus," which goes with it in the Bursar's Accounts and in the Buttery Book. Hereafter, as we trace him week by week and shilling by shilling through the Buttery Book and through the scholarship accounts in the Annual Audits, we find Marlowe less and less in Cambridge. Ancient papers are all that time has left of that eager, high-spirited university youngster who trod the old streets; who on the banks of the Cam and the Granta "walkt along a streame for purenesse rare," where bending trees with "their garland tops the brooke orespread"; and who as "the passionate sheepheard" sat[1]

> vpon the Rocks,
> Seeing the Sheepheards feed theyr flocks
> By shallow Riuers, to whose falls
> Melodious byrds sings Madrigalls

—these, plus a handful of sometimes too bombastious plays, one immortal lyric and two lovely fragments, stored here and there in libraries where he himself as a student once bent eagerly over quite other books, never dreaming that his own plays and poems, most of which he never lived to see in print, would be treasured there too, one day. But from the old books of accounts and records in the Bursary of Corpus Christi and in the University Registry, with their crabbed, faded writing; from what we know of his life in London; and above all from the man's own mind as we find it in his work, we may permit ourselves some wholly warranted deductions.

In the first trimester of 1584/5, Dominus Marlin is present in Cambridge but three weeks, if we may judge by the three shillings of his scholarship payments, though the Buttery Book shows that he was not absent for the full ten weeks that this implies. In his second trimester he is drawing scholarship payments for but seven and a half weeks and the Buttery Book again shows absences. In his third trimester, he draws scholarship payments for but four weeks; and in his fourth trimester for but five. The records of academic payments for the next year are lost; but the Buttery Book comes conveniently to the rescue and shows that he is absent at intervals which total nearly four months.

Thereafter the later volumes of the Buttery Book are lost; but the scholarship accounts begin anew. In them we find Dominus Marlen present nine weeks in the first trimester and five and a half in the second. Thereafter Corpus Christi and the Bursar know him no more. This disgraceful genius's successor is elected as usual in November, 1587; but by this time Corpus Christi is eager to forget that such a scandalous personage as Marlowe ever darkened its worn stone doorways or paced the grassy enclosure of the Old Court. Usually, when a new scholar is placed upon the books, the Bursar records the name of the scholar whom he succeeds. But here the Bursar will not so much as sully his goose-quill with the abhorrèd name. The University had not wished to grant Marlowe a master's degree. It had been compelled to do so by the Queen's own Privy Council. But it could—and for the sake of Puritanism, it did—at least make sure that the man's name should be named no more.

The circumstances under which Marlowe received his M.A. have been elucidated by the discovery of a resolution of the Privy Council bluntly directing the University to award the degree whether it wanted to or not, and ask no questions. In the Queen's name, learnèd gentlemen!

When Master Robert Norgate, of Corpus, and Mr. Vice-Chancellor received word like that from London, they knew what they had to do, else their learned heads might stand very unsteady on their scarlet-hooded shoulders. They did as they were ordered, albeit with very wry faces. Marlowe became Magister Artium and departed his Cambridge life for London, fame, and death, leaving some highly indignant dons, outwitted, discomfited, and overruled, fuming behind him in their dignity.

As an example of governmental interference in University affairs, this document is remarkable even for the sixteenth century. It deserves to be quoted in full, though it is not at all the sort of communication that University heads are accustomed to receive. Thus it stands in the minutes of the Privy Council: [2]

> Whereas it was reported that Christopher Morley was determined to haue gone beyond the seas to Reames [Rheims] and there to remain, their L*ordships* thought good to certify that he had no such intent, but that in all his acc*i*ons he had behaued him selfe orderlie and discreetelie wherebe he had done her Majesty good service, and deserued to be rewarded for his faithfull dealinge. Their L*ordships*' request was that the rumor thereof should be allaied by all possible meanes, and that he should be furthered in the degree he was to take this next Commencem*ent*: Because it was not her Majestes pleasure that any one employed as he had been in matters touching the benefitt of his countrie should be defamed by those who are ignorant in th' affaires he went about.

This is not the way the Privy Council usually writes a letter. Formal communications of that kind are always introduced into the Minutes as "A letter." This entry seems merely to record a resolution; but the grim Lord Burghley sat in the Privy Council as Lord Treasurer at that particular meeting; and doubtless in his other capacity as Chancellor of the University he saw that the resolution reached Cambridge with no diminution of its emphatic language.

It is not really very hard to see about what must have happened. This was the year before the Spanish Armada descended on the coast of an England that was not quite sure whether it was really Protestant or Catholic, nor any surer whether Protestantism meant the Church of England, or Puritanism; an England that wavered between the stout ghost of Henry VIII, the doctrine of Luther, and the doctrine of Calvin. There were grimly honest men who espoused all these views. Catholic families still remained, loyally English for the most part, but so far as they dared, still practising "the old religion" in secrecy. Devout English Jesuits, not so loyal, slipped into the country from the English Catholic seminary at Rheims, disguised as laymen. Plotters against the Queen and the state as well as against the established religion, they took their lives in their hands when they came, and usually lost them for their faith in the end—lost them, not by simple, comfortable heading or hanging, but by torture or by the horrible death of traitors, hanging, drawing, quartering.

They came to hearten the lingering faithful of the Church of Rome, and to convert wavering Protestants, but also to intrigue against the heretic Queen—in their eyes no Queen at all, but merely an upstart royal bastard—and her usurping government.

The rulers of England, ecclesiastical and governmental, were nervous. The University authorities, being a little of both, were more nervous still. Serious-minded and devoutly inclined University students who found themselves turning to the ancient faith, often under the skilful urging of the disguised Jesuits, usually continued their education at Oxford and Cambridge, veiling their real Catholic convictions; and then slipped off to the Continent to complete their studies for the Roman priesthood. A royal proclamation had some years before ordered all loyal subjects to recall their sons studying in the foreign seminaries and to refuse support to any who declined to come home; but devout Catholics ignored it.[3]

It is possible to judge Dr. Robert Norgate, Master of Corpus, a great deal too severely. What was he to think? Converts to Catholicism notoriously disappeared shortly before receiving the master's degree. And here was one of his own scholars—ostensibly in training for the priesthood of the Church of England—interrupting his studies for weeks at a time; moving mysteriously about the country; and said by rumour to have made a journey to Rheims—a city filled with wicked English Jesuits engaged in training Roman Catholic pupils to overthrow the Queen's throne, the Queen's government, and the Queen's faith.

It is quite possible that Marlowe really did make a secret journey to Rheims, acting on secret instructions from some one very high in Elizabeth's affairs of state. The Queen's secret service was directed by Sir Francis Walsingham, second cousin and friend of that same Thomas Walsingham who was Marlowe's patron. His spies were everywhere, listening to tavern conversations in England, watching the English Catholic students in Rome, reporting the casual conversations of suspected Englishmen abroad. Their reports still linger in the archives, sometimes straightforward letters telling the worst in plain English; again darkly mysterious and conspiratorial in tone, signed only with a numeral forming part of the secret code.

Nor were these the comic sleuths of fiction. Sir Francis's

secret service was vigilant and efficient. Did an Englishman in Germany call the Queen an atheist? Walsingham had a spy on the spot to hear him and write it down.[4] The secret service was clever enough to intercept and read all the letters that passed between the captive Mary Queen of Scots and Anthony Babington's Catholic conspirators, who sought to free her and murder Elizabeth. It was also clever enough to speed those letters on their way again without the least suspicion among the conspirators. And Robert Poley, one of the operatives engaged on this very work, was an agent of Sir Francis Walsingham's, an acquaintance of Marlowe's patron, Thomas Walsingham, and an associate of Marlowe's—he dined with the poet, indeed, on the very day of his death! [5]

This man deceived the unfortunate Babington so thoroughly that even when the Catholic conspirator had been betrayed, he was still not quite sure whether Poley was the faithful member of the conspiracy he seemed to be, or the government spy he really was. As Babington fled in a vain effort to escape the death which soon overtook him, he sent Marlowe's treacherous friend a letter which is one of the most pathetic of all the pathetic documents that have come down from those bad, dark days, showing as it does both his suspicion that his friend had betrayed him and at the same time his unwillingness to doubt his friend's fidelity: [6]

> ffarewell, sweet Robyn, if as I take the, true to me. If not Adieu, *omnium bipedum nequissimus* Retorne me thyne answere for my satisfaction, and my dyamond & what els thow wilt. The fornace is prepared wherin our faith muste be tryed. ffarewell till we mete, which God knowes when.

Poley's character being what it was, Babington probably never got his diamond; but he was hanged, drawn, and quartered so speedily that he had no time to worry about it.

If the Queen's government—as it certainly did—wanted secret information about the Jesuit college at Rheims, Marlowe was an ideal agent. He was about to take a master's degree—was, in other words, at the very stage in his studies when converts usually fled to the Catholic seminary on the Continent. He was looked on with disfavour by the Puritans of Corpus. He was, as the reports of other spies later made abundantly evident, able to advocate Papist doctrine with alarming enthusiasm.[7]

Moreover, he seems to have been in direct personal touch with one of Sir Francis Walsingham's confidential messengers. In *Tamburlaine*, Marlowe quotes from a book on *The Practise of Fortification*, by a certain Paul Ive, which was not published until 1589, when Marlowe's play had probably been complete for some years. How did he find his quotation? Almost certainly in Ive's own manuscript. Paul Ive appears repeatedly as a messenger for Walsingham (to whom he dedicates his book) in the very year when Marlowe was also involved in secret affairs of state.[8]

Marlowe may really have gone to Rheims; and it would not be strange if rumour of his journey reached the ears of Dr. Norgate or the Vice-Chancellor. If so, there was only one course for them to take: to refuse the degree, which Marlowe had probably not done very much to earn, and cast out the cut branch for the burning.

Marlowe, alarmed at the prospective loss of a greatly coveted distinction, dashes up to London, sees some friend powerful enough to move the Privy Council in his behalf, returns to Cambridge, and triumphs. His friend must have acted with great speed, since the degree was taken only a couple of days later.

Vice-Chancellors and Masters of Colleges do not like being compelled to yield to wild and careless students. Whatever they may now have thought of Marlowe's loyalty to the crown, his academic labours had for three years certainly not been assiduous, and his religious views were certainly not orthodox. There had been trouble with religious scepticism at Corpus for more than a decade—from the time of the heretic Francis Kett who had resigned his fellowship six months before Marlowe entered but who was still living at Corpus among the dons for several months while Marlowe was in residence, on down to the days of Thomas Fineux, another Kentishman said to have been "made an atheist" by Marlowe, who entered just as Marlowe was leaving, but whose career, like the heretical Kett's, overlapped the poet's. Cambridge was probably the first of many places which in the next six years were rather glad to see the last of fiery Kit Marlowe, who combined in more than ordinary degree the madman and the poet.

The master's degree was highly esteemed by Englishmen of the Renaissance, when learning was cherished like an art, and when no unreal distinction was drawn between art and scholarship. It represented as much study for as many years as a modern doctorate; and many university students dropped out, discouraged by the rigour of the course, before they had even attained the baccalaureate. All the greater, therefore, was the pride of the masters.

The University itself ordered "that no master or scholar shall presume to sit by any master of arts in any church, or at any lecture in the schools." The dignity of the master was recognized by special privileges and academic costume of special silken splendour. It was a proverb that "a Royston horse, and a Cambridge Master of Arts, are a couple of creatures that will give way to nobody." The village of Royston near Cambridge made malt and its horses carried it on their backs to London; the horses could not very well turn out of the road and the Cambridge masters, feeling themselves equally laden with learning, would not.[9]

The boast of Marlowe's enemy, Robert Greene, that he was "Master of Arts in both Universities," his contempt for the "upstart crow," Shakespeare, who had not even a bachelor's degree; Ben Jonson's satisfaction in becoming a master "in both ye Universities by yr favour not his studie"; or Doctor Samuel Johnson's devious stratagems to capture an honorary Oxford M.A., two hundred years later, are thus entirely comprehensible.

The cobbler's son is henceforward almost invariably referred to as "gentleman." He is in close association with the aristocratic great and powerful of Elizabeth's Court. In Cambridge, he spends much more than the stipend of his scholarship. In London, he writes not nearly enough to support him, and yet there is never any hint that he is in any straits for money. He had a powerful friend somewhere, or perhaps several powerful friends; and it is no wonder he turned to these mysterious patrons to get him that M.A.

It would be interesting to know the exact nature of Marlowe's work for the government. It was obviously confidential, and its nature is not specified even in the Privy Council's resolution. It was probably secret service of some sort, which almost certainly included the carrying of confidential letters and the dispatch of confidential business. Elizabethan literary men were often used in this way. Anthony Munday, a very minor dramatist, spied upon the English Catholics in Rome for the benefit of the Queen's government. James Welsh, a student of Magdalene College, Cambridge, also did espionage. William Fowler, a minor Scotch poet, and William Vaughan, author of *The Golden Grove*, sent in secret reports; and Marlowe's friend Matthew Royden was accused of secret dealings with the King of Scots. Even Ben Jonson has been suspected of being an intelligence agent.[10]

Marlowe was a protégé of Thomas Walsingham, second cousin of Sir Francis Walsingham, Secretary of State in charge of the government secret service. Sir Francis took a lively interest in his kinsman's affairs and acquaintance with Thomas Walsingham was a useful shortcut to the notice of the powerful Sir Francis. Moreover, Marlowe's friend Thomas Watson, the poet, was also acquainted with the Walsinghams.

This was a period of great activity in the government's secret service. Catholics were plotting at home. The Armada was being outfitted in Spain. Spanish forces were collecting in the Low Countries to invade England when the Armada should have cleared the seas. Mr. Secretary Walsingham received between March of 1587 and June of 1588, a total of £3,399 for secret service, the largest sum ever given him within so short a time.

Some of that money quite probably went to Christopher Marlowe, while he was still a B.A. of Cambridge University and perhaps after he left the University. Spies were sometimes employed as confidential messengers, carrying secret dispatches of special importance. Robert Poley, for example, who was later present at Marlowe's murder, acted both as spy and as diplomatic courier. This dual rôle may explain why we find an official letter from Utrecht, addressed to Lord Burghley October 2, 1587, mentioning "Mr. Morley" among "the messengers from you." [11] If Marlowe—who is called "Christopher Morley" in the Privy Council's resolution—had really been doing confidential errands for the Lord Treasurer, who was also Chancellor of the University, it is no wonder that the Privy Council were a trifle emphatic about his degree. But we must not be too sure, for there seem to have been other Morleys in the Exchequer.

Then, too, Marlowe may have been abroad aiding in some way the negotiations with the Duke of Parma, sponsored by Sir James Crofts, a Spanish sympathizer who still hoped that peace might be maintained. Robert Cecil, son of Lord Burghley, a former Cambridge student of about Marlowe's generation, was engaged in these negotiations which were still in progress in Belgium the next year, at the very instant when the little English warships were riddling the hulks of the Armada with their shot. More likely, however, Marlowe stood with the Walsingham family; and Sir Francis, at least, was bitterly opposed to the peace negotiations.

7.

London and Fame

"That like I best that flyes beyond my reach."
Massacre at Paris

The London to which Marlowe turned, as the gates of Corpus Christi closed with a final disapproving bang behind him, was the London of a very short period in Queen Elizabeth's long reign. Marlowe knew the literary life of the great Queen's little capital only from 1587 to 1593.

Some time during those six years, or perhaps a little earlier, young Will Shakespeare had come up from Stratford. These are the lost years of Shakespeare's life. We do not really know anything about him until the early 1590's, when he suddenly begins to publish highly erotic but beautiful verse like *Venus and Adonis*, a poem which probably owes its being to a vogue started by Marlowe's *Hero and Leander*. We do know that after his marriage young Will drops out of Stratford records, save for the premature birth of a daughter and the entirely decorous and respectable birth of some later offspring.

But Shakespeare's life covers the whole of the great period of English literature under Queen Elizabeth and the greater part of that under King James. No matter when he came to London, Shakespeare certainly lived there until late in life—late in life, that is, for those days of swift and sudden death. He saw almost the whole of the most brilliant epoch in English letters, before he retired—rich, respected, famous—to tiny Stratford, one of the biggest frogs the world has ever known in one of its tiniest puddles.

Shakespeare saw the last of the old theatrical inns, saw the new theatres go up, one after another, to supplement the first two or three, which were all that Marlowe knew. He lived through the rising of the Earl of Essex, in which his *Richard II* was used as propaganda; went to Court as actor and as playwright; wrote (says a legend of respectable antiquity) one play at the Queen's own command; won the honour of a coat of arms and gave the Stratford Shakespeares a place among the better people; intervened to help on the marriage of his landlady's daughter; stole a girl from Richard Burbage; bought property and set up as a land-owner; affably lent his influence to help forward the affairs of fellow-townsmen, back in Stratford; saw the foundations of the Empire laid, once the Spaniards were conquered; saw the Queen grow old and haggard and ridiculous, yet hold the hearts of her subjects all the while and match her wits against the best of her foemen to the very end; saw the new King ride down from Scotland; and himself, as a King's player, walked in the royal procession clad in a royal gift of scarlet cloth.

Of all these things, mad, kind young Kit Marlowe knew nothing. He slept in the churchyard at Deptford, while along the Thames, a waterman now and then sang a few lines of his *Hero and Leander*, and on the Bankside, illiterate, greedy old Philip Henslowe, money-lender and theatrical producer, watched with gleaming, covetous eyes the money that rolled in from production after production of the dead poet's plays; and in the booksellers' shops around St. Paul's an eager public spent its sixpences for fifty years upon those shabby little pamphlets in which the plays and poems first appeared, early editions which to-day sell literally for much more than their weight in gold.

Marlowe was killed a few months after his twenty-ninth birthday. His life was short; and of that short life, most was spent in Canterbury and in Cambridge. Fame came quickly when he reached London at last, but the whole space from fame to death was five or six years at most. The years between July of 1587, when he took his degree, and May 30, 1593, when he took a dagger thrust above the eye from his friend Ingram Frizer and died, included all the fledgling eagle ever knew of London and its life. It is worth while to study carefully the narrow stage that London set for his brief scene.

Marlowe never heard most of the greatest names of Elizabethan literature. He knew Spenser's poems well and almost certainly knew the poet, too. He must have met Sir Philip Sidney. But Shakespeare to him was a raw young beginner, who looked as if he might eventually amount to something. Marlowe never heard of *Othello*, *Macbeth*, *Lear*, or *Twelfth Night*. If he knew *Hamlet* at all, it was as some anonymous early play, botched and bloody, perhaps the work of his friend Thomas Kydd, which Shakespeare revised years afterward. Francis Bacon to him was a rising young lawyer, lucky enough to have a seat in Parliament and powerful friends at Court. Francis Beaumont was a child of less than ten. John Fletcher was a boy, still at Corpus Christi. Ben Jonson was a bricklayer's stepson in his 'teens; certainly no one had ever heard of him.

The Elizabethan writers whom Marlowe knew were minor figures, mostly pitiable hacks, whose reputations have for the most part ill endured the test of time—envious Robert Greene, malignant Gabriel Harvey, satiric Thomas Nashe, learned Thomas Watson, grave George Chapman, dissolute George Peele, and Sir Walter Raleigh, whose romantic life has never been forgotten and whose books are never read.

The city of London that Marlowe knew, including neighbouring Westminster, sprawled along the river for three or four miles. From North to South, including Southwark on the opposite bank of the Thames, it reached about two miles.[1] It was a city of 100,000 or 120,000 inhabitants, obviously of some degree of piety, since they worshipped in 119 churches, whose steeples broke the low Elizabethan sky-line, dominated by the squat tower of St. Paul's—not the great dome-crowned edifice of Sir Christopher Wren, but the old Cathedral which had already lost its spire and which perished in the Great Fire seventy years later.

Municipal affairs were dominated by the sour but solid London burghers, of Puritanical leanings. Social life and gaiety were dominated by the gallants and light wenches at the Court of the Virgin Queen. Over them all, during Marlowe's first year in London, hung the shadow of Spain, fear of the Armada and the Duke of Parma's soldiery, ready to bring back to Merry England the terrible days of Bloody Mary. Then came the victory of Howard and Drake and Hawkins, a great joy and a new buoyancy in the English spirit, a proud exultation in England's new freedom and power, all expressed in a great outburst of poetry.

Splendid though its citizens thought it, Marlowe's London would in modern eyes have appeared at most quaintly picturesque and at worst rather mean. The streets were narrow, ill-lighted, and unsafe. The police were constables much like Dogberry and his aides in Shakespeare's *Much Ado*. Two of the Shoreditch constables about this time went in fear of their lives because of the poet Marlowe and appealed to the courts for protection against him.[2] The streets which they guarded were filthy, in spite of the sanitary decree of some early enthusiast for public health, which forbade householders to empty waste into the streets before nine o'clock at night, thereby adding a new peril to nocturnal rambles.

But if the streets that Marlowe trod were filthy, they were also inimitably picturesque. Their narrow passages were thronged with lusty 'prentices like those bound to his father's cobbler's-bench back in Canterbury, sturdy tradesmen like old John Marlowe himself, soldiers home from the wars, gallants of the Court. They resounded with street-cries which an old playwright has preserved: [3]

> "Kitchen-stuff, maids!"
> "Hot fine oat-cakes, hot!"
> "Whiting, maids, whiting!"
> "I ha' white radish, white hard lettuce, white young onions!"
> "Salt—salt—white Wor-stershire salt!"
> "Small-coals here!"
> "Lanthorn and candle-light here!"

These were the cries, so rhythmically delivered that they could be bundled together to make a single lyric for Thomas Heywood's play on Lucrece.

Elizabethan gentry, gallants, nobles, and prosperous merchants—who wanted to keep their fine white ruffs unspotted, their silken doublets and fine velvet cloaks free from the street mire flung up by galloping riders or by the new-fangled coaches that were becoming fashionable and creating a traffic problem—much preferred to travel by water. The "silver christall streame," [4] of the River Thames—in those days still free from the contaminations of modernity—dominated communications. The old plays that deal with London life are full of allusions showing that the river was the city's principal highway. Up and down stream and across the current, north and south among the swans, bobbed the "watermen," their little boats darting wherever their fares demanded, with cries of "Eastward ho!" "Westward ho!" to warn other craft and the gliding swans as well.

It is no wonder that Elizabethan lyrics are full of swans, for the graceful white birds, protected by the Queen who owned them, were everywhere. Sailing thirty miles down the Thames to London, a German traveller found that "all the time the river was full of tame swans, who have nests and breed in small islands." And, said another, "the sight of them and their noise is vastly agreeable to the fleets that meet them in their course."[5] These, evidently, did not include Orlando Gibbons's "silver swan that living had no note."

On state occasions, the Thames bore the Queen herself in her royal barge, her watermen in splendid liveries. In Marlowe's time, there led down from the palace at Whitehall "a verye statlye passage to the Thamise for her Matie to take bardge, to pass at her pleasure the pleasant streame."[6] The nobility built their palaces along the main-travelled thoroughfare, with water-gates leading down to its bank; and like their royal mistress travelled in stately barges of their own. The Lord Mayor and city dignitaries, not to be outdone, voyaged upon the Thames, as a visitor records, in a barge "covered with red taffetas ornamented with a white cross," while "each guild or company had its own barge, ornamented with numerous flags by which each company might be distinguished."

Between the courts and the Tower of London, plied the prison barges—frequent enough to be familiar sights—bearing state prisoners to and from their trials. The headsman sat grimly in the same barge with his prospective victim—the blade of the axe turned from him if acquitted; the blade turned toward him if convicted. Somehow, in most cases, the blade did turn toward the prisoner eventually. As a foreigner remarked, it was hard to find a nobleman who had not had at least a few relatives beheaded. During Queen Elizabeth's reign it is estimated that the government executed 6,476 men and women for various offences in London and Middlesex alone![7]

The river itself was dominated by London Bridge, the only means of crossing on foot. Marlowe's friend, Sir Walter Raleigh, made a fetish of crossing the river always by the bridge and refusing—despite innumerable voyages on perilous seas—to use the little boats of the watermen. On the bridge, tenements had risen to a height of several stories and in them scores of families lived, their houses fronting inward on the bridge as on a narrow lane, the rushing waters beneath them. "In the midst," says an ancient account contemporary with Marlowe,[8] there was "a drawe bridge, and vpon the same bridge on either side, the houses so artificially combined, that the whole bridge seemeth not onely a mayne and faire streete, but men seeme to passe vnder a continuall roofe." The way was so narrow that two coaches could barely pass each other.

To support all this, twenty thick stone piers obstructed the water, so that the bridge became almost a dam, the Thames rushing between them as if through sluices. "Shooting the bridge" was a minor adventure. On the southern end of London Bridge, the "Surrey Side," the heads of traitors stood on long, spiked poles. The number varied, but some thirty heads usually stood there until they mouldered away or were replaced with others, as silent warning to the throngs of the great Queen's subjects passing underneath. Jesuit missionary priests who had crossed in disguise from the Continent and who, having landed at Dover, often passed this way, could glance up at their predecessors and see what their own fate was pretty certain to be. One of these priests later used "Christopher Marlowe" as a convenient alias. The Tower of London, grim place of torture, imprisonment, and execution, stood farther down the river, much as it had stood for centuries, much as it stands to-day—"strong and ample, well walled and trenched about, beautified with sundrie buildings, semblable to a little towne."[9]

London, amid this grimness mingled with splendour, was developing a taste for a new kind of drama which was both grim and splendid. The miracle, mystery, and morality plays, lingering on into the latter half of the sixteenth century, touched the boyhood of Marlowe and of Shakespeare, both of whom show in their writings their familiarity with these old plays. The Universities had long made a practice of producing plays in Greek and Latin—usually with the approval of their rulers—but these were for the educated few.

The mass of the English people had formed the habit of play-acting (for half the population of a town might take part in the performance of one of the mystery cycles); and they had also formed the habit of play-going. These popular plays were crude for the most part, but hearty and roughly vigorous. They were also exciting. They may have been unreal; but they were full of stir and colour, tales of far away and long ago that broke the monotony of life in Tudor villages and shops. The nobility shared the popular taste for plays; but, better educated, they sought in English plays the grace of classic finish and style that they had learned to know in the Universities.

Religion no longer monopolized the drama. Since early in the century, small groups of players had wandered about the kingdom, setting up their stages of barrel-heads and planks in the courtyards of the inns (with their tiers of balconies for the spectators all around). Legally, these players were rogues, vagabonds, and masterless men; the godly burghers of London disapproved of them as much as the Queen and her nobles encouraged them.

It was this favour of the upper classes that saved the day for the actors. There was always a way to circumvent the law. The nobility had the right to maintain "servants," ministering to their own amusements. It was, therefore, always easy for a manager to get some actors together, buy a few costumes, find some manuscripts, and then persuade the Lord Admiral —or the Lord Chamberlain, or the Lord Warden of the Cinque Ports—that it would be a fine thing to have a company of actors wearing his badge. Thus the actors became the nobleman's privileged servants. Naturally, the noble lord never paid his actors; but the protection of his name enabled them to make a living for themselves and the drama to flourish.

In one of these companies Christopher Marlowe may have acted when he first came to London. So runs an old and by no means improbable story, which, alas! no one now believes—solely because the nineteenth century scholar, John Payne Collier, perpetually itching to "prove" things, calmly forged an entire "Elizabethan" ballad telling the story of how Marlowe

> Brake his leg in one lewd scene
> While playing on the stage.

As usual, Collier wrote his forgeries into a quite genuine manuscript. About the time of Charles I's execution, some one had copied out in manuscript *Eikon Basilike,* the book dedicated to his memory. Unfortunately, this enthusiast copied the book on one side of the paper only. A century or two later, Collier found the manuscript, and proceeded to forge on each blank page "poems" of his own, written in his usual imitation of Elizabethan handwriting, which employed an alphabet quite unlike that of modern days. Such was the forger's misplaced ingenuity that he even tried to make the poem seem more authentic by alluding to Marlowe, not under his own name—that would have been too transparent—but under the anagram of "Wormall." Then, to make sure the reference to Marlowe might be more noticeable, he gave his fraudulent creation the title of *The Atheist's Tragedie.* In spite of this, the forgery was very badly managed—so badly that Collier even uses the modern letter "r" side by side with the old letter, which is very different.

As soon as this and various other of his forgeries had been exposed, every one refused to believe any statement that he made. The fact that Collier held an opinion was enough to damn it; hence no one to-day believes that Marlowe was ever an actor. Yet there are innumerable printed references to his acting. These are quite genuine and they begin in the seventeenth century—they are almost as old in fact as the Collier forgery pretended to be in fiction; but the forgery had done its work. When Collier's library was sold after his death, the British Museum—perfectly aware that it was buying a forgery —purchased the lamentable document that had done all this damage and carefully preserves it still as an awful warning to future generations.

If Marlowe really was an actor, he must have exhibited his art in the early theatrical inns rather than in the playhouses. At least five inns in early Elizabethan London were quite as much "common osteryes turned to playhouses," as they were shelters for travellers. These were the Bull, the Bell, the Bell Savage, the Cross Keys, and the Boar's Head.[10] But there was always trouble. The bedrooms of the inns opened directly on the balconies where upper-class spectators sat to watch the plays. Small wonder that the citizens of London objected when they found how frequent was the "inveigling and alluring of maids, specially orphans and good citizens' children, under age, to privy and unmeet contacts." [11]

The Puritan element in the city objected to plays anyhow, on general principles. One of their number asserted that the devil gave theatrical performances in hell every Sunday evening to offset any possible good the churches might be doing at the same time. The clergy complained that the competition of the plays was hard to meet. The perpetual danger of plague often gave the London burghers good excuse to forbid the gathering of audiences for fear of contagion. Elizabethan impresarios found themselves perpetually harassed.

Scattered here and there about London were "liberties"—districts which were geographically in the city but legally outside it. They were policed by the Queen's indulgent government, not by the stern city of London. These offered haven to the players—Marlowe himself went to live in the Liberty of Norton Folgate, and Shakespeare in the Liberty of Shoreditch, six doors away. The first Blackfriars Theatre was set up in the Liberty of Blackfriars to enable the actors and their noble patrons to snap their fingers at the Puritans. But this little "private" theatre was too small for really profitable theatrical ventures.

It was James Burbage, father of Richard Burbage—star of Shakespeare's company, creator of the first Hamlet and many other leading Shakespearean rôles—who first found a way out of the difficulty. North of the city was Finsbury Fields—open country with a few houses, just outside London, near enough to attract audiences, but completely beyond the legal jurisdiction of the Lord Mayor.

Here, in 1576, while Marlowe was still growing up in Canterbury, the elder Burbage and his brother-in-law set up the first real theatre that England had possessed since the Roman legions withdrew in 411. It was more than a thousand years since any one had built a theatre in England. The architect did not know quite what was needed; but he had a model in the theatrical inn-yards. He hit upon a brilliant idea. He would simply build an inn-yard with its balconies and stage, and leave the inn off. Thus was created the first purely British theatre, to which its creators gave the obvious name. It was *the* Theatre. There was no other.

Here the actors, unmolested, plied their craft. Here Marlowe's *Doctor Faustus* was certainly produced, and probably *Tamburlaine*.[12]

As usual, when one business pioneer embarks upon a new and successful venture, imitators were not far behind. Within a year or two there was another theatre—the Curtain, whose name still lingers in "Curtain Road," now a part of roaring metropolitan London.

We know a good deal about these early theatres. Wandering foreigners came, beheld, and wrote descriptions home. One such, with a sketch attached, turned up in Holland a few centuries later. The artists who drew laboriously detailed panoramas of Elizabethan London put the theatres in with as much painstaking detail as if they had guessed how interesting their sketches would be to later generations. The contract for the Fortune Theatre remains, and we know that Shakespeare's Globe was built to the specifications of that very contract.

Even without all this detail, we can almost reconstruct these old playhouses in our minds' eyes from allusions and stage directions in the old plays. The buildings were rounded or octagonal. That is why Shakespeare's prologue to *Henry V* calls the theatre "this wooden O." The inn-yards had been open to the sky? Why, then, so were the theatres. The strolling players of the older days had performed on improvised stages of barrels and planks projecting out into the inn-yard? Then the new theatres would have permanent stages just like it. The gallants who could afford to pay for inn rooms had found seats on the balconies of the inns? Then let them sit on the balconies of the new theatres. The common herd had stood in the mud of the inn-yard? Then let them stand in the corresponding part of the theatre. In the old, rounded bull-rings this had been "the pit"? Then let it be the pit in the new theatres—and cheap seats in London theatres remain "the pit" to-day.

In 1589, by the time Marlowe had won a reputation with his earliest plays, the Burbages and their Theatre were in worse than usual difficulties. The widow of James Burbage's former partner turned up one day, accompanied by an attorney with a claim; and there followed a scene which is recorded in all seriousness in an extant legal document of incredible solemnity.[13] It is lamentable to record that Mrs. Burbage received her guests with something less than cordiality. In fact, she told them that her son, Cuthbert Burbage, would "break their knaves' heads" at the earliest opportunity, while the elder Mr. Burbage, from an upper window, so far forgot himself as to call the importunate widow a "murdering whore" and her companions "villaines, rascals, and knaves."

"If my son come," continued Mr. Burbage, who did not really like his visitors, "if my son come he will thump you hence." Just then Cuthbert did come, "and in very hot sort bid them get hence." After what the widow and the lawyer had heard of Cuthbert's pugilistic prowess and his impetuous disposition, they stood not upon the order of their going, but "went their ways," appalled by a final series of "great and horrible oathes" from the Burbages, father and son.

When the lawyer appeared upon a later visit, the other son, Richard Burbage, and his mother "beat him with a broom staff, calling him murdering knave." When a second attorney ventured the opinion that this was no way to treat the bearer of a court order, "the said Richard Burbage, scornfully and disdainfully playing with this deponent's nose, said that if he dealt in the matter, he would beat him also." [14]

They were a happy, united family, the Burbages; and the Burbage boys, Cuthbert and Richard, were a great comfort to their ageing parents; but there seems to have been an impression among outsiders that they were all just a little bit impulsive.

Some timorous soul among the actors—it was the brother of the great Edward Alleyn, who starred in most of Marlowe's plays—even murmured a few cautious words about assault and battery, but—

"Tush," replied the proud father, as he explained, "my sons, if they will be ruled by me, shall at their next coming provide charged pistols, with powder and hempseed, to shoot them in the legs."

The Theatre, it is not surprising to learn, stayed under the control of the Burbages. When it came down at last, in 1598, it was the Burbage heirs who took it down, to build Shakespeare's Globe out of its timbers and to found a new stock company in which Master William Shakespeare was a prominent share-holder, as well as actor, playwright, and general handyman.

"Southwark," the south bank of the Thames, also known as the "Surrey Side," had two theatres during at least part of Marlowe's life in London. One was the rather mysterious theatre at Newington Butts, standing well back from the river, which does not seem to have been popular and about which little is known. The other was the Rose, standing near the Clink Prison, in the "Liberty of the Clink," directly on the Bankside and close to the southern end of London Bridge. Newington Butts seems to have been little used after 1592.[15] The Rose was probably the theatre where Marlowe saw most (though not all) of his plays performed; for it was built about 1587/8 [16] and was largely controlled by Philip Henslowe, father-in-law of Edward Alleyn, who starred as Tamburlaine, Faustus, and Barabas.

The Rose was a circular building of timber, lath, and plaster, with the usual stage projecting into the pit, a "heavens" over the stage—where "j dragon in fostes" doubtless hovered —the whole crowned by a thatched roof and flagpole, where a banner announced the beginning of a play. It was thoroughly overhauled in 1591/2, by which time Henslowe was in complete control of its management. His accounts [17] at this time are full of such purchases as "hallfe a lode of lathes," "elme bordes," "ij thowssen of lathe naylles," "fur powles," and "ij gystes to bear the chymne." So fantastic is his spelling that one often has to pronounce the words once or twice to see what he means.

All this re-furbishing was in preparation for the coming of Lord Strange's players, with Edward Alleyn at their head. These actors were, just about this time, making a great success with Marlowe's *Jew of Malta*, taking in fifty shillings or more at the box office for a single performance.

The Bankside, where they played, was not a particularly reputable section of London, though no Elizabethan playwright or producer ever worried greatly over such matters. There were taverns, bull-rings, bear-rings, kennels for the dogs that tormented the poor beasts; and along the river stood a row of famous brothels, owned by the Bishop of Winchester, whose episcopal palace stood a little farther down the river, nearer the Bridge and respectability. The frail sisterhood to whom the Bishop leased his property were known as "Winchester geese" or "Winchester pigeons." Theirs had been a vice district for centuries. When Henry II laid down regulations to control this sorry traffic, he was merely maintaining "the old customs that had been there used time out of mind." [18] The "stew-holders" were forbidden to keep any inmate "against her will that would leave her sin," forbidden to sell food or drink, forbidden to keep open on holidays. Further, "no man to be drawn or enticed into any stew-house." The police were to exercise supervision and there was some effort at sanitary regulations. The dead harlots, forbidden Christian burial, lay in what was euphemistically called a "Single Woman's Churchyard appointed for them far from the parish church."

"The stews" were more or less legal establishments until

the time of Henry VIII. In 1545/6, that exponent of morality suppressed the whole district by statute, though as Bishop Fuller explains, many suspected that "he rather scattered than quenched the fire." [19] The stews were no longer under legal protection, but references in the old plays make it abundantly evident that they were still flourishing. A few plays—like *Holland's Leaguer,* named for a famous brothel—even laid their scenes in the vice district, to which Shakespeare occasionally alludes.[20] Ben Jonson, in his parody of Marlowe's *Hero and Leander,* degrades the story of that exquisite idyll to make "Hero a wench of the Bankside, who going over one morning to Old Fish street Leander spies her land at Trig-Stairs and falls in love with her." [21]

Conveniently at hand stood the Clink, a prison "for any such as should brabble, fray, or break the peace in the said bank or in the brothel-houses." Marlowe, so far as we know to-day, was cast into but one prison and it was not the Clink—a somewhat dubious testimony to his sobriety.[22]

Upon this scene enters the young man from Cambridge. Wild, reckless, and brilliant, he came down to the metropolis to try his fortune. Distinctly in the foreground were some very riotous companions. Somewhere in the background were powerful friends. Thomas Walsingham—later to be the fourth Sir Thomas—kinsman and friend of the powerful Secretary of the Queen, Sir Francis Walsingham, was his patron. The brilliant Raleigh and the learned Harriot were his friends. He was in some way attached to the circle of the Countess of Pembroke, Sidney's sister, for whom the *Arcadia* was written—at least he writes a dedication to her.

He had his education, his pen, his genius, and his way to make. He was disgraced at Cambridge; and Canterbury, incurably ecclesiastical, was none too friendly to a former candidate for holy orders now writing for the stage. Ahead lay swift and dazzling success—and death almost as swift.

He plunged into the life of London.

8.

A Young Career

> "Nature that fram'd vs of foure Elements,
> Warring within our breasts for regiment,
> Doth teach vs all to haue aspyring minds."
>
> *I. Tamburlaine*

It was a growing practice at this time for young University men to seek their fortunes in the literary life of the capital. John Lyly, down from Oxford, disgusted with a university where he had "tyr'd at a dry breast three years," had made a sensational success with a novel, written in a new and highly artificial English prose of his own devising, *Euphues, The Anatomy of Wit;* and had followed it quickly with a sequel when he saw its success—*Euphues and His England.* The books were written in a new style—one might almost say a new jargon. Elaborate bits of strange natural history, borrowed from Pliny, supplied most of the metaphors, which dealt with unicorns, mermaids, basilisks, and elephants. Every sentence balanced and many of the pairs of balanced metaphors also alliterated. It was a strange, lifeless, artificial language, which Shakespeare was to ridicule and parody a few years later.

But as so often happens, the very strangeness of the jargon made it popular. And Lyly, seeing that his work had become the fashion, plunged into dramatic writing with no more misgivings as to his special dramatic talents than a popular modern novelist assailing the cinema or attempting to lecture. The result was a series of weakly pretty and fanciful comedies, known to modern readers chiefly by a few exquisite lyrics which find their way into all anthologies under Lyly's name, though they were quite possibly not his work at all. Elizabethan writers took what they wanted where they found it; there never was a race that troubled their heads less over literary ethics.

After Lyly came suddenly a whole group of University graduates, some like Marlowe's friend Thomas Watson to become poets and live in obscure dependence on noblemen and gentry who were at once friends and patrons; others, like Marlowe's friend Thomas Nashe and his bitter enemy Robert Greene, to plunge into that wild variety of hack-work by which the professional Elizabethan man-of-letters made his scanty living—plays, verse, and those "scald, triviall, lying pamphlets" which were sold for a sixpence around St. Paul's. These were the cheaper journalism of the day, fiction of a falsely moralistic sort, occasional bits of unblushing bawdry, handbooks of this and that, religious tracts, and most irreligiously savage criticism by one author of another—anything that would keep the needy hacks alive in their obscure lodgings.

This was the first group of professional, university-trained literary men that London had ever known. As such, they were promptly dubbed "the University Wits," and by that name the group has come down the ages. The name did not, to the Elizabethan mind, imply that they were witty in the modern meaning of the word. None, as a matter of fact, was witty in our sense, and Marlowe least of all. Not for them the rapier-play of a Horace, a Martial, a Wilde, or a Whistler. Even humour was notably lacking in most of them. Their attacks were downright, savage, brutal sneers—what their contemporaries called "snarling satires." The Archbishop of Canterbury had to intervene in some of their quarrels eventually, calling in and burning the volumes of laborious abuse with which Thomas Nashe and the Cambridge don, Gabriel Harvey, had assailed each other.

"The University Intellectuals" would be a pretty fair rendering of the school's name into modern English. It meant that their work had a certain polish derived partly from the classics and partly from rhetorical training. It meant also that their work had an elegance which had been lacking in most secular writing in the hundred and fifty years since Chaucer. It meant also that here were men who could write out of a wide intellectual background, not the "riming motherwits" at whom Marlowe aims a barbed shaft in the opening lines of *Tamburlaine.*

The group included not only Marlowe, Nashe, and Greene, who were closely associated, but also George Peele and Dr. Thomas Lodge, that early example of a since familiar type, the literary medico.

Most of these men knew Marlowe personally. We know that from the tone of their allusions to him, whether they praise or whether they sneer. None of them, in fact, could very well avoid knowing him and knowing all about him. London was still (by modern standards) a small city; literary London was still smaller—a group of madcap, spendthrift writers; sober, money-seeking stationers, who printed their work; the actors who did their best to see that plays, at least, were *not* printed, so long as their performance could still draw a crowd; an aloof group still at the Universities, critical of modern letters (the Bodleian Library for a long time accepted no English plays and sold its First Folio when a new and "better" edition came out); a few intellectual coteries like Sir Walter Raleigh's "School of Night," which included Marlowe and many of his friends, interested in letters, science, and speculative philosophy.

Plays for the popular stage had always suffered because the playwrights could never quite make up their minds what kind of verse they wanted to write. For some strange reason, it never occurred to any of them to go about with their ears open, listen to the real dialogue of daily life, and then write the realistic, racy prose of the actual speech about them.

Instead, they experimented with any and every kind of verse form. The writers of the early religious plays tried to make their characters talk in stanzas. (The young Shakespeare, years later, quietly popped an entire sonnet into a particularly long speech in *Love's Labour's Lost.*) But dialogue in stanzas was hopeless. It was too glaringly artificial; it made any quick movement of the play impossible; repartee in stanza form is as near impossibility as literature can come.

John Lyly had written his plays in prose. The two authors of *Gorboduc* had produced very nearly the dullest tragedy in the world—in itself a considerable achievement—and had produced at the same time a stupendous idea: The classical dramatists of Greece and Rome had written blank verse. It now appeared perfectly possible to write blank verse in English and use it on the stage. It is hard to see why no one had ever thought of it before, since every schoolboy was brought up on Latin blank verse, learning to read it and even trying to write it, throughout his school days.

Even when the earliest English blank verse began at length to be written, it was merely the old rimed couplet with the rimes left off. Each line stood by itself. A pause at the end marked each off as a separate unit in the rhythmic scheme. The "run-on" line was unknown. There was none of that merging of one line into another, with subtle variation in the pauses, or with no pause at all, to give the verse variety, beauty, even flow and movement, and some feeling of real life. English blank verse was all a clattering march of monotonous iambics, a parade of wooden soldiers, unrelieved. Small wonder that it found few imitators.

Some years after *Gorboduc,* blank verse was tried again on the stage in a play—long since and most justly forgotten—called *The Misfortunes of Arthur.*

But plays like these were somewhat "precious" affairs, intended for the private stage and the upper classes. Blank verse reached the practical, commercial stage one day in 1587 or 1588, when young Christopher Marlowe walked into the Theatre or the Curtain with the manuscript of *Tamburlaine* under his arm. It is not by any means certain that his play was the first blank verse to astonish the ears of the groundlings. *The Spanish Tragedie,* a flamboyant, blood-soaked melodrama supposed to have been written by Thomas Kydd, who at one time shared rooms with Marlowe, may have preceded it on the stage.

It does not make a great deal of difference. Both helped to make blank verse popular; both plays made a tremendous impression; both were certainly written about the same time, perhaps in the same room; both suffered from a lamentable tendency to blood and bombast; both were admired and imitated; both were in blank verse. But there was one enormous difference. *Tamburlaine,* with all its noise and rant and its frequent moments of unrelieved hokum, was redeemed by the unearthly beauty of its finest passages, sometimes even the most violent passages; by an intense and genuine feeling; and by occasional passages of the purest lyricism, which in its own special kind has never been surpassed.

This was "Marlowe's mighty line," and no matter how clumsily it was imitated, no matter how much it was ridiculed and parodied, and no matter how much it deserved both ridicule and parody, it brought to the English stage for the first time "the heady music of the five marching iambs," the pentameter line, which was to be modified and sweetened by Shakespeare, to be gradually reduced almost to the level of conversational English by Beaumont and Fletcher, but never to be lost from the English stage so long as plays were written in verse at all, and to remain forever after in the poetry that is written in books.

When one is told how important *Tamburlaine* was in the development of the English popular drama; how long its influence lasted; and how great its greatest passages really are, reading the play is something of a shock. It is long, noisy, tedious, and frequently absurd. Its characters are designed to be superhuman but succeed merely in being not human. It is blood-thirsty with a more than Elizabethan blood-thirstiness. It is full of mere rant, and it is often bombastic.

But in spite of all that, there is good reason for calling *Tamburlaine* an important play, even in its own way a great play. It ushers in an entirely new period in drama. It introduces a new medium, blank verse. It stirs its hearers sufficiently to keep its memory alive for a century or more. It contains some of the finest lyric passages ever written. It marks the first step toward a drama which is at once literate and popular.

Tamburlaine is a play on the theme of power, which obsessed the poor shoemaker's son so completely that it dominated almost everything he ever wrote. *Tamburlaine* deals with political and military power, the armed might of the conqueror. *Doctor Faustus* deals with power of the intellect, unlawful power through black magic. *The Jew of Malta* deals with the power of wealth, gained through unscrupulous Machiavellian "pollicie." *The Massacre at Paris* returns again to the theme of political power to be attained by violence, as in *Tamburlaine*, and also by "pollicie," as in *The Jew of Malta.*

The soliloquy of the Duke of Guise, one of the few bits of pure, if violent, poetry in *The Massacre at Paris*, which is at best a very dull play, is the epitome of Marlowe's own mind, and the minds of the fiery and rebellious heroes who echo it:[1]

> What glory is there in a common good,
> That hanges for every peasant to atchiue?
> That like I best that flyes beyond my reach.
> Set me to scale the high Peramides,
> And thereon set the Diadem of Fraunce,
> Ile either rend it with my nayles to naught,
> Or mount the top with my aspiring winges,
> Although my downfall be the deepest hell.
> For this, I wake, when others think I sleepe,
> For this, I waite, that scornes attendance else.

That spirit is Tamburlaine, Faustus, Barabas, Guise—and Christopher Marlowe, gentleman, of London—all in one. Only in *Dido, Queene of Carthage,* where he had Nashe as a collaborator, or in *Edward the Second,* last and nearest perfection of Marlowe's plays, in which he shows for the first time signs of restraint and mastery of his medium and the prospect of growing into something newer and greater, does Marlowe vary from his formula.

Marlowe's *Tamburlaine* is an early example of a kind of play common enough in Elizabethan days. It is neither tragedy nor comedy, but a chronicle play, based on more or less authentic history, re-written and adapted for the stage. The Tamburlaine of history was Timur Lenk (Timur the Lame), the Asiatic conquerer of obscure birth whose armies swept across southwestern Asia, conquered the Turkish Emperor, Ylderim Bajazeth, and died about 1404, something less than two centuries before young Marlowe, casting about for a subject, stumbled on some books at Cambridge, and began to regard him as a possible means of success in the theatre.

The Timur Lenk of history really did most of the things that Marlowe astonished the London audiences by making him do upon the stage; and one may have a very interesting time tracing down all the strange avenues along which news of the far-off Asiatic warrior reached the young English University "scholler" in Cambridge or London. As the play opens, the weakling King of Persia is dispatching his general, Theridamas, to suppress [2]

> Tamburlaine, that sturdie Scythian thiefe,
> That robs your merchants of Persepolis.

Tamburlaine wins the Persian general and his men over to join his own band, captures the "Soldan of Egypt's" daughter, Zenocrate—obviously so named because the poet remembered a Greek philosopher—then joins forces with a second Persian army and places the king's brother on the throne of Persia, then overthrows the new monarch and makes himself King of Persia. All this by the end of the second act.

It was this crowded action, this rush and bustle of mimic armies across the stage, as well as the beauty of the verse, that thrilled Elizabethan audiences. Here was a play that told its story in orotund and thrilling language, where its predecessors had relied on inanely artificial dialogue, or else called in a chorus to explain to the long-suffering audience what the play was really all about.

The rest of the drama is equally stirring. The Turkish sultan, Bajazeth, enters with "the kings of Fess, Morocco, Argier, with others, in great pompe." (It is a little difficult here to recognize Fez, Morocco, and Algiers, the Barbary states of North Africa, which were actually under Turkish suzerainty and which Marlowe had picked up, spellings and all, from the map of Ortelius in the Corpus Christi Library.) Bajazeth's army encounters Tamburlaine's off-stage, while "they sound the battell within." Zabina, the Turkish Empress, and Tamburlaine's Zenocrate sit watching it from the stage and taunting each other, until Bajazeth is overcome.

Enter now the Soldan of Egypt, coming to save his daughter from worse than death with an army—and a speech that became a by-word in Elizabethan London. It was the kind of passion in the kind of resounding language that a robustious actor with a big, resonant voice and a talent that way could take down to the front of the platform stage and use to make the theatre ring:[3]

> Awake ye men of Memphis, heare the clange
> Of Scythian trumpets, heare the Basiliskes,
> That roaring, shake Damascus turrets downe.
> The rogue of Volga holds Zenocrate,
> The Souldans daughter for his Concubine,
> And with a troope of theeues and vagabondes,
> Hath spread his collours to our high disgrace.

The lords and their masked ladies in the galleries were as thrilled as the crowd of groundlings in the pit, and

> Awake ye men of Memphis!

went around London. We know that because other playwrights promptly went off and tried to write speeches like it, some of which survive.

Tamburlaine has in the meantime besieged Damascus, which Marlowe apparently regards as part of the Soldan of Egypt's domains. The besieged city is first surrounded by Tamburlaine's army with white tents, displaying white banners, to indicate that if the governor will surrender,[4]

So shall he haue his life, and all the rest.
But if he stay vntil the bloody flag
Be once aduanc'd on my vermilion Tent,
He dies, and those that kept vs out so long.
And when they see me march in black aray,
With mournfull streamers hanging down their heads,
Were in that citie all the world contain'd,
Not one should scape: but perish by our swords.

The historical Tamburlaine's custom of displaying first white tents and banners in token of mercy, then red meaning that only the fighting men must die, and finally, after continued resistance, black to indicate that no living soul would be spared, is mentioned in most books of the period. Marlowe, recognizing an excellent bit of pure theatre, seized on it at once. He also uses the pathetic scene in which a deputation of young girls come out from the doomed city to plead for mercy and are handed over to Tamburlaine's cavalry to be speared to death. Pope Pius II gives vivid accounts of this episode in a book which was in the Corpus Christi Library while Marlowe was still a student [5] and which is still there.

From this perfect bit of blood-and-thunder, Tamburlaine goes on into his long soliloquy on his love for Zenocrate,[6]

Ah faire Zenocrate, diuine Zenocrate,
Faire is too foule an Epithite for thee,—

containing that exquisite apostrophe to Beauty which is blank verse as perfect as Marlowe or any other poet was ever to write:

What is beauty saith my sufferings then?
If all the pens that euer poets held,
Had fed the feeling of their maisters thoughts,
And euery sweetnes that inspir'd their harts,
Their minds, and muses on admyred theames:
If all the heauenly Quintessence they still
From their immortall flowers of Poesy,
Wherein as in a myrrour we perceiue
The highest reaches of a humaine wit.
If these had made one Poems period
And all combin'd in Beauties worthinesse,
Yet should ther houer in their restlesse heads,
One thought, one grace, one woonder at the least,
Which into words no vertue can digest.

The soliloquy is pure lyric and pure ornament. It advances the plot not a whit. It is wholly without action. But it is the sort of passage that Marlowe loved to write for his great interpreter, Edward Alleyn, just as Shakespeare was later to write another soliloquy which would allow Richard Burbage, as Hamlet, to display his talents.

Do you see the picture? The old Theatre in Finsbury Fields is crowded. The groundlings are agape at the scene with the pleading virgins and agape too at Tamburlaine's savage order —flung out in Alleyn's best martial manner to his horsemen:

> . . . straight goe charge a few of them
> To chardge these Dames, and shew my seruant death,
> Sitting in scarlet on their armed speares.

There is much shrieking and screaming and clashing of steel, offstage, while Alleyn, frowning fearsomely, declaims:

> I will not spare these proud Egyptians,
> Nor change my Martiall obseruations. . . .
> They haue refusde the offer of their liues,
> And know my customes are as peremptory
> As wrathful Planets, death, or destinie.

The spell of the great actor lays itself upon the house, that sunlit afternoon; and then the mood changes. Alleyn, in all the splendour of "Tamberlaynes cotte, with coper lace," and "Tamberlanes breches of crymson vellvet" (items later dutifully recorded in Henslowe's account books), strides slowly down the stage, out on the platform where every line of his face is visible, where he can sense every least change in his audience's feeling, where every syllable can have full value, and swings into the lines of the love soliloquy.

Why, Tamburlaine, the scourge of God, is not a monster but a man, after all—a man, and a man in love.

An instant later we wade in blood again. Bajazeth beats his brains out against the bars of his cage. So does his Empress, amid the enthusiasm of the pit. The King of Arabia, Zenocrate's discarded suitor, enters mortally wounded. The Soldan of Egypt is defeated and captured. But love stories must have a happy ending, and the Soldan announces himself

> . . . pleasde with this my ouerthrow:
> If as beseems a person of thy state,
> Thou hast with honor vsde Zenocrate.

The conqueror of the world, the scourge of God, crowns his Zenocrate, announces their coming marriage, and is reconciled with the Soldan.

The play ends. The play-goers turn homeward or pause in the taverns to spread word of the new and amazing talent of this miraculous young man, said to be "a Cambridge scholler." They undoubtedly spread it to good effect; for we can see that effect in the account book of Master Philip Henslowe. These accounts do not begin until long after, when Marlowe is already dead and *Tamburlaine* is an old play; but even then it can still draw an audience. Between September, 1594, and November, 1595, Henslowe enters receipts for fourteen performances, the takings for each ranging between eighteen and forty-five shillings—very respectable by Elizabethan standards, especially for a play that was already six or seven years past its prime.

John Taylor, the "water poet," a Thames boatman with a talent for minor verse, wrote years afterward that "Tamburlaine perhaps is not altogether so famous in his owne countrie of Tartaria as in England"; and we have an allusion to productions at the Red Bull Theatre and by players wandering in the provinces, which show that *Tamburlaine* held the stage, one way or another, for some fifty years. The play became so familiar that Shakespeare, in writing *Henry IV*, could still be sure that his casual allusion to a single line would be instantly familiar to his hearers.[7]

The obvious course for an ambitious young man who has just made a tremendous success with a first play is to write a new one as fast as possible; and there is no doubt at all that the actors, seeing *Tamburlaine's* success, clamoured for another play. But Marlowe did not have another play to give them. His secret government missions and such study as he had been doing at Cambridge must have kept him fairly well occupied. The thing to do was to write, not a new play, but a sequel to the first one, whose characters and materials he had well in mind already. This duly appeared, some time in 1588, as *Tamburlaine the Great. With his impasſionate furie, for the death of his Lady and Loue faire Zenocrate.* The poet is quite frank about it in the prologue:

> The generall welcomes Tamburlain receiu'd,
> When he arriued last vpon our stage,

Hath made our Poet pen his second part,
Wher death cuts off the progres of his pomp.

The Second Part of *Tamburlaine* is obviously more hurried and more careless than the first. Young Marlowe glances through his sources again and sees that there is a good deal about Tamburlaine of which he has so far made no use. He trims the point of his goose-quill and begins: The Turkish vassals of the conquered Bajazeth gather to redeem his defeat. In order to be free to attack Tamburlaine in the east, they swear a holy truce with their Christian foe, Sigismund of Hungary, on the west. Sigismund, however, acts on the theory that his oath is not binding because the Turks with whom he made it are infidels. Breaking his pledged word, he attacks. The Turks appeal, not to Allah, but to the Christ by whom the perfidious Christian King has sworn, to avenge the broken oath by which the Christians have themselves dishonoured His name.

This episode gives Marlowe a chance to write into the play a typical bit of heresy like that which later appears in *Doctor Faustus*. While in these days it lacks the startlingly unorthodox ring it had in its own, the passage is a good example of the bold speculation which already occupied the poet's mind and which had probably already helped to bring him into bad odour at the University. It was a tendency in Marlowe's thought which later led to the wild, irreligious tavern talk that horrified government spies reported secretly. But it is, after all, only speculation as to the nature of the one true God. Modern ears will have a hard time finding it shocking in the least degree; standards of orthodoxy were stricter in the sixteenth century.

The Turkish leader cries out in fury: [8]

Then if there be a Christ, as Christians say,
But in their deeds deny him for their Christ:
If he be son to euerliuing Ioue,
And hath the power of his outstretched arme,
If he be iealous of his name and honor,
As is our holy prophet Mahomet,
Take here these papers as our sacrifice
And witnesse of thy seruants periury.
Open thou shining vaile of Cynthia
And make a passage from the imperiall heauen
That he that sits on high and neuer sleeps,

> Nor in one place is circumscriptible,
> But euery where fils euery Continent,
> With strange infusion of his sacred vigor,
> May in his endlesse power and puritie
> Behold and venge this Traitors periury.
> Thou Christ that art esteem'd omnipotent,
> If thou wilt prooue thy selfe a perfect God,
> Worthy the worship of all faithfull hearts,
> Be now reueng'd vpon this Traitor's soule. . . .
> To armes my Lords, on Christ still let vs crie,
> If there be Christ, we shall haue victorie.

The Turks meet and defeat the Christians in the West. But in the meantime, in the East, Tamburlaine's various armies join into one enormous host. Each of the leaders describes the countries over which his army has marched—taking the names verbatim, mistakes and all, from the map of Ortelius, which Marlowe had seen at Cambridge. Tamburlaine meets, and of course conquers, the Turks.

At this point, however, Marlowe is shrewd enough to see that he cannot go on for ten acts with nothing but a series of speeches, clashes of arms, and mighty conquests. He has already done his best to make Tamburlaine a human and credible figure by developing with all his might the love story of Tamburlaine and Zenocrate at which the sources of the play barely hint.

There was in the Orient a tradition that mighty Tamburlaine had one favourite wife whom his armies had originally brought to him as a captive, whom he greatly loved and whose death greatly distressed him. This tale, current in Asia in various Persian histories, nowhere appears in the European printed sources available to the dramatist; but in some mysterious way he got hold of it and used it to vary his play by making his conqueror more humanly appealing—a figure who in spite of all his blood-and-thunder could stir an audience to sympathy. Tamburlaine has loved as other men; the pit shall now see him suffer as other men.

Zenocrate falls ill and dies; and for her death, Marlowe writes another of those great lyrical passages many of which might fall flat enough on the modern stage because of their length; but which gave an actor like Edward Alleyn a chance to stalk down the platform-stage and tear a passion to tatters. They are splendid, fantastically poetic stuff, these highly ornamented passages, though to enjoy them one must leave a good share of one's common sense and all one's modern tastes behind.[9]

> Blacke is the beauty of the brightest day,
> The golden balle of heauens eternal fire,
> That danc'd with glorie on the siluer waues:
> Now wants the fewell that enflamde his beames
> And all with faintnesse and for foule disgrace,
> He bindes his temples with a frowning cloude,
> Ready to darken earth with endless night.

—Thus it begins, ending with a purple patch of purely lyrical blank verse, built around the refrain, one echoing, haunting line:

> To entertaine deuine Zenocrate.

It is a passage that cries aloud for music and that almost sings itself. Probably the early stage managers saw their chance and did let their actor read it over music, for at the end a stage direction says: "The musicke sounds, and she dies."

Critics have sometimes objected to the unrestrained violence of emotion in it; quite forgetting that we have here the words of a barbarian chieftain who proudly styles himself "the scourge of God," a half-savage Scythian who is stricken to the heart with grief, mad with his anguish, and not likely to express himself with the sedate restraint of a Victorian bishop:

> Now walk the angels on the walles of heauen,
> As Centinels to warne th'immortall soules,
> To entertaine deuine Zenocrate.
> Apollo, Cynthia, and the ceaslesse lamps
> That gently look'd vpon this loathsome earth,
> Shine downwards now no more, but deck the heauens
> To entertaine diuine Zenocrate.
> The christall springs whose taste illuminates
> Refined eies with an eternall sight,
> Like tried siluer runs through Paradice
> To entertaine diuine Zenocrate.
> The Cherubins and holy Seraphins
> That sing and play before the king of kings,
> Vse all their voices and their instruments
> To entertaine diuine Zenocrate.
> And in this sweet and currious harmony,
> The God that tunes this musicke to our soules:
> Holds out his hand in highest maiesty
> To entertaine diuine Zenocrate.

For the rest of his life, Tamburlaine carries the beloved body about with him, wherever his armies go,

> Embalm'd with Cassia, Amber Greece and Myrre,
> Not lapt in lead but in a sheet of gold.

The defeat of the Turks gives the young dramatist a chance to devise another stage spectacle that lingered long in the memories of the London play-goers. Many later writers allude to it, half smilingly; and Shakespeare himself uses a scrap of it in *Henry IV*, when mine Ancient Pistol, very drunk, indulges in a ranting speech full of half-remembered scraps from the playhouse.

Long before, in 1566, when Marlowe was only two years old, George Gascoigne's *Jocasta,* the first Elizabethan adaptation of Greek tragedy, had used a scene in which a king appears, "sitting in a Chariote very richely furnished, drawne in by foure Kinges in their Dublettes and Hosen, with Crownes also upon their heades." Marlowe (or the stage manager) remembers this; and so Edward Alleyn makes a sensational entrance as "Tamburlaine drawen in his chariot by Trebizon and Soria with bittes in their mouthes, reines in his left hand, in his right hand a whip, with which he scourgeth them," while two other kings are "led by with fiue or six common souldiers." It gave Alleyn one of the most successful bits of his long career: [10]

> Holla, ye pampered Iades of Asia:
> What, can ye draw but twenty miles a day,
> And haue so proud a chariot at your heeles,
> And such a Coachman as great Tamburlaine?

Even the phrase "pampered jades of Asia" had probably been borrowed from Arthur Golding's translation of Ovid, with its "pampered jades of Thrace"; but that made no difference to the electrified audience.

The ale-houses, the great Queen's Court, the palaces of the nobility echoed with the line; and other English writers for three centuries rang the changes on it. There are at least ten variations, ranging from Beaumont and Fletcher to George Eliot. [11]

The last act is a final series of conquests and speeches, ending in the death of Tamburlaine. Babylon is captured and the governor hanged in chains upon the city walls, as many a poor wretch had been hanged on the Canterbury walls. Tamburlaine falls ill. A map is brought in and the hero traces his life of conquest, exactly following Ortelius again. Zenocrate's hearse appears for the last time, while her lover exclaims:

> Now eies, inioy your latest benefite,

and then—in a speech of thirty-odd lines—vehemently dies at last.

The death scene is a curious illustration of the purely dramatic limitations of Marlowe's earlier work. The man is primarily a poet, who cannot resist the temptation to a resounding line; and his final scene is in consequence much too full of life and vigour. The dying hero can rise to recite a reverberating speech of great length, filled with elaborate metaphors, classical allusions, all the approved rhetorical devices and "high astounding terms" that Marlowe loved.

It is all completely artificial and it is saved from absurdity only by the splendour of the language and the extensive willingness of the Elizabethan audience to swallow unreality. Far different is the death scene in which Shakespeare, after a few years' advance in stage craft, lets his Antony die—in blank verse still, but in a blank verse now whose very rhythm has the choking gasp of a dying man:

> I am dying, Egypt, dying.

Marlowe was like most of the writers of his time, who never had the least idea of inventing stories of their own. A playwright's first step was to look around for a source, either in some older play which he could re-write and bring up to date, or in some old book of tales, which he could adapt to the stage. Far from being shame-faced about it, these old writers seem to have felt that it was hardly respectable to write an original plot.

Only two of Shakespeare's plays have any claim to originality in plot; and for nearly every one of the few hundred other Elizabethan plays that have come down to us, a prototype can usually be found somewhere or other. Almost all of their originals have been unearthed by the patient labour of scholars, who have been examining this curious aspect of letters for more than a century.

Often these sources have no particular importance, except that they reveal the quarry whence the stone was digged for later shaping. With Marlowe, however, it is worth a little effort to discover sources, because their discovery tells us so much about the kind of man he was and the way his mind worked. Most writers of his day were content with a single source. When Shakespeare wanted to write an historical play, he took down his trusty volume of Holinshed's *Chronicle,* a quaint early collection of stories from English history; chose what he wanted; let his imagination play freely around it; and wrote his play from that. When Ben Jonson wrote his *Catiline,* he simply translated copiously from Cicero's orations and put them on the stage without even troubling to adapt them. When Shakespeare wrote *Hamlet,* he was content to re-write an old and fairly well-known play.

But Marlowe was a highly trained University graduate, who had read in the finest libraries of the day. Nothing so simple would do for him. Wherever possible, he reads as many books as he can find before he begins to write; and *Tamburlaine* is the play for which he appears to have read more books than for any other. Half a dozen books about Tamburlaine himself, some of Spenser's poems, Ariosto's *Orlando Furioso,* a treatise on fortification to get the conqueror's military terminology right, and the maps of Ortelius which set his geography marvellously awry—these were some of the materials that went to make the play that took London by storm. More mysterious are the echoes that we catch of distant Oriental sources in languages Marlowe cannot possibly have known, whose materials appear in no European books but nevertheless do appear in the two parts of the play.

The search for Marlowe's sources thus ceases to be mere amusement for scholarly dilettantes and becomes a genuine search for the mind of a poet. Until a few years ago, it seemed plain enough that Marlowe had used only two books. One of these was a Latin life of Tamburlaine, *Vita Magni Tamerlanis,* by an Italian who Latinized his name as Petrus Perondinus. The other was a queer volume of literary odds and ends quite unconnected with each other—something like a magazine with but a single issue—which the Spaniard, Pedro Mexia, published as *Silva de Varia Leccon,* and which one Thomas Fortescue, otherwise unknown to fame, "Englished" as *The Forest.*

From these two books, Marlowe could have gathered most of the historical details which he used in writing *Tamburlaine;*

but his play also contains a great many other elements that could not possibly have come from these sources. Among the most interesting details of this sort are such minute matters as proper names and titles, the exact number of Tamburlaine's troops at the beginning of his career, the use of the captive Bajazeth as a foot-stool, Tamburlaine's love for Zenocrate, and their children.

Where did the young poet get it all? At the end of his account of the historical Tamburlaine, Mexia adds a little list of his authorities, in the most approved modern manner: "This then that I héere giue you, that all haue I borowed of Baptista Fulgotius, Pope Pius, Plantina vpon the life of Boniface the ninth, of Matthew Palmier, and of Cambinus a Florentine writing the History and exploits of the Turks."

It so happens that all these old authors have survived. Plantina and Matthew Palmier have really very little to say about Tamburlaine and are unimportant. But the writings on Tamburlaine of Baptista Fulgotius and of Pope Pius II (both listed by Mexia) were actually in the library of Corpus Christi College while Marlowe was a student. So also was the work of Baptista Ignatius (or Egnatius), whom Mexia does not include in his book list but whom he does, in the body of his work, mention approvingly as "a diligent sercher of ancient antiquities."

Going beyond Mexia's authorities, Marlowe seems also to have used the writings of Paulus Jovius, the learned bishop of Nocera in far-off Italy, whose works were in both the Corpus Christi and University libraries, and Philip Lonicer's *Chronicorum Turcicorum Libri.*

These books abound in details that are in the play but not in Mexia and not in Perondinus. Most of the details they yield are exceedingly minute; but that very fact adds to their significance as proof where Marlowe has been browsing. They are in themselves too unimportant for any one to bother to invent. If Marlowe used them at all, he copied them—perhaps unconsciously. And where would he be so likely to look as in the old books just across the court in his own college, or in the library of the University? This is the more plausible because both libraries together amounted to a very few hundred volumes—so few that with nearly seven years to browse among the shelves Marlowe could not very well miss them.

Take, for example, the names of Bajazeth's son. Perondinus

says that he was called "Celebinus," but Marlowe gets mixed up and gives that name to one of Tamburlaine's sons by mistake. Baptista Ignatius says that the Turkish prince was "Orchanes, whom others call Calepinus." His book was actually published as part of the same collection of Turkish chronicles that contained the life of Tamburlaine by Perondinus. Cambinus gives the name as "Calapino," and Paulus Jovius explains that many people "for Cyryscelebes, named him Calepyne." Somewhere, also, Marlowe had—as we know from another quotation—discovered Philip Lonicer's *Chronicorum Turcicorum Libri,* which devotes a chapter to "Calepinus Cyricelebes, qui Cibelinus," and also refers to him as "Calepinus Cyricelebes, whom they also call Cibelius."

After all that, it is not hard to guess why Marlowe's play describes the Turkish prince as "Calepinus Cyricelibes, otherwise Cybelius." [12] It is interesting also to note that Marlowe is too economical to waste a high-sounding name like "Orchanes." He uses it, not for one of Bajazeth's sons, but for one of his vassals. And he uses the name Calapine all over again when he writes *The Jew of Malta.* The man loved words, loved the sound and tone and colour of them; and he could not bear to see a good one go to waste.

Again, Marlowe's Tamburlaine delights in calling himself "the scourge of God." Nothing like this appears in Mexia or Perondinus; but it does appear in several of the other books, notably in the Corpus Christi copy of Pope Pius's *Asiae Europaeque Elegantissima Descriptio* (1531), where Tamburlaine is made to say: "I am the wrath of God and the destruction of the world."

Yet again, while most sources say that the Persian kings sent out a thousand soldiers to capture Tamburlaine, most of them are silent as to the number of Tamburlaine's own troops. But Baptista Fulgotius and Philip Lonicer give the same figure that Marlowe gives: "The number came to five hundred." [13]

"We fiue hundred foote," says Marlowe's hero.

One of the favourite stories about Tamburlaine was his degradation of the captive Bajazeth, who had to get down on all fours and serve as a foot-stool for his conqueror. Mexia does not mention the tale and Perondinus alludes to it without using Marlowe's word, "foot-stool." But Baptista Fulgotius and Philip Lonicer are very specific about this detail: "Using him for a foot-stool" *(eo pro scabello utens).*

One can almost see the poet's brain at work. Marlowe has been reading the old books. He is scribbling at his play one night in the old storehouse where the Parker scholars lodged in the Old Court at Corpus Christi. He gets half a line. His hero is going to say:

"Bring out my—"

And then the poet's memory of the old books supplies the missing word, and he unconsciously leaves a clue to his literary browsings, to be traced centuries later. Such is the origin of a famous scene which his imitators were to refer to and reproduce for years after Marlowe's own death—as late, indeed, as Dryden's *Conquest of Granada.*

It is hard to explain just where Marlowe found the story of Tamburlaine's love for Zenocrate. Johan Schiltberger, a Bavarian traveller, who had actually visited the court of Timur Lenk, mentions a favourite wife whom Timur beheaded for infidelity, after which regret for her caused him to fall ill and die. Laying aside the infidelity, this is essentially the story as Marlowe tells it; but the poet certainly never heard the tale from Schiltberger, whose account of his adventures lay in manuscript until 1859.[14]

A queer old sixteenth century book of sermons [15] also alludes to a wife's influence over the conqueror; but most of the learned books on Tamburlaine simply ignore his marriage, though Perondinus mentions it casually.

Strangest of all is the close correspondence between Marlowe's story and Oriental documents, some of which have never been translated and none of which were translated until long after Marlowe was dead. One of these is the *Mulfuzat Timury,* which mentions a favourite wife who accompanied her heroic husband in the field, shared his perils and conquests, and died while he was in the midst of his victories. The Persian historians, Mir Khwand and Ali-i-Yazdi, also tell the story of the captive princess whom Timur married, whom he loved exceedingly, and at whose death he was so distressed that he withdrew from affairs of state.[16]

It is simply impossible to think that Marlowe hit upon the same story that these Oriental writers tell, by mere chance; and yet it is equally impossible to show how he could ever have become acquainted with such obscure documents. Perhaps he heard the tale as it was brought back from the East by word-of-mouth. This is not by any means incredible, for there was more passage between East and West than one might suppose. The Spaniard, Ruy Gonzalez de Clavijo, went on an embassy to the Court of Timur not long before the monarch's death; and Timur's Court was at least once in touch with the Court of France.[17]

It was not, therefore, impossible for such tales to reach Europe orally. The whole Continent was interested in stories of the Asiatic conqueror—one can see that by the numerous books about him. English sailors roved the world. Back and forth between the island kingdom and the seven seas there was a constant stream of travel, much of it pouring through Canterbury. Is it too much to assume an eager English lad with a keen ear for travellers' tales of Tartar kings and far-off conquests, simple tales which blossomed into art, years after?

So we have an Asiatic chieftain, and a young English poet. Between them, league upon league of tossing seas, of burning desert, of snow-capped mountain—plus the greater gulf of nearly two centuries. But all of these are not enough to sever them completely. They are linked by priestly chroniclers, upon the vellum covers of whose pious labours the dust of four centuries now lies thick; by the strange screed in which a barbarian chief tells the story of his life: by the tales of old historians. Between these two minds, so distant in time and space, there are as links the maps of strange regions, the hurrying ships of England, old books, the living word upon the lips of men.

9.

"The Watch Strikes"

"Faustus is gone, regard his hellish fall."
Doctor Faustus

Marlowe's *Doctor Faustus* is the first work of conscious literary art to tell the story of John Faustus, the partly legendary and partly historical German scholar who bartered his soul to the devil in exchange for twenty-four years of power and pleasure, won through diabolical aid. The essence of the story was already more than a thousand years old. It had long circulated throughout Germany and elsewhere in the world, in various folk legends, but no serious writer with any pretensions to literary power had ever given it permanent and artistic form.

The story that Marlowe tells is not quite the same as the version which Goethe's play and the operas of Gounod and Berlioz have made familiar. Never interested in love stories, Marlowe ignores the Marguerite episodes entirely. In his hands, the story of Faustus becomes another drama of the soul of man in quest of boundless power.

Faustus is a learnèd doctor of the University of Wittenberg. Being a Marlowe hero he is inevitably a superman whose achievements have already exceeded any ordinary human capacity. He is a doctor in theology. He is a physician so skilled that his prescriptions are

> . . . hung vp as monuments,
> Whereby whole Citties haue escapt the plague,
> And thousand desprate maladies beene easde.

He is learnèd in the law. He is a master of the liberal arts, particularly the logic of Aristotle. In other words, he has mastered all of the traditional "four faculties" of the early universities, any one of which was a lifework for anybody except the hero of a Marlowe play. Marlowe may have been an idle student in his last three years at Cambridge; but he is full of sharp interest in learning and has as hearty a respect for

Faustus's conquests in the golden realms of the intellect as for Tamburlaine's conquests of kings and provinces.

But as Faustus sits in his study brooding, all merely human learning seems hollow. Theology teaches what? That we must sin and sinning die—it is mere fatalism.

> What doctrine call you this, *Che sera, sera,*
> What wil be, shall be? Diuinitie, adieu.

Faustus will none of it. Medicine is nothing but the palliation of disease, nothing but the prolongation of a life that is doomed to end at last.

> Yet art thou still but Faustus, and a man.
> Wouldst thou make man to liue eternally?
> Or being dead, raise them to life againe?
> Then this profession were to be esteemd.

Nothing ordinary ever satisfied Marlowe; nothing ordinary can therefore satisfy Faustus, in whose aching longing for the impossible we come closer to the high aspiring mind of Marlowe than in any other of his heroes. Since the physician's science must ultimately be overcome by death, Faustus will scorn it.

For the law, he feels the disgust that so many sensitive minds experience when they face for the first time the carefully preserved records of the trivial squabbles of petty and dishonest folk through the centuries that stretch illimitably back. To Faustus the law is merely "a pretty case of paltry legacies." It is a kind of learning that

> fittes a mercenary drudge,
> Who aimes at nothing but externall trash,
> Too seruile and illiberall for me.

Faustus has thus exhausted all legitimate learning and remains unsatisfied. There remains the black art, which is forbidden to Christian souls; but Faustus scorns such scruples. He will be greater than Tamburlaine himself:

> All things that mooue betweene the quiet poles
> Shalbe at my commaund, Emperours and Kings
> Are but obeyd in their seuerall prouinces:
> Nor can they raise the winde, or rend the cloudes:
> But his dominion that exceedes in this,
> Stretcheth as farre as doth the minde of man.

A sound Magician is a mighty god:
Here Faustus trie thy braines to gaine a deitie.

A Good Angel appears to beg him to "lay that damned booke aside," an Evil Angel to urge him on: [1]

Go forward Faustus in that famous art,
Wherein all natures treasury is containd,

and Faustus, "glutted with conceit of this," calls in learned magicians and then begins to conjure for himself.

A devil appears, heralding Mephastophilis, who bargains for the magician's soul. A deed is drawn in Faustus's own blood, which congeals rather than be used for the horrid purpose, and has to be warmed at the fire before the document can be written. To the modern reader, these scenes lose much of the thrill of horror that they had for the Elizabethan. To us, they appear at best amusing flights of fantasy. To the Elizabethan spectator in the old Theatre of the Burbages, they were daring and deadly realism. Sober citizens of London believed that at some performances of Marlowe's wicked play the horrified actors suddenly found that there was "one devell too many amongst them"—Satan's own imp of darkness had suddenly appeared on the stage to mingle with the players and act his part as one of the company!

Thomas Fineux, still a student at Corpus Christi where he had known Marlowe, took it all so seriously that he "learnd all Marlo by heart," and actually went out at midnight to pray that the devil might appear. The only effect of this mumbo-jumbo was to imperil, not Thomas's soul, but his Cambridge degree. Yet these earnest efforts at black magic at Corpus Christi, just after Marlowe left, by a man who had lived in college with him and knew him personally, suggest the fascinated horror with which their original audiences viewed these alarming scenes.[2]

To them, "Enter the ghost" in *Hamlet* meant that a real actor glided upon the stage, impersonating a real ghost. "Enter Mephastophilis with a chafer of coles" meant a real devil with a whiff of brimstone about him, no bloodless abstraction of purely metaphysical evil. The people who saw these scenes believed in the ghost and believed in the devil, believed so thoroughly that they almost forgot that what they saw was, after all, but the mimic world of the theatre.

And yet Marlowe was able at the same time to make sublime verse out of the wholly impersonal abstraction of good and evil. In *Tamburlaine,* he had speculated on a deity who was simply "endlesse power and puritie," a being omnipresent "with strange infusion of his sacred vigor." In *Doctor Faustus,* there is one glimpse of the spiritual agony that pure evil produces, which terrifies even the devil himself and makes him for a moment weaken and almost beg even his victim to bethink him what he does and repent in time. Faustus has asked Mephastophilis how it is possible for him to leave hell. The reply is unforgettable: [3]

> Why this is hel, nor am I out of it:
> Thinkst thou that I who saw the face of God,
> And tasted the eternal ioyes of heauen,
> Am not tormented with ten thousand hels,
> In being depriv'd of euerlasting blisse?
> O Faustus, leave these frivolous demands,
> Which strike a terror to my fainting soule.

It is the stubborn Faustus who must encourage the faint-hearted fiend. "This word damnation terrifies not him," he cries: [4]

> Had I as many soules as there be starres,
> Ide giue them al for Mephastophilis.

"Come, I thinke hell's a fable," he tells his tempter, who replies with sardonic grimness: "I, thinke so still, till experience change thy minde."

Faustus now enters upon his promised twenty-four years of complete power, "letting him liue in al voluptuousnesse." He flies about the world, seeing all the stateliest cities, guided by Mephastophilis and drawn through the air by winged dragons. It was for these scenes that Philip Henslowe bought the "j dragon in fostes," which we find mentioned in his account books. Faustus performs miracles at the Emperor's court, brings fresh fruit by magic from Africa in European midwinter, plays clownish tricks in the Pope's palace, to the delight of the anti-Catholic audience, and finally raises Helen of Troy from the dead.

In this scene are lines by which the poet Marlowe is still known wherever the English language is spoken or poetry is treasured. As the fair ghost of Troy's immortal wanton appears, the doomed magician exclaims in rapture: [5]

Was this the face that lancht a thousand shippes?
And burnt the toplesse Towres of Ilium?
Sweete Helen, make me immortall with a kisse:
Her lips suckes forth my soule, see where it flies:
Come Helen, come giue mee my soule againe.
Here wil I dwel, for heauen be in these lips,
And all is drosse that is not Helena:
I wil be Paris, and for loue of thee,
Insteade of Troy shal Wertenberge be sackt,
And I will combate with weake Menelaus,
And weare thy colours on my plumed Crest:
Yea I wil wound Achillis in the heele,
And then returne to Helen for a kisse.
O thou art fairer then the euening aire,
Clad in the beauty of a thousand starres,
Brighter art thou then flaming Iupiter,
When he appeard to haplesse Semele,
More louely then the monarke of the skie
In wanton Arethusaes azurde armes,
And none but thou shalt be my paramour.

This was another of those purple patches, highly toned in its emotions and exquisitely wrought and phrased in its language, intended to give Edward Alleyn a chance at an adroit bit of elocution. We happen to know that Alleyn did act Faustus, because an old poem with a passing allusion to "Allen playing Faustus" is by chance preserved.[6]

The origin of the "thousand ships" passage is an example of the way in which a poet's pen can transmute the least promising source material. In the little chapbook from which Marlowe took the Faust story, he found an allusion to "fayre Helena of Greece for whom the worthy town of Troie was destroyd and razed down to the ground." Classical tradition was pretty clear about the number of ships that sailed against Troy. The "thousand ships" are mentioned in the *Aeneid* and in *Iphigenia in Tauris*.[7] There is also a passage in the Eighteenth *Dialogue of the Dead*, written in the fourth century by the late Syrian Greek satirist, Lucian. In this, a character looking upon the skull of Helen ponders: "And for this a thousand ships were launched from all Greece, and so many Greeks and barbarians and so many cities were destroyed."

Out of such stuff—a few legendary naval statistics, a commonplace passage in a cheap little popular work of his own day, and an equally commonplace bit from a forgotten Syrian

Greek—Marlowe fused together the deathless lines which rise to the mind wherever his name is heard.

The famous phrases of these famous lines are not wholly new, but are mostly the poet's re-working of earlier and less successful experiments. He had already alluded to the "thousand ships," once in *Tamburlaine* and once in *Dido*,[8] an unimportant play which is nevertheless of interest because it shows Marlowe's early fumbling with lines and phrases which he later re-casts into perfection. In it he describes the ocean's waves as "toplesse hilles" and makes Dido, dreaming of Aeneas, murmur:

> And heele make me immortall with a kisse.

Marlowe is often like Keats; and it is interesting here to find the poet in his workshop making, like Keats, a first experiment, then catching it up and re-casting it more perfectly. Keats often does this in the manuscripts that have come down to us; and had we Marlowe's original "foul sheets," as the Elizabethan writers called their first drafts, we should doubtless find him doing the same thing over and over again.

After this high point, the play moves swiftly to its catastrophe. Faustus has had occasional qualms throughout the play. The Good and Evil Angels have continued their solicitings. Finally, a virtuous Old Man endeavours to persuade Faustus to abandon the damnable black art; but he is tormented and driven off by devils who are determined not to be baulked of their prey.

As his dreadful end approaches, Faustus in his agony takes counsel with fellow-scholars—again in terms of that Cambridge which Marlowe knew so well and which permeates this tragedy of a scholar damned by the pride of his own overweening intellect. Addressing one of his comforters, Faustus exclaims:[9] "Ah my sweete chamber-fellow! had I liued with thee, then had I liued stil, but now I die eternally." It is tempting to suppose that here, for an instant, Marlowe, who has abjured the cloth for which Archbishop Parker's bounty had destined him and who like Faustus has given himself over to forbidden speculation, looks back for an instant to the corner room in the Old Court at Corpus Christi, where he had had as chamber-fellows, Lewgar, Pashley, and the other Canterbury scholars who had duly proceeded in divinity and were now decorous parsons in rural English villages.

This is one of many places in *Doctor Faustus* where one feels an autobiographical touch, feels it keenly, too, though such things are in their very nature beyond proof. It was with some such idea that Josephine Preston Peabody, in her play on *Marlowe,*[10] made him cry:

> Why, sir, I am the man who wrote the play
> Of Faustus who did sell him to the Devil!
> I am the man, the devil and the soul.

For sheer dramatic effect, pure poetry, intense agony of feeling, and metrical skill, the solitary closing scene of *Doctor Faustus* is one of the highest points in Marlowe's art and in the whole of Elizabethan drama. It is a long soliloquy of nearly sixty lines which, upon the stage, is supposed to last for an entire hour. When one reads it slowly in a quiet study (preferably at midnight), it occupies only a few minutes. Even the utmost of Alleyn's skill in facial expression, gesture, chilling silences, and pantomime, cannot have dragged it out beyond five or ten minutes. Yet between the opening stage direction, "The clocke strikes eleauen," to the menacing side note, "The watch strikes," indicating the half hour at the exact middle of the scene—at which the doomed wretch shrieks, "Ah, halfe the houre is past"—onward to the stroke of fate in the final stage direction, "The clocke striketh twelue," reader or hearer has the feeling that he has lived through a full hour. No ordinary hour, either, but an hour that begins an eternity of damnation.

Though Marlowe builds this passage firmly on the conventional iambic line, he varies it amazingly, so that his metre is a perfect mirror of the gasping agony of the damned magician's last hour on earth. Lines which stand alone like "Ah Faustus," "No, no," "Oh God," have enough gasping horror in them to make one understand why the startled theatre-goers were ready to swear again and again that they had seen real devils. Nor is it hard to understand why the audience was terrified when at one performance "the Old Theatre crackt and startled the audience."[11]

Most terrible of all is the quotation from Ovid, Marlowe's favourite among the Latin poets, whom he quotes perpetually but never to such effect as here:

> O lente, lente curite noctis equi.

This is the line which Ovid utters when he finds himself at length within Corinna's arms. It is the conventional lover's plea to the dawn to be slow, at his moment of full ecstasy. Here, with fearful irony, it rises naturally to the lips of the despairing scholar in his ecstasy of terror, as he pleads with the night to go slowly because midnight begins damnation.

The devils enter upon the stroke of twelve and carry Faustus away forever, while the Chorus begins the solemn epilogue which dismally foreshadows the future course of Marlowe's own career:

> Cut is the branch that might haue growne ful straight,
> And burned is Appolloes Laurel bough
> That sometime grew within this learned man.

Strange to say, these prophetic lines are not altogether Marlowe's own, but are adapted from the half-forgotten poem on *Shore's Wife* by the wholly forgotten court poet, Thomas Churchyard:

> They brake the bowes and shakte the tree by sleight,
> And bent the wand that mought haue growne full streight.

This had been published in the 1563 edition of the *Mirrour for Magistrates* a year before Marlowe's birth, but the book was well known in his lifetime.[12] If Marlowe ever read the poem of Churchyard, its lines must have lingered in his subconscious memory, rising again to his pen's point when he needed them most to finish off the play that traced the course of his own tragic destiny. The same book contains an account of the bold and defiant Young Mortimer, who is one of the leading figures in Marlowe's last great play, *Edward the Second.*

Except for a few reminiscences like this, however, *Doctor Faustus* is wholly based on a little popular chapbook, the kind of thing that was hawked around the country for sale to lovers of sensation. This was *The Historie of the Damnable Life and Deserved Death of Dr. John Faustus,* which is a very free translation of the original German *Faustbuch.* There is a certain mystery about the matter, for the English Faust Book was not published until 1592, two or three years after Marlowe is supposed to have written the play. It has even been suggested [13] that *Doctor Faustus* was not written in 1588 or 1589, but in 1592 or 1593; since otherwise the play seems to have been published prior to the source from which it is derived.

This is not necessarily the case, however. In *Tamburlaine*, Marlowe quotes from Spenser's *Faerie Queene* a year or two before publication; and from Paul Ive's *Practise of Fortification* at least a year before the publication of the only known edition of this military treatise.[14] Books often circulated in manuscript among the author's friends—some books were never meant to circulate in any other way. Moreover, it is quite possible that there was an earlier edition of the English Faust Book, all copies of which have since been destroyed. It is, unfortunately, not at all unusual for an edition to disappear completely.

That *Doctor Faustus* as we now have it is a poet's re-writing of this cheap little popular pamphlet, there is not a shadow of doubt. The play follows it throughout, event by event, incident by incident. Sometimes Marlowe hardly troubles to adapt its material but copies it almost verbatim. Thus the English Faust Book describes Faustus's visit to "the Castle of St. Angelo, wherein are so many great cast peeces [of artillery] as there are days in the year." This plainly re-appears in Marlowe's lines: [15]

> Vpon the bridge call'd Ponto Angelo,
> Erected is a Castle passing strong,
> Within whose walles such store of ordonance are
> And double Canons, fram'd of carued brasse,
> As match the dayes within one compleate yeare.

A little further on, the English Faust Book mentions "the Pyramids that Iulius Caesar broughte out of Africa." Marlowe promptly turns this into verse as

> . . . high piramides,
> Which Iulius Caesar brought from Affrica,

scarcely altering the wording. Neither of these passages appears in the German, a language which Marlowe would hardly have known in any case.

Rather more human and amusing is a slip in Faustus's allusion to the city of Trier, which he visits in company with Mephastophilis and describes as surrounded by "ayrie mountaine tops." There is no reference to mountains at Trier in the Faust Book; but there *is* a reference to "monuments." Master Marlowe was writing hard and fast that night, and as he scanned the page rather hastily, "monuments" and "mountains" looked very much alike. Three centuries later, he is caught in his blunder.[16]

The Faust story is, of course, much older than either of these books. Its germ is probably as old as the story of Simon Magus, the wicked magician who attempts to purchase divine power from St. Paul in the Book of Acts.[17] That episode is the only one which Holy Scripture mentions; but several apocryphal gospels—which the Fathers of the Church refused to admit into the Canon of Scripture—have a great deal more to say about him. Such apocryphal books as the *Acts of Peter*, the *Acts of Paul*, the *Passion of Peter and Paul* and the *Epistles of the Apostles* describe a character who might very easily be an historical prototype of the legendary Faustus.

Like Faustus, Simon is a highly educated man, who becomes a professional wizard. Like Faustus, he flies through the air. Like Faustus, he creates a magic horse who disappears, leaving only the "bottle" [bale] of hay that he has eaten. Finally, he is described by St. Clement of Alexandria, whose father and brother are both named "Faustus," or "fortunate"—a rather common name in the later Roman Empire. It almost looks as if their names slipped into the narrative by accident.

Down the centuries, these old stories seem to have clustered around various Christian tales of temptation by the devil, until we reach the sixth century story of Theophilus of Syracuse, who sold himself to the devil, forswore God, and renounced the saints, though he did not renounce the Holy Virgin, who eventually saved him—an oversight on the devil's part. A disciple averred that he had beheld Theophilus conversing with the foul fiend and signing a compact in blood. The story of Cyprian of Antioch is much the same and was probably combined with the Faust story.

It never seems to have occurred to the early Christians that pagan deities simply did not exist. They remained real enough, in the minds of their erstwhile worshippers, even when those worshippers became Christian converts. Only, now they had ceased to be gods and had become demons, were no longer friends, but foes to the soul. Genuine miracles were due to divine grace; but signs and wonders could also be produced by diabolical aid through those "curious arts" against which St. Paul preached at Ephesus. Although this black magic involved the soul's damnation, it remained and could not be put down (it flourishes mildly even to this day); for it was supposed to provide wealth, women, and limitless power so long as the devil's contract held good. And the devil was a gentleman who honoured his bond.

Early in the fifteenth century, this accumulation of legend gathered about a real and perfectly historical student of theology at the University of Heidelberg—not Wittenberg, as Marlowe has it. The record of his degree in divinity still stands upon the pages of the Heidelberg archives. This was Johannes Faust, of Simmern, who in 1509 began his damnable career in the odour of sanctity by virtuously taking the degree of bachelor of divinity. The old Register still reminds us by the notation "d"—for "dedit"—that this devil's disciple honestly paid the fee required for his degree.[18]

Faust seems to have been known to Melanchthon, Luther's fellow-reformer; and he is described by one of Melanchthon's pupils as a "cesspool of many devils." German town records and the correspondence of German humanists for several decades represent him as a wandering magician, boastful and vicious, but skilful in his horrifying art. At least once, he casts a bishop's horoscope, and the payment of ten florins for this illicit service still stands in the episcopal accounts. The accounts describe him as "philosophus," and he describes himself as "philosophus philosophorum." He deals in "chiromancy, nigromancy, the art of visions, visions in the crystal, and other arts of the sort."

The story of his death first appears in a volume of *Sermones Conviviales*, by the theologian John Gast: "The wretched man came to a terrible end; for the devil strangled him; his corpse lay on the bier on its face all the time, although it was turned round five times." More sceptical generations have inclined to the view that some one anticipated the devil by giving Faustus a pinch of poison. His permanently twisted corpse presents the usual symptoms of strychnine, which induces muscular spasms that arch the body so that it will not lie upon the back; but this strange condition was enough to start the story that the devil whom Faust had served undid him at the last.[19]

Scarcely had printing been invented—with a certain Johann Fust, or Faust, as one of Gutenberg's associates—when these stories began to appear in books. In 1493, one Schedel published a *Chronik* which includes some of the very travels of Doctor Faustus that find their way first into the German Faust Book, then into the English one, and then—with very little change—into Marlowe's play.

The German Faust Book first appeared at Frankfurt in 1587 and immediately ran through several German editions before it was picked up and translated into English by one "P. F., Gent[leman]," who is otherwise unknown. The story may have reached Marlowe before his departure from Cambridge, where German influence had been strong for at least half a century.

It is a curious and regrettable circumstance that practically none of the works of the elder authors have come down to us exactly as they were written. The Greek and Latin classics have suffered from centuries of copying and re-copying, during the course of which the scribes have introduced many errors and have occasionally even copied marginal annotations by ancient readers into the text, as if they were part of the book itself.

Elizabethan dramatists have suffered in much the same way when printed; and their work has usually been lost entirely when left in manuscript. Since the actors were chary of letting their parts get into the hands of printers, and since no author seems to have taken any great interest in the publication of a play, once it had been written and sold to the actors, most of the printed plays are in bad condition.

The printers got their manuscripts in various and devious ways, mostly illicit. A treacherous actor might sell his part, secretly, to a publisher, the rest of the play being built up around the lines and business of this one character by stenographers who slipped into the theatres as spectators and secretly took down the dialogue. Two new stenographic systems were being introduced in London while Marlowe's plays were popular, one during his life, the other just after his death—though both were too cumbersome to be of much use. Sometimes the actors were willing to sell a play that had lost its drawing power; but the manuscripts that they had for sale to printers were usually old ones that had lain around the playhouse for many years. They were likely to be scribbled over with the producer's stage directions and notes, and even with lines and whole scenes which the actors themselves had introduced.

Comic dialogue was often left to the company's clown, who "ad libbed" such dialogue as he could think up on the spur of the moment to raise a laugh. In *Doctor Faustus*, Marlowe gives his clown the line, "You are but an &c.," leaving the rest to the actor. A stage direction in another old play says simply: "Exit clown speaking anything." Even when such liberty was not specifically allowed by the author, the clown was very likely to take it anyhow, with results that may be imagined.[20]

To complicate matters still further, theatrical managers made a practice of sending out for dramatic hired hands to revise an old play and bring it up to date. Ben Jonson was thus employed to inject new life and "ginger" into the old *Spanish Tragedie*, originally produced in his boyhood; and Henslowe in his diary quite shamelessly enters payment of four pounds to William Birde and Samuel Rowley, minor writers of the period, "for ther adicyones in doctor fostes."[21] As this was—judging by Henslowe's other payments—a good round sum, the "adicyones" must have been very considerable.

Any one or all of these mishaps might befall a play before its manuscript eventually reached a publisher. Upon this already mutilated text, the printer exercised the right of such excision as seemed good to him. Richard Jones, the printer of *Tamburlaine*, tells us in his preface to the 1590 edition, that he had purposely "omitted and left out some fond and frivolous Iestures, digressing (and in my poore opinion) far vnmeet for the matter." These comic passages have, he admits, "bene of some vaine conceited fondlings greatly gaped at, what times they were shewed vpon the stage in their graced deformities." Nevertheless, for them "to be mixtured in print with such matters of worth, it would prooue a great disgrace to so honorable & stately a history." So they are gone, and with them any way of explaining why *Tamburlaine* was entered in the *Stationers' Register* as a "commical discourse" instead of a tragedy. Marlowe's *Jew of Malta* has been so barbarously mangled that it is an open question whether it was he or Thomas Heywood who wrote most of the last half of the play as we now have it.

Doctor Faustus is a particularly malignant example of the dire state into which a few decades of this treatment could bring an originally great work. Indeed, among the learned gentlemen who spend their lives bringing order into the chaos of other writers' work, its intricacy is almost proverbial. Says J. P. Postgate, in his article on "Textual Criticism" in the *Encyclopaedia Britannica*, "where there is great or complicated divergence between the editions, as in the case of Marlowe's Faustus, the production of a resultant text of the author is well-nigh impossible."

Mr. Postgate is really a little too pessimistic. The revisions have certainly produced two different versions of the play, with a discrepancy between them of something more than five hundred lines. But this, after all, is nothing when compared with the text of *Hamlet,* which shows a difference of fifteen hundred lines or more between the first and second quartos. What time has left us is certainly not the play that Marlowe wrote; but even in its shattered state, *Doctor Faustus* remains a great and profoundly moving work; and the revisers at their worst have had sufficient taste to leave unspoiled the greatest passages, like the soliloquy in the study, which opens the play, the "thousand ships," and the death scene. It is easy enough to ignore the tedious comic relief, in which the clowns discourse of wenches and their plackets—the result either of Marlowe's ill-judged attempt to write humorous lines for which he had no talent, or of the clowns' own efforts to make good the poet's deficiency and give humorous relief to the stark tragedy of a damned soul.

The thrillingly theatrical qualities of the old play made it deservedly popular and ten separate editions have come down to us, while an earlier and now lost edition is with good reason believed at one time to have existed. The first three editions of 1604, 1609, and 1611 agree closely with each other. Then in 1616 comes an entirely new text. When this text was reprinted in 1619, the changes—as we can see from the title page of the sole surviving copy—were noted on the title as "new Additions," and with minor changes they run through all subsequent editions of the play including that of 1663, the last of Marlowe's works to appear until interest in him began to revive again in the early nineteenth century.

These alterations may represent the re-writing by Birde and Rowley in 1602, more than a decade after *Doctor Faustus* first appeared. More probably, however, these were made much earlier; and it is quite possible that all of the Birde and Rowley changes were lost in manuscript; and that the play as we now have it in both texts is essential Marlowe.

We know this—or we can at least hazard a very shrewd guess—thanks to *The Taming of A Shrew,* the old source play which Shakespeare long afterwards re-wrote as *The Taming of The Shrew.* The unknown author of *A Shrew* had a certain comic gift which enabled him to write a fairly amusing play; but his soul yearned after the high-flying Marlowe style; and being unable to produce it himself, he quite unscrupulously borrowed a dozen or more passages direct from Marlowe. Luckily, he borrowed from the second text of *Faustus,* usually called the "1616 text." Now, *A Shrew* is a very early play, probably written in Marlowe's own lifetime, though certainly not (as a few indiscreet critics have surmised) written by Marlowe himself. The unknown author's quotations from *Doctor Faustus* thus prove that certain passages in the later, expanded text were actually in existence before Birde and Rowley began their revisions in 1602; and that these passages actually existed while Marlowe was still alive.

Like *Tamburlaine, Doctor Faustus* was a tremendous success on the stage. The inventory of Philip Henslowe's theatrical properties, made in 1598, shows that he still thought it worth his while to keep his dragon ready in the store-room; and this terrifying bit of stage machinery probably creaked back to life when Birde and Rowley made their revision of 1602. Marlowe's old play remained part of the repertory for years after his death; and we have records of steady performance from October 9, 1594, when a single production brought in forty-four shillings, until January 5, 1596/7, when the takings had fallen to five shillings. No wonder Henslowe began to think that the play needed revision!

The old companies of actors gave the play as much sensational costuming and stage machinery as possible. There is one casual reference to "a head of hayre like one of my Divells in Dr. Faustus," and as late as 1620 a contemporary author is still describing what one may behold when "men goe to the Fortune in Golding-lane to see the Tragedie of Doctor Faustus. There indeede a man may behold shagge-hayr'd Deuills runne roaring ouer the Stage with Squibs in their mouthes, while Drummers make Thunder in the Tyring-house, and the twelue-penny hirelings make artificiall Lightning in their Heauens." [22]

The "hirelings" were actors not members of the company

but employed at a salary, and the "heavens" were, of course, the canopy projecting over the stage.

Edward Alleyn played the title rôle in *Faustus,* and we have a pretty fair idea what he looked like from the wood-cut which, with minor changes, adorns most of the early editions of the play. The conjurer is arrayed in a long black robe and square academic cap (which must have eased the mind of Lord Burghley), the robe embroidered with cabalistic symbols and adorned with a white ornament at the throat. All about him are magic appliances; and he has drawn on the stage the magician's circle with its magic symbols, while just outside it a devil is appearing through the trap door in the stage.

All this made an enormous impression. Allusions to "the devil and Doctor Foster" were still known in Daniel Defoe's day, two hundred years later; and there are three separate accounts of how the Devil in person appeared, to take a hand in the play as one of the actors.

William Prynne, who later had his ears clipped for referring to the Queen's actresses as "notorious whores," describes in *Histrio-Mastix* (1633), his book attacking the stage, "the visible apparition of the Devill on the Stage at the Belsavage Play-house, in Queene Elizabeth's dayes, (to the great amazement both of the Actors and Spectators) whiles they were prophanely playing the History of Faustus (the truth of which I have heard from many now alive, who well remember it,) there being some distracted with that fearfull sight."[23]

The same thing happened at Exeter, according to a manuscript notation in an old book, now lost. On this horrifying occasion, "as a certain number of Devels kept everie one his circle there, and as Faustus was busie in his magicall invocations, on a sudden they wer all dasht, every one harkning other in the eare, for they were all perswaded there was one devell too many amongst them; and so after a little pause desired the people to pardon them, they could go no further with this matter; the people also understanding the thing as it was, every man hastened to be first out of dores. The players (as I heard it) contrarye to their custome spending the night in reading and in prayer got them out of the town the next morning."

By the end of the seventeenth century the story was being told of Alleyn himself, who was "in the midst of the play surpriz'd by an apparition of the Devil, which so work'd on his Fancy that he made a Vow, which he perform'd at this place"—that is at Dulwich, where Alleyn's College of God's Gift still educates British youth in decorous ignorance of the fact that the College really owes its foundation to His Satanic Majesty in person. It is the kind of thing that an educational institution naturally prefers to keep dark.

One understands why the Puritans objected to plays in general and to *Doctor Faustus* in particular. One also understands why the general public continued to flock to Marlowe's play for the better part of a century. Samuel Pepys saw it performed May 26, 1662, "but so wretchedly & poorly done that we were sick of it." Charles II saw it in 1675, performed by the Duke of York's Company, one of the relatively few Elizabethan plays that survived the Restoration. English actors had early begun to carry the Faust story back to its native Germany. Wandering companies performed it at Graetz in 1608, together with *The Jew of Malta*, and it was also taken to Vienna by English actors. Gradually, the old play degenerated into a mere spectacle. By the time Alexander Pope saw it, it had become what he describes in the notes to the *Dunciad*—"a set of farces, which lasted in vogue two or three seasons, in which both playhouses strove to outdo each other in the year 1726, 27."[24] However sadly Marlowe's play had come down in the world, it was still "frequented by persons of the first quality in England, to the twentieth and thirtieth time." Pope tells how the spectators

> . . . look'd, and saw a sable sorc'rer rise,
> Swift to whose hand a winged volume flies:
> All sudden, gorgons hiss, and dragons glare,
> And ten-horn'd fiends and giants rush to war.
> Hell rises, heav'n descends, and dance on earth:
> Gods, imps, and monsters, music, rage, and mirth,
> A fire, a jigg, a battle, and a ball,
> Till one wide conflagration swallows all.

The *Spectator* also describes the puppet shows of *Faustus* under the Covent Garden piazzas. By this time its authorship had been completely forgotten, and Marlowe's name was not even mentioned. It was perhaps just as well.

The enormous impression that *Doctor Faustus* made upon its original public is naturally reflected in other plays. Robert Greene's *Friar Bacon and Friar Bungay* is flat imitation of

Marlowe. Shakespeare alludes to Faustus four times[25] and there are clear traces of Marlowe's play in the work of at least a dozen other dramatists in the years immediately following.

Most fascinating of all is the question how far Marlowe's play affected Goethe, Byron and the Spanish dramatist, Calderón. Goethe's *Faust* closely resembles Marlowe's; but since they were both telling the same story, this was to be expected. Goethe uses two elements of the Faust legend that Marlowe ignores—the Marguerite story and the story of the homunculus whom Faustus fashions out of air. The story was by Goethe's time a permanent part of German legend; and the poet had undoubtedly seen the innumerable puppet shows which also told the story. He had no special need of Marlowe's play and its version of the old story.

Nevertheless, the resemblances of *Faust* and *Faustus* are very striking. Both open with the monologue on the vanity of learning, which appears neither in the Faust Books nor in the puppet shows. Both ridicule jurisprudence and both praise medical science. There are a good many verbal echoes, as if Goethe while he wrote was remembering Marlowe's lines, half-consciously. Marlowe's Faustus, for example, exclaims:[26]

> This night Ile coniure though I die therefore.

Goethe's says to himself:

> Du musst! du musst! und kostet es dein Leben.

Marlowe's Faustus hails Lucifer, master of Mephastophilis, with the line:

> O who art thou that lookst so terrible?

while Goethe's Faust salutes the Erdgeist, also master of Mephastophilis, with the words, "Schreckliches Gesicht!" It is, to be sure, a quite natural way to greet the devil; but there are so many similar parallels that it is hard to believe they are mere accident.

There is no doubt at all that toward the end of his life, long after he had finished the first part of *Faust* which tells Marlowe's part of the story, Goethe was interested in Marlowe's play. That odd literary dilettante, Henry Crabbe Robinson, enters in his diary a conversation with the German poet in 1829: "I mentioned Marlowe's 'Faust.' He burst out into an exclamation of praise: 'How greatly is it all planned!' He had thought of translating it. He was fully aware that Shakespeare did not stand alone." [27] There is a somewhat similar allusion in 1829 to Eckermann's *Conversations,* and also a record in 1824 of another occasion when the two men discussed Elizabethan dramatists, including Marlowe.

This was a period when German literary circles were taking a keen interest in Elizabethan authors. Goethe had contemplated a work on *Hero and Leander,* another of Marlowe's subjects not very well known except in his poem—and this as early as 1796, when the Faust story was very much in Goethe's mind.

After his death, Goethe's library contained no copy of Marlowe's play; but this is probably because he gave the book away to Charlotte von Schiller, widow of the poet. Frau von Schiller writes June 5, 1818, to thank Goethe for a book containing, like Marlowe's *Doctor Faustus,* a passage dealing with the Seven Deadly Sins. On the eleventh, Goethe mysteriously enters in his diary: "Dr. Faust von Marlowe," with no further explanation of what he was thinking about.

It is clear enough, then, that Goethe wrote a play which in general outline is very much like Marlowe's; and that in the latter part of his life he was perfectly familiar with Marlowe's work. There are, however, two reasons for questioning whether Goethe really imitated his Elizabethan predecessor. One reason is that the parallels between the plays are not quite close enough to constitute absolute proof, since two plays on the same theme are bound to be more or less alike. A second reason is that at the time when Goethe was working on the first part of his *Faust,* no edition of Marlowe's play had appeared for more than a century. A few obscure copies of early editions may have lurked in European libraries, but even professed scholars had no idea of their existence. When Oxberry and Chappell's English reprints and Wilhelm Müller's translation appeared in 1818, Goethe seems to have been quick to discover them; but by that time his version of the Faust story had long been published.

Lord Byron's *Manfred* also closely resembles the Faust story. Manfred is a necromancer who raises spirits in his study; prescribes, like Faust, the special form in which they shall appear to him; seeks forbidden knowledge; laments the vanity of learning; raises Astarte (instead of Helen) from the dead; and obdurately resists a pious old Abbot's entreaties to repent. Contemporary critics were quick to point out these similarities, to the indignation of Byron's admirers on the *Edinburgh Review* and *Blackwood's*. Said Henry Maitland in *Blackwood's:* "The mixed, rambling, headlong and reckless manner of Marlowe, in that play, must not be put into competition with the sustained dignity of Byron." The noble lord himself was caustic: "As to the Faustus of Marlowe, I never read, never saw, nor heard of it." If that was true, his lordship was simply imitating Goethe instead of Marlowe, and keeping quiet about it; for the close resemblance of *Manfred* to the Faust story cannot be an accident.

Calderón's *Magico Prodigioso* shows the same resemblances, but seems to be rather a working-up of the story of Cyprian of Antioch, one of the other branches of the Faust epic.

The last trace of the literary influence exerted by the old story that took shape in Marlowe's mind in the roaring, roistering Liberty of Norton Folgate some time in 1588 or 1589, appears in Mr. Brian Hooker's translation of Edmond Rostand's *Cyrano de Bergerac,* as produced by Mr. Walter Hampden. The thousand ships passage is adroitly slipped into Cyrano's famous speech about his nose:

> Or—parodying Faustus in the play—
> "Was this the nose that launched a thousand ships
> And burned the topless towers of Ilium?"

—a grotesque conclusion to a hundred and fifty years of literary influence, but an aid to the depiction of a swashbuckling, poetic character conceived so completely in Marlowe's own mood that the lines fit perfectly.

Thus the Faust legend, beginning dimly amid the religious upheaval of early Christian days, in the confused Greco-Roman world, slips down the centuries. The stories gradually cluster about the name of Johann Faust, theologian and charlatan of the early German Renaissance. They pass, with much embroidery, into folk-lore. The early printers see a chance of honest profit with a popular sensation. The old tales attract the lively mind of Christopher Marlowe, M.A. of Cambridge, gentleman of London. In some way, they also reach the minds of Calderón, Goethe, and Byron. Over a period of eighteen hundred years, Saint Paul and his foe, the Samaritan impostor, Simon Magus, the deacon Theophilus, Cyprian of Antioch, and the German Johann Faust merge to produce a Spanish classic, one of the great dramas of England, a national monument of German letters—and one of my Lord Byron's less successful performances.

10.

Bloody, Bold, and Resolute

"I know sir, what it is to kil a man."
II. Tamburlaine

While Marlowe was thus moving from triumph to triumph, he was, like most successful men, making enemies. The Cambridge rhetorician, Gabriel Harvey, hated Marlowe bitterly, had probably hated him since they were both in the University, hated him so completely that he poured ridicule on all his works and ideas and made no secret of his exultation when the dramatist was murdered a few years later. His brother, Richard Harvey, rector of Chislehurst, Kent, the parish of Marlowe's patrons, the Walsinghams, may on Christian principles have concealed his enmity toward the outspoken and impetuous Christopher; but he had certainly not enjoyed being called "an asse," even by the most successful playwright in London. Robert Greene was also venomous against the man who had written better and more successful plays than his own; who was an associate of the great, the brilliant, the rich, and the powerful, while poor Greene himself had to write cheaply sensational pamphlets for a shabby living.

But there were others who disliked "kynde Kit Marlowe" still more completely. One of these was William Bradley, the son of a London inn-keeper. Young William Bradley was a quarrelsome fellow. He was twenty-six years old, one year older than Marlowe; and he resembled a good many other people in feeling that something must be done immediately to take that obstreperous fellow down a peg. Like the elder Harvey, he had probably formed that unfavourable impression at Cambridge—if he was indeed the same William Bradley who had matriculated as a pensioner of St. John's College in 1580, only a little while before Marlowe.

Not only did Bradley look with disfavour on Christopher Marlowe; he had no greater fondness for Marlowe's friend, the poet Thomas Watson. And furthermore, William Bradley —a hater of no ordinary capacity—looked with a jaundiced eye upon a certain Hugh Swyft, Watson's brother-in-law, and upon John Alleyn, brother of the actor Edward Alleyn, that same John Alleyn who had endeavoured in vain to soothe the irate Burbages one historic day at the Theatre.

The first permanent record of these rumblings in Bradley's bosom is a record of the Court of Queen's Bench, probably made during the summer of 1589. An entry on a parchment four or five feet long records that Bradley was already praying "sureties of the peace against Hugo Swyft & Johannes Allen & Thomas Watson, being in fear of death."[1] The record is exactly like the one in which a certain William Wayte was to ask for sureties against a certain William Shakespeare a few years later.[2]

A good many Londoners in those turbulent days had reason to go to court asking for protection, and this particular roll is full of their petitions. Bradley was following excellent example when he demanded that each of these three men be required to provide bond in their own names and in the names of two sureties to guarantee their "good abearing" toward himself.

One or more of the Queen's judges heard the plea and made it returnable on the fifteenth of St. Martin—the usual clumsy legal way of dating at that period, which meant fifteen days after the Feast of St. Martin, or, in plain English, November 25. This, however, was but another example of the law's delays and this time the law delayed too long. What it was all about, we shall never know, for ere the appointed date arrived, Bradley's fears had been only too fully justified. He himself was in his grave and Watson and Marlowe had been charged with his murder.

Whatever the dispute was about, it must have been fairly serious, for Bradley was a stout man of his hands, not easily frightened and quite ready to do battle on occasion. Seven years before, as a mere boy, he had been in a fight with a jerkin-maker's apprentice, from which both he and his brother Richard emerged with wounds.[3] The unfortunate outcome of that encounter may, perhaps, have inclined him to see what the courts could do for him, this time.

The courts, as it turned out, could not do very much. On the 18th of September, 1589, between two and three o'clock in the afternoon, there was a rattle of steel along Hog Lane, an obscure street running from the Liberty of Norton Folgate, where Marlowe lodged, toward Finsbury Fields, near the

Theatre and the Curtain, whither Marlowe walked to see his plays performed. Bradley and Marlowe were engaged in savage battle, sword to sword. It was the usual sort of Elizabethan duel in which each man fought with his sword in his right hand and his dagger clutched in the left, ready for any chance to close in and give his enemy quietus with the bare bodkin. The quality of the steel was usually excellent, because the armourers and cutlers of London did their best to prevent the sale of "naughtie and deceiptfull sworde blades." [4]

The scene of the duel was toward the north end of Hog Lane, beyond the point where the street crossed into the parish of St. Giles, Cripplegate—we know that from the detailed description of the place given in the inquest which the coroner was to hold over Bradley's body the next day. Marlowe had probably been walking out from his lodgings. It was after the mid-day Elizabethan dinner, and dinner in the Liberty of Norton Folgate meant wine, and plenty of it. It was in this very year that Marlowe's friend, Thomas Nashe, wrote of "the blacke pot; which makes our Poets vndermeale Muses so mutinous, as euerie stanzo they pen after dinner, is full poynted with a stabbe." [5]

Marlowe's undermeal muse was in a particularly violent mood that day; and as another friend, his former chamberfellow Thomas Kydd, said later, he had a habit of "attempting soden pryvie iniuries to men." That is what he proved on this occasion.

Luckily for Marlowe, he got no further than the attempt. His friend Thomas Watson was also walking out in the neighbourhood that afternoon. A crowd had quickly gathered about the spot where Marlowe and Bradley were thrusting, cutting, and parrying. Elizabethans delighted in these sudden frays, and there was a babble of excited shouts, advice, and exclamations, which the legal documents learnedly describe as "clamorem populi ibidem adstant*is*." Watson heard the noise and made for the scene of battle. As he came up, Bradley, seeing his enemy Watson coming to the aid of his other enemy, Marlowe, showed no dismay at all. Bradley might appeal to the law upon occasion, but he was not in the least afraid of a fight and he showed remarkable confidence in the chivalry of his opponents. They were two to one but he knew that they would fight only man-to-man.

"Art thowe nowe come?" yelled Bradley, in words whose

English form the Latin inquest carefully records. (They are, in fact, the only English in the document.) "Then I will haue a boute with the." He used the insultingly familiar "thou" and "thee," which in the English of that day was nearly equivalent to using German "du" or French "tu."

It was the exact situation of the duel between Tybalt and Mercutio, with Romeo interposing. Shakespeare, who certainly knew Marlowe and who certainly heard all about this particular duel, might easily have modelled the fight in *Romeo and Juliet* upon it. But Marlowe, wiser than Mercutio, dropped out of the fight as he saw his friend approaching, and Bradley turned his sword against Watson alone.

So far, no one had been hurt. There had been much rattle of blades, much noise from excited by-standers, and no blood whatever. Marlowe was handy enough with cold steel, and a few years later gave Ingram Frizer, his murderer, several wounds with his own dagger before succumbing; but on this occasion he had not even succeeded in injuring his opponent.

Watson was willing enough to meet Bradley, and the swords clashed again; but, being a much older man than either of the other two, Watson was at a disadvantage. He was wounded. The record of the inquest says he was so badly wounded that he despaired of his life—a claim he would not have dared to make unless he had some pretty severe gashes to show the inquisitors next day. But it was to his advantage to make his own personal danger seem as great as possible, and he was under strong temptation to exaggerate. However badly Watson may have been hurt, he was quite strong enough to kill his man; and Marlowe, standing by, seems to have felt no need of coming to his aid, in spite of the fact that Watson was plainly getting the worst of it.

He gave ground before Bradley's impetuous onset, and then gave more ground, until at length he had been forced against the ditch that ran along Hog Lane. With this behind him, there was nothing for it but to make a stand; and as Bradley continued his thrusts, Watson decided that he could not go on parrying them forever and that he was in very real danger of his life. He took the offensive and speedily ran Bradley through the right breast. The stab was six inches deep, almost through the body, and one inch wide, about the breadth of the sword blade. Coroners' inquests were very precise about such small matters (they followed a fixed legal form) and always gave the price of the lethal weapon, which was forfeit to the crown. In this case, Watson's sword is valued at three shillings four pence.[6]

Watson cleared his blade and saw his opponent dead or dying at his feet, with a great gush of blood from the wound. Such, at least, is the story that Marlowe and Watson told a few days later, when they were trying to prove that the killing was a necessary matter of self-defence and that they were innocent of murder.

There is no need to wonder where the police were, all this time. Even when they tried, they often could not get near the duellists in a combat of this sort. The populace enjoyed these sudden street-fights; and, rather than have them broken up, would form a ring close and dense enough to keep the constables off while the duel was fought out undisturbed.[7]

But very often, the constables did not try. The "watch" of Elizabethan London was not a very intrepid or very efficient organization. They were not quite so stupid nor so cowardly as Dogberry and his fellow constables, whom Shakespeare ridicules; but when they saw two rake-helly, dare-devils of poets with swords in their hands, courage forsook them. They much preferred to close one eye or look the other way with both eyes. Two constables of Shakespeare's own Shoreditch sought the protection of the courts against Christopher Marlowe a few years after this very duel, alleging that they went in fear of their lives because of that violent young madcap.

Master Stephen Wyld, tailor and constable of Norton Folgate, was not really very eager to leave his needle and thread and interfere with two combative poets who had blades in their hands and had just demonstrated their complete willingness to use them. He did not arrive on the scene of battle until all was over. When he did at length appear, he found Marlowe and Watson standing by the body as evidence of their innocence, instead of fleeing for their lives, which would have been taken as a testimony to their guilt. The situation in which they found themselves was common enough in Elizabethan life, and these literati knew the law.

Constable Stephen Wyld, doubtless with a sigh for the doublet he was leaving half-finished, arrested them both without difficulty and took them before the Lieutenant of the Tower of London. Manslaughter was a matter for the Royal Government, not for the city authorities. Sir Owen Hopton, the lieutenant, committed them to Newgate Prison, where their arrival "*pro Suspicione* Murdri," is duly entered.[8]

The following day the unfortunate Bradley's body was exhibited to a coroner's jury and was then buried in the church or churchyard of St. Andrew's, Holborn.[9] Having assembled the day after the murder, as was usual, the jury had access to all the facts and cleared Marlowe, who had "withdrawn himself and ceased from fighting" (seip*sum* ret*ra*xit & a pugnando desistit) before the actual killing; and Watson, who was able to prove self-defence. The coroner, however, had no power to order their release.

Under Elizabethan law, Watson's claim of self-defence meant that he would be required to prove that the other man had made the attack; that he had himself withdrawn as far as he possibly could; and that he had killed only when flight was impossible and he saw no other means of preserving his own life. It is about what modern law demands, in similar cases. The coroner's jury found that Bradley had beaten, wounded, and ill-treated (v*er*b*er*auit, vuln*er*auit & male t*ra*ctauit) the unfortunate and innocent Watson; that he "fled from the aforesaid William Bradley for the salvation of his life as far as to a certain ditch in the aforesaid lane" (a p*re*d*ict*o will*elm*o Bradley pro saluac*ion*e vite sue vsq*ue* ad quoddam fossatu*m* in venella p*re*d*ict*a fugijt); and that "beyond this certain ditch Thomas Watson could not flee without peril of his own life" (vlt*ra* quodquidem fossatum idem Thomas Watson absq*ue* p*er*iculo vite sue fug*er*e non potuit.)

Only then did the guileless, the innocent, the madly used and much abused Watson smite "the aforesaid William Bradley with his aforesaid sword, giving him a mortal injury or wound in and upon the right part of the breast of the same William Bradley near the nipple, of the depth of six inches and the width of one inch, of which injury the same William Bradley at Fynnesbury aforesaid in the aforesaid county of Middlesex instantly died"—as the jury put it, carefully following the approved legal form. (P*re*d*ict*um Will*elmu*m Bradley cum gladio suo p*re*d*ict*o tunc & ibidem p*er*cussit dans ei vnam plagam mortalem siue vulnus in & sup*er* dextram partem pectoris ip*s*ius will*elmi* Bradley p*r*ope mamillam p*r*ofunditatis sex pollic*um* & latitudinis vnius pollicis de qua quidem plaga mortali idem Will*elmus* Bradley apud ffymesburye p*re*d*ict*am in p*re*d*ict*o Com*itatu* Midd*lesex* instanter obijt.)

Therefore, said the coroner's jury, upon their oath, the aforesaid Thomas Watson, though he had indeed regrettably —against the peace of their Lady the Queen and her dignity— killed the aforesaid William Bradley, had done it only in self-defence and not as a felony nor in any other way than as aforesaid. They were pretty long-winded about it, but no more so than the law required; and their verdict meant ultimate release for Watson as well as for Marlowe.

After the inquest, both men went back to Newgate Prison; but on October 1 Marlowe secured his temporary freedom by giving bond, with two sureties, for his appearance at the next gaol delivery.[10] Marlowe appeared to give bond before William Fleetwood, Recorder of London, and was admitted to bail of forty pounds with proper security. He may have found the justice rather friendly. Officially, the Recorder sometimes found it necessary to denounce plays, playwrights, and players, but unofficially he read them on the sly, as modern justices read detective stories. Marlowe must have impressed him, for the judge seized an early opportunity to buy a copy of *Tamburlaine*. The play in an edition which must have been either that of 1590 or that of 1592—since neither the justice nor the prisoner lived to see any later editions—was listed as part of his library when it came up for sale two hundred years later.[11]

Marlowe's sureties were Richard Kytchine, of Clifford's Inn, gentleman, and Humphrey Rowland, of East Smithfield, a horner—that is, an artisan who made thin slices of horn, which were used in lanterns, and perhaps also carved horn for knife handles and the hilts of daggers. Richard Kytchine was of a temperament akin to Marlowe's own. He was indicted for an assault with a dagger in 1594; but there are also records of his professional appearances in court, which suggest the prosperous man of law in active practice, and he is repeatedly described as "gentleman." Humphrey Rowland was a less prosperous but still eminently respectable person. Lord Burghley describes him as "a very honest poore man" in 1583;[12] and he became Church Warden of St. Botolph Aldgate in 1586. He is a fairly frequent surety for others and is sometimes in legal toils himself.

Both these men were average, respectable Londoners, and their willingness to become sureties for the playwright—who is in this bond for the first time described as "gentleman"— suggests that Marlowe was already fairly well regarded in

London. He was at least a good risk. The fact that Recorder Fleetwood was willing to accept so poor a bondsman as Rowland may mean that he did not regard the murder charge very seriously.[13]

The next gaol delivery was on December 3, 1589, at "Justice hall in Le Olde Bailie"—that is, a building on the site of the Central Criminal Court of modern London. Marlowe came to court to fulfil his bond. Watson, after eleven weeks in Newgate Prison, was brought from confinement. The facts as determined by the coroner's jury were rehearsed. Marlowe was released—against his record stands the note: "freed by proclamation" (del*iberatus* per proclam*acionem*)—and Watson was returned to prison to "await the queen's grace."

The Queen's grace was a long time coming. Poor Watson actually spent almost five months in "that infamous Castle of Misery" before he received the royal pardon on February 10, 1589/90. The pardon, still extant, again rehearses the coroner's inquest, word for word.

Affrays of the sort in which these two had been involved were not unusual among the riotous actors and authors of the London theatrical world and among Londoners in general. Ben Jonson, who boasted of having killed his man and taken spoil from his body in open warfare in Flanders, also killed the actor, Gabriel Spencer—himself a killer—in a private affray, and escaped alive only by pleading "benefit of clergy," calling for the Bible, reading the "neck verse" which saved his neck from the gallows, and submitting to be branded.

These were the milder punishments that the Elizabethan law provided for the educated man. There had been nothing remarkable about the Bradley-Marlowe-Watson duello except the literary distinction of two of the combatants. The Elizabethans were always fighting; and the lower classes, though supposed to settle their differences by fisticuffs or by round blows with the cudgel, were as quick to use cold steel as their betters. It is proverbial that "no Englishman uses the knife" in these days; but in those days it was not at all unusual for a man who had been knocked down in an honest rough-and-tumble to draw a small knife while lying on the ground and stab the unarmed opponent kneeling above him. The yellowing court parchments in the Middlesex archives are full of yeomen, tradesmen, tailors, and shoemakers intent upon mayhem and murder with rapier, short-sword, bill, knife, or dagger.

Death was swift and sudden and omnipresent. Tavern-haunters, the worse for drink, settled their differences upon the spot. The gentry might sometimes indulge in the formalities of challenge and meeting by appointment—Marlowe's friend Raleigh acted as second in one such affair. But tempers were high in the Tudor age and the avenging blow followed so quickly on the offensive word that often the avenger had hardly time to realize what he was doing before he looked down upon the gasping form of a friend with whom he had been exchanging pledges of friendship a few moments earlier.

Rarely did duellists trouble to seek the privacy of the open fields. The Elizabethans were not a reticent race. The public streets, a tavern room, St. Paul's Churchyard were places good enough to kill your man; and everywhere a crowd gathered quickly, delighted with the entertainment that mortal combat offered.

Marlowe and Watson could certainly have escaped the gallows in the same way as Jonson. Branding was uncomfortable and a little disgraceful, but it was a great deal better than hanging. The clergy had long enjoyed a limited exemption from capital punishment, partly because their duties made them sacred, partly because men who could read and write were too valuable and too scarce to hang. Gradually their privilege was extended, and the rule grew up that a criminal who could read one verse of the Bible might claim "benefit of clergy," whether he was actually in holy orders or not. Court documents of the time contain many annotations recording how the accused, when convicted, "calls for the book, reads like a clerk, and is relieved." There is even one pitiful record of a condemned criminal who, though illiterate, in his utter terror of the noose, "asked for the book, could not read, and was remanded"—for hanging.[14]

The abuses of this privilege eventually compelled a modification of the law. A man might claim benefit only once. Thereafter a cleric, no matter how learned, must hang like anybody else, one murder being regarded as enough for the lifetime of any reasonable man. But how to prove that the criminal had already enjoyed his one legitimate murder? The legal solution was to mark the brawn of the thumb deeply with a branded letter "T" for Tyburn, where the gallows stood, near the modern Marble Arch. The letter was seared in by a red-hot iron, so that it could not possibly be effaced.

There are legends that in later and humaner generations, the gaolers could be bribed to use the iron so carefully that the scar could later be effaced, or even to brand with a lukewarm or completely cold iron; but these weak-kneed evasions of the law's majestic demands were impossible under Elizabeth. The statute was then relatively new and was enforced with full rigour.

Marlowe and Watson would certainly have been branded, if they had not been able to prove their innocence of murder—unless they had been able to persuade the authorities to change the indictment from murder to manslaughter. It was this device which saved the very minor dramatist, John Day, Marlowe's collaborator in *The Maiden's Holiday*, who in 1599 killed the equally minor playhouse hack, Henry Porter.[15]

The coroner's inquest on the unfortunate Bradley has a special interest because it is the only way of telling where Marlowe lived in London. The documents describe him as a gentleman of Norton Folgate. This might mean the main street leading from London Bridge, north through the city, a short stretch of which is called by this name. It is more sensible, however, to suppose that Marlowe lived in the Liberty of Norton Folgate, south of the scene of the duel and conveniently close to the Theatre and the Curtain, where his plays were being frequently performed.

The old manager, William Beeston, who had known most of the Elizabethan poets in his younger days, told John Aubrey, later, when the antiquarian was gathering material for his life of Shakespeare, that Shakespeare had "lived in Shoreditch," which is close to Norton Folgate. Beeston himself had lived in Shoreditch and when he talked with Aubrey was living "at Hoglane, within 6 dores—Norton-Folgate," almost on the scene of the crime which turned out not to be a crime after all.

Another and less innocent resident of Shoreditch about this time—we know that he was living there by 1591—was the government spy and diplomatic courier, Robert Poley, who in 1593 was present in the room where Marlowe was murdered. Norton Folgate, though a bit Bohemian, was a good residential district and it probably required a fair income to live there. Near it, says old John Stowe, there were "many faire houses builded, for receipt and lodging of worshipfull persons," of whom Marlowe was one.

It is perfectly certain that Marlowe's lodgings were close to Shakespeare's. Unhappily, there is no way of proving that they occupied these lodgings at the same time. But though there is no exact proof to show precisely when Shakespeare lived in Shoreditch and Marlowe in Norton Folgate, it is very probable that they were in these lodgings during the same year, passing each other casually in the street and acquainted as every one in the small theatrical world was acquainted with every one else.

It was in all probability here that the rising young man from Stratford met and admired the brilliant and successfully established young man from Canterbury and Cambridge, whose plays and poems and perilous adventures were the talk of London. Here, then, was formed the friendship of which we catch an echo in Shakespeare's wistful allusion to the "dead shepherd" in *As You Like It.* Here, too, they must have laboured long together over those scenes which bear Marlowe's stamp so strongly, in *Henry VI,* and which first appear, not in Shakespeare's play, but in the two earlier and anonymous plays, *The Contention of the Two Noble Houses of York and Lancaster* and *The True Tragedy of Richard, Duke of York.*

The roistering young Marlowe must have swaggered through the dubiously respectable streets of Shoreditch pretty frequently; and it is certain that here he fell foul of the law once more. It was a little matter of friction between the poet, a constable, and the constable's assistant. On May 9, 1592, Allen Nicholls, "constabularius" of Shoreditch, and Nicholaus Helliott, "subconstabularius," went before Sir Owen Hopton, Lieutenant of the Tower, and demanded that "Christopher Marle, of London, gentleman," should be bound over to keep the peace toward all of Queen Bess's subjects, and particularly toward themselves. Sir Owen, who by this time must have begun to find the appearance of the poet before him a little monotonous, obliged the Dogberries of Shoreditch by binding their enemy over to the next general sessions, under bond of £20, "good and legal money of England." No record has ever been discovered to show what came of all this, or whether Marlowe suffered any further penalty. At any rate, his troubles with the constables do not seem to have interfered with his literary productiveness.[16]

About this time or even earlier, Marlowe was sharing a room with Thomas Kydd, author of *The Spanish Tragedie,* chief rival of *Tamburlaine* in the esteem of the theatre-going public. It was not an entirely happy arrangement. Kydd's "first acquaintance w*i*th this Marlowe" came about through a mysterious and entirely unknown nobleman, whom Kydd is careful never to name. This peer soon came to disapprove of Marlowe's riotous ways and heretical opinions and "never knewe his service but in writing for his plaiers." Indeed, "never cold my L*ord* endure his name, or sight, when he had heard of his conditions." But Kydd was exceedingly anxious to "reteyne the fav*our*s of my Lord," and being under arrest when he wrote this and knowing that Marlowe was dead, he painted his murdered friend in the very darkest colours, hoping to save himself.

It was this extreme regard for the safety of his own skin that made Kydd so obviously unhappy as Marlowe's chamber-fellow. "Ffirst," he complained, "it was his custom when J knewe him first & as J heare saie he contynewd it in table talk or otherwise to iest at the devine scriptures gybe at praiers, & stryve in argum*en*t to frustrate & confute what hath byn spoke or wrytt by prophets & such holie men." This was perilous talk with a Queen like Elizabeth on a throne which derived its authority from the validity of a Protestant marriage.

It amused Marlowe to see Kydd's horrified visage at some of his heretical remarks, and he kept on making them to see if he could shock his unfortunate chamber-fellow still further. These appalling remarks, as Kydd also complains, "he wold so sodenlie take slight occasion to slyp out," that a pious poet like himself never knew what was coming next. But "J & many others in regard of his other rashnes in attempting soden pryvie iniuries to men did ouerslypp though oft reprehend him for it." In other words, Kydd was afraid of violence, for he was at best a timorous soul.

Eventually their relations became so strained that "aswell by my lord*es* commaundm*ent* as in hatred of his Life and thoughts J left & did refraine his companie." Unfortunately for himself, in breaking off his association with his unorthodox friend, Kydd failed to dispose of some incriminating manuscripts that belonged to Marlowe—that, at least, was Kydd's own story. These were relics of a heresy charge of some forty years earlier. In 1549 a Unitarian heretic had been arrested and Archbishop Cranmer had permitted him to write out a statement of his beliefs, especially his reasons for doubting the divinity of Christ. This paper was copied by various persons interested in theological speculations and went about from hand to hand for years. One copy fell into the hands of a certain John Proctour, who printed the heretical statements *seriatim*, adding his own refutation of each in a rare little volume called *The Fal of the Late Arrian*.

One of the manuscripts setting forth these heretical views—which roughly parallelled the Arian heresy of the early days of Church history—had in some way found its way into the room where Kydd and Marlowe wrote. In 1593, Kydd was arrested; his papers were searched; and among them the minions of the law discovered these heretical papers. Kydd, who was in obvious terror of what might happen to him, wrote a long letter[17] to Sir John Puckering, Lord Keeper of the Great Seal, explaining that the incriminating documents were not his at all. They belonged, he said, to Marlowe, and had been "shufled w*i*th some of myne (vnknown to me) by some occasion of o*u*r wrytinge in one chamber twoe yeares synce." They were in no sense a reflection of Kydd's own ideas but "fragment*es* of a disputation toching that opinion affirmed by Marlowe to be his."

They were also in a handwriting closely resembling one of the two hands that Kydd uses in his letter; but it will not do to be too sure of the identification of Elizabethan handwritings. The original copies of the heretical documents have been preserved at the British Museum.[18] They are in the "Italian" hand, practically print, which was so completely stylized that one man's handwriting was almost identical with another's. The hand of the documents also resembles very closely that of Marlowe's free-thinking, scientific friend, the mathematician Thomas Harriot, who often used the "Italian" hand for copying out his notes and documents.[19]

If we could be quite sure that Kydd was not trying to lie his way out of a predicament, we might regard these notes as genuine examples of Marlowe's own handwriting. But Kydd is so evidently in an agony of anxiety to save himself that his statements are almost worthless. He is telling a good deal of the truth but he is also obviously lying whenever he thinks it likely to be useful. Marlowe was already dead when Kydd wrote his letters to Sir John. Kydd probably felt that he could do no harm to Marlowe by pushing the whole responsibility off on him; and that he might—as he actually did—save his own life.

The Bradley duel and the terror of the two constables, however, give point to Kydd's statement that Marlowe "was intemp*er*ate & of a cruel hart," and his allusion to Marlowe's "rashnes." Except for that, the two rival authors would have shared their chamber as amicably as Beaumont and Fletcher. Unlike Robert Greene, Kydd does not seem to have envied Marlowe the success of his plays; but then, Kydd had had a resounding success of his own and was more inclined to be tolerant—so long, at least, as there was nothing to be gained by blackguarding the character of his dead friend.

11.

A Great Play Botched

"Thinke vpon the Iewels and the gold."
The Jew of Malta

During these exciting years of duels, gaols, charges, bonds, and law-courts, Marlowe went steadily onward in the theatre. The last two really distinguished plays that he wrote belong to this period. These are *The Jew of Malta* and *Edward the Second,* the one a wreck of what its author meant it to be and what he probably created, only to have it mangled later; the other almost perfect in its form and substance, foreshadowing a promise of future greatness that Marlowe never lived to fulfil. *The Jew of Malta* is especially interesting because it gave Shakespeare an inspiration and because it established two new traditions in the English theatre, the stage Jew and the stage miser. *Edward the Second* is interesting because, though not so great in sheer poetry as *Faustus,* it is, as a technical production, the top of Marlowe's performance for the stage.

Bailiffs, judges, constables, and sureties could not interfere with this determined young man's steady development in his craft. *The Jew of Malta* was almost certainly written in 1589 or 1590, about the time of the Bradley murder, perhaps while Marlowe was sharing rooms with Thomas Kydd near Shakespeare's lodgings. The prologue refers to the murder of the Duke of Guise,—the villain-hero of Marlowe's palpably inferior play, *The Massacre at Paris,*—on December 23, 1588. Marlowe was later sufficiently interested in this political killing to weave an entire play around it; and as an intimate of persons closely associated with the event itself, he had often heard it discussed. It thus slipped easily and naturally, almost unconsciously, out of his mind and into the prologue to his *Jew of Malta.*

In February, 1591—that is, 1592, by modern reckoning—old Philip Henslowe notes in his accounts the performance of "the Jewe of Malltuse." He does not mark it "ne," his usual note in entering new plays, and we may assume that this was the revival of a play already old upon the boards. (If it had really been a new play, we should find a series of performances instead of only one.) Date the play 1589 or 1590, then, and everything is logical.

The Jew of Malta is an early version of the story of the rich and wicked Jew, whose beautiful daughter falls in love with a Christian and steals her father's wealth, a story which Shakespeare—borrowing with both hands from his friend Marlowe—in after years gave immortal form as *The Merchant of Venice*. The rest of Shakespeare's play—the story of the caskets, the pound of flesh, Portia's legal masquerade, Lorenzo, Nerissa, and the clown—the acquisitive bard borrowed elsewhere.

The Jew of Malta is Barabas, who, as the play opens with some of Marlowe's finest verse, sits in the little inner stage at the rear of the broad Elizabethan platform stage, gloating over his wealth. It was for this scene that Marlowe wrote the famous line:

> Infinite riches in a little roome,

borrowing it, strange to say, from William Harrison's *Description of England*, a commonplace geographical work, but transmuting it from prose to purest poetry by the deft change of two words.[1] Harrison had written a casual reference to "great commoditie in a little room."

This is the passage at which Shakespeare glances a few years later—after Marlowe had been murdered in the little room of a Deptford tavern, in a brawl over an inn-keeper's reckoning—when he makes a character in *As You Like It* say that something "strikes a man more dead than a great reckoning in a little room." This is also the line that gruff old Ben Jonson—who knew Marlowe's works well, though he did not wholly approve of them—remembers when he makes his own miser in *The Sad Shepherd* allude to "the sacred treasure in this blessed room." George Chapman, Marlowe's friend who finished the poem on *Hero and Leander* which the dying Marlowe left incomplete, remembers it too, when he writes the line

> And show their riches in a little room

in his poem, *Ovid's Banquet of Sence.*

Elizabethan writers habitually quoted each other—without

giving credit—to an extent that is unbelievable to-day; but this series of borrowings goes beyond even the Elizabethan practice. Everything that Kit Marlowe wrote clung to the memory of his contemporaries then, as a few passages like the "thousand ships" still cling to the memories of after generations.

Three other Jewish merchants now enter with news of fresh commercial successes; but they have scarcely finished their tidings when the Christian governor of the island, faced with a demand for Turkish tribute, decrees that all the Jews living in Malta must either become Christians or pay over half their estates to satisfy the Turks. When Barabas protests, all of his estate is seized as a punishment.

Finding that his house, after seizure, has been turned into a Christian nunnery, Barabas persuades his daughter Abigail to pretend conversion, enter the nunnery, and secure the gold he has secreted there. Meantime, he provokes a duel between two young Christian gentlemen who love his daughter and both are slain. Abigail, really in love with one of them, now turns sincerely to the Church and is genuinely converted. Barabas—who slowly changes from a human and believable figure in the first part of the play to a mere Elizabethan stage monster in the latter half—poisons the entire nunnery to punish his recreant daughter; but Abigail, before her death, reveals his villainy.

Barabas saves himself by murdering a Christian friar and then setting up the body where another friar, to whom Abigail has confessed all, knocks it down. The second friar is then accused of murder and hanged—a reminiscence, perhaps, of the fate of the unfortunate Friar Stone in Canterbury. Barabas, however, is betrayed by his villainous slave, Ithamore, who has been a partner of his crimes. Once more, however, the wicked Jew of Malta escapes—this time by deserting to the Turkish army which is besieging Malta. Through his treachery Malta falls—in defiance of history—into Turkish hands, and Barabas as a reward is made governor. The villain-hero, now doubly perfidious, offers to betray his Turkish masters to the Christians for a hundred thousand pounds. He hates equally

> Damn'd Christians, dogges, and Turkish Infidels.

A banquet is prepared, at which the floor is to fall in, beneath

Barabas's Turkish guests, precipitating some of them into a boiling cauldron and some into depths below. But the humane Christian governor is content merely to capture the Turks alive, and Barabas himself is precipitated into the boiling cauldron—again like Friar Stone, of Canterbury.

The Jew of Malta, as even this barest of outlines makes only too clear, is a rather crude play, filled with the cheapest blood-and-thunder, which alternates with the keenest characterization and lines of clear human understanding expressed in the finest verse. Barabas, in the first half of the play, is an entirely credible and human figure, often a pathetic one—a miser, indeed, who gloats over his wealth, but a father also who sincerely loves his daughter and whose savagery toward his Christian foes is explained by the deep wrongs done him and justified by legal sophistry. As he sardonically reminds the Christian governor, who is virtuously protesting his excellent intentions:

> Your extreme right does me exceeding wrong.

So far in the play, Marlowe's villain-hero has good stage reasons for everything he does; and his yearning for revenge is something any reader can believe in.

Then, of a sudden, the poetry—save for infrequent snatches of a few lines—has disappeared. The character of a man who is vindictive with good reason changes; and he becomes the least credible of theatrical villains, indulging in miscellaneous iniquities merely to cause shudders in the uncritical pit. The rush and action of the play is sufficient to conceal these flaws when it is produced on the stage; but they are hopelessly revealed when one sits down to read. Barabas has now become the kind of villain who boasts:

> As for my selfe, I walke abroad a nights
> And kill sicke people groaning under walls:
> Sometimes I goe about and poyson wells.

His villainy has long

> kept the Sexton's armes in vre
> With digging graues and ringing dead mens knels.

In the wars he has slain "friend and enemy with my stratagems." And worst of all—

> Then after that was I an Vsurer,
> And with extorting, cozening, forfeiting,
> And tricks belonging vnto Brokery,
> I fill'd the Iailes with Bankrouts in a yeare,
> And with young Orphans planted Hospitals,
> And euery Moone made some or other mad,
> And now and then one hang himselfe for griefe,
> Pinning vpon his breast a long great Scrowle
> How I with interest tormented him.

This enthusiastic confession of villainy is evidently not the sort of thing in which any one can be expected to believe. Barabas has become, not a genuine character, but a bogey man to startle the groundlings for a moment and provide a rather cheap thrill.

This sudden collapse of the play in its latter half is not proof positive that some one else has re-touched and ruined Marlowe's original handiwork. Brave beginnings and botched endings are no novelty in dramatic literature; nor was Christopher Marlowe a steady-going young man who could be relied on to finish, with painstaking care, every work that he began. It is quite possible that Marlowe started the play with the best intentions, got tired of it, or needed money in a hurry, and finished it in the quickest, easiest way he could. All the speculations of all the learned critics upon this point may have been wasted on nothing more than a sudden need for cash on the part of a rather dissipated young man who happened to have the kind of genius that did not always last through five acts.

It is more likely, however, that the play owes its present mangled condition to the handiwork of one Thomas Heywood, man-of-all-work to various theatres until well on in the time of Charles I, who boasted that he had had "either an entire hand, or at the least a main finger" in two hundred and twenty plays, as well as in others that he could not remember.[2]

The Jew of Malta exists to-day only in Heywood's adapted edition of 1633, "as it was playd before the King and Queene, in His Majesties Theatre at White-Hall, by her Majesties Servants at the Cock-pit." The other four important Marlowe plays—the two parts of *Tamburlaine, Faustus,* and *Edward the Second*—exist in numerous editions. *Faustus* ran to ten or perhaps even eleven if we allow for a supposed lost edition, and was still being published after the Restoration of Charles

II. The two less important plays, *Dido* and *The Massacre at Paris*, also exist, like *The Jew of Malta*, only in single editions; but the correctness of their text is a matter of relatively slight importance, since they are obviously Marlowe's inferior work.

The Jew of Malta in its present form is an adaptation of Marlowe's original, made for Charles I and his court and for the audience of the Cock-Pit Theatre. It was probably made from a manuscript that had already suffered forty years of re-writing to suit the tastes of several generations of theatre-goers, before it finally fell into the hands of the conscienceless Heywood, who cut and re-cast it to suit his own rather erratic taste.

Heywood at any rate it is who writes the "Epistle Dedicatory" in which he avers that he "vsher'd it unto the Court, and presented it to the Cock-pit." He also claims credit for two new prologues and two epilogues, one of each for the Court performance and for the performance in the public theatre. The story of the friar condemned to death because he thinks he has killed a body already dead appears in Heywood's own play, *The Captives*, and in his *Gynaikeion, or Nine Bookes of Various History Concerning Women.* It is fairly certain, then, who must bear responsibility for the general mishandling of Marlowe's play—a mishandling that can never be corrected, since we lack any other edition for purposes of comparison.

It may be said in Heywood's extenuation that his adaptations, however offensive from the purely literary standpoint, are usually exceedingly good theatre, as modern producers have found to their amazement.[3] They were written into the manuscript by a man who understood audiences perfectly, and they still produce the effect that he intended when placed upon the stage—as he also intended.

Next to *Doctor Faustus*, *The Jew of Malta* has had a longer stage history than any of Marlowe's other plays. After its first production from Marlowe's manuscript, the actors seem to have let *The Jew* alone for a year or two; and there are no records of performance for some time after Henslowe's solitary entry in February, 1592. Then in 1594, a year after the author's death, it was suddenly recalled to the stage and to a burst of unexpected popularity by nothing less than a scandal at the Court of Queen Elizabeth. Not that scandals there were unusual occurrences; but this was a scandal with a fillip all its own: The Queen's personal physician was charged with attempting to poison her, and—the royal physician was a Jew!

According to the strict letter of the law, there were not supposed to be any Jews in Elizabethan England. Edward I had banished them all in 1290, and none could lawfully return till Cromwell called them back in 1650. The historian J. R. Green asserts that "from the time of Edward to that of Cromwell no Jew touched English ground."[4] If that were true, it would be hard to understand why the Elizabethan play-goers were so interested in plays about Jewish characters and how the playwrights were able to catch so adroitly so many of the subtle traits of the Jewish character. A play called simply *The Jew* had been popular as early as 1579. Then came Marlowe's play and after it Shakespeare's, to be followed by numerous other plays with Jewish characters of much the same sort. Both Marlowe and Shakespeare have caught and reproduced typically Jewish traits—strong family affection, habitual quotation from the Old Testament, clan feeling, religious strictness, and rigid observance of dietary regulations. Jewish commercial acumen is an essential element in both plays.

All this, of course, may be unconscious on the writer's part, but that sort of thing is not accidental. Both playwrights had been observing Jews. And how could they do that if there were no Jews in England?

The answer is, of course, that—law or no law—there were a good many Jews in Queen Elizabeth's England. Henry VIII had brought a rabbi to England. His daughter Elizabeth numbered among her ladies-in-waiting during Marlowe's life-time, a Portuguese Jewess, who rejected an English nobleman's offer of marriage rather than abandon her ancient faith. There are even casual allusions to the custom of hiring court costumes from Jewish pawnbrokers; and throughout Elizabeth's reign a house for converted Jews was maintained in Chancery Lane. Their signatures in Hebrew characters still exist. And, as the study of Hebrew was essential to the education of Christian divines, the Universities seem to have welcomed men learned in Jewish literature and not to have been unduly curious as to their religion. Marlowe might easily have known one or two Hebrew scholars in his Cambridge days.

Dr. Rodrigo Lopez was the royal physician whose untimely elevation on a Tyburn gallows furnished the Queen's subjects with a reverberating sensation and restored Marlowe's play to the stage. "Doctor Lopus portingale howsholder Denizen" is listed among the returns of strangers in London in 1571 as one who "came into this realme about xij yeares past to get his lyvinge by physicke."[5] He had already become a member of the College of Physicians, was attending Sir Francis Walsingham,[6] and soon became household physician to the Earl of Leicester, the royal favourite. In 1586, while Marlowe was still at Cambridge, Lopez became chief physician to the Queen. He helped the Earl of Essex to secure secret intelligence from Spain. When Essex brought over Don Antonio Perez, half-Jewish pretender to the throne of Portugal, who could be so useful an interpreter as Dr. Lopez, with his command of five languages?

But the doctor, alas! was learned rather than discreet. Waxing merry while revelling with Don Antonio, "Lopez began to inveigh against the Earl of Essex, telling some secrecies, how he had cured him, and of what diseases, with some other things that did disparage his honor."[7] The noble Earl, quite normally furious, began to use his enormous influence to turn her Majesty's fickle mind against her medical adviser. It is doubtful whether Lopez was in the least guilty; but like most Elizabethans, he was not above accepting "gifts"; he had certainly received 50,000 crowns from Spain; and he had threatened Don Antonio's life. Under torture, he made other confessions, which he subsequently retracted.

The Queen, as usual, hesitated over the death warrant—a few years later she was to hesitate in just the same way over the death warrant for Essex himself. But she signed at last, and the brilliant physician dangled from a noosed rope at Tyburn, June 7, 1594, almost exactly a year after Marlowe's death.

By the usual custom, the condemned man was allowed to make a dying speech. His assertion that he loved the Queen as he loved Christ amused the highly Christian mob who had turned out to enjoy the hanging, and as the drop fell the crowd hooted: "He is a Jew!" The Queen, who still suffered some compunctious visitings of nature, did not seize the estate, as she was legally entitled to do, but left it to the widow. She took nothing but one jewel, said to have been sent to Lopez by the King of Spain, and wore it at her girdle the rest of her life.[8]

Lopez had long been a familiar London figure—Marlowe or

one of his adapters has tucked a casual allusion to him into *Faustus:* "Doctor Lopus was neuer such a Doctor." [9] His trial and execution created a tremendous stir in the little Elizabethan capital, which had many of the characteristics of a big village. The public became suddenly interested in Jews—especially rich and wicked ones, with murderous intentions, like Lopez.

A hint was enough for Henslowe. A man of his shrewd judgment and experience in estimating the public taste needed nothing more. The manuscript of Marlowe's *Jew of Malta* was dug out of the playhouse dust and put into immediate rehearsal. Edward Alleyn refreshed his memory of the part of Barabas.

Henslowe proposed to make some money. Lopez was not formally arraigned until February, but on "the 18 of Jenewary," the players were already producing *The Jew of Malta* —which had not previously been on the stage for at least a year—before the biggest house the play had ever had. The takings were three pounds. Two productions followed in February, the month of the arraignment; two more in April; and one in May. In June, when Lopez was hanged, there were four productions; and the Londoners were by this time so deeply interested in the wicked Jew of Malta that the play ran on with at least one, and sometimes several, productions a month, until February of the following year. Never was any man so literally "butchered to make a holiday" as Lopez. The interest in *The Jew of Malta* did not entirely die out until June, 1596, two years after the hanging. When the takings dropped in that month to a meagre thirteen shillings a performance, Henslowe took it off the stage for good.

The Jew of Malta did not vanish from the boards entirely, however. It continued to be played in the provinces, along with *Tamburlaine;* and there may have been occasional metropolitan revivals. Henslowe lent money "to bye divers things for the Jewe of malta," in 1601, and then "lent mor to the litell tayller for the same daye for mor things for the Jewe of malta." This sounds like re-costuming; but there is no actual record of production in London until Heywood's revival in 1633, when Perkins replaces Alleyn—"so unimitable an Actor," says Heywood—as Barabas. Edmund Kean revived the play in 1818, playing the rôle of Barabas himself. Since then it has appeared only in amateur productions and a Phœnix Society revival in London in 1922.

The play helped to start a costume tradition on the English stage. Marlowe's lines show clearly enough that Barabas must have been made up like the "bottle-nosed knave" [10] there described, and a contemporary pamphlet actually describes Alleyn's make-up as "the artificiall Jew of Maltae's nose . . . upon which nose two casements were built, through which his eyes had a little ken of us." The "casements" were, of course, spectacles.

This emphasis on Jewish features is something new in English literature. The Old Testament figures of the early mystery plays had been Jewish; but they seem to have been regarded merely as Scriptural personages, without effort to indicate their racial characteristics.

The red wig and beard which became identified with the part of Shylock may also have begun with Marlowe's Barabas. According to the old actor Thomas Jordan, writing in 1664,[11] the original Shylock's

> beard was red; his face was made
> Not much unlike a witches.
> His habit was a Jewish gown,
> That would defend all weather;
> His chin turned up, his nose hung down,
> And both ends met together.

Not only did *The Jew of Malta* start a fashion in stage costume; it started something more important—a fashion in villains, just as *Tamburlaine* and *Faustus* had started fashions in heroes. *The Jew of Malta* is followed by an epidemic of misers and usurers on the stage; while *Tamburlaine* is followed by a series of grandiloquent conquerors, and *Faustus* by one stage conjurer after another. The new style of usurers as villains which *The Jew of Malta* introduced is also marked by a Machiavellian philosophy, which Marlowe seems to have imported from Cambridge and made popular.

Machiavelli had by this time been translated into French and Latin, though not into English; but the gist of his thought was reported—for the highly moral purpose of refutation—by a learned and indignant French Huguenot, Innocent Gentillet. Gentillet, like a good many Frenchmen, especially the Protestants, objected to the influx of Italians who came to

France with Catherine de' Medici; and after the St. Bartholomew's Massacre, his book with the long-winded title which began *Discourse on the Meanes of well governing and maintaining in Good Peace a Kingdom,* ran through a number of editions. Gentillet's full title is a good deal longer; but it always ends with the words, "against Nicholas Machiavel," and thus it came to be known as the "Anti-Machiavel."

"The end and scope which I haue proposed unto my selfe," wrote Gentillet, was "to confute the doctrine of Machiavell," which he regarded as "beastly vanitie and madnesse, yea full of extreame wickednesse." [12] As "extreame wickednesse" was just what Marlowe was looking for when he wrote *The Jew of Malta,* he took Gentillet's statements and mis-statements of the true Machiavellian doctrine at their face value, and let his villain-hero advocate them impartially—especially the passages that fell in with his own unorthodox religious views.[13]

Machiavelli had applied his cynicism only to affairs of state; Marlowe applied it also to personal life. Machiavelli did not necessarily oppose the special conception of power which he called "virtù" to ordinary moral virtue; Marlowe did. Machiavelli employed virtù to enhance the power of the state; Marlowe's heroes seek it for its own sake. There are traces of Machiavelli in Tamburlaine and Faustus; and the Duke of Guise in *The Massacre at Paris* is a pure Machiavellian hero. It is only natural that he should be, for he was one of the chief enemies of the Huguenots, for whom Gentillet was spokesman. It is from Machiavelli, too—or rather, from Gentillet's perversion of his ideas—that Marlowe's Barabas derives his eagerness for revenge, his contempt for religion as mere self-seeking and hypocrisy, his idea that one is bound to keep faith only when it is profitable to do so, and his complete egoism, a quality that he shares with Marlowe's other heroes.

When the actor costumed as Machiavel stepped on the stage to speak the prologue to *The Jew of Malta,* the sinister Florentine made his first appearance in an Elizabethan play; and there entered with him a motif new to the English stage: the ruthless, selfish, unscrupulous execution of devious schemes. Tamburlaine was after all a mere barbarian; Faustus was hesitant and beset by scruples, inadequate Machiavellians both. But the Duke of Guise in *The Massacre at Paris,* the evil favourites in *Edward the Second,* and Barabas himself are cunning, sinister, cold-blooded schemers of the same sort that appear in anonymous plays like *The Contention* and *The True Tragedy*, where Marlowe's hand is rather more than suspected. This is the type that Shakespeare catches up in his *Richard III* and that John Ford and John Webster carry on into later plays. It is a type that never afterwards quite drops out of English literature—Old Scrooge is a very late and very Victorian version of Barabas.

Machiavellian usurers are particularly plentiful in the later Elizabethan plays. There are forty-five of them in all; and nine are accompanied by a loveable, reckless gallant of the sort introduced by Marlowe and Shakespeare, a gallant who is tricked by the wicked money-lender but saved by the love of the usurer's daughter, niece, or ward.[14] Queen Bess's playwrights knew a good thing when they saw it!

The sources of Marlowe's play are numerous and rather confused. The figure of Barabas is in some way related to the lives of two historical Mediterranean adventurers. These were the Portuguese Jew, João Miques, alias Joseph Nassi, and a certain David Passi. Nassi became confidential adviser to the Sultan. Like Marlowe's Barabas, he was in political and financial touch with the courts of France and Germany, and false to both. Like Barabas he was rich—the French Government at one time owed him 150,000 ducats.[15] Finally—again like Barabas—he became the Jewish governor of a Christian island, ruling over Naxos and even providing himself with a crown in the hope that he would be made King of Cyprus.

David Passi aided the Turks in constructing models of Crete and Malta, in preparation for their attacks upon the islands; kept the Sultan informed of events in Christendom; and became so powerful that the Venetian diplomats report him as "able to do great harm and great good." They add that "this David for one truth tells a hundred lies"—which would certainly qualify him as the original of Barabas were such habits at all remarkable either in diplomacy or in the Near East. There was also a converted English Jew, Edward Brandon, who was wealthy, who was involved in political intrigue, and who became governor of the Channel Islands.

As a friend of many courtiers, Marlowe might easily have heard tales of all these men. Nassi was actually described by Philip Lonicer,[16] in a book which Marlowe had used in writing *Tamburlaine*, and in Belleforest's *Cosmographie Universelle*, which also contains an episode that duly appears in *Tamburlaine.*

A few other clues to the dramatist's literary browsings are preserved in the play. Barabas betrays to the Turks a weak place in the walls where [17]

> The rocke is hollow, and of purpose digg'd,
> To make a passage for the running streames
> And common channels of the City.

There still exists an old book by "T. Washington the younger," on *The Navigations, peregrinations, and voyages made into Turky by Nicholas Nicholay,* published in 1585, which tells how, at the siege of Tripoli, a traitor "informed the Turks of the weakest places of the castle"—weak because of "having underneath it the cellars." In other words—Marlowe's words —"hollow, and of purpose digg'd."

Again we watch the poet following up his author's hints, and doing some further reading. Nicholay's account mentions the *Discours de la Guerre de Malte,* by one Nicholas de Villegagnon. This repeats the story of Tripoli's fall; but it also mentions one "Octauio Ferneso," and "le seigneur Fernese." That is why Marlowe names his governor of Malta "Ferneze," ignoring the gallant Lavalette, who as a matter of genuine history actually defended the island of Malta. As if to clinch the matter, the accounts of Tripoli and Malta stand close together in Villegagnon's book.[18]

Two other names linger in the poet's head. His ruffian Ithamore is named for the saintly bishop Ithamar, a manuscript of whose miracles (said to be the only one extant) was in the Corpus Christi Library; and when the Turkish leader addresses a pasha as "Callapine," we know that the name has been carried over in the poet's mind from the days when he was writing *Tamburlaine.*

12.

Maturity Achieved

"Is it not passing braue to be a King?"
I. Tamburlaine

From *The Jew of Malta,* Marlowe turned to the last and in many ways the greatest of the four great plays by which his name is remembered. All critics agree—it is one of the very few points on which they do agree—that this is the maturest of Marlowe's plays and, except perhaps for the insignificant *Massacre at Paris,* the latest. It is one of those strange situations in which there is very little dispute about a question, in spite (or perhaps because) of the fact that there is very little evidence. Different authorities date the play differently, but the earliest date given is 1590 and the latest is 1592, while more recent authorities prefer to believe that *Edward the Second* was written either in 1591 or 1592.

The play is entered for publication in the *Stationers' Register* for July 6, 1593—a few weeks after Marlowe's sensational assassination. Only a manuscript copy of the 1593 edition has come down to us, but it is clear that the bookseller, William Jones, was quick to take advantage of a murder that had amazed London and that provided admirable publicity for the first edition of a new work of the dead author. In 1594, there was another edition which has completely disappeared from England, but of which two stray copies still exist on the Continent. The title page of this quarto says that "it was sundrie times publiquely acted in the honourable citie of London, by the right honourable the Earle of Pembrooke his seruants." This particular company of actors is unknown after 1575/6 until it suddenly re-appears in December, 1592.[1] It seems certain, then, that about the time when he was writing in one room with Thomas Kydd and shocking him with unorthodox philosophy while he terrified the guardians of the uncertain public peace in Shoreditch, Marlowe was also quietly scribbling away at this one play of his which is the most perfectly planned, most perfectly finished, and most perfectly preserved of all his writings.

In *Edward the Second,* Marlowe for the only time in his career chooses a weakling as his hero; and the eager struggle for power which is the chief characteristic of his other works is handed over to secondary characters—to the sycophantic favourites of the King, and to the rough, ambitious barons who struggle against them. In the main, Marlowe follows history as he found it in Holinshed's *Chronicle.*

Piers Gaveston, already the degenerate favourite of the weakling King, is hurrying back to Court at the news that the old King is dead and that his patron reigns. Already Gaveston is cynically planning to entrap the young monarch's mind: [2]

> I must haue wanton Poets, pleasant wits,
> Musitians, that with touching of a string
> May draw the pliant king which way I please,

when the King enters, arguing with a group of barons, who urge him to part company with the favourite. In this dialogue the two Lords Mortimer, father and son, take the leading part, while Gaveston stands silently by, listening but observed by none—a stage convention of which the Elizabethan dramatists freely availed themselves.

Rejoining the King, Gaveston is received with open arms. When the Bishop of Coventry protests, he is flung into the Tower and his estate handed over to the royal favourite. When the protests of the barons grow stronger, Edward is forced, sorely against his will, to exile Gaveston, who has already sown dissension between King Edward and Queen Isabel. The Queen nevertheless pities her husband's sorrow, intercedes with the barons, and procures Gaveston's recall. His return instantly produces fresh dissension, which is embittered when the elder Mortimer is captured by the Scots, and the King refuses to pay his ransom from a captivity incurred in the royal service. The barons now rise in open rebellion, seize Gaveston, and execute him.

The besotted Edward adopts a new favourite in Young Spenser, a mere adventurer, who is joined by his father. The barons, again alarmed, continue their rebellion but are defeated. Young Mortimer, however, escapes, and with the aid of the neglected Queen, whose wavering affections are at length transferred to him, raises the rebellion anew and defeats the royal party. The King flees, but is captured and compelled to abdicate, in a scene which Shakespeare later copies in *Richard II*. He is sent to prison in Berkeley Castle, after suffering the indignity of being shaved in "puddle water" from the nearest ditch. At Berkeley, he is the victim of a peculiarly horrible murder. But the barons and the Queen have gone too far. Young Edward III, in horror at their crime, executes Mortimer and sends the suspected Queen to the Tower.

Such in outline is the story which Marlowe took over—sometimes word for word—from the old chronicle. Outlines of the plots of great plays are the least profitable form of writing known to man; but even from this bald summary, the immense advance that Marlowe has made since the early days of *Tamburlaine* leaps to the eye. *Edward the Second* is the story of a king, his favourites, and his wars; *Tamburlaine* is also the story of a king, his favourites, and his wars. But *Edward the Second* is an intricately knit piece of structure; *Tamburlaine* is no more than a succession of more or less thrilling episodes. The characters in *Edward the Second* are individuals, real people; the characters in *Tamburlaine* are nothing but lay figures—and it is all a reader can do to tell the subordinate chieftains, Techelles, Usumcasane, and Theridamas, apart.

Most of all, Marlowe has advanced in the treatment of his women characters. In *Tamburlaine,* Zenocrate is a pale and patient shadow of her fiery lord; in *Edward the Second,* Queen Isabel is a real woman, whose devotion shifts slowly through the play; yet so gradually, so deftly, so subtly is this indicated that there is never a line where one can lay a finger saying: "Here is the change." Life is like that, when an emotion fades.

As the play opens, Queen Isabel is the faithful wife of an impatient, indifferent King, who is plainly tired of her. As the play closes, she is the shameless paramour of Young Mortimer. Yet the stages between these two extremes are as imperceptible as such changes are in life itself. The reasons why the change takes place—the King's harshness, his indifference, his neglect of his wife for his favourites, and the virile attractiveness of Young Mortimer as compared with the fainéant King—are always dextrously slipped into Marlowe's dialogue just at the right moment, the causes for the alteration in the Queen's affections being so slowly assembled in the reader's mind that he never sees it taking place, yet finds it perfectly natural when he can no longer fail to see it.

In *Tamburlaine* this is not so at all. The stage events happen because the source books said so, or because the actors wanted another scene. Sometimes they almost seem to happen because young Marlowe was carried away by the gorgeous sound of his own words and the thunder of the mighty line. In *Edward the Second*, Marlowe has at last reached the ultimate stage of perfection in dramatic writing. The action happens because, these characters being what they are and being placed in the situations that the dramatist has devised, the action of the play *has* to follow. It is an inner, spiritual necessity, as clear and as evident as are the forces that bring Macbeth to his downfall, drawn forward to destruction by a glittering bait and pushed to his own undoing by a ruthless and dominating spouse; as necessary as the crime of Othello, when once his blunt and simple mind is ensnared by Iago's subtleties.

Edward is a weakling, hopelessly under the sway of his favourites. His contemporaries, whose accounts of him have come down to us, certainly regarded him as a degenerate; but Marlowe (whose mind had played about this subject in several passages of *Dido* and of *Hero and Leander)* is surprisingly chary in handling it here. All through the first part of *Edward the Second*, his allusions suggest nothing worse than a fundamental weakness in the King's character, a weakness which leads to the domination first of Gaveston, then of the Spensers, father and son; but he never specifically states what that weakness is.

When misfortune falls upon the King and he is compelled to yield, first his throne and eventually his life, a degree of manhood appears in him for the first time; and the spectator's or reader's sympathy is entirely transferred to Edward as the play closes. This change in the reader's attitude is almost as subtly contrived as the change in the love of the wavering Isabel.

In this play, Marlowe overcomes for the first time his tendency to be carried away by the splendour of mere words. He has learned to restrain his love for resounding but bombastious lines. The scene in which "the King rageth" would have been written six years earlier with all the rant of Tamburlaine's dying speech. Now, as Charles Lamb said,[3] "the reluctant pangs of abdicating royalty in Edward furnished hints, which Shakespeare scarcely improved in his Richard the Second; and the death-scene of Marlowe's king moves pity and terror beyond any scene ancient or modern with which I am acquainted."

Marlowe probably remembered most of the story of King Edward II from his student days at Corpus Christi. There is no doubt whatever that he took most of his play from Holinshed's *Chronicle,* whose narrative he follows closely and whose very language he sometimes copies unconsciously. This was a new book, which had appeared in 1586, and a copy had been presented to Corpus Christi by a former fellow, Henry Clifford. It bears the date in ink, 1587, apparently the date of its presentation; and this is the very year in which the future playwright took his master's degree. The faded inscription in old brown ink is still upon the title page, and the old folio itself still stands in its place on the shelves of Archbishop Parker's quiet old library.

The books that Marlowe used are unique in Elizabethan study. We can usually point to the titles of the source-books that Shakespeare and the other dramatists worked from, and even to the passages that they copied. But how and where they found their books and where those books are now, no man can say. Thanks, however, to the pious care of Cambridge librarians for the last three or four hundred years, it is still possible to point to many a volume standing to this day upon their shelves and say with tolerable certainty that young Christopher Marlowe, student of Corpus, used those very books!

Marlowe follows the account of Holinshed, his main source, with surprising fidelity. Only in *Dido* and in *Doctor Faustus* has he adhered so closely to the original, and in these cases the *Aeneid* and the English Faust Book were the only sources from which he could get the story at all. Taking Holinshed's *Chronicle* as he sits down to write *Edward the Second,* the poet has simply run through the volume, selecting facts for their stage value and condensing time for the same reason. He makes the Spensers follow Gaveston immediately, as royal favourites; as a matter of history there was a long period between—a period far too long for the two hours' traffic of the stage. Just as in *Dido* and *Doctor Faustus,* so here it is possible to run through the play and the source together and indicate by actual passages in the original exactly where the poet's lines come from.

Occasionally, Marlowe takes a whole phrase bodily from his source; but usually he is careful to re-write Holinshed's rather wooden narrative into his own incomparably richer, though now restrained, style. Thus, Holinshed makes the Earl of Pembroke go "to visit his wife lieng *not farre from thence,*" Marlowe gives him a speech beginning: "My house is *not farre hence.*" When Spenser outbids Mortimer and secures a coveted property, both Holinshed and Marlowe use the phrase "in hand" to buy. When Holinshed says: "The king came to Bristow," Marlowe simply reverses the order of the words and gets the line: "Come, friends, to Bristow." When Holinshed quotes a Latin line or two from the historian, Polydor Vergil, about the unhappiness of crowned heads, Marlowe translates them along with his own verses.

Even the riddling Latin message ordering Edward's murder, which conveys contradictory instructions according to the place where a single comma stands, was taken over whole from Holinshed in simple Latin which the young university man scorns to translate:

> Edwardum occidere, nolite timere,
> Edwardum occidere nolite, timere.

Put the comma before the last two words or leave it out entirely, and the treacherous Latin says: "Don't be afraid to kill Edward." Move the comma a single word backward and the Latin says: "Do not think of killing Edward. Fear it."[4]

It is a strange fact that this play, Marlowe's finest technical performance, should have enjoyed a relatively slight success in production. At least we have to-day no evidence that it was ever much performed. Henslowe's Diary is obstinately silent, except for cryptic allusions to one play called *Mortymer* and another called *The Spencers.* The only light as to *Edward the Second's* fortunes upon the stage comes from the conflicting statements on the title pages of the 1622 edition. For some reason, this edition appears with two title pages. One form agrees with the other four editions, which show that the play was first produced by the Earl of Pembroke's servants, while a second state of the title attributes the later production to the Queen's players at the Red Bull Theatre in St. John's Street. Other records show that during the reign of James I,

Queen Anne's men did play at the Red Bull, some time between 1604 and 1606. The performance by Pembroke's men accounts for the Latin dedication to the Countess of Pembroke, which Marlowe wrote for *Amintæ Gaudia,* a book by his friend Thomas Watson.[5]

The dates show that Marlowe's most finished play was at least kept in production for a period of some years; and Henslowe's silence is probably explained by the fact that he had very little interest in what the Pembroke Company was acting—his main interest was in the Lord Admiral's men, whose star was his son-in-law. It may be added that *Edward the Second* has been rather fortunate in its twentieth century productions. William Poel produced it for the Elizabethan Stage Society, August 10, 1903, with Granville Barker as Edward. It was produced at Birkbeck College, London, in 1920; at the Regent Theatre, London, by the Phœnix Society in 1923; at Cambridge by the Marlowe Dramatic Society in 1926; by Christ Church, Oxford, in 1933. There was a highly modernistic Czech production in Prague in 1922.

13.

Friends and Foes

> "It lies not in our power to loue, or hate."
> *Hero and Leander*

Marlowe arrived in London, not as the usual struggling and obscure youngster from the University with vague literary aspirations, but as a young man who had already been commended by Her Majesty's Government for useful service, and who in consequence had powerful friends at Court and in the Privy Council. He had left the cobbler's shop behind for good, and he probably entered the metropolis with a play or two already stowed somewhere in his luggage.

It is one of the remarkable facts of a remarkable career that in the short space of six years, this youth of the humblest possible birth had become associated with the highest and most powerful—as well as with some of the lowest and least important—in Elizabeth's London: with an unknown but very pious Lord, to whom Thomas Kydd darkly alludes; with Sir Walter Raleigh, the by no means pious Captain of Her Majesty's Guard; with a philosophical, sceptical, literary and scientific group who gathered about Raleigh; with the wealthy and prominent Walsingham family; and with a sinister underworld group of tricksters, petty criminals, spies, and secret agents who killed him at the last.

It all ended with tragedy, but between the middle 1580's and the dagger thrust at Deptford in 1593 lay as thrilling a half dozen years as ever young man lived, even in the stirring age when the Virgin Eliza reigned. In 1580 one is a mere nobody, a shoemaker's son, lucky to be even a pensioner in the University, preparing for holy orders without the least inclination for them. By 1586 or '87, one is in touch with the great and powerful of England, handling darkly secret affairs of state, with the dismal prospect of the Church cast aside forever, but with a high and greatly treasured academic degree remaining as the tangible reward of those years of toil.

Another year, and one is a brilliant theatrical success, the talk of London, envied, admired, applauded, imitated—and also hated. Almost every new year sees another new play and another new success. One's poetry goes from hand to hand, appreciated and applauded by a literary coterie of high renown, which mingles social and intellectual distinction. One is a welcome guest at the country houses of the landed gentry. One deals familiarly with the most brilliant intellects of the age, suggests mathematical problems to one of the first scientific men of Europe, discusses theology casually with the same brilliant writer, lends young Shakespeare a helping hand up the ladder.

Closest akin to Marlowe's spirit among all his London friends was Sir Walter Raleigh, "a handsome hasty stout fellow, very bold and apt to affront,"[1] twice imprisoned for brawls, a fluent Latinist, an ardent student, a religious sceptic always ready to "venture at discourse which was unpleasant to the churchmen," the idol of the sailors he commanded, sailor himself, and likewise soldier, poet, explorer, philosopher, historian, and in all the brilliant things he undertook surprisingly brilliant.

Born of Devonshire gentry in 1552, he was some twelve years older than Marlowe, when that young man arrived from Cambridge. Raleigh was already a familiar figure at Court. He had caught the Queen's fancy in 1581, while Marlowe was just settling to his Cambridge studies, and it is in that year that he is said to have made his famous gesture with his new plush cloak.[2] Within two years he held the wine monopoly of England—he alone could license vintners, a privilege which the Cambridge dons disputed in vain. This monopoly brought in an income of from £800 to £2,000 a year.

That plush cloak may have been ruined by the mud puddle over which the Virgin Queen walked dry-shod; but it was a good investment. Within the next five years Raleigh not only achieved the wine monopoly; he was also made Lord Warden of the Stanneries (in charge of the Cornish tin mines), he was knighted, and he was made Captain of the Queen's Guard, a body of picked men chosen for their magnificent physique. Raleigh himself attended to the recruiting.

Raleigh's portraits more or less justify the praises of his robust physical charm, but there were two opinions even about that, for Raleigh had enemies enough in all ranks of society. Said note-gathering old John Aubrey, he had an "exceeding high forehead, long-faced, & sour eie-lidded, a kind of pigge-eie," while "his Beard turnd up naturally." [3] The description at least justifies Aubrey in adding that Raleigh had "a most remarkeable aspect," to which he added all the typical Elizabethan extravagance in dress. One of his costumes was of pure white satin, embroidered with pearls, with a pearl necklace as the final touch. He was fond of these gems, which suited the Queen's punning nickname for him, "Water," and occasionally in poetical outbursts alluded to himself as "Ocean," who madly loved the Queen as "Cynthia." He is credited with one suit in which every button was made of forty pearls, and was so fond of finery that even as a prisoner in the Tower he wore "a velvet cap laced, and a rich gowne, and trunke hose." [4]

The Queen was not the only virgin whose affections were entangled by the glamour of his personality and the foppishness of his garments. Contemporary gossip records an unseemly tale of the ardour of his wooing of Elizabeth Throckmorton, maid of honour to Her Majesty. By a tree in a wood, Raleigh made such violent love to his future wife that "something fearfull of her honour, & modest, she cryed, Sweet S*ir* Walter, what doe you me ask? Will you undoe me? Nay Sweet S*ir* Walter! Sweet S*ir* Walter! S*ir* Walter!" But gossipy old John Aubrey records that these shrieks of feminine protest eventually sank to a mere mumble of "Switter Swatter, Switter Swatter!" and the lady capitulated.[5]

When this impetuous lover finally married his Lady, Queen Elizabeth was furious—as she usually was with any courtier who dared prefer any charms to her own—and the newlyweds went to the Tower of London for a somewhat grim honeymoon, whence they were later banished to Raleigh's country estates.

Yet though "he loved a wench well," and though his garments were of an outlandish splendour after the extreme Elizabethan mode, Raleigh was a man of brilliant intellect, an eager inquisitive mind, much like Marlowe's own, "still climing after knowledge infinite," full of fire and imagination but also capable of coldly intellectual inquiry. A contemporary remarks of the explorer that "in his youth, his companions were boisterous blades, but generally those that had witt"—and a more precise description of the fiery young poet of Norton Folgate and the Lord Admiral's company it would be hard to find. Like Marlowe, Raleigh loved both wit and learning. When he was at home in England and much occupied with affairs of state, he nevertheless contrived to give his early mornings to study. He employed the brilliant Thomas Harriot as his personal mathematical tutor. But "he studyed most in his sea-voyages, when he carried always a truncke of bookes along with him, and had nothing to divert him." It was true enough, as Aubrey's disjointed notes declare, that "he was no slug, without doubt, had a wonderfull waking spirit."

With all this brilliance and success, Raleigh was "damnable proud." Learned though he was, Oxford educated though he was, he disdained to speak anything but "broad Devonshire to his dyeing day." The drawling burr of a rural dialect acquired distinction enough, Raleigh thought, if it passed *his* lips. Blunt, self-satisfied, he could be downright rude, as when in a room filled with persons of quality, he "took a pipe of tobacco, which made the ladies quitt it till he had done," like shrinking Victorian maids rather than robust Elizabethan lasses.

His pride extended to his authorship. One of his books "sold very slowly at first and the bookeseller complayned of it, and told him that he should be a looser by it, which put Sir W. into a passion." Authors are always like that, but few of them are so passionate over a publisher's plaint that they destroy the next volume in manuscript.[6] Nor was Raleigh one who suffered fools gladly. Annoyed by a chatterbox, "one time in a tavern, Sir W. R. beates him and seales up his mouth his upper and neather beard with hard wax."

Pride like this may be justified, little pranks like this may be amusing, but people do resent them. No wonder the rimed gibe went about, punning on the words "raw" and "lye" which made up one of the sixty-six Elizabethan spellings of his name:[7]

> The enemie to the stomack, and the word of disgrace,
> Is the name of the Gentleman with a bold face.

It was the same pun that James I—who hated him—made a little later: "On my soule, mon, I have heard rawly of thee."[8]

Marlowe's six years in London corresponded with some of the most dramatic incidents in Raleigh's life—the rivalry with Essex for the Queen's favour in 1587, just as Marlowe came up from Cambridge; Raleigh's return from Ireland with the poet Spenser and three books of *The Faerie Queene*, from which Marlowe quotes; Raleigh's liaison with Elizabeth Throckmorton, ending in the marriage which infuriated the Queen; and finally the dark rumours of irreligion which gathered about Marlowe's and Raleigh's names in 1593 and 1594. The rest of Raleigh's long career—the attack on Cadiz, the enmity of James I, the false charges of treason, the long, tiresome years in the Tower, the hapless voyage to Guiana; its failure, and Raleigh's death on the block—all these lie outside the shorter life of Marlowe.

Three contemporary allusions testify to their acquaintance. One is the poem, *The Nymph's Reply,* written in answer to Marlowe's lyric, *The Passionate Shepherd,* and attributed to Raleigh on fairly good early authority. A second is the assertion in a government spy's report that Marlowe told a friend how "hee hath read the Atheist lecture to Sr Walter Raliegh and others." A third is another government spy's reference to a known friend of Marlowe's as Sir Walter's "man." [9]

One might add a fourth odd, telltale bit of verbal evidence. A spy also reported that Marlowe "hath coated [i.e., quoted] a number of contrarieties out of the Scriptures." Now, "contrarieties" is a very odd word, a rather unusual word, the sort of word that one first hears a friend using and then employs unconsciously one's self. Marlowe had used it. And what do we find in Sir Walter's book, *The Skeptic?* Nothing less than a warning against the logical error of believing "contrarieties." [10] A small matter, no doubt, but pretty clear evidence of many a philosophical discussion between Sir Walter and young Christopher.

Raleigh and his philosophical intimates delighted to debate on religious subjects. In this circle were Thomas Harriot (1560-1621), mathematician and astronomer; Walter Warner (fl. 1600), another mathematician; George Chapman, translator of Homer, the poet who completed *Hero and Leander* after Marlowe's death; and Matthew Royden (fl. 1580-1622), a poet admired in his own day and remembered by nobody now. Thomas Kydd, in his first letter to Sir John Puckering about Marlowe,[11] remarks that "Harriot, Warner, Royden, and some stationers in Paules churchyard" were "such as he conversd withall." Since Harriot and Warner were in the group it must also have included Robert Hues (1553-1632) and the Earl of Northumberland, another patron of Harriot's. Harriot, Warner, and Hues were jointly known as the Earl's "three magi." When Raleigh went to the Tower, "the Earle of Northumberland was prisoner at the same time, who was patrone to Mr. Harriot and Mr. Warner, two of the best mathematicians then in the world, as also Mr. Hues [who wrote] *De Globis.*"[12]

These men were among the most brilliant of their age. Raleigh and Northumberland were rare figures in that world of courtly climbers who were themselves brilliant enough to know the worth of such men. Harriot improved algebra; anticipated Descartes in analytical geometry; turned his telescope toward the stars about the same time as Galileo; predicted seven comets and observed nine; was one of the first astronomers to observe sunspots; and corresponded with Kepler on optics. The Earl of Northumberland gave him lodging at Sion House, Isleworth, from 1607 to 1621, and there he devoted himself to "the calm, still air of delightful studies" and stored away those masses of notes, calculations, and diagrams, four or five thousand foolscap sheets of which still exist. One is a set of observations noted down day by day for a long period—and it gives one a shiver down the spine in these after years to see the scientific student's notes going calmly on through the fatal 30th of May, 1593, when Marlowe was stabbed to death and also through the months of plague before and after. Harriot was the true man of science. Friends might die and disease might rage but not for an instant would he neglect his data.

It is interesting also to note a shopping list in which the old scholar jots down the things that he must buy—pipes, tobacco (for all the Raleigh circle smoked the little silver pipes that were handed about from man to man like Indian peace pipes), "my jerkin," "my scarfe," "a riding cloke," and—"a horse for Kit." On another page Harriot jots down a long and involved scientific note about the plain sphere constructed by the early sixteenth century mathematician, Gemma Frisius, adding: "This Morly told me to consider what benefit followeth,"—clear evidence of the breadth of the poet's intellectual interests,[13] unless we regard it as an allusion to his supposed kinsmen, Captain Edmund Marlowe, whom Harriot also knew.

Harriot was with Raleigh's American colonists in Virginia who were rescued by Drake, and it was he who made the first Virginia survey and wrote the first book about the new-found land. Less is known of Warner and Hues, but their studies were evidently much the same, though pursued with less distinction.

Such studies in that age of superstition were inevitably misunderstood by outsiders, and "the voice of the Countree reported thereof strange things." Harriot was especially a victim of this early fundamentalism. At Raleigh's trial he was called "that devil Harriot." Marlowe's friend Nashe is alluding to him when he writes in *Pierce Penniless* (1592): "I heare that there be Mathematicians abroad that will prove men before Adam." [14] Aubrey reports that Sir Walter himself "was scandalized with atheisme," and recalls that the "first lord Scudamour sayd ''twas basely sayd of Sir W. R. to talke of the anagramme of Dog.'"

One of the Jesuit Fathers sent as missionaries to Protestant England writes indignantly of "Sir VVwalter Rauleys schoole of Atheisme by the way, and of the Coniurer that is Master thereof"—a palpable dig at Harriot. He also complains gravely that "the olde and new Testaments are iested at, and the schollers taught amonge other thinges, to spell God backwards." Harriot's notes still survive to show that he had been carefully calculating the chronology of Genesis and they leave little doubt whence Marlowe derived the idea—solemnly reported by the government's indefatigably theological spy system—that "the Jndians and many Authors of antiquity haue assuredly writen of aboue 16 thousand yeares agone wher as Adam is proued to haue lived w*i*thin 6 thowsand yeares." Immediately after this scandalous thought (a commonplace in most theological seminaries to-day), the terrible Christopher adds: "that Moyses was but a Jugler, & that one Heriots being S*i*r W Raleighs man Can do more then he." [15] The spy listened in horror, then wrote it all down in an original report still carefully treasured in the British Museum.

Anthony à Wood later asserted of Harriot that "notwithstanding his great skill in mathematics he had strange thoughts of the Scriptures and always undervalued the old story of the Creation of the World, and could never believe that trite position, *ex nihilo nihil fit*. He made a Philosophical theology wherein he cast off the Old Testament, so that consequently the New would have no foundation."

Actually, the diabolical Harriot turns out to have been a quiet, gentle scholar of marked piety. In 1616, when already afflicted with the incurable disease of which he died years later, he wrote to his physician: "I believe in God Almighty, I believe that medicine was ordained by him; I trust the physician as His minister. My faith is sure, my hope is firm." In Virginia, just before Marlowe made his acquaintance, he preached to the Indians with fervour; and the sober old poet, George Chapman, praises his "most blameless life, and the right sacred expence of his time."[16] Raleigh himself was hardly the mocking sceptic that his enemies picture. He once sat up all night to discuss religion with a captive Jesuit, and on the scaffold he affirmed his belief in deity as the headsman stood grimly waiting by the block for him to finish the dying speech that custom granted him.

The general sort of thing that this company of wits and daring philosophers discussed together is made clearer by an official investigation into Raleigh's religious beliefs in the spring of 1594, just after Marlowe's death. The commission was to investigate the views of Sir Walter and his brother Carew, as well as "one Heryott of Sir Walter Rawleigh's house," and various others.[17] Elizabeth's ministers delighted to draw up lists of questions for their suspects to answer, and the list used by these inquisitors gives a pretty clear idea of the sort of thing they were after:

> Whome doe you knowe, or have harde to be suspected of Atheisme; or Apostacye? And in what manner doe you knowe or have harde the same? And what other notice can you geive thereof?
>
> Whome doe you knowe, or have hard, that have argued, or spoken againste? or as doubtinge, the beinge of anye God? Or what or where God is? Or to sweare by god, addinge if there be a god, or such like, and when and where was the same?
>
> Whome doe you knowe or have harde to have sayde, when he was dead his soule shoulde be hanged on the topp of a poale, and ronne god, ronne devill, and fetch it that woulde have it, or to like effecte? or that hath otherwise spoken againste the beinge; or imortallitye of the soule of man? or that a mans soule shoulde dye & become like the soule of a beaste, or such like; and when & where was the same?
>
> What can you saye more of anye of the premisses? or whome have you knowne or harde can geive anye notice of the same? And speake all *your* knowledge therin.

Raleigh, Marlowe, and their circle enjoyed horrifying the

unco' guid. One way of doing it was by smoking tobacco—a new and dreadful practice introduced by Raleigh and his Virginia colonists, regarded with suspicion partly because it was new and partly because it was supposed to blacken the human interior with soot, like a chimney. Harriot's personal notes are full of memoranda about tobacco. Raleigh called for a last whiff of his pipe as he went to the block. Marlowe averred "that all they that loue not Tobacco" were fools.

Unfortunately, one of these enthusiastic lovers of the weed, a certain friend of Raleigh's named Thomas Allen, had torn leaves from a Bible to dry tobacco on. The inquisitors naturally wanted to know all about anything so sinful. Worse still, Allen's servant Oliver, walking home from church with two pious and talkative ladies, Mistress Whetcomb and Mistress Brewer, complained that the sermon was too long. His companions, simple souls who admired the parson, replied that "they were blessed, having so good a ma*n*."[18]

"He vsed many words," said Oliver maliciously, "but might have ended it in fewer, to as great effect."

"He did nothing but out of the word of God," said Mistress Whetcomb, appropriately shocked. "If you love to heare the worde of God you cannot be wearye with hearinge it."

"The word of god saith that Moyses had 52 whores," grinned the flippant Oliver.

"Whores?" cried the indignant Mistress Whetcomb.

"Nay, Concubines," qualified Oliver, intent on getting all possible fun out of the situation, but a little mixed in his Scripture.

"Yt was Salomon," put in Mistress Brewer, who knew her Bible and who also knew men; for she advised Oliver "to goe home to sleepe," since, as she explained to the inquisitors, "she did well p*er*ceaue he was gonne with drincke."

How Oliver managed to get into that deplorable state while attending service must remain a mystery; but both ladies later declared that "there eares did glowe, and that they neu*er* harde such mounsterous speches from anye man." Their lives, perhaps, had been too sheltered.

In the summer of 1593, about the time of Marlowe's death, Raleigh and his brother Carew had been equally incautious in conversation with a local parson, the Reverend Ralph Ironside, and a local magnate, Sir Raulfe Horsey—no less a person than the Queen's Deputy Lieutenant of the County, who was afterwards one of the inquisitors. Like Marlowe, Raleigh enjoyed choosing the very people who could make him the utmost possible trouble and then airing his heresies before them. Raleigh managed very neatly to horrify both hearers.

As the Reverend Mr. Ironside told the commissioners later, he went to the house of another Deputy Lieutenant, Sir George Trencharde, where he found "the knight Sir Walter Rawleigh, Sir Raulfe Horsey, Mr. Carewe Raleigh, Mr. John Fitziames," and some others, talking theology. After supper, Sir Raulfe Horsey felt that "some loose speeches" of Carewe Raleigh ought to be "gentlye reproved,"[19] and he quoted St. Paul in Latin: "Evil communications corrupt good manners." Carewe Raleigh asked "what daunger he might incurr by such speeches."

"The wages of sinn is death," growled the Reverend Mr. Ironside, who like Sir Raulfe Horsey was a little too fond of solemn quotations to be a really merry supper companion. "As that liffe w*hi*ch is the gifte of God through Iesus Christ is liffe eternall: soe that Death w*hi*ch is p*ro*perlye the wages of sinne is death eternall."

"Soule," q*uo*d Mr. Carew Raleigh, "what is that?"

"Better it were," said the Reverend Mr. Ironside, growing more solemn as he grew more indignant, "that we would be carefull how the soules might be saved then to be curiouse in findinge out ther essence."

At this Sir Walter took a hand in the conversation.

"Heitherunto," he said in his Devonshire burr, "in this pointe (to witte, what the reasonable soule of man is) have I not by anye ben resolvd."

The Reverend Mr. Ironside replied with one of his irritating quotations. This time it was Aristotle's *De Anima*—just a little heavy for after supper, especially when he added a few observations on the nature of deity.

"Marrye," cried Sir Walter with impish delight, "These 2 be like, for neither coulde I lerne heitherto what God is." Yet this horrifying free-thinker ended the conversation by calling for prayers.

"For that," q*uod* he, "is better then this disputacon!"

At conversations of this sort, Marlowe must often have made one, and that fact undoubtedly helped on the difficulties that closed in about him toward the end. Raleigh on the other hand, perhaps because of his greater social position, had no great difficulty in clearing himself. The investigation led to nothing. He was soon restored to royal favour and off on another expedition.

THE CAMBRIDGE GROUP

Marlowe's Cambridge acquaintances for the most part became his bitter enemies. He must have been a difficult man to live with. Thomas Kydd certainly found him so when they had lodgings together, and association with him at the University certainly caused very few to love him, though he made friends more easily in later life in London. Thomas Nashe, Robert Greene, and Richard Harvey had all been fellow students at Cambridge. The William Bradley of the duel may have been identical with the William Bradley who was at St. John's College in Marlowe's time. Gabriel Harvey, bitterest of Marlowe's enemies in later life, was a Cambridge don while Marlowe was at Corpus. Robert Poley, who stood by while Ingram Frizer killed the poet, may have been another Cambridge man of the elder Harvey's generation.

Of them all, only Thomas Nashe seems—in spite of one sneer at Marlowe's verse—to have been friendly, and even he sometimes found it difficult to maintain his friendship with Greene and Marlowe at the same time. Still, he heartily hated Gabriel Harvey, who hated Marlowe and Greene impartially. That made it easier, and he wrote pamphlet after pamphlet against Harvey, to which that worthy replied with such asperity that the bishops ultimately stopped the controversy by burning all their books and forbidding them to write any more.

Nashe seems to sneer at Marlowe once or twice, usually when he is defending Greene; but he collaborates with him in *Dido*, he is supposed to have written an elegy paying tribute to his memory, and his pamphlet, *Christ's Teares Over Jerusalem,*[20] alludes to "poore deceased Kit Marlow" in terms of apparently sincere regret. Even when he parodies *Hero and Leander*, it is with a note of admiration for his old associate. It is, he says, a story of lovers whom "diuine Musæus sung, and a diuiner muse than him, Kit Marlow."

Not so Robert Greene, who could find nothing good whatever in his rival Marlowe, whom he admired and hated in about equal degree. Greene's life after the University was a long and rather squalid tragedy. He had always done rather better than Marlowe at Cambridge, and his rival's swift and sudden success in after life was the bitterest of all his many blows. Greene had matriculated at the University in 1575 among the "quadrantarij," the poorest and lowest group among the undergraduates, ranking even below the sizars, whilst Marlowe had been among the pensioners, next to the highest rank. The "quadrantarij" were really only college servants, or "famuli," who were permitted to study. Few of them ever succeeded even in matriculating in the University and fewer still in struggling through to the degree. Greene took five years to secure the bachelor's degree which others took in four years and which is to-day taken in three. Undismayed by this struggle, however, he took an M.A. in 1583, and so was for at least three years at the University at the same time as Marlowe. Nashe was at Cambridge with both at once, studying from 1582 to 1586, when he took his B.A. He seems to have lingered at the University a little longer, then became involved in trouble of some kind, and left in something very like disgrace.

Starting his literary life in London four years earlier than Marlowe, Greene never approached his success. After 1588, he found himself in the humiliating position of a writer who must imitate a junior, grinding out *Alphonsus of Arragon* in imitation of *Tamburlaine;* and *Friar Bacon and Friar Bungay* in imitation of *Doctor Faustus*. But while Marlowe always seems well-to-do, always associates with the rich and powerful, Greene sinks lower and lower. In addition to his plays, he turns off pious and hypocritical pamphlets, one after another—all written in a fluid curiously compounded of ink and tears and alcohol. Married to a gentle and charming girl, he proves himself a faithless and dissolute husband, though some scholars have played with the fancy that in the exquisite character of Greene's heroine in *James IV*, the dramatist is paying tribute to her. Poverty forces him to such straits that he is accused of selling the same play to two rival dramatic companies at once. Involved with a serving wench who bears him a bastard child, he names the wretched infant Fortunatus Greene, and he and the child die not many months apart. The keepers of Greene's shabby lodgings, impressed by the fact that the man was after all an author of sorts, crown his corpse with bay leaves. The body has scarcely been carried away for burial, when the malignant face of Gabriel Harvey pushes in at the doorway, come to learn the worst and triumph over his literary foe. The hatred of authors could go no further.

It is no wonder that after the success of *Tamburlaine* and the first successes of Shakespeare, Greene bursts out in virulent denunciation of his rivals—denunciations so bitter that they were gently pruned by Henry Chettle, who saw Greene's last writings through the press. Even with this decorous editing, Greene's malignant fury almost seems to shriek from the page. He explains the failure of one of his own plays because "I could not make my verses jet upon the stage in tragical buskins, every word filling the mouth like a fa-burden of Bow-bells, daring God out of heaven with that atheist Tamburlaine."[21]

That passage calls for a bit of explanation. Marlowe's *Tamburlaine* does contain the line:

> What daring God torments my body thus?

and Greene seizes upon this to give point to his sneer. To "jet" in Elizabethan English is to "strut"—a hit at the bombast with which *Tamburlaine* and other Marlowe plays are filled. "Bow-bells" are the bells of St. Mary le Bow, known to every Londoner for centuries. "Burden" is a musical term and "fa" is of course a particular note to which the bells are tuned.

Greene also sneers at "mad and scoffing poets that have poetical spirits, as bred of Merlin's race." In the English of that day, "Merlin" was pronounced "Marlin," just as in modern English "clerk" is "clark." Greene had known Marlowe at Cambridge where his name is usually given as "Marlin." The allusion of the word "spirits" is probably to the demons that rise in *Doctor Faustus*. It was all instantly apparent to readers of the day.

Again, Greene sneers at a love passage as a mere "Canterbury tale," told "by a propheticall full mouth that as he were a Cobbler's eldest sonne would by the laste tell where another's shoe wrings." Marlowe might have achieved the rank of gentleman, but if Greene had anything to do with the matter, his humble origin was to be flung in his teeth whenever possible. In his *Farewell to Folly*, published in 1591, Greene shows the typical author's jealousy of another author's sales.

He sneers at "the life of Tomliuclin"—*Tamburlaine*, of course. Pedlars, he says, were wrapping their trinkets in "those vnsauorie papers" which no one would buy otherwise. The first edition of Marlowe's play had appeared a few months earlier.

Greene died September 3, 1592, but not even the approach of death could still his malignant voice. His dying hands penned a tract called *A Groatsworth of Wit Bought with a Million of Repentance*, in which he attacks Marlowe, Nashe, Shakespeare, and others while pretending to exhort them to repentance. The address to Marlowe runs:

> Wonder not, (for with thee wil I first begin), thou famous gracer of Tragedians, that Greene, who hath said with thee like the foole in his heart, There is no God, should now giue glorie vnto his greatnesse: for penitrating is His power, his hand lies heauie vpon me, he hath spoken vnto me in a voice of thunder, and I haue felt he is a God that can punish enimies.

Marlowe, in other words, was not only Greene's enemy—he was God's enemy, too. It was a pleasant thought; and, revolving it deliciously within his darkening brain, Robert Greene died.

Thomas Nashe later[22] called the *Groatsworth of Wit* "a scald triuiall lying Pamphlet"; but he had at one time written an introduction for Greene's novel, *Menaphon*, in which he ridiculed "idiote art-masters, that intrude themselues to our eares as the alcumists of eloquence; who (mounted on the stage of arrogance) think to outbraue better pens with the swelling bumbast of a bragging blank verse." This is "conceited" Elizabethan prose at its obscure worst. It is, indeed, hard to see exactly what it does mean; but it certainly means Marlowe—an "art-master," who had a reputation for arrogance, and who certainly wrote a "bragging blank verse"; and it also certainly means to be unpleasant. Evidently Nashe later repented of his effort to carry water on both shoulders—to be Marlowe's friend and yet abuse him to please Greene.

THE HARVEYS

But none of all these mighty haters hated Marlowe with quite such outspoken virulence as Gabriel Harvey. There were three Harvey brothers, sons of a rope-maker of Saffron Walden, a village near Cambridge. Only two of them—Gabriel and Richard—come into the story. Gabriel, the elder, was fourteen years older than Marlowe. An indefatigable scholar, he was by 1585 B.A., M.A., LL.B. of Cambridge, and D.C.L. of Oxford. In that year, while Marlowe was at the University, he was elected Master of Trinity Hall, but the election was set aside by the Queen, whose advisers evidently knew something of Harvey's temper and the academic furies to which his mastership would probably lead. He had been deputy proctor in 1583, and as such in an excellent position for friction with the obstreperous young man from Canterbury.

Harvey was a close friend of the poet Spenser, with whom he corresponded at length, and is the "Hobbinol" of *The Sheepeardes Calender*. Foiled in his aspirations after academic heights, he retired eventually to his native Saffron Walden and there—on the strength of four degrees in other subjects! —practised medicine.

Why Gabriel Harvey hated Marlowe, no one knows. His brother, Richard, author of *The Lamb of God*, and other works on piety and astrology, had better reason for hatred; of him "Kit Marloe was wont to say that he was an asse good for nothing but to preach of the Iron Age." Marlowe was probably right. As to Richard Harvey's asininity there was a certain unanimity, and even Robert Greene for once agreed with Marlowe. He called the unfortunate Richard "a vaine glorious asse,"[23] though his opinion was later suppressed by the startled publisher and appears in only one surviving copy of his book, *A Quip for an Upstart Courtier*, now in the Huntington Library.

Whatever else may be said of Richard Harvey, he had a nice taste for beautiful books. Gonville and Caius College, Cambridge, still possesses an illuminated manuscript of the Gospels that once was his. The title page has his inscription, which makes the book itself say to the reader: "Sum Ricardi Haruei, 1627 in Chi*f*leherst, in Kent," and there are occasional notes in the beautifully round and flowing calligraphy of the "vaine glorious asse." Looking at it to-day, one thinks of quiet hours in a country rectory, rather than of the savage rancours of the Elizabethan literary world; and to do Richard Harvey justice, there is no record that he ever struck back at his foes. His vehement brother Gabriel was entirely capable of conducting literary hostilities for the entire Harvey family. From about the time of Greene's death in 1592 until after Marlowe's death in 1593—plague or no plague—Harvey was living in London, engaged in some legal business for which, with his two law degrees, he was well qualified. He thus received prompt and accurate news of Greene's death; but of Marlowe's murder he received more confused reports. He thought Marlowe had died of the plague, then raging.

Gabriel Harvey hated Nashe nearly as much as he hated Marlowe and Greene, comparing him—for Nashe had an undeniable liking for the composition of very bawdy verses—to the obscene Italian, Pietro Aretino; Greene to Julian the Apostate; Marlowe to the Greek sceptic, Lucian. He alludes to "no religion but precise Marlowisme," and in his exultant poems on Marlowe's death he describes the murdered poet as

> He that nor feared God, nor dreaded Diu'll,
> Nor ought admired, but his wondrous selfe.

One longs to know the reason for all this malignity writ large. Doubtless there had been long and violent—and very picturesque—squabbles, but to their nature there is no clue today.

GENTRY AND NOBILITY

Raleigh and Northumberland were not the only gentlemen of high degree with whom Marlowe was on terms of intimacy. Kydd alludes to Marlowe's "bearing name to serve my Lord although his Lordship never knew his service, but in writing for his plaiers, ffor never cold my Lord endure his name, or sight, when he had heard of his conditions, nor wold in deed the forme of devyne praier vsed duelie in his Lordships house, haue quadred [i.e., "squared," or "agreed"] with such reprobates." [24] Translated out of Kydd's hysterical epistolatory style, this means that Marlowe wrote for the actors of a certain nobleman. The nobleman was very pious. When he learned that Marlowe was not very pious, he could have nothing more to do with him. Marlowe wrote for the players of Lord Strange, the Lord Admiral, and the Earl of Pembroke; but the description does not fit any of them and probably refers to some other nobleman.

Mr. Thomas Walsingham, of Scadbury, Chislehurst, Kent, is usually regarded as Marlowe's patron When some years after Marlowe's death, Elizabeth visited his home and knighted him, he became the fourth Sir Thomas Walsingham. Of his acquaintance with Marlowe we can be entirely sure. The Privy Council directs its messenger to Walsingham's house when it wants Marlowe arrested, as if it were quite sure of finding him there; and the publisher of one of the two 1598 editions of *Hero and Leander* dedicates the poem to Sir Thomas in the name of "the vnhappily deceased author of this Poem," upon whom the knight had "bestowed many kind fauors, entertaining the parts of reckoning and woorth which you found in him, with good countenance and liberall affection." Marlowe, he said, would have been especially pleased with "the gentle aire of your liking: for since his selfe had ben accustomed thervnto, it would prooue more agreeable and thriuing to his right children [i.e., poems], than any other foster countenance whatsoeuer."

Walsingham was on friendly terms with his second cousin, Sir Francis, Secretary to the Queen and head of the secret service, who had intervened to assist him when he came into his estate. Even after Sir Francis's death, the Privy Council were willing, for his sake, to aid his kinsman when they heard that he was "in danger to suffer great domage in his patrimony by the rigor of divers bondes and statutes." [25]

Many of Marlowe's other associates seem also to have been associates of the Walsinghams. Sir Roger Manwood, whose epitaph Marlowe wrote, was a relative by marriage. Thomas Watson, the poet, had travelled abroad with one of the Walsinghams, either Sir Thomas or his son, probably at the time when Sir Francis was Ambassador in Paris. And of the three men present at Marlowe's murder, two at least were acquainted with his patron.

SPIES, MURDERERS, PERJURERS, ADULTERERS

Ingram Frizer, who killed Christopher Marlowe, is alluded to in legal documents of the time as an agent of Sir Thomas and his daughter, Lady Audrey, for whom he continued to do business long after the murder. Robert Poley, government secret agent who sat in the room while the murder was committed, was acquainted both with Sir Thomas and Sir Francis Walsingham, dealings with whom his letters describe at length. It is a perplexing tangle of relationships.

Ingram Frizer, the murderer, first appears in history in

1589, when he buys the Angel Inn at Basingstoke for £120. He was in and out of the courts most of his life—the Elizabethans were addicted to litigation—and at his death his estate was thrown into the courts and distributed by a judge's "sentence." His most famous exploit was the fraud by which he persuaded a foolish young man, of the sort described in Elizabethan London as a "gull," to buy some old artillery—"a certayne number of gunnes or great Iron peeces." The "gull" signed a bond for £60. Frizer then undertook to sell them for his victim but pretended he could get no more than £30, —his own money, of course. The unfortunate gull now had £30 in hand and a debt to Frizer of £60, while Frizer had recovered his old iron. Later, with the assistance of Nicholas Skeres (also present at the murder), Frizer tricked the credulous youth into signing two fraudulent bonds. One was on behalf of Sir Thomas Walsingham, who is described as Frizer's "master." Long after these events, the youth's indignant mother haled the wily Frizer into court—to meet the defence, not that the charges were false, but merely that it was all a long time ago and they were now outlawed by the passage of time.

Later, Frizer retired to Eltham, Kent, where he became church-warden, tax-collector, and in legal eyes one of the "good and lawful men of the county." He and his wife both died in 1627, leaving one daughter and never dreaming that centuries after his career of fraud and petty scheming had closed forever, people would still be interested in him because of the man he killed.[26]

The mysterious and sinister figure of the government spy and confidential messenger, Robert Poley, may have come into Marlowe's life very early. Many of his original letters, ciphers, and secret reports survive; and they are obviously the work of a man of education. This makes it tempting to identify him with the Robert Pollye who was a chorister of King's College, Cambridge, in 1564 and who matriculated as a sizar of Clare in 1568.[27] As a Cambridge man a few years older than Marlowe, already in the secret service, he may well have been the connecting link between Marlowe's Cambridge and his London life. Spy, adulterer, treacherous friend, only too probably a religious and political turn-coat, he was the least edifying of all Marlowe's associates.

He first appears in the records when sent to the Marshalsea

prison by Sir Francis Walsingham, and thereafter he bobs in and out of prison with reasonable regularity every year or two. Sir Francis was not the first chief of intelligence who found that gaol-birds can be useful in espionage. Released from prison, Poley entered the government secret service, headed by the very man who had sent him to gaol already and was soon to do so again. Poley apparently bore no ill-will and was always ready to go back to his spying when released.

Although a seminary priest had married him to "one Watson's daughter," Poley had long been deep in an amorous intrigue with Mistress Joan Yeomans, wife of a London cutler, William Yeomans. For a time he lodged at Yeomans's home, but for respectability's sake he later went to live at the home of his mistress's mother. The good old soul had no idea what was going on until, coming in from the garden unexpectedly one day, she found her daughter "sittinge vppon the said Polleys knees the sight whereof did soe stryke to her hart that she shoulde never recover yt." She "prayed God to cutt her of verie quickly or ells she feared she shoulde be bawde vnto her owne daughter."[28] Shortly afterward the poor old mother really did die. Poley contrived to get the unfortunate Yeomans thrown into prison, so that he might continue his intrigue with Mistress Yeomans unhampered by an inconvenient husband; and when the husband finally got out of gaol, Poley and the faithless wife eloped together.

Poley was also deeply involved in Anthony Babington's conspiracy to murder Queen Elizabeth and place Mary Queen of Scots on the throne of England. But the secret agent played a part so dark and devious that it is still hard to decide which side he was really on, or whether he changed from side to side. It is most likely that he was on both sides at once. Elizabeth's secret service certainly employed him as a spy; but then, so did the Catholic conspirators. Elizabeth's secret service certainly distrusted him; but then, so did the Catholic conspirators. Both sets of employers were at times inclined to believe in him and at other times to fear he played them false. Both were probably right about that.

As nearly as this tangled web of deceit can be unravelled three centuries later, it appears that Sir Francis Walsingham sent Poley as his spy to join the conspirators. Babington was instantly suspicious. In a letter still extant he writes to Mary's secretary: "I would gladlie understand what opinione you hould of one Robert Pooley whome I find to haue intelligence with her M*aies*tyes occasions. I am private with the man and by the meanes thereof knowe some whate but suspect more."[29] Thomas Morgan, one of Mary's foreign agents, writes that his friends "dout the sayd Poley was sent by England to practise my death in prison." Because of this suspicion, Morgan "wrote not one line with him." Morgan was a wise man, for presently Poley's letters began to be "accidentally" intercepted by the government.

In spite of this bad beginning, Poley soon wormed his way into the conspirators' confidence; and as a result, this double-spy, who was already spying for the government, was placed by the conspirators "to be Sir Phillipp Sidney's man." Sidney was at this time living in the household of his father-in-law, Sir Francis Walsingham. The innocent conspirators thought, in their guileless way, that Poley was "therebye able to picke owt many things."

All this time, the government kept the conspirators' letters passing through official hands, took copies, deciphered them, and sent them on to their destination, occasionally forging a few additions. When at length the police struck, Father Ballard, one of the conspirators, was arrested in Poley's very lodgings, and Poley went to the Tower of London, where he remained for at least two years. The Catholic party asserted that this was a trick to mask the fact that he was a government spy; but with all the conspirators promptly hanged, it is hard to see why he had to be immured for two whole years. More probably the government was a little uncertain what kind of rôle Poley really had been playing and yielded to a long-standing and prevalent impression that gaol was usually a good place for Master Robert Poley.

Poley had been caught with prohibited books about 1586, and had had a stormy interview with Sir Francis Walsingham. But he himself "saied that he putt Mr. Secretary into that heate that he looked out of his wyndoe and grynned like a dogge." Poley denied the charges but told a friend privately that "I will sweare and forsweare my selffe rather then I will accuse my selfe to doe me any harme." Later he admitted "receyvenge, and keepenge of a feawe purposeles Bookes" for a friend—the friend being then in gaol, as seems natural for a friend of Poley's. It was this obvious liar and admitted perjurer whose testimony helped to get Frizer off after the Marlowe murder.

Like Frizer, Poley knew Marlowe's patron, for in one letter he tells of having "attended Mr. Thomas Walsingham for my secrett recourse to Mr. Secretary." [30] In other words, Marlowe's murderer was an accredited agent of Thomas Walsingham, and his friend Robert Poley was acquainted with both branches of the family.

Frizer and Poley must have died about the same time, if we can identify the secret agent with Robert Pooley, "citizen and habberdasher of London," whose will on May 9, 1626, divided a small estate among his family.[31]

Nicholas Skeres is a much less important person than either Frizer or Poley. William Fleetwood, Recorder of London, describes him as one of the "Maisterles men and Cutpurses whose practice is to robbe Gentlemen's Chambers and Artificers' shoppes in & about London." [32] Later, he is listed with Babington "and others of this crew." After Marlowe's murder he appears "in very dangerous company," goes to gaol, and is described as "seruant to the Earl of Essex." Like Poley, he seems to have carried secret messages, and after the Essex rebellion is clapped in gaol once more. Thereafter, he fades into the dim light of the Elizabethan underworld, whence he had emerged.

Thus Marlowe's associates range up and down the scale of social, moral, and intellectual life: the brilliant Raleigh, favourite of the Queen; Harriot, devoted man of science; virtuous old George Chapman; the Walsinghams, respectable country gentry, influential in government; Frizer, the swindler; Poley, the spy; Skeres, the cut-purse and gaol-bird. Strange company in which to write the mighty line.

14.

"Stabd with a Dagger"

"His life like a Canne too full spills vpon the bench."
John Earle: *Micro-Cosmographie* (1628)

In the spring of 1593, the impetuous poet was again in trouble with the authorities—as he had been almost constantly since his last year at Cambridge. If we look back over the six years of his literary career, we find him with amazing regularity in a scrape of some kind. In 1587, the University of Cambridge disapproves of Marlowe so strongly that it will not grant him the usual degree until the Privy Council intervenes. In 1589, he is duelling with Bradley and is sent to prison on murder charges, of which he eventually clears himself. In 1592, he is quarrelling with the constables of Shoreditch. In 1593, the Privy Council, which had been his ally in the squabble at Cambridge, is sending its messenger after him; Thomas Kydd, another erstwhile friend, is making the gravest charges against his conduct and character; government spies are secretly dogging his footsteps and listening to his casual conversation; and he is saved from the trouble that is obviously brewing, only by the unexpected stroke of an assassin's dagger.

Even that may not have been the accident it seems; for there are those who hold that the assassination was secretly arranged by powerful figures in the aristocratic world, who feared the revelations Marlowe might make and procured a murderer to stop the troublesome poet's mouth forever.

Some of this turmoil can be attributed to mere bigotry and stupidity in high places. Cambridge University probably had had nothing more serious against its master of arts than a suspicion of Roman Catholicism. No one knows who was at fault in the quarrel that led to Bradley's death; at all events, it is quite certain that Marlowe did not kill him. A pair of constables who go in fear of their lives because of a single poet are figures of farce, not tragedy. No one knows why the Privy Council demanded Marlowe's presence before it in 1593; Her

Majesty's Councillors frequently called Her Majesty's subjects into their august presence on very trivial grounds.

There were two obvious reasons for the disfavour into which Marlowe was obviously falling. One was the suspicion of atheism which was gradually growing against the whole Marlowe-Raleigh circle, sometimes called the "School of Night." This culminated in the investigation of the religious views of Raleigh and his friends the following year, from which, after much testimony and pious palaver, every one emerged unscathed and Raleigh, restored to royal favour, went on to fresh official preferment.

The other was certain placards, or "libels," against Flemish immigrants, which had been surreptitiously posted up about London and which had led to riots. Thomas Kydd had been accused of having a hand in this—that is why his letter to the Lord Keeper [1] says that he was "suspected for that Libell that concern'd the state." Whatever they were, the libels showed the hand of a literary man. Hence the accusation of Kydd. It turned out that Marlowe and Kydd had roomed together; and the search of Kydd's papers revealed heretical documents. Hence suspicion of both Marlowe and Kydd. That is why Kydd has so much to say about "Marlowe's monstruous opinions," especially "concerning Atheisme, a deadlie thing w*hi*ch J was vndeserved chargd w*i*thall." [2]

There had been a steady immigration of European Protestants to escape the Catholic persecutions; and their increasing number in London and their competition in trade had offended the Elizabethan mob. It is fairly clear that Kydd, finding himself legally involved, was so anxious to clear himself that he made every charge he could think of against his dead friend, though he does not say specifically that Marlowe was involved in the libels. Just treason and atheism—that was all.

Most of this is speculation on reasonable grounds. What we do know positively is that in the middle of May, 1593, a little less than two weeks before Marlowe was murdered, the Privy Council became suddenly very eager to interrogate Christopher Marlowe. On May 18 it issued "a warrant to Henry Maunder one of the Messengers of her Ma*jesty's* Chamber to repaire to the house of Mr Tho: Walsingham in Kent, or to anie other place where he shall understand C*hris*tofer Marlow to be remayning, and by vertue thereof to apprehend and bring him to the Court in his Companie." [3]

The reference to Walsingham makes it perfectly clear that among the eight or nine Christopher Marlowes then flourishing in London, we have the right man.

The plague was at this time raging in the capital, the theatres were closed, and every one who could do so had left the city. Marlowe could not go down to Canterbury, where the plague was equally severe. In less than a month that summer it wiped out Thomas Arthur, supposed to have been the poet's maternal uncle, his wife, and four children. Dorothy Arthur, the only survivor of that stricken family, came to live in John Marlowe's house. It is about this time that the Canterbury accounts contain the grim entry: "Gave to Goodman Eccles for watching at Anthony Howe's Door in the Morning after the Watch was broken up when his House was first infected with the plage. 2d. Abel Payne for watching at several other Doors on the like cause." It was the only thing to do with plague patients: shut them up and let them die.[4]

Elizabethan medicine had no idea of the complex interrelation between the lives of the plague bacillus, rats, lice, and humankind. All the sages of the day knew was that, in some mysterious way, the dreadful disease was "catching." They rather suspected that it was due to divine wrath at the abomination of stage plays; but however that might be, they took both moral and sanitary precautions. They closed the playhouses (a precaution which contained a little of both elements); they burned the bodies of the dead; and they closed all suspected dwellings. A memory of the terror of those fearful visitations still survives in our modern proverb about avoiding something "like the plague."

Marlowe, having nothing to do in London, with the theatres closed and the actors travelling in the provinces, and being unable to return to his father's house (which there is no record of his having seen since his departure for the University), bethought him of his friend Thomas Walsingham. He went down to the Walsingham estate at Scadbury, Chislehurst, which is far enough out of London in the Kentish countryside to be safe from infection, and close enough to London to keep in touch with his literary and theatrical interests there, as soon as the outbreak of plague ceased.

Since there was no market for plays at the moment, he was probably peacefully at work upon his poem of *Hero and Leander*, when Master Henry Maunder and his warrant arrived together. The Queen's Messenger had had very little difficulty in finding his man; for two days after the issue of the warrant—barely time to ride down to Chislehurst and back—the Privy Council records that [5]

> This day Chr*ist*ofer Marley of London gent, being sent for by warrant from their Lord*ships* hath entered his appearance accordinglie for his Jndemnity therein, and is commaunded to give his daily attendaunce on their Lord*ships* untill he shalbe lycensed to the contrary.

With that, the whole matter vanishes from the records. Within a few days, Marlowe was dead. Whatever the Privy Council wanted, it could not get it now—unless, as three hundred years later, scholars began to whisper, some powerful personage wanted Marlowe hushed up about something and to attain this end took the most direct means of silencing him. In that case, some one—not necessarily on the Privy Council—had gained exactly what he wished.

That is, in all likelihood, too sinister an interpretation of the facts, though not by any means impossible. Her Majesty's Council do not seem to have been greatly worried about young Marlowe. They wanted him, so they sent for him. After his appearance, they decided that they still wanted him, so they ordered him to appear daily. If they had been really worried about him, they would have clapped him in the Tower without further ceremony.

The Lords of the Privy Council often sent urgently for the Queen's subjects, both of very great and of very little importance; and then did practically nothing about it when they appeared. The President of Corpus Christi, Oxford, for instance, had been summoned like Marlowe a few weeks earlier, but he seems to have suffered no further inconvenience. A certain Mistress Anne Rolles, summoned before their Lordships in a dispute over an estate, simply sent word that she "was not well at ease, and thereby (thoughe she was in towne) not in case to repair hether." Their Lordships, gallantly unwilling to disturb a lady, politely agreed to await Mistress Anne's convenience, stipulating only that she "shuld not depart till leave were graunted unto her," [6] which was really all they insisted on in Marlowe's case.

The whole affair, whatever it was, may have been trivial, and it may be mere coincidence that it was preceded by charges of atheism and followed by murder. At least, the Reverend Richard Harvey, rector of Chislehurst and brother of the malignant Gabriel, seems never even to have heard of the arrest; and Gabriel Harvey, who a few months later is whooping with delight over Marlowe's death, never mentions the affair. Gabriel Harvey was not a man who ever failed to bring out anything to Marlowe's discredit. The arrest at Chislehurst must have been very quietly managed indeed if no hint of it reached the long and eager ears of the Harveys, either of whom would have rejoiced at any bad news affecting Marlowe; partly because they resented his bitter tongue; partly also because they must have held him to blame for some of the bitter attacks on them by his friends Nashe and Watson.

Marlowe was now rather at loss for lodgings. The plague-stricken city was dangerous, yet he was officially bidden to be there daily, attending the Privy Council's wishes. It would have been a little embarrassing to go back to Chislehurst from which Master Henry Maunder had taken him, under arrest, only a day or two before. Then, too, Chislehurst was a little too far out from London to make it convenient to go back and forth daily. Probably Marlowe went to the little village of Deptford, just across the Thames from London and a few miles down stream, where, it has been surmised, the wealthy and respectable Anthony Marlowe, agent for the Muscovy Company, may have been a kinsman.[7]

In Deptford, at least, we find him ten days later when he walks through the door of a tavern kept by Dame Eleanor Bull, widow, at Deptford Strand, about ten o'clock in the morning of May 30, 1593. With him were three extremely doubtful characters: Ingram Frizer, Robert Poley, and Nicholas Skeres.

The four men had no desire for the company of the ordinary folk who frequented Dame Eleanor's tavern, but called for a private room "& there passed the time together & dined & after dinner were in quiet sort together there & walked in the garden belonging to the said house until the sixth hour after noon of the same day & then returned from the said garden to the room aforesaid & there together and in company supped."[8]

There was obviously something extremely private in the wind. All except Frizer—and perhaps Frizer too, though of that we have no evidence—had been concerned in minor affairs of state, which were sometimes shady and which were always confidential. The four stayed away from the tavern ordinary, at which Elizabethan gallants usually mingled freely. They took two meals in private, had enough private conversation to keep them busy from ten in the morning until six at night, and seem in every way to have kept very much to themselves.

Poley, who had gone to The Hague earlier in the month, hurried home that very day, carrying official correspondence [9] which may or may not have had something to do with the conversation. Frizer, being associated with Thomas Walsingham, would know all about Marlowe's difficulties with the Privy Council, and probably all about the difficulties in which Marlowe's former roommate, Thomas Kydd, found himself. Skeres had been privy to Frizer's schemes several times before.

The quartet had had two meals together, which almost certainly means that they had between them consumed a good deal of drink—Marlowe's buttery account at Corpus Christi indicates pretty clearly that he was not averse to the glass that cheers. After supper in their private room, Frizer, Poley, and Skeres sat down to a game of "tables," or backgammon,[10] while Marlowe lay down on a bed behind them—perhaps in tribute to the potency of Dame Eleanor's liquors. His three companions were sitting side by side on a bench—chairs being rare articles of furniture in Elizabethan taverns—with their knees under the table, intent upon their game. Frizer was wearing the usual dagger at his side, and finding it in his way, slung it around so that it hung down behind him over the edge of the bench—temptingly within reach from where Marlowe was lying. The others were probably similarly armed; but it is this twelve-penny dagger of Frizer's that matters. The four may also have had their swords with them; but if so they had probably been taken off and left with their cloaks.

While the game went on, Marlowe fell into a dispute with Frizer over the bill. According to one account,[11] Marlowe was the guest of "one named Ingram [Frizer, of course] that had invited him thither to a feast." If that is true, it is no wonder that when Marlowe was confronted with the bill, he and Frizer "were in speech & uttered one to the other divers malicious words for the reason that they could not be at one nor agree about the payment of the sum of pence, that is, le recknynge." Thomas Kydd was probably at this very moment in prison meditating the letters in which he declares that Marlowe was "intemperate & of a cruel hart," and accuses him of "rashnes in attempting soden pryvie iniuries to men."[12] Once again Marlowe proved the correctness of Kydd's estimate of his character, just as he had in the Bradley duel.

Infuriated by the dispute and probably more than a little drunk, he snatched at Frizer's dagger, got it out of the sheath before any one could stop him, and "maliciously gave the aforesaid Ingram two wounds on his head of the length of two inches & of the depth of a quarter of an inch." It is hard to see how an angry man striking downward at a seated opponent with a stout steel blade could have inflicted nothing worse than a couple of scalp wounds, if he was really trying to kill. But Marlowe may have reversed the dagger and tried to "knock out" his opponent with the heavy hilt, so as to do no fatal injury.

That would leave the blade of the dagger pointing upward and toward his own face. Frizer was caught with his knees under the table and a man on each side of him, while the furious poet was slashing at him from above. Unable to rise, he turned round and caught Marlowe's arm. Or, as the official record has it, Frizer "in his own defence & for the saving of his own life, then & there struggled with the said Christopher Morley to get back from him his dagger aforesaid; in which affray the same Ingram could not get away from the said Christopher Morley."

Finding himself caught and unable to disarm his opponent, Frizer seized Marlowe's hand and the dagger together, and drove the blade back. His blow caught Marlowe in the right eye and crashed back into the frontal lobe of the brain. Or, as the coroner's report rehearses the story, "So it befell in that affray that the said Ingram, in defence of his life, with the dagger aforesaid of the value of 12*d.* gave the said Christopher then & there a mortal wound over his right eye of the depth of two inches & of the width of one inch; of which mortal wound the aforesaid Christopher Morley then & there instantly died."[13]

As a matter of fact, injuries to the frontal lobe of the brain, though fatal, do not cause instant death but a prolonged coma, which is followed by death. This was a fact perfectly familiar to Elizabethan coroners to whose attention circumstances often forcibly directed it. There was, for a specially violent and gory example, the murder of one James Feake by Gabriel Spencer, the actor whom Ben Jonson killed a year later. The men quarrelled, "Feake having in his hand a certain candelabrum of copper called a candle stick, worth sixpence, which he then and there had in his right hand, and held with the intention to throw it at the said Gabriel Spencer, having a sword called a rapier of iron and steel of the price of five shillings, being in the scabberd." Without waiting to draw, Spencer struck "with the sword being in the aforesaid scabberd," and inflicted, as one might expect, "a mortal wound, six inches deep and two inches wide, on the face, that is to say, between the pupil of the right eye, called the ball of the eye, and the eyebrows, penetrating to the brain." Yet, though thus horribly mangled, Feake "languished and lived in languor 3 days," before he finally died.[14]

The statement that Marlowe "then & there instantly died" is either the careless use of a common legal phrase; or else the three excited men, looking down at the victim, mistook his coma for death.

This assumes that the story they told the coroner was true; but none of them was remarkable for veracity. If the men were lying, their story—which is, medically speaking, impossible—may cover cold-blooded and deliberately planned assassination. If so, their lie succeeded, for its accuracy was never questioned until in recent years the evidence has been examined by modern physicians.[15] The coroner was not even curious enough to ask why three men were unable to overpower one man and disarm him without killing him. If the official version of the murder is true, Marlowe must indeed have been a terrible fellow, against whom two constables, or even three ordinary mortals, were entirely helpless.

If we accept the view that there is more here than appears on the surface, and that Marlowe was deliberately put out of the way, much that is hard to understand in the official papers becomes clear enough. His three companions did not try to overpower and disarm Marlowe because they were in a plot to kill him. Their demand for privacy was part of the plot; and the long time they spent together was necessary to get Marlowe drunk enough so that he could be easily dealt with. Frizer shows only two scalp wounds after this desperate encounter because he never was in any real danger. He may have given himself a few slashes to make his story credible—an old device. The coroner may have been so notably incurious because he had been given a quiet hint from some one in authority not to ask too many questions. After all, he was an official of the Queen's own Court, amenable to influence from powerful courtiers. The statement that Marlowe died instantly from a wound that could not possibly have killed him instantly may be part of the general fabrication necessary to cover up the murder.

And the motive? If this idea is correct, the whole atheistic Marlowe-Raleigh circle was becoming suspect. Kydd had been arrested, charged both with atheism and with the "Libell that concern'd the state." Kydd was in prison, where he could be controlled. But Marlowe was at large, was about to come before the Privy Council, and might tell too much. It was wise to silence him.

It is a pretty theory but not really very convincing. We have only the conclusions of the coroner's jury; we do not know what witnesses they summoned or what evidence they heard. Very likely they checked with the utmost care all statements made to them. The only powerful courtier who could have been in danger at this time was Sir Walter Raleigh. The investigation of his religious views the following year seems to have made him little trouble—though of course that may have been so because Marlowe was out of the way.

Whatever the motive for the murder, its sequel is fully recorded. Frizer "neither fled nor withdrew himself," action which helped establish the presumption of his innocence. Queen Elizabeth happened to be somewhere in the vicinity—probably at Kew, from which Frizer's pardon[16] is dated—and this brought Deptford "within the verge," a circle of twelve miles which surrounded the person of the Sovereign wherever she went. The Marlowe murder thus came within the jurisdiction of the Queen's own coroner, William Danby, and not under that of the local authorities. Frizer seems to have had little difficulty—much less than Thomas Watson had had four years earlier when he killed William Bradley.

Marlowe was killed on Wednesday evening, May 30, 1593. The inquest was held Friday, June 1. His body could not be buried until the coroner's jury had viewed it; but it was taken to the Church of St. Nicholas, Deptford, and buried the same day—probably in the churchyard, since burial within most

Elizabethan churches was a privilege rigidly restricted. It was all very well for a solid and respectable citizen like William Shakespeare, Gent., of Stratford, one of the wealthiest men in the town, to be buried within the parish church—though even he feared that a later and impious generation might "digge the dust" enclosed there. But burial within the church was hardly to be hoped for by a scapegrace poet, known to be of "monstruous opinions," who had been killed in a tavern brawl.

The Court of Chancery issued a writ of certiorari on Friday, June 15, inquiring of Coroner Danby whether Frizer had killed Marlowe with malice aforethought (and therefore feloniously) or whether the killing was in self-defence (and therefore innocent, or at least such as to entitle him to a pardon). The coroner reported the finding of his jury, that Frizer had killed Marlowe in self-defence; and Frizer was a free man. Thomas Walsingham, Marlowe's supposed patron, continued to employ him, as a later transaction, recorded in the legal documents of the time, shows.

The murder created a sensation even in plague-stricken London; and the Puritan divines soon found in it evidence of heaven's judgment against all "play-makers and poets of scurillitie." But the first on the scene of the tragedy, as usual, was that carrion-crow, Gabriel Harvey, who had been engaged in legal business in London for nearly a year.[17] Just as he had rushed off with glee to learn the worst the moment he heard of Robert Greene's death, so now he bursts into print with an unintelligible farrago called *A Newe Letter of Notable Contents.* This contains a "poem" called "Gorgon, or the Wonderfull Yeare," the poem being quite as wonderful as the year it purports to describe—obviously 1593, since the title page is so dated. This contains the line:

> Weepe Powles, thy Tamberlaine voutsafes to dye,

and then adds a "glosse," quite as obscure as the poem it pretends to interpret, which tells how death,

> smiling at his tamberlaine contempt,
> Sternely struck-home the peremptory stroke.

It is not possible to make anything intelligible of this windy nonsense, which is really only a savage's war-whoop at a foe's death. "Tamberlaine" is a clear allusion to Marlowe, and

"Powles" is, of course, St. Paul's Cathedral—the haunt of "some stationers in Paules churchyard," whom Kydd mentions [18] among "such as he conversd w*i*thall." The only thing these drivelling lines are intended to convey—in their vague and cloudy way—is that Harvey, never what you might call a sensitive and scrupulous person, has heard of his enemy's death and is hugely pleased. He does not mention the murder, because he is under the impression that Marlowe has died of the plague. Harvey would probably have been still happier and would have reached even more confused lyric heights if he had known the truth.

To Puritan preachers in search of edifying and also thrilling sermon material, the murder was a godsend; and they rang the changes on it through one edition after another of their devotional books of moral counsel. Theirs was the only account of the murder that got beyond the official records, which soon disappeared into the official files, where they lay forgotten for the next 330 years. As a result the Puritans, with the very best intentions, started a story about Marlowe's death and "atheism," which had a very long life and acquired various trimmings—notably the tale of the "lewd wench," for the sake of whose sinful favours Marlowe was supposed to have battled with his foe. For most of this there was not a scintilla of evidence; but a story which is at once thrilling, horrifying, edifying, and a trifle sexy, has a long life; and the apocryphal lady and her apocryphal sins were described by moralists for centuries.

The first of this crew is the Reverend Thomas Beard, a divine noted for the Puritan zeal with which, as a contemporary says, he "painfully preached the word of God." [19] He was a school-master who taught Oliver Cromwell, and who—surely no ordinary man—is said to have flogged the Lord Protector in early youth.

Beard was heart and soul in the Puritan cause. In his highly popular book, *The Theatre of Gods Judgments,* he set out to discredit the stage and the Papacy, together with all anti-Puritans. Here, ready to his hand, was the sensational murder of "a play-maker and poet full of scurrilitie," who had long been suspected of Roman Catholic leanings and who was certainly no Puritan. The result was a passage which, though mostly a tissue of well-intentioned lies, deserves to be quoted if only for the vehemence of its rhetoric:[20]

> Marlin, by profession a scholler . . . but by practice a playmaker and a poet full of scurrilitie, who by giving too large a swing to his own wit, and suffering his lust to have full reines, fell (not without just desert) to that outrage and extremitie, that he denied God and his sonne Christ, and not only in word blasphemed the Trinitie, but also, as it is credibly reported, wrote bookes against it, affirming our Saviour to be but a deceiver, and Moses to be but a conjurer and seducer of the people, and the holy Bible to bee but vaine and idle stories, and all religion but a device of pollicie. But see what a hooke the Lord put in the nostrils of this barking dogge!
>
> It so fell out, that in London Streets, as he purposed to stab one whome hee ought a grudge, unto with his dagger, the other party perceiving so avoided the stroke, that withall catching hold of his wrest, he stabbed his owne dagger into his owne head, in such sort that notwithstanding all the meanes of surgerie that could be wrought, he shortly after died thereof; the manner of his death being so terrible (for he even cursed and blasphemed to his last gaspe and together with his breath an oath flew out of his mouth) that it was not only a manifest sign of God's judgment, but also a horrible and fearefull terror to all that beheld him. But herein did the justice of God most notable appeare, in that he compelled his owne hand which had written those blasphemies, to bee the instrument to punish him, and that in his brains which had devised the same.

Like so many of the devout, Beard found moral abuse and moral fervour rather easier than the pursuit of fact, and fell into several errors. Marlowe was not killed "in London Streets." But in Greenwich, which immediately adjoins Dame Eleanor's Deptford tavern, there is a thoroughfare called "London Street." It may be said in Beard's favour that he corrected the blunder by omitting the words in his second edition.

If Marlowe was really stabbed where the coroner's jury, after viewing the body and its wounds, said he was stabbed, it is certainly not true that he "cursed and blasphemed to his last gaspe and together with his breath an oath flew out of his mouth." Marlowe must have been unconscious long before the end; but Beard's version was a good, sound, conventional picture of the atheist's death-bed, the sort of thing people liked and expected; and the story spread.

It spread to Canterbury, where it came to the ears of an old gentleman of no particular importance named Simon Aldrich. He had a friend in one Henry Oxinden, scion of a family of Kentish gentry, who spent his life largely in pruning his fruit trees, tending his garden, reading his large library, and writing down his thoughts on the margins of his books and in two large commonplace books. The two latter have survived and they provide an entirely independent version of the Marlowe murder as it was told by old Simon Aldrich, a contemporary who must often have passed old John Marlowe and his wife in the narrow Canterbury streets.

Oxinden wrote down the story as Aldrich told it to him in February of 1640, in a commonplace book now in the British Museum. He copied it again in a later and better commonplace book, now in the Folger Shakespeare Library; and for some strange reason he wrote it out still a third time on a fly-leaf of his copy of the now rare 1629 *Hero and Leander.* There it was found about 1830; but unfortunately it was found and published by John Payne Collier, the notorious forger. After his earlier frauds had been exposed, no one would believe anything Collier said; and Aldrich's account of the matter was completely discredited until a few years ago, when both commonplace books turned up to confirm the story. In the meantime, the mysterious copy of *Hero and Leander* which few had ever seen disappeared completely. The London book dealer, P. J. Dobell, sold it to an unknown purchaser; and even the photograph of the all-important inscription which had been made about 1880 also disappeared.

But the commonplace books remain, the earlier one in the British Museum, the other in the Folger Shakespeare Library. No one questions their authenticity. They deal mostly with Marlowe's supposed atheism, but each ends with the sentence: "He was stabd with a dagger and dyed swearing," thus confirming Beard.[21]

Beard's book had an enormous influence. It ran through at least four editions; and as late as 1659 still a fifth version had been prepared in manuscript.[22] Its story of the atheist's death was instantly caught up by other pious writers, among them one Edmund Rudierd, in a lurid tome entitled *The Thunderbolt of God's Wrath.*[23]

More than fifty years after the murder, Beard's account of it was still being copied for purposes of moral edification by a London parson, the Reverend Samuel Clark, or Clarke, whose *Looking-Glasse both for Saints and Sinners* appeared in March, 1645/6, at a time when the Puritans were masters in London and players and playwrights had been completely suppressed. The Reverend Samuel had himself written a *Life of Tamerlane the Great;* but he had probably never heard of Marlowe's play, and certainly did not admit it if he had. His story is nearly word-for-word from Beard.

William Vaughan, however, the author of *The Golden Grove,* which appeared in 1600, seems to have done a little independent investigating for himself. His account of the murder gives Frizer's first name and the place of the murder correctly.[24]

The Return from Parnassus, an anonymous Cambridge University play which comments freely on many of the poets and playwrights of the day, echoes ancient Cambridge rancours in its four lines about Marlowe:[25]

> . . . happy in his buskine muse,
> Alas, vnhappy in his life and end,
> Pitty it is, that wit so ill should dwell
> Wit lent from heauen, but vices sent from hell.

The tale about the "lewd wench" is first set afloat by a certain Francis Meres, who in 1598 published a book called *The Wits Treasury.* A great admirer of contemporary writers, he gives a great deal of valuable early information about Marlowe, Shakespeare, and their fellows; but literary enthusiasm carried him away. He was eager to compare Marlowe with "Iodelle, a French tragicall poet, beeing an epicure and an atheist," and with the Greek poet-actor who, Ovid says, was killed by a rival in love. Hence, after explaining how "our tragicall poet Marlow for his Epicurisme and Atheism had a tragical death," he refers to Beard and closes his own account with a passage that explains how:[26] "As the poet Lycophron was shot to death by a certaine rival of his: so Christofer Marlow was stabd to death by a bawdy servingman, a rival of his in his lewde loue."

That was enough; the tale was started; and nearly a hundred years later the antiquary Anthony à Wood, writing the lives of Oxford graduates (with whom Marlowe had nothing to do), drags a thinly disguised quotation from Meres, sinful lady and all, into his *Athenae Oxonienses:*[27]

> He being deeply in love with a certain woman, had for his rival a bawdy serving-man, one rather fit to be a pimp, than an ingenious amoretto as Marlo conceived himself to be. Whereupon Marlo taking it to be a high affront, rush'd in

> upon, to stab him, with his dagger: But the serving-man being very quick, so avoided the stroke, that withal catching hold of Marlowe's wrist, he stab'd his own dagger into his head in such sort, that notwithstanding all the means of surgery that could be wrought, he shortly after died of his wound, before the year 1593.

It ought to be clear by this time how this story arose. Meres touches up his copy with some apt comparisons, and thereby starts a slander which lasts until publication of the official documents describing Marlowe's death—in 1925. Anthony à Wood is so entranced by the spiciness of the tale that he drags the Cambridge poet into a book about Oxford. Thereafter, one industrious chronicler after another quotes his predecessors, the tale growing larger and larger and the lady wickeder and wickeder down the centuries.

Had there been any evidence for the existence of this wench, Frizer would have been glad enough to bring her out at the inquest; and the Puritans would not have missed so choice a morsel for an instant. If the admiring Meres had only been able to control his enthusiasm for comparative literature, this particular libel against Marlowe's memory would never have gained a start upon the truth. As it is, the erring lady simply will not die. Born in Meres's too fertile brain, she lives merrily on until the year 1917, when she makes (let us trust) her last and positively final appearance in a devout cleric's article upon "Marlowe and the Heavy Wrath of God," [28] which concludes darkly that "the evils of Marlowe's chief characters were also Marlowe's own, and he, like these characters, fell to be plagued in hell."

The chief contributors to the long life of this frail and fictitious damsel were the compilers of theatrical handbooks. Toward the end of Queen Bess's reign, the book-buying public was not only eager to buy play-books, but also began to develop an interest in the lives of the dramatists—something entirely new. This demand was met under William and Mary by a flood of little "playhouse companions," alphabetical "Who's Who's" to the British stage for the last century, giving thumbnail biographies of the authors, lists of their plays, and even lists of the sources from which those plays were taken.

The book-sellers soon hit upon the modern device of including a list of their other plays in an advertising page inserted at the back of each edition. By the middle 1600's, these had become voluminous catalogues, giving rough lists of all the important authors and all their plays, usually with a good many other plays that they had not written. Four reasonably complete lists of this sort appear between 1656 and 1671.[29] Similar compilations were numerous in the middle and latter eighteenth century.

These industrious hacks copied from each other and reviled each other with equal impartiality, and they snatched up information of all kinds without very carefully examining its source. One of them, William Rufus Chetwode, in his *British Theatre* (1752), reveals the talents of a cinema scenario writer born a hundred and fifty years too soon:[30]

> Having an intrigue with a loose woman, he came unexpectedly into her Chamber, and caught her in the Embraces of another Gallant. This so much enraged him, that he drew his Dagger and attempted to Stab him; but in the Struggle, the Paramour seized Marlow, turnd the Point into his Head, and killed him on the spot in 1592.

J. P. Kemble, the actor, noted in his copy of the *Theatrical Intelligencer* that Marlowe "died about 1592 of a wound received in a brothel from his own sword being forced upon him." Fortunate, indeed, for Kemble that Dame Eleanor Bull never heard her tavern so described!

Modern writers have operated on these misleading data with lamentable results. The third edition of the *Encyclopaedia Britannica* describes the lady as a "low girl." The brothers Didot in their *Nouvelle Biographie Générale* explain her as "une fille de basse condition"; Hippolyte Taine calls her a "drab"; and Iwan Bloch in 1912 casts her into the rough embraces of a brutal and licentious soldiery as simply "eine Soldatendirne." There is not a trace of real evidence for any of this, but in 1917 she still remains "a disreputable wench." Three hundred years of sound and fury and bad names over nothing, all because Master Francis Meres's pen slipped into a needlessly fine flourish one day in 1598! He got a little sex-interest into his story; but he misled history for three hundred years.

The true story was revealed by Dr. John Leslie Hotson's discovery of the coroner's inquest, the chancery writ, and Ingram Frizer's pardon, which he published in 1925.[31] The long series of errors which these documents corrected had really begun when the vicar of the Church of St. Nicholas, Deptford, blundered in entering the record of Marlowe's burial in his register on June 1, 1593. That entry, correctly read, runs:

Christopher Marlow slaine by ffrancis ffrezer; the . 1 . of June.

As there had never been a *Francis* Frizer, this placed a first stumbling block in the way of future researchers, but as there was no particular interest in the matter for the next two hundred years, it did not really matter very much. In 1820, the English antiquary, James Broughton, author of the first extensive critical account of Marlowe and his work, inquired of the vicar of St. Nicholas and was told that the murderer's name was given as "Ffrancis *Archer*."[32] This set scholars questing for a mysterious being, both of whose names were wrong, of whom nobody had ever heard and of whom no one could ever find a trace, except the usual Bacon-Shakespeare sciolist who presently discovered the non-existent Archer in the usual cryptogram.

The two innocent vicars of St. Nicholas, between them, thus misled scholars completely; but the later one, at least, must not be too greatly blamed. The "ff," often used in Elizabethan times instead of a capital, with which his predecessor had begun Frizer's name, *does* look a good deal like a capital "A" to any one not thoroughly familiar with Elizabethan handwriting. Hasted's *History of Kent* later gave nearly the correct reading, "Frezer," another investigator made it "Frazer," and Sir Sidney Lee, in writing Marlowe's life for the Dictionary of National Biography, hesitated to decide; but none of this was any use so long as the first name stood as "Francis," the original vicar's blunder.

Meantime a clue lurked undetected in the account of the murder given by William Vaughan, who in 1600 had said that the murderer was "one named Ingram"—which every one mistook for a surname. Actually, Elizabethan records frequently use the Christian name in preference to the surname. In Dr. Hotson's own documents, Frizer is called "the said Ingram" and Marlowe "the said Christopher." The Corpus Christi records occasionally refer to Archbishop Parker as "the said Mathu." Gabriel Spencer, whom Ben Jonson killed, is twice called simply "one Gabriel" in the indictment.[33]

When, therefore, Dr. Hotson stumbled on the name of "Ingram Frizer" at the Public Record Office, he instantly suspected the truth. The document in which he found it had nothing to do with Marlowe; but it did prove that Queen Elizabeth numbered among her subjects a man with *both* the names that had been given as the murderer's. If there was an Ingram Frizer in existence, then Vaughan might be right about one half of the name and the Burial Register at Deptford might be right about the other half.

Following up this fragmentary and still doubtful clue, Dr. Hotson discovered in a list of pardons an entry recording a grant to "Ingramo ffrisar" on June 28, 1593, just four weeks and a day after Marlowe had been killed. At that very instant, the Public Record Office closed for the day—a proceeding about which there is always a certain firmness—and the discoverer was left the whole of one very long night to wonder whether he had made one of the literary discoveries of all time, or whether he had merely found another mare's nest. In the morning he was able to send for the documents themselves, which told the true story already recounted here. The secret of Marlowe's death was a secret no longer.

15.

Poetic Interludes

"And from my hands the reines will slip away."
Elegies

Of Marlowe's three minor plays, two were written in collaboration; and of these two, one is completely lost. It would have made little difference to his reputation if all three had been lost; but we should have been denied some fascinating and unexpected glimpses into the poet's mind.

Still a fourth play bears Marlowe's name upon the title page; but the evidence for his authorship is late and untrustworthy, and it is a full century since any critic has ventured to include it in a collected edition of his works. This is *Lust's Dominion, or the Lascivious Queen*—a much milder play than one might guess from its flamboyant title. There is no real reason for regarding this as Marlowe's, except that the publisher who brought out the first edition in 1657 placed his name upon the title page and repeated it in the editions of 1658 and 1661, of which the title pages alone survive.

A few early writers on the theatre attribute the play to Marlowe; and it was actually included in the two earliest editions of his complete works, while both William Hazlitt and Charles Lamb regarded it as genuine. Further study, however, shows how impossible this is. The death of Philip of Spain is an important part of the play, too completely integral to have been written in by any possible reviser; and it did not occur until 1599, six years after the poet's death. To make matters clearer still, several lines are copied from a source pamphlet, also published after Marlowe's death.

Since 1825, no one has seriously regarded the play as Marlowe's. It is now generally believed that it dates from 1600, a period when other playwrights were still doing their best to imitate Marlowe; that it is the work of some writer strongly under his influence; and that perhaps it may even be a rewriting of some very early and completely forgotten Marlowe manuscript, preserving here and there a few lines of his genuine handiwork.

In one way or another, a number of other old plays have survived, like this one, without any indication of authorship; and critics who believe that they can tell by looking at a play or poem the name of the man who wrote it, have busied themselves for generations with speculation as to their authorship. Many of these have been fathered on Shakespeare—sometimes for the most ludicrous reasons. The banal tragedy of *Mucedorus* was claimed for him on no better grounds than the accident that Charles II's bookbinder had bound it with his accepted plays. Critics who can believe in the plenary inspiration of bookbinders can believe in anything; and some have not been slow to impute to Christopher Marlowe a number of the better waifs and strays and orphans of Elizabethan drama, who still lack authors. Occasionally their attributions may be right, as when the two source plays which preceded Shakespeare's *Henry VI* are on highly rational grounds believed to have been at least in part from Marlowe's pen.

More frequently the reasoning seems to run: "Here is a play bereft of an author. Here is Marlowe, an author almost certainly bereft of several lost plays. Let us put the two together, and all will be well."

Among the plays thus claimed for Marlowe have been *Selimus, Locrine, Edward III, The Troublesome Reign of King John, The True History of George Scanderbage, An Alarum for London*, and *Arden of Feversham*. The first two, which deal with the legendary history of Britain, to which Milton makes some allusion in *Comus*, are closely related to each other and are probably by the same author, but there is no reason to suppose that author was Marlowe, except that the style is vaguely like his or an imitator's—and his imitators were extraordinarily abundant.

The only reasons for assigning *Edward III* to Marlowe are a supposed resemblance in the style, and a passage in Robert Greene's *Francesco's Fortunes:* "If the Cobler hath taught thee to say Aue Cæsar, disdain not thy tutor." People who enjoy riddles have assumed that "the Cobler" was Marlowe, and have pointed out the undoubted fact that the words, "Ave Cæsar" appear in *Edward III* and in no other Elizabethan play. So far as evidence from style is concerned, it is enough to say with Swinburne that "the author of 'King Edward III,' was a devout student and humble follower of Christopher Marlowe." The other argument is hardly evidence at all.

Arden of Feversham is a fine piece of work, which has also been assigned to Shakespeare. The unknown author has caught a few of Marlowe's tricks of expression and occasionally quotes a line or two of his known work; but on such a basis, Marlowe might be the author of the entire first half of the Elizabethan drama, for nearly all the early authors imitate him and quote him copiously. There is no better reason for regarding the other plays as Marlowe's, though in some cases writers may be influenced by him or may even be re-writing still earlier plays in which he really had had a hand years before.

The two authentic Marlowe plays which still survive are *The Massacre at Paris*, a violently Protestant historical play, based on the Massacre of St. Bartholomew's and subsequent events in the French wars of religion, which were both bloody and violent enough to suit Elizabethan theatrical taste; and *Dido, Queene of Carthage*, written in some kind of collaboration (there is a good deal of doubt just how much or what kind) with his friend Thomas Nashe. Still another Marlowe play, now lost, was *The Maiden's Holiday*, which disappeared forever when an unappreciative eighteenth century cook used the sole surviving manuscript to put under her pies.

This play was entered for publication in the Stationers' Register, April 8, 1654, more than half a century after Marlowe's death, and is there ascribed to his collaboration with John Day (1574?-1619). As Day had been a mere boy at Marlowe's death, it is hard to see how they could have collaborated, though Day may later have brought an old Marlowe manuscript up to date. The play is described as a comedy, which may mean that we have lost Marlowe's only experiment in this vein; or may mean only that the publisher is making the same mistake as that other publisher who described *Tamburlaine* as "twooe commicall discourses."

No printed copy has survived, and there is some doubt whether the publisher ever issued any. The only reason for thinking that he did is a remark in David Erskine Baker's *Companion to the Playhouse* (1764) that Marlowe "also joined with Day in the Maiden's Holyday. 1654";[1] but Baker may merely have been reading the Stationers' Register and have taken it for granted that the play was really published.

Most of the Marlowe editions printed as late as this survive in several copies, which is an additional reason for doubting that this totally unknown play ever saw print at all.

On the other hand, there is always the chance that copies may still be lying about old country houses in forgotten lumber rooms, or may be concealed in Continental libraries, where so many rare English plays have been discovered. If such a copy is ever found, it will be worth its weight in gold, for it will be the only copy in the world of a play that no one has seen for at least two hundred years. Marlowe's play on *Dido* was likewise eagerly sought by collectors for many years and its existence seriously doubted, but in the end three copies turned up.

The unique manuscript of *The Maiden's Holiday*—which only too probably contained specimens of Marlowe's handwriting, of which not a scrap that can be proved genuine now survives—found its way into the hands of John Warburton, an English collector, who died in 1759. In his own catalogue of his library, which still survives in the British Museum, he has entered it as "The Mayden Holaday by Chris. Marlowe," without mention of Day's collaboration, probably because Marlowe's name stood alone on the manuscript.[2]

Warburton seems to have taken a very languid interest in his collection, and there is no reason to suppose that he ever so much as read this unique part of it. He makes no notes of its nature or contents, and there is absolutely no record of what it may have been like.

He carelessly left his manuscripts where Betsy, his cook, could get them, and did not discover what was happening until the artless Betsy had "unluckily burnd or put under pye bottoms" the Marlowe manuscript and several others as well.[3]

There is no real way of telling at what stage in his career Marlowe wrote the two extant plays. *The Massacre at Paris* cannot have been earlier than the death of Henri III, of France, on August 2, 1589. Henslowe enters "the tragedey of the gvyes" in his diary as "ne" on January 30, 1593/4, exactly seven months after Marlowe's death. The takings on this occasion were £3. 14s., a large amount which suggests that audiences streamed to the last work of a popular playwright who had died in sensational circumstances. Henslowe's "gvyes" was the Duke of Guise, the central figure of the play, whose name really provides a much more logical title than that by which it is usually known, the Massacre of St. Bartholomew's being merely an episode of the opening part.

The play starts with the marriage of Henry of Navarre to Margaret, daughter of Catherine de' Medici, Queen Dowager of France. The mood of Machiavellian "pollicie" in which the play is written closely resembles the tone of *The Jew of Malta,* and suggests that Marlowe's mind was running very much along the same lines when he wrote them, probably not very far apart. The history of this stormy period in France provides an abundance of that blood-and-thunder in which Elizabethan audiences delighted; and this particular story came close home because every man in the theatre had seen the Protestant refugees who had streamed from France to England.

Although *The Massacre* is a scamped and hasty play, carelessly written, with only occasional flashes of the mighty line which was Marlowe at his best, he has been shrewd enough to take full advantage of the opportunity this provided. For once he can punctuate his play with murders and take no liberty with his sources whatever. The Duke of Guise, villain-hero of the play, sends an assassin to murder the Admiral Coligny. The shot only wounds its victim and in a later scene we have the stage direction, "Enter the Admirall in his bed"—meaning either that the bed, Admiral and all, was thrust in from the wings; or else that the curtain along the rear of the stage was drawn, revealing him wounded in his bed. (The first device would not in the least have surprised an Elizabethan audience—one of Shakespeare's plays has the direction, "Bed put forth," at the moment when that article of furniture is required in the play.)[4]

The Old Queen of Navarre, mother of the bridegroom, is poisoned with a pair of perfumed gloves, an episode from history which made such a great sensation that it was still being referred to as late as Sir Richard Steele's oddly titled comedy, *The Funeral.* Then follows the massacre itself, with much mimic slaughter and much rushing of armed men back and forth across the little platform stage. The wounded Admiral is assassinated in his bed; and Marlowe is particularly careful to depict in full the murder of the philosopher Petrus Ramus.

Henry of Navarre, the Protestant champion, escapes from Paris. The Duke of Guise taunts the weak French King for his subserviency to his minions and is met by taunts about the

Duchess of Guise's infidelity with the courtier, Mugeroun. Guise procures the courtier's murder. The King procures the murder both of Guise and his brother the Cardinal. A friar, in retaliation, murders the King, and the Protestant Henry of Navarre, very nearly the only surviving character, comes to the throne of France.

The play is obviously badly plotted—indeed, hardly plotted at all—clumsily motivated, and saved from complete dulness only by some splendid passages written for the Duke of Guise and by the rush and bustle of the fast-crowding deeds of blood. These were the kind of thing that most delighted the Elizabethan public, and even to-day they give the play the only interest it still possesses.

In spite of all that, it had the ingredients of a fair popular success. It played throughout the year 1594 to respectable houses and was revived and re-costumed in 1598 and 1601. Philip Henslowe makes many loans to the actors for the new costumes. He "lent vnto Wm Bon[ne] the 19 of novemb*er* 1598 vpon a longe taney [tawny] clocke [cloak] of clothe the some of xij s. wch he sayd yt was to Jmbrader his hatte for the gwisse." On November 27 the same actor received a pound "to bye his stockens for the gwisse" and another gets the same amount "to bye a payer of sylke stockens to playe the gwisse." In 1601 the actors are buying "stamell cllath for a clocke for the gwisse"; and there was a complicated transaction whereby Henslowe "lent vnto the company to lend the littell tayller to bye fuschen [fustian] and lynynge for the clockes for the masaker of france." Later, he "lent vnto the company the 13 of novmb*er* 1601 to paye the littell tayllor Radford vpon his bill for the gwisse." Finally, Henslowe "pd at the apoyntment of the company vnto the littell tayller in fulle payment of his Bille for the gwisse the 26 of novemb*er* 1601." Obviously, this was a revival of no ordinary splendour.

Even with these elaborate fittings, *The Massacre at Paris* was far from rivalling the success of *Tamburlaine* or *Faustus*. Unlike most of Marlowe's other works it is never referred to and rarely if ever imitated by his contemporaries; but it does possess the distinction of having helped to set two governments at odds. In 1602, Sir Ralph Winwood, English Ambassador in Paris, discovered that Queen Elizabeth's dignity was being affronted on the Parisian stage. As he wrote to Lord Burghley from Paris on July 7, "certaine Italian Comedians did set up upon the Corners of the Passages in this Towne that that Afternoone they would plaie *l'Histoire Angloise contre la Roine d'Angleterre.*"[5]

When Sir Ralph protested, the French government told him that he had no legitimate ground for complaint, because the French monarchy had suffered similar treatment on the London stage. The performances to which they objected can only have been the revival of Marlowe's *Massacre* in 1601. As the Ambassador tells the story: "It was objected to me before the [French] Counsaile by some Standers by, that the Death of the Duke of Guise hath ben plaied at London; which I answered was never done in the Life of the last King [of France]; and sence, by some others, that the Massacre of St. Bartholomews hath ben publickly acted, and this King represented upon the Stage."

There seems to have been general agreement that no living Christian monarch could be presented on the stage. The Italian comedians had violated this convention by using Queen Elizabeth as a stage character. The assassination rate and general royal mortality in France being what it was at this time, practically all of Marlowe's characters were safely dead long before 1601. But Henry of Navarre lives clear through the five acts of *The Massacre at Paris* and as Henri IV he was still upon the throne of France. One sees why nothing further is heard of Marlowe's play, upon the boards.

The French Ambassador in London made a similar protest against *The Tragedy of Charles Duke of Biron,* by Marlowe's friend, George Chapman, in which the French King also appears; but the later dramatists were not deterred from other attempts to give their audiences the pleasure of seeing the mighty of their own day upon the stage. Thomas Middleton put King James I and the Spanish Ambassador Gondomar into his *Game at Chesse* under a disguise so thin that the Spanish government objected strongly. Later the English government made Philip Massinger revise *Believe as You List,* because it was afraid of offending Spain again.[6]

Disappearance of *The Massacre at Paris* was no great loss to literature. The play is a blood-soaked piece of commercial writing, built to fit the rather bad taste of the worst element among the theatre-goers of its time—crude, violent, gory, relieved only by purple patches of poetic interlude stitched in between assassinations, mainly because Marlowe simply could not stay down upon the lowest level of his own play.

The best example of this is the great soliloquy of the Duke of Guise, already quoted,* in which Marlowe lays bare all his own aching longing for the glory and the splendour that eluded him in life but not in poetry. The words are the words of a character in a play; but the mood belongs to the shoemaker's son who could not bow his proud and discontented spirit to be a country clergyman like the other meek and proper Canterbury scholars of his day in Cambridge; who associated with the noble, great, and powerful of the brilliant world in Elizabeth's Court and yet was never one of them; and who made up for humble birth and lodgings in a liberty and drudgery for the players by spinning gorgeous webs of magnificent verse to give his longings vent.

Marlowe's friends probably helped provide material for the play. The murdered Admiral Coligny had been a friend of Marlowe's friend Raleigh, who had himself fought in the French wars of religion. Sir Francis Walsingham had been Ambassador in Paris during the horrible night of the massacre itself. He had known the murdered Ramus, and under the diplomatic immunity of the Embassy Sir Philip Sidney himself had sought refuge. That Marlowe knew Sir Francis personally there is no proof; but he seems to have been more or less in touch with the whole Walsingham circle; and he certainly wrote a dedication to Sidney's sister, Sir Philip being Walsingham's son-in-law. It is tempting to believe that from Raleigh, Sidney, or the Walsinghams, Marlowe picked up some of his knowledge of the massacre; while he probably gained still more from the Huguenot refugees who had streamed to Canterbury in his youth.

However much Marlowe may have learned from his distinguished and his humble friends, he had also read a great deal in preparation for writing his play—almost as widely, in fact, as he had read when he was writing *Tamburlaine*. He probably depended on diplomatic gossip for the scandals about the Duchess of Guise and the Duc d'Epernoun. Writers in France who wished to keep their nostrils unslit, their ears intact, and their heads firmly on their shoulders did not print such things; but it is the business of diplomats like Sir

* See p. 87.

Francis Walsingham to know all about the seamy side of the courts to which they are accredited.

Printed sources were abundant, for the Massacre of St. Bartholomew's and the French wars of religion had enjoyed a very good press. The journalism of the day consisted principally of "newsbooks" and controversial pamphlets, predecessors of the genuine periodicals which were to spring up in the next century. Whenever anything so sensational as the massacre happened, every printer hastened to pick up an honest penny by bringing out a newsbook or broadside telling just as much of the truth as he could learn and as he thought safe. The discovery of America had been thus reported in a news broadside which ran through seventeen editions. Sometimes these pamphlets reported the news with extreme speed. Thus, while Marlowe's career is at its height, the Stationers' Register for September 25, 1590, contains the entry of "The true news from Ffraunce broughte by the laste post the 23th of September 1590." [7] The entry is made only two days after the arrival of the news, and by that time the old-fashioned hand-presses had probably been clanking for some time.

Sensational and dramatic stories of the struggles in France and the series of assassinations were not, therefore, hard to come by. As a contemporary remarks, after the murder of the Duke of Guise, "There was no foolish Poet nor Ballet-singer within Parris, that deuised not one couple of songs touching this action." [8] Both Catholics and Protestants were eager to spread their own interpretations not only of the massacre itself but of the assassinations. As another contemporary remarks,[9] "Bokes are extant on both parts." A good many are still extant, and we can find in them the very events out of which Marlowe made his play.

Eager to pacify the horrified Protestants outside France, the French government took some highly modern steps to distribute secret propaganda, justifying the massacre. A letter from Charles IX of France still exists in which His Most Christian Majesty orders his Ambassador in England to have certain propagandist pamphlets "secretly published and passed from hand to hand without any one's knowing that they come from you or from me" [10]—exactly the kind of thing that both sides did in the World War.

In a sense, therefore, Marlowe's *Massacre at Paris* is a "news play," like *Arden of Feversham, A Warning for Fair*

Women, The Yorkshire Tragedy, or Ben Jonson's *Page of Plymouth,* which dealt in the manner of the sensational press of to-day with exciting murders. His play had for its audience the same sort of interest that any current sensation has for the modern reader of the tabloid newspapers. The modern reader insists on getting his sensations a little fresher; that is the main difference.

The newsbooks and contemporary histories that Marlowe used are among the most ephemeral of publications. Hastily run off the press in small editions to catch an immediate market among buyers interested in the particular event described, they were rarely bound and they disappeared quickly—as yesterday's newspaper always does. Hence, while it is possible to be quite sure what kind of material Marlowe was using, we can never be positive that we have the exact books. He almost certainly used the tenth book of a long-winded volume called *Three Partes of Commentaries Containing the whole and perfect discourse of the Ciuill warres of Fraunce,* which had appeared in Latin and English in four successive editions between 1570 and 1574. Marlowe's lines show so many verbal echoes of this work that it is hard to doubt his use of it; but as usual he seems to have gone further afield in his search for material. It is reasonably certain that he also used the highly Protestant *Tocsain contre les Massacreurs* (1579)—which mentions Ramus's efforts to buy his life, omitted by most books but mentioned by Marlowe; and perhaps also a Catholic pamphlet called *Le Martire des Deux Freres,* which describes the assassination of the Duke and Cardinal de Guise, and which also has some surprisingly plain-spoken allusions to the royal favourites.

Dido, Queene of Carthage is in itself of no more interest to modern readers than *The Massacre at Paris;* and Elizabethan readers seem to have felt much the same way about it. But it is intensely interesting as a kind of unconscious first draft of many of Marlowe's most felicitous lines and phrases, to which he owes much of his enduring reputation. In this one play, Marlowe seems to be groping his way through his immaturity toward the greater work that he was eventually to do as his mind became mature, his technical skill increased, and he acquired a firm hold upon his craft. There is no really good way to date this play; but the constant curious anticipation of passages that in his later work become perfection could belong only to the early work of an unpractised hand. It is probable enough that Marlowe wrote his part of it while he was still at Cambridge.

All writers are likely to echo themselves more or less; but the Elizabethan poets echoed themselves and each other in a degree quite inconceivable to their successors; and Marlowe was particularly inclined to this failing. He is always repeating himself, from play to play or from poem to poem; and doubtless if he had had more predecessors worth echoing, he would have plundered their best lines, showing the same blithe unscrupulousness that his immediate followers showed, when they took what they pleased from his works and forgot about quotation marks.

The lines of *Dido* which echo in later plays are not, however, like Marlowe's ordinary self-repetition. Almost invariably they are less fortunate, less happy, less inevitably right than the versions in which they reappear in the newer and more brilliant dress which the poet gives to his own creation when it rises to his mind anew, as he works upon another play later in his career. It is as if the youthful writer, labouring over *Dido,* had inspirations and ideas with which he was not yet competent to deal; as if there was genius enough in him for the inspirations, but not skill and experience enough to deal with inspirations when they came. Marlowe did the best he could with his unpractised hand; and later, when mastery over his craft had come, remoulded them nearer to his heart's desire.

Many of the most famous bits in *Doctor Faustus*—three of them in the famous passage about the "thousand ships"—make their appearance first as rough, experimental drafts, in *Dido.*[11] In all, some five and twenty passages from *Dido* appear and reappear in this way in Marlowe's other works.* They range from an entire line,[12]

> Threatening a thousand deaths at eurie glance,

which is transplanted bodily into *Hero and Leander,* to mere echoes of small phrases or slight turns of speech. Occasionally the poet hits upon a phrase like "quenchles fire" or "blubbered cheeks" or "lawles spoyle," which he promptly repeats in another play. "Quenchles fire" is repeated in *Dido, Edward the Second,* and twice in *Tamburlaine.* It had a rather pleasant sound, Marlowe liked it, it was running in his head, and it

* See p. 108.

slipped off his penpoint so easily that he probably never knew he was repeating himself.[13] The repetitions are most common in *Tamburlaine* and *Doctor Faustus;* but they turn up in all the plays and most of the poems. While Marlowe elsewhere often catches up and reproduces a line from one or another of his plays, he never does this with a frequency in any wise approaching that with which he borrows again and again from his own work in *Dido, Queene of Carthage.*

Probably this is because *Dido* is an early play, perhaps written while Marlowe and Nashe were at Cambridge together, or just after Nashe had followed Marlowe to London. Nashe had been at the University from 1582 to 1588; but when in the latter year he found it expedient to leave Cambridge as soon as possible, it would have been natural for him to turn to his old friend Marlowe, then at the beginning of his meteoric London career. It would be equally natural for two young university men to take a classical subject—*Dido* is nothing but a re-writing of the first part of Vergil's *Aeneid;* and Nashe's inferiority to Marlowe as a writer, which shows in all his published work, would account for the odd way in which lines of an excruciating badness alternate with other lines that plainly foreshadow the brilliance of Marlowe's later manner.

The changes that Marlowe makes in Vergil's story tell us a good deal about the poet himself. He is clever enough to see that the plot will gain interest if there is more conflict. He therefore takes the obscure character, Iarbas, whom Vergil barely mentions, and transforms him from a neighbouring prince of no great importance into a noble at Dido's court and the rival of Aeneas for her love.

Marlowe's own impetuous nature led him to make still further changes, which amusingly demonstrate the difference between the classical restraint of an Augustan like Vergil and the flaming romanticism of an Elizabethan like Marlowe. Vergil's hero is always "pius Aeneas." Marlowe uses that adjective just once; *his* Trojan is an Elizabethan adventurer, a little like Drake and a great deal more like Raleigh. Vergil's Aeneas leads a band of warriors against the Greeks; Marlowe's Aeneas attacks them all alone. Vergil's Aeneas, like a prudent soldier, slips out of doomed Troy under cover of the shadows; Marlowe's fights his way out through the enemy. Vergil's Aeneas carries the aged Anchises to safety; Marlowe's carries

Anchises on his back and Iulus in his arms, while he leads Creusa by the hand. Vergil's Aeneas describes the building of Carthage by the Carthaginians; Marlowe's hero builds the city himself. The changes are typical of the poet and only a little less typical of the age.[14]

The fantastic result is in some queer way related to the passage mouthed by the player-king before the critical prince in Shakespeare's *Hamlet*. Late in the eighteenth century, when all copies of *Dido* had disappeared, it was supposed that Shakespeare had simply copied these lines from his friend Marlowe's play. When two or three copies of *Dido* were finally discovered and the two plays could be compared, it was evident that this was not the case. Nevertheless there is a kind of resemblance, almost as if Shakespeare were slyly poking fun at the elder play by exaggerating some of its exaggerations. Marlowe, for instance, had written[15] how the Greek hero, Pyrrhus,

> . . . disdaining whiskt his sword about,
> And with the wind thereof the King fell downe.

Master William underlines and emphasizes the ridiculous side of this, ever so slightly, adding just a word or so too many, so that it becomes:

> But with the whiff and wind of his fell sword
> The unnerved father falls.

Later Shakespeare himself becomes a victim to Marlowe's habit and repeats his own parody in all seriousness in *Troilus and Cressida:*

> The captive Grecian falls
> Even in the fan and wind of your fair sword.

Like the play which Hamlet discusses with the strolling players, *Dido* "pleas'd not the million," and it is no very great exaggeration to say that "it was never acted; or, if it was, not above once," though it would be flattering Marlowe too far to say that this was because *Dido* was "an excellent play, well digested in the scenes, set down with as much modesty as cunning."

But it all does sound very much as if the Globe Theatre's literary main-stay was recalling, not too clearly, the touch of a vanished hand and the sound of a voice that had been stilled a decade before.

16.

"Marlowe's Mighty Line"

> ". . . how farre thou didst our Lily out-shine,
> Or sporting Kid, or Marlowes mighty line."
> *Ben Jonson in Shakespeare's First Folio*

The real test of a writer for the theatre is production in the theatre; and dramatic genius of the first rank must withstand this test without regard for changing fashions or the lapse of time. Such a claim can hardly be made for Marlowe. Only one or two of his plays hold the stage to-day save as brief revivals for the delectation of curious literary folk. It is for their pure poetry, far more than for their dramatic quality, that they live—Tamburlaine's lyric passages, "What is beauty saith my sufferings then?" the death of Faustus or his apostrophe to Helen, the Jew of Malta gloating over the infinite riches in his little room, the "reluctant pangs of abdicating royalty," which Charles Lamb praised so highly in *Edward the Second.*

Not only do the plays live as poetry, but Marlowe's best lyric and narrative verse belongs to the top flight of English poetry—the unfinished fragment of *Hero and Leander;* the lyric properly entitled *The Passionate Shepherd,* but better known by its first line,

> Come liue with mee, and be my loue,

for which Sir Walter Raleigh wrote a reply; and one fragment, without a title, beginning,

> I walkt along a streame for purenesse rare.

Marlowe's less significant verse—the rather amusing translations of *Ovid,* the work of a very young man intent on a little daring bawdry; the rather dull version of the first book of Lucan's *Pharsalia;* and one Latin epitaph—might have been forgotten without any detriment to his memory and without any great loss to literature. Nor—if the five surviving lines are a fair sample—need one mourn unduly the group of sixteen sonnets and the eclogue, "Amor Constans," supposed to be Marlowe's, which came to light in the nineteenth century and then disappeared again.

The sonnets seem to be addressed to an Elizabethan painter named Seager, of whom nothing else is known:

> Whilest thou in breathinge cullers, crimson white,
> Drewst these bright eyes, whose language sayth to me,
> Loe! the right way to heaven; love stoode by the,
> Seager! fayne to be drawne in cullers brighte.

The eclogue begins with the line:

> For shame, man, wilt thou never leave this sorrowe?

the rest being lost. These mysterious verses were found together with a manuscript translation by Henry Howard of the last instructions given by the Emperor Charles V to his son, Philip of Spain. The poems were signed "Ch. M."—a signature frequent on Marlowe's title pages—and were in a hand different from the rest of the manuscript. They are supposed to have been transcribed by a certain Paul Thompson, of whom nothing whatever is known, about the end of the sixteenth century.[1]

Though these poems seem to have been of no particular value, their loss suggests that a good deal of Marlowe's lyric verse has long since disappeared. Such a loss could happen very easily. Elizabethan poets and playwrights were unlike their modern congeners in having no very great desire for print. To them there was no magic about publication. The act of creation itself and the quiet appreciation of his manuscript work by a small, discerning circle, were enough for an Elizabethan poet. Sir Walter Raleigh never published any of his poetry; and one of the earliest allusions to Shakespeare's Sonnets describes them merely as "his sugred Sonnets among his private friends." Publishers frequently had to steal the manuscripts of poems in order to publish them at all.

The poet's friends took copies freely of anything they liked. Every gentleman kept a commonplace book, in which he scribbled odds and ends of notes, extracts from favourite classic authors, together with English poems that he had happened to see in print or manuscript and that had happened to strike his fancy, sometimes mingling them with philosophical reflections of his own. Some of these commonplace books are a curious mingling of tawdry obscenities with some of the finest lyrics in the language. Sometimes they have been the sole means of preserving poems or biographical facts known only from their scrawled and scribbled pages. No one would ever have been sure that Marlowe wrote his Latin epitaph on Sir Roger Manwood, Chief Baron of the Exchequer, if old Henry Oxinden had not copied it out twice in his Commonplace Book and named the author; and we owe three different versions of *The Passionate Shepherd* to the fact that it, too, was copied into commonplace books. Marlowe's lost eclogue and lost sonnets were apparently part of a similar collection.

For an Elizabethan poet, it was enough that his friends admired his verses. For an Elizabethan playwright, it was enough to have seen his work upon the stage—and to have received old Philip Henslowe's grudging payment of a few stingy pounds. But the publishers whose shops clustered around St. Paul's Cathedral were eager snappers-up of such unconsidered trifles. Sometimes commonplace books fell into unauthorized hands, and lyrics were gathered up from manuscript or print and brought out in that amazing series of English anthologies which begins with *Tottel's Miscellany* in 1557 and extends well into the seventeenth century, preserving many poems, good and bad, the manuscripts of which are lost and which would not otherwise have survived at all. It is to such anthologies that we owe two other versions of *The Passionate Shepherd* and Raleigh's reply, as well as the surviving fragment of Marlowe's untitled lyric.

When Marlowe was killed, he had already finished, but had not published, some 800 lines of his *Hero and Leander*. These are to-day known as the first two "Sestyads"—a word which we owe to the misplaced ingenuity of George Chapman, who completed the poem. As Homer, whom Chapman translated, had written an Iliad on the city of Ilium, so he, Chapman, would write a series of "Sestyads" about the town of Sestos, where Hero dwelt.

Marlowe had written the story of the immortal lovers to the point where they are united and then parted; and the first edition of 1598 consists merely of this part of the poem without any division at all. Chapman later divided Marlowe's fragment into two parts and then added four more, in respectable but uninspired verse of his own, to complete the story.

There is an old tradition, founded on a very obscure passage in Marlowe's part of the poem, that Marlowe, anticipating his own death, asked Chapman to finish the poem. It is hard to see just how this was possible, in view of what we now know about the suddenness and violence of Marlowe's taking-off. Chapman was certainly not at Dame Eleanor Bull's tavern when Marlowe was stabbed; and though the poet was probably a long time dying, there is every medical reason to believe that he lay to the end in a coma from which he never recovered. Marlowe neither "dyed swearing," as his foes averred; nor was he able to think to the very last about his unfinished poem, as his faithful admirers have long liked to believe.

But he may have for a long time suspected that he was in danger of some sort. He had been under a cloud for several weeks at least. He had perhaps some premonition of his end; or he may have known that he went in peril of his life for any one of half a dozen reasons; and he may well have asked Chapman, another member of the Raleigh circle, to finish the poem if he did not live to finish it himself.

In his Third Sestyad, Chapman has a passage that is as strangely moving as it is incomprehensible, hinting at something of the sort: [2]

> Then thou most strangely-intellectuall fire,
> That proper to my soule hast power t'inspire
> Her burning faculties, and with the wings
> Of thy vnspheared flame visitst the springs
> Of spirits immortall; Now (as swift as Time
> Doth follow Motion) finde th'eternall Clime
> Of his free soule, whose liuing subiect stood
> Vp to the chin in the Pyerean flood,
> And drunke to me halfe this Musean storie,
> Inscribing it to deathles Memorie:
> Confer with it, and make my pledge as deepe,
> That neithers draught be consecrate to sleepe.
> Tell it how much his late desires I tender,
> (If yet it know not) and to light surrender
> My soules darke ofspring.

John Donne himself, at his worst, could scarcely thicken such obscurity; and yet it is reasonably clear that beneath all his elaborate verbiage, Chapman is saying something like this: "Spirit of poetic inspiration, strangely intellectual fire, visit the haunts of the immortals. Seek out Marlowe, who when alive plunged deep into the Pierian spring of the Muses and wrote half this poem. Tell him, if yet he know not, that I cherish his late desires; that I have, as he wished, finished the poem, offspring now of my mind as well as his; and that I here surrender it to the light of publication."

This is dismally bald prose; but unless Chapman was hopelessly involved in a tangle of images and a rumble of fine-sounding words, without any real significance, this is what he meant.

The exquisite, Keats-like quality of Marlowe's part of the poem deserved a better completion; but most modern readers prefer to take Marlowe's work as a beautiful fragment, sufficient in itself, even though unfinished; and let Chapman's lengthy continuation pass unread.

Like Marlowe, Chapman bases the story on a little-known and very late Greek poem, attributed to a certain Musæus. Marlowe and Chapman undoubtedly thought of this author as a very early Greek poet of the classical age. That is how he was described in the ancient *Lexicon* of Suidas, of which there were two copies in the University Library, Cambridge, in Marlowe's day. But more modern criticism has first shown that the Greek dialect of the original poem is very late; and has then pursued its destructive course by showing that Musæus himself is more or less a myth. The poem, whoever wrote it, is in good, respectable Attic Greek; but it is Attic dating from some time in the decadent Alexandrian period, probably from the fourth or fifth century, A.D. A new Latin version had appeared in 1587, as the poet was leaving the university; but as a Cambridge-trained scholar he would naturally prefer to go directly to the original Greek.

Hero and Leander tells the story of the young Leander, dwelling in Abydos, and his love for Hero, a maiden of Sestos, on the other side of the Hellespont; how Leander swam the Hellespont nightly for her sake; how he won her—and here Marlowe's fragment breaks off, after a love scene described in the most delicate verse and with the most complete frankness of aesthetic paganism.

Chapman tells the rest of the story: how Leander is drowned returning from Sestos; how the waves wash his body to the foot of Hero's tower; how, seeing it, she throws herself from its heights and dies; and how the lovers' souls pass into[3]

> two sweet birds surnam'd th'Acanthides,
> Which we call Thistle-warps, that neere no Seas
> Dare euer come, but still in couples flie,
> And feede on Thistle tops, to testifie
> The hardnes of their first life in their last.

Musæus, with classic restraint, had told the whole tale in 343 lines. Marlowe, with romantic exuberance, expands and elaborates, making an entirely new work out of the old story and breaking off with the tale half told after 818 lines.

Shortly after the poet's death, on September 28, 1593, the publisher John Wolf entered in the Stationers' Register "a booke entituled HERO *and* LEANDER beinge an amorous poem devised by CHRISTOPHER MARLOW." Like other publishers, he is plainly trying to take advantage of the stir caused by Marlowe's assassination, for sales purposes; and though no copy of this 1593 edition now survives, he must certainly have carried out so promising a business enterprise.

Five years later, there was a sudden revival of interest in *Hero and Leander*. In 1598 there appeared a new edition, containing only the first two Sestyads; then in the same year another edition with Chapman's continuation; and also an entirely independent continuation by one Henry Petowe. Thereafter the poem appears in a new edition every few years until 1637. The amazing abundance of copies of the last edition shows the waning interest in the old story. People bought the little chapbooks but were not interested enough to read them to pieces like the earlier issues.

Except that he was a dull fellow and a liar in a mild way, almost nothing is known of Henry Petowe; and his continuation, like his other works, is now so obscure that it is almost impossible to find a copy.[4] He was Marshal of the Artillery Garden (the Artillery Lane of modern London), where the gunners from the Tower went for training. He wrote a book called *Philocassander and Elanira*, which is supposed to show traces of Marlowe's poem, and also to record Petowe's own courtship. Of his various other works only one, a funeral poem on Queen Elizabeth, ever roused enough interest to require a second edition.

In his continuation of *Hero and Leander*, Petowe professes reverence for "that admired poet Marloe," but he is not willing, like Marlowe, to follow the story as the Greek original had told it. Instead, he pretends in his "Epistle Dedicatorie," that he has been "enriched by a Gentleman, a friend of mine, with the true Italian discourse, of those Lovers further Fortunes." As the original Greek of Musæus is perfectly well known, and as no such "Italian discourse" has ever been discovered, it probably never existed. Petowe lied about it because he felt that the authority of a source was more reputable than the exercise of his own ingenuity and hesitated to invent his own plot—exactly the reverse of what a modern writer would feel.

However dreadful Petowe's poem may be, it is mercifully brief, reaching only 628 lines, and contains a second tribute to

> Marlo admir'd, whose honney flowing veine,
> No English writer can as yet attaine,
> Whose name in Fames immortall treasurie,
> Truth shall record to endless memorie,
> Marlo late mortall, now fram'd all divine.

Petowe's original plot is extremely weak and artificial. Duke Archilaus falls in love with Hero and banishes Leander. The Duke dies and Hero, accused of poisoning him, submits her fate to ordeal by battle. Leander returns as her champion, is victorious, and—in defiance of all classical tradition—lives happily with Hero "full many yeares" as ruler of the city and "heire of Sestos right."

THE PASSIONATE SHEPHERD

In 1599 there appeared a small book entitled *The Passionate Pilgrim*, by William Shakespeare. At the back of the little volume there is a second title page, which does not repeat Shakespeare's name and which introduces "Sonnets to Sundry Notes of Music." The poems which follow are not all what we should call sonnets to-day; but that was not a matter of importance among Elizabethans, who were likely to describe any short poem by that name. Even Shakespeare wrote a sonnet with fifteen lines!

Among these poems is one which is nearly as well known as the famous lines in *Doctor Faustus*, and which has found a place in every English anthology from that day to this, *The Passionate Shepherd to His Love*. The poem is unsigned and but four stanzas are printed; but a new anthology, *England's Helicon*, which appears in 1600, prints the fuller version, which has since been accepted, after comparison with various other printed manuscript versions, as about what Christopher Marlowe must have written. As printed in *England's Helicon,* the poem runs:

> Come liue with mee, and be my loue,
> And we will all the pleasures proue,
> That Vallies, groues, hills and fieldes,
> Woods, or steepie mountaine yeeldes.
>
> And wee will sit vpon the Rocks,
> Seeing the Sheepheards feede theyr flocks
> By shallow Riuers, to whose falls
> Melodious byrds sings Madrigalls.
>
> And I will make thee beds of Roses,
> And a thousand fragrant poesies,
> A cap of flowers, and a kirtle,
> Imbroydered all with leaues of Mirtle.
>
> A gowne made of the finest wooll,
> Which from our pretty Lambes we pull,
> Fayre lined slippers for the cold,
> With buckles of the purest gold.
>
> A balt of straw and Iuie buds,
> With Corall clasps and Amber studs,
> And if these pleasures may thee moue,
> Come liue with mee, and be my loue.
>
> The Sheepheards Swaines shall daunce & sing
> For thy delight each May-morning.
> If these delights thy minde may moue,
> Then liue with mee, and be my loue.

There had been no signature in *The Passionate Pilgrim,* but this version is, in *England's Helicon,* signed "Chr. Marlow." At about this time there appeared a black letter broadside of which but a single copy is preserved.[5] This can be roughly dated because it is "Printed by the Assignes of Thomas symcock," a printer flourishing in the 1620's. In 1653, Izaak Walton tells in *The Compleat Angler* how he heard a milk-maid sing "that smooth song which was made by Kit Marlowe, now at least fifty years ago," and then prints the text. In his edition of 1655 he prints a somewhat different version.

In recent years three early commonplace books containing still other versions of the poem have come to light. One of these, now in the Folger Shakespeare Library, was kept by John Thornborough (1551-1641), chaplain to Queen Elizabeth. Another, of unknown origin but obviously dating from Elizabethan times, is in the possession of Dr. A. S. W. Rosenbach. The third is in the Ashmolean Collection at the Bodleian Library, Oxford.[6] The Rosenbach book contains a great many other verses, some highly erotic and a few which the owner, grown shamefaced, has carefully scratched out. These include a few snatches from Marlowe's licentious translation of Ovid.

Charles Lamb copied Walton's version of the lyric and of Raleigh's reply out by hand in the book of poetry that he made for his adopted daughter, Emma Isola. The manuscript, which still survives though broken up into separate pages, remained in the possession of the little girl's descendants for generations—at least as late as 1907.[7]

The companion piece, *The Nymph's Reply*, universally attributed to Marlowe's friend, Sir Walter Raleigh, is very nearly inseparable from it, and from the beginning the two poems have almost always been printed together. *The Passionate Pilgrim* printed but one stanza of the reply. *England's Helicon* printed it more fully and even added a second reply, now forgotten. All of the manuscript versions also give the reply in one form or another.

The Passionate Shepherd in a most curious way pervades all Marlowe's work. Just as in *Dido, Queene of Carthage*, we find him conceiving (rather vaguely and badly) the exquisite lines and phrases which were later to make his name immortal, so through all his plays from the very beginning, we find hints, phrases, and even one entire and perfect line of *The Passionate Shepherd*. This is in *The Jew of Malta*,[8] where the ruffianly slave Ithamore, making love to the courtesan, Bellamira, falls into the rime and—for the last two lines—into the measure of the lyric:

> Where painted Carpets o're the meads are hurl'd,
> And Bacchus vineyards ore-spread the world:
> Where Woods and Forrests goe in goodly greene,
> I'le be Adonis, thou shalt be Loues Queene.
>
> The Meads, the Orchards, and the Primrose lanes,
> Instead of Sedge and Reed, beare Sugar Canes:
> Thou in those Groues, by Dis aboue,
> Shalt liue with me and be my loue.

Tamburlaine woos Zenocrate[9] in very much the same words:

> A hundreth Tartars shall attend on thee,
> Mounted on Steeds, swifter than Pegasus.
> Thy Garments shall be made of Medean silke,
> Enchast with precious iuelles of mine owne:
> More rich and valurous than Zenocrates.
> With milke-white Hartes vpon an Iuorie sled,
> Thou shalt be drawen.

Tamburlaine wins over Theridamas who has been sent to capture him; Callapine, the captive Turkish prince, persuades his jailer to let him escape; Venus bribes Ascanius; Dido woos Aeneas; even Mephastophilis persuades the hesitant Faustus to his doom—in lines of invitation to ornately catalogued joys which are exactly in the tone of the Shepherd's promises to the Shepherdess. Mr. R. S. Forsythe has detected[10] no less than fourteen passages which show Marlowe writing in the mood of this poem, with one or more examples from every one of his important works.

VERSES IN "ENGLAND'S PARNASSUS"

The anthology, *England's Parnassus,* which appeared in 1600, reproduced one bit of Marlowe's poetry which is otherwise unknown. It is without title, except for the general heading, "Description of Seas, Waters, Rivers, & c.," which the publisher gave to the whole section of the book in which they appear. Almost unknown to the average reader, these verses deserve quotation both because they are beautiful in themselves and because they are the only known poem by Marlowe in any form except the couplet or blank verse:

> I walkt along a streame for purenesse rare,
> Brighter then sun-shine, for it did acquaint
> The dullest sight with all the glorious pray,
> That in the pibble paued chanell lay.
>
> No molten Christall, but a richer mine,
> Euen natures rarest alchumie ran there,
> Diamonds resolud, and substance more diuine,
> Through whose bright gliding current might appeare
> A thousand naked Nymphes, whose yuorie shine,
> Enameling the bankes, made them more deare

Then euer was that glorious Pallas gate,
Where the day-shining sunne in triumph sate.

Vpon this brim the Eglantine and Rose,
The Tamoriscke, Oliue, and the Almond tree,
As kind companions in one vnion growes,
Folding their twindring armes as oft we see
Turtle-taught louers either other close,
Lending to dulnesse feeling Sympathie.
And as a costly vallance ore a bed,
So did their garland tops the brooke orespred:

Their leaues that differed both in shape and showe,
(Though all were greene) yet difference such in greene,
Like to the checkered bent of Iris bowe,
Prided the running maine as it had beene—

and there, without even completing the sentence, the poem breaks off, perhaps to be completed some day when a fuller version is found in some Elizabethan commonplace book lying as yet undiscovered in the proverbial dusty attic.

The grace and beauty of these poems, strangely suggestive of Keats, is of a piece with the finer lyric passages in the plays. What is not so apparent to the modern reader, familiar with three centuries of lyric verse in which the lessons Marlowe had taught were applied by Shakespeare, Milton, Keats, and a hundred others, is the amazing newness and strangeness that Marlowe's Elizabethan confrères discerned in his poetry easily enough.

English poetry was in rather a bad way when Marlowe burst upon the scene. Chaucer was the last great poet who had written gracefully, clearly, and beautifully in English. Spenser was exquisitely ornate, no doubt; but even Sir Philip Sidney had his hesitant moments. The fifteenth century had been a long lyric nightmare. When Henry Howard, Earl of Surrey, and Sir Thomas Wyatt come back from Italy and begin to experiment with English lyrics, it is painfully apparent to later readers (though not to admiring readers of their own day) how incompletely they have grasped the real problems of English versification. Both of them have to twist ordinary English words out of their ordinary pronunciation in order to make them scan at all, using false accents like "bannér," "captáin," and others quite as bad.

Sidney and Spenser had gone beyond this; but the principles on which they worked were very imperfectly understood. A powerful school, led by Gabriel Harvey, was still trying to write English verse which should scan quantitatively, with a metre produced, not as in all English poetry before and after this time, by alternation of accented and lightly-stressed syllables, but by the alternation of long and short, as in ancient Greek and Latin verse. It was a natural attempt, for all these men were brought up in the schools upon this kind of verse; but it was, for the English language, a completely wrong method.

No one really knows why the stubborn Anglo-Saxon tongue has always refused the burden of quantitative verse, any more than any one knows why the six feet of the hexameter which are so beautiful in Homer and Vergil are so flat and dull when English poets use them. The fact remains that both efforts have always failed, and that Harvey and his school were trying their best to turn English poetry into a hopelessly blind alley. Their failure was apparent enough to Marlowe and others of his school, notably his friend Thomas Watson, who, to exemplify and ridicule Harvey's pretension simultaneously, wrote a couplet about him with one line in pentameter and the other in hexameter, and both in a roughly quantitative measure:

> But, o, what newes of that good Gabriell Haruey,
> Knowne to the world for a foole and clapt in the Fleet for a Rimer?

There was much bitter dispute over these matters; and the sudden appearance of half a dozen treatises upon the "Arte of English Poesie" and similar subjects shows how keenly literary folk of the day were interested in the relative merits of blank and rimed, quantitative and accentual verse.

Marlowe's great successes came in the late 1580's and early 1590's. They introduced a number of technical devices which, though not absolutely new, had certainly not been very widely employed by many of his predecessors, though used to the very best of their ability by the poets who came after him.

The easiest way to understand the changes that followed Marlowe's brief career is to place side by side three passages from poems written a few years apart—first a battle scene from Nicholas Grimald's *Death of Zoroas*, published in *Tottel's Miscellany* in 1557, one of the two or three earliest English poems in blank verse; then a similar passage from the Earl of Surrey's translation of the *Aeneid;* and then the same passage, which Marlowe has translated with very slight adaptations of his own in *Dido.*[11]

The passage from *Zoroas* describes a scene nearly like the emergence of the Greeks from the wooden horse, which the other two poets borrow from Vergil. Grimald wrote:

> Now clattering arms, now raging broyls of warr
> Gan passe the noyes of tarantara clang:
> Shrowded with shafts, the heven; with clowd of darts,
> Covered, the ayre: against fulfatted bulls,
> As forceth kindled ire the Lions keen:
> Whose greedy gutts the gnawing hoonger pricks:
> So Macedoins against the Persians fare.

Note the harsh and unpleasing sound of almost unpronounceable word-groups like "shrowded with shafts," or "fulfatted bulls," or the somewhat less than euphonious "greedy gutts." Note also the hit-or-miss way of distributing the pauses in the verse itself, adding nothing to the sound; helping the sense not at all; and sometimes, as in the fourth line, resulting in a jangle of consonants that can hardly be pronounced without positive muscular effort.

The Earl of Surrey had advanced somewhat beyond this. His work is far more smoothly regular, though even he cannot quite make "the great captáins" obey orders and march where they should in the line. Yet in his poem there is little emotional lift, and still less of the charm of sound, adroitly used to reinforce the meaning:

> Simon, preserved by froward destiny
> Let forth the Greeks enclosed in the womb:
> The closures eke of pine by stealth unpinn'd,
> Whereby the Greeks restored were to air.
> With joy down hasting from the hollow tree,
> With cords let down did slide unto the ground
> The great captains.

Marlowe's freer translation differs entirely from both of these. It is something entirely new, a piece of life and movement, a verse in which every line falls neatly into the pattern of subtle sameness and still more subtle variation, the whole a vivid picture of living men in action, in which the movement of the verse fits the action it describes and the sound mysteriously echoes the sense:

Then he vnlockt the Horse, and suddenly
From out his entrailes, Neoptolemus
Setting his speare vpon the ground, leapt forth,
And after him a thousand Grecians more,
In whose sterne faces shin'd the quenchles fire,
That after burnt the pride of Asia.

This was the "mighty line," or at least an early experiment in it, which Marlowe swiftly re-moulded into a subtle instrument to catch the minds and imaginations of his hearers and his readers, and to set all the other scribblers in Queen Bess's London to imitating everything he did—among the rest not least that promising youngster from Stratford, two months younger, who was now beginning slowly and clumsily to follow in the way that Marlowe had marked out for him.

Marlowe's verse introduces at least a dozen new technical devices. These are not all of Marlowe's original invention; one can find some of them, or their rudimentary beginnings, here and there among his predecessors; but it is Marlowe who first uses most of them freely and effectively; and Marlowe seems to have been the first writer to use some of them at all.

The technical side of poetry is at best a mysterious business. Poetry is not, like music, pure emotion expressed in sound without anything that really deserves to be called intellectual content. On the other hand, it is not in the least like the sterner forms of prose, in which the intellectual content is all, and such grace and charm of style as the author can compass is merely an incidental, added gift from heaven. Poetry uses rime and metre and often adds to them that "language enriched with every kind of ornament" that Aristotle prescribed for what he considered the highest form of poetry. Sometimes it uses these things solely for the sound's sake, solely to get the pure beauty of sound and the mysterious throb of rhythm, which always heightens emotion. (Even prose tends toward rhythm whenever the writer's emotional state is heightened, and there are passages in some of the greatest prose writers that can be cut out of their prose context and rearranged as a kind of rhythmic "free verse," without a single change of wording.)

On the other hand, poetry can never pass whole into mere beauty of sound. It must always "say something," though in lyric verse the intellectual content, the "something" that the poetry "says" may become very thin indeed. Prose summaries of the "ideas" expressed in one of Shakespeare's sonnets, or in a lyric by Robert Herrick, would show their purely ideational element to be alarmingly slight. The value of these poems is not in what is said; it is in the perfect form that gives a very old truth or a very small idea a value that will last forever.

An important element in that form is the sound of the words themselves. Marlowe is the first writer for the stage and one of the first lyric poets to make a skilful (and probably deliberate) use of the music inherent in speech itself. This is one of the most ticklish questions in prosody; yet any one who can hear verse at all can tell instantly the difference between a thoroughly bad line which definitely offends the ear, like Matthew Arnold's[12]

> Who prop, thou askst, in these bad days my mind

and the pure music of Keats's

> Charm'd magic casements, opening on the foam
> Of perilous seas, in faery lands forlorn,

—lines which after all mean next to nothing when you come to test them (as they were never meant to be tested) by cold reason; but which have the kind of wistful beauty that outlasts philosophies.

Keats himself explains the difference in the next line:

> Forlorn! the very word is like a bell.

Any one who will go out and listen to a church bell and then listen to the word, will see how, even in the cold and scientific sense, Keats was right. It is the boom of the *o*'s and the rumble of the *r* and *l* and *n* that give the word the curious beauty which it transmits to the whole passage. No one pretends that devices of this sort were new in poetry. They are at least as old as Homer, who in his "poluphloisboio thalasses" had accurately caught the lift, halt, and surge of billowing water; and who in the famous line in the Odyssey,[13]

> Δεῦρ' ἄγε νῦν, πολύαιν' Ὀδυσεῦ, μέγα κῦδος Ἀχαιῶν,

had produced exactly that "vowelled undersong" which Marlowe was later to use so adroitly.

Such writing was rare among the Elizabethans before Marlowe, and usually confined to lyric poetry—the most natural place for it, though not the only one. It simply does not appear on the stage before Marlowe. One does find it in all of Marlowe's dramatic, as well as his lyric, verse. One does find it in all Marlowe's verse for the stage, used frequently, appropriately, and just as effectively as in his lyrics—lines like [14]

> And all combin'd in Beauties worthinesse

or

> Are smoothly gliding downe by Candie shoare,

or

> Faire as was Pigmalions iuory gyrle,
> Or louely Io metamorphosed,

in which the poet is obviously seeking the pure melody of speech.

Marlowe is the first poet to see this element of resonance linked with other imagination-filling qualities in the geographic names which he culls from the atlas of Ortelius, with much more regard to sound than to anything else. That is why Usumcasane recruits Tamburlaine's soldiers

> From Azamor to Tunys neare the sea

and why the faithful Techelles recruits his Moorish host

> From strong Tesella vnto Biledull

—magic, golden-sounding names of far-off, strange, and magic places.

Being thus in love with pure sound, it is strange that Marlowe did not use rime more frequently. So delicate was his ear, so adroit his pen, that in poems like *Hero and Leander* or *The Passionate Shepherd* he rimes with the utmost grace when he wills; and—as the fragmentary *I Walkt Along a Streame* shows—he was entirely deft in manipulating a delicate and difficult stanzaic scheme. Often in the plays one can see him barely avoiding a rime, as if by a sturdy exertion of the will he were resisting a stylistic temptation. In *Tamburlaine* [15] we have lines ending: "witnesses . . . for this"; ". . . home . . . Dame"; "followers . . . Emperours"; "one . . . possession"—almost rimes but not quite; "false rimes," if you will, almost exactly like the assonances which some modern lyrists think superior to rime and use deliberately. In the whole play of *Doctor Faustus* there are but eight rimes, and these probably accidental or inadvertent.

Marlowe seems to have known instinctively—or to have had it pointed out to him by extremely practical stage-managers—that though lovely, golden sounds gave Alleyn a chance for magnificent down-stage declamations, they were out of place in the swiftly moving portions of the plot. He might have learned as much from Aristotle's *Poetics,* but wherever he learned the rule, he observed it strictly. All of the great lyric passages which run on for twenty to fifty lines in a single speech, the "verse paragraphs," which Marlowe invented to take the place of stanzas, are placed in the "quiet" portions of the plot, moments of emotional tension but not moments when the stage events are running swiftly through their mimic life. These passages are not really drama; but they are magnificent as poetry; and Marlowe wrote them so melodiously that he gives the effect of rime, yet does not burden his play with its final touch of unreality. Thus, all unknowing, he gave the lie, in advance, to that slander which Dryden laid upon all Elizabethans, when he said a century later that Shakespeare "to shun the pains of continual rhyming" wrote blank verse.

Shakespeare, who burdened his own early plays with over-abundant rime, might well have learned from his great predecessor the lessons which he actually did learn only after a decade of effort. If like Marlowe he had rimed less and had played with mere verbal conceits less eagerly, he might have leaped into greatness as swiftly as Marlowe.

Marlowe's blank verse owes much of its beauty to its variety. Most important among the variations that he introduces is the use of "run-on," or "run-over," lines—the device that French critics call *enjambement*. When blank verse began to be written in England, it was written by poets who for generations had used rime of one sort or another. Familiar though they were with the unrimed verse of classic Greek and classic Latin, they do not seem to have noticed that much of the charm of the great classic poems is due to the frequent running of the voice without an instant's pause from the end of one line to the beginning of the next. The English poets, on the other hand, began by regarding blank verse as merely rimed verse with the rime left off. They made up for the point which the rime marks in the reader's memory at the end of the line, by using a pause. Every line was thus "end-stopped," and the resulting monotony is scarcely conceivable to any one who has not heroically delved among the worst of the minor and deservedly forgotten bards. *Gorboduc*, one of the dullest plays ever written in any land or age in any language, is a dreadful example of what happens when the end-stopped line predominates. The trouble, of course, is the relentless pause.

Marlowe begins to vary this, so that line flows smoothly into line, often without any pause at all for several lines, or at most with very brief pauses, until thought and verse-pattern end together in a final pause which marks the climax of his thought. This is the so-called "verse-paragraph," of which the passage on beauty quoted on p. 90 is a superb example. A much shorter verse-paragraph in *Edward the Second* runs on for four lines without a single perceptible pause at a line-end:

> . . . A heauie case,
> When force to force is knit and sword and gleaue
> In ciuill broiles makes kind and country men
> Slaughter themselues in others and their sides
> With their own weapons gorde, but what the help?

Not only does Marlowe run these lines over, one after the other, thus giving the ear a change from the end-stopped lines which begin and close the passage; he also introduces a certain variety within the lines themselves, so that no one line sounds exactly like any other; and yet the fundamental basis of the pentameter verse—what Tucker Brooke once aptly called "the heady music of the five marching iambs"—is never lost to the memory, no matter with how much variety the ear may be indulged.[16]

The caesura, or pause within the line, falls first after the word "knit," the end of the third foot. In the next line it falls after the word "broiles," the end of the second foot. In the next line, it is a very slight, barely perceptible pause after "others," again at the end of the third foot. In the last line it is a very sharply marked pause in the same place, after "gorde," giving the actor time to get in a telling gesture. Thus no one line is rhythmically like any other, yet all conform to pattern, giving that odd mingling of diversity and sameness, surprise and expectation fulfilled, that is the mind's delight in rhythm.

Occasionally Marlowe varies his verse still more by boldly admitting an alexandrine, the typical French line with six instead of the conventional five iambic feet. The continual use of hexameter lines is practically impossible in English, but an occasional hexameter is effective enough. Spenser had placed an alexandrine as an intrinsic part of his verse pattern at the end of every "Spenserian" stanza. Marlowe's best-known alexandrine is actually in a passage in *Tamburlaine* which Marlowe lifted bodily from *The Faerie Queene,* telltale hexameter and all.

Marlowe must have known Spenser's works well, for he frequently quotes them;[17] and he probably knew the poet himself, for Spenser had come home from Ireland with Raleigh in 1589, bringing the first three books of *The Faerie Queene,* the only part of the poem from which Marlowe quotes. His lines in *Tamburlaine* are almost word-for-word from Spenser:

> Ile ride in golden armour like the Sun,
> And in my helme a triple plume shal spring,
> Spangled with Diamonds dancing in the aire,
> To note me Emperour of the three fold world,
> Like to an almond tree ymounted high,
> Vpon the lofty and celestiall mount,
> Of euer greene Selinus queintly dect,
> With bloomes more white that Hericinas browes,
> Whose tender blossoms tremble euery one,
> At euery little breath that thorow heauen is blowen.

The last line, having originally been the close of a Spenserian stanza, has six instead of the usual five feet. Marlowe's earliest editors, shocked at this apparent irregularity, solicitously amputated one foot to make the line conform.

Quite possibly, Marlowe simply remembered Spenser's lines, sub-consciously, thought they were really his own, did not realize that he was plagiarizing, and let this alexandrine slip accidentally into his verse. But there are plenty of other alexandrines in his work that are not accidental, since they are used either to open or close scenes or to give special emphasis to an appeal or an entreaty.

It is not always possible to tell whether Marlowe really meant certain lines to be scanned as alexandrines. This doubt is caused by his addiction to the so-called "tumbling ending." Most Elizabethans pronounced words like "nati-on," "executi-on," as if the last three letters represented two distinct syllables.[18] Marlowe liked to give these syllables their full Elizabethan value; and lines like

Bláck are his cóllours, blácke Pauíllión

will not yield even their conventional five feet, unless this peculiar pronunciation is used. Sometimes, however, Marlowe writes a line like

Why mán, they sáy there ís great éxecútión.

This must either be scanned as a six-stressed line, or else the last four syllables must be counted as one foot—what is sometimes called a "tumbling ending." [19]

It is lamentably probable that the poet troubled his head very little about many of these wire-drawn distinctions. Like other men, he had five fingers and like other poets he could count his stresses on them. Many of the alexandrines are probably accidental. Many of his tumbling endings are doubtless equally accidental. For Marlowe was certainly far less conscious of the technical devices of his own scansion than the learned gentlemen of a later day, who discourse at length upon his art. He had an exceptionally sensitive ear, a gift for beauty, a feeling for language. If a verse struck fire from his imagination, pleased his own ear, his actors', and his audiences', it may be doubted whether Marlowe himself tumbled uneasily on his midnight pallet in Norton Folgate worrying whether his endings tumbled too, and whether they were wholly legitimate in English verse. The play—that was the thing.

But whether he meant to do it or whether it was partly accidental—unconscious would be a more accurate word, were it not worked to death in these Freudian days—Marlowe did start the long process of releasing English poetry from a hopelessly inadequate technique. Later poets improved on his improvements. Where he had used a few cautious substitutions of other feet for the orthodox iambus, his successors employed many. Where he had occasionally added a syllable or two, or had dropped in an alexandrine, his successors eventually took so many liberties with their verse that in the hands of Beaumont and Fletcher it almost ceased to be verse at all. But all of this begins with the relatively cautious experiments of Christopher Marlowe—who in all his life was never cautious in anything save in his experiments with metre.

A few of his less important poems are important merely as indicating stages in his development. No literary interest at all attaches to the epitaph on Sir Roger Manwood, which is the only evidence now remaining for Henry Oxinden's note in his Commonplace Book that Marlowe "made excellent verses in Latin." Manwood had been on the bench when Marlowe was let off so easily after the Bradley killing; he was often associated with Marlowe's patrons, the Walsinghams; he was well known for philanthropy in and near Canterbury. It was natural enough that Marlowe should write his epitaph, though it does not seem to have been greatly appreciated. Sir Roger's tomb still stands at St. Stephen's, near Canterbury, but it bears another's verses.

Until John Payne Collier discovered Marlowe's Latin lines written in the Prideaux copy of *Hero and Leander* (now lost), no one had any idea of its existence; and even then—in view of Collier's bad reputation for forgery—the epitaph was set down as doubtful, until the discovery of the Oxinden Commonplace Book in the Folger Shakespeare Library set all doubt at rest.[20] Oxinden had twice copied the epitaph and had given Marlowe's name.

He had also tried to translate the Latin, with the result that he very nearly added one more libel to the innumerable others that have blackened the unfortunate poet's name. Beside his copy of the Latin verses he had written: "a hanter of baudrie," "a ruffian, a ravener of a dilicate meates, a gluttoun, a votary of sinn." This sounds very much like another of the Puritan diatribes against Marlowe's personal character; but it turns out to have nothing to do with Marlowe at all. It is simply Oxinden's gloss on Latin words in the epitaph, whose meanings he had had to look up. Marlowe had described Sir Roger as a terror to evil-doers, and these were some of the evil-doers whom (with the best intentions) he had mentioned as the particular objects of a just judge's wrath. It would have been the final irony of fate if these charges had been permanently attached to Marlowe's name!

Proof of Marlowe's authorship of this obscure bit of Latin verse is of special interest because another bit of Latin has recently been shown to be his. This is the prose dedication of Thomas Watson's *Amintæ Gaudia,* which is signed "C. M." Though this had long been suspected to be Marlowe's work, proof was lacking until Mr. Mark Eccles's discovery of the

Marlowe-Watson-Bradley duel showed that Marlowe and Watson were friends, thus leaving no doubt that the initials were Marlowe's.

This, in turn, suggests that still a third doubtful work may also be Marlowe's. The Bodleian Library at Oxford contains the only copy in the world of a strange little black-letter pamphlet, *The Nature of a Woman,* also signed "C. M." It is a very dull story in prose, based on a classical version of the ancient legend of the child who grew up among wild beasts. It is entered in the Stationers' Register in 1595, at a time when the publishers seem to have been looking for Marlowe manuscripts; and the odd way in which the other two suspected works have in recent years turned out to be authentic suggests that this, too, may some day be proved genuine. If so, it will not matter very much, for the story is one of the least readable ever written; though as Marlowe's only known prose work it would—could its authorship be proved—have a certain interest, if only because its dull insignificance is in such curious contrast with the flame and passion of the mighty line.

THE TRANSLATIONS

Of Marlowe's two extant translations, neither has much greater literary interest. One is so hopelessly dull that, except in collected editions, it has never been reprinted since it first appeared. The other has only that interest which the fillip of a *succès de scandale* gives to any book. It may not be a very brilliant poem—but at least it was condemned by two bishops and burnt by the common hangman!

The first is Marlowe's version of Lucan's *Pharsalia,* which records the wars of Cæsar and Pompey. Marlowe renders the original Latin, which is not particularly inspired, line-for-line, and the result is quite as bad as could be expected. There is a certain interest in the dedication written by Thomas Thorpe, publisher of Shakespeare's Sonnets, to Edward Blount, publisher of *Hero and Leander.* This alludes to "that pure Elementall wit Chr. Marlow; whose ghoast or Genius is to be seen walke the Churchyard in (at the least) three or foure sheets." The "Churchyard" is St. Paul's, where the living Marlowe had had friends among the book-sellers, and where his plays and poems were on sale. The "sheets" were, of course, the printer's broadsheets of paper, large enough to print from four to twelve pages of the small books of those days. "Three or foure sheets" were thus sufficient for the average Marlowe edition and in a very special sense a wrapping for his "ghoast or Genius."

The translation of Ovid was a much more serious affair. Publius Ovidius Naso had about the time of Christ written in his *Amores* some of the most licentious verse that even imperial Rome itself ever produced. In the end he shocked even that cynical and debauched society and had to go into exile. Yet in spite of the erotic nature of so much of his poetry, Ovid remained—decorously edited, let us trust—an accepted classic read both in schools and in the university. He was an especial favourite of Marlowe's, who shows traces of Ovid's poems in practically everything he ever wrote.

At some period in his career—probably very early, though the matter is still in dispute—Marlowe made a translation of the three books of the *Amores*. Since they were written in Latin elegiac metre, some one gave them the unfortunate title of "Ovid's Elegies," which to the English reader suggests poems like *Lycidas* or Gray's *Elegy*. A more misleading title for a collection of some of the least decorous love poetry ever written can hardly be imagined. Publius Ovidius Naso, gaiest, wildest, giddiest and wickedest blade of all the gay young blades of Augustan Rome, had found other uses for the antique metre. Marlowe found and translated these bawdy bits—translated them, it is sadly to be feared, even while he was still within the grey old walls of Corpus Christi, an ostensible candidate for the priesthood of the Church of England. Some time in the middle 1590's—1596 is the date usually given—one or more publishers found them, too.

Now these particular poems of Ovid's have equal claims to be regarded as art and as pornography; and the scale is so nicely balanced that a reader whose mind inclines to either side of the scale is quite safe in indulging in a good, smug sneer at the expense of any one whose mind tips in the opposite direction. But the publishers had no doubt at all which way the mind of the Bishop of London would incline. And the Bishop of London was in control of all printing within the city, and armed besides with fearful penalties against any printer who offended.

This particular publisher—whoever he was—had every intention of offending, for he judged, quite rightly, that there was a very pretty penny in it; but he had at the same time a wholesome respect for the safety of his own skin. Consequently he made sure of protecting himself. The poems were printed without the name of publisher or printer and without date. As a joke, the anonymous publisher added a false place of publication—Middleburg.

Time has evaporated the full flavour of that rich Elizabethan jest; but it must have drawn many a chuckle from the slightly bawdy gallants and 'prentices who bought the little books. Middleburg was the Dutch town where the Brownists and other Puritan sects were accustomed to print their tracts, which were banned from England because of an undue piety that the state church did not approve. Ovid was—or soon would be—banned too, but not on account of piety. Why not pretend that they came from the same place?

As a matter of fact, two of the six extant editions bear the peculiar form of signature markings used only by Robert Waldegrave, King's Printer in Edinburgh—and Waldegrave had been driven out of England for printing Puritan tracts! [21]

With the Elegies were coupled the "Epigrames" of "J. D.," or John Davies. Marlowe's name had also been given only in initials. There does not seem to have been much doubt about the authorship, for many of the surviving copies have the names filled in by hand, and the indignant bishops in 1599 described them quite accurately as "Davyes Epigrams, with Marlowe's Elegyes."

By 1599, the scandalous little books had begun to attract public attention. At the same time, Marlowe's friend Thomas Nashe and his enemy, Gabriel Harvey, had been abusing each other in print so bitterly that the quarrel was becoming almost as great a scandal as the licentious books. The Archbishop of Canterbury and the Bishop of London decided to suppress them entirely, together with some other questionable works. They therefore listed nine books and wrote to the Wardens of the Stationers' Company, ordering that "any of the bookes aboue expressed lett them bee presentlye [i.e., immediately] broughte to the Bishop of London to be burnte." The Bishops further ordered "That noe Satyres or Epigrams be printed hereafter," and "that all Nashe's bookes and Doctor Harvyes bookes be taken wheresoeuer they maye be found and that none of their bookes bee euer printed hereafter"—which is a blow for any author.

These orders reached the Stationers' Company on June 1, 1599, and seven of the titles listed were actually burnt later in the month, Marlowe included. Most of the condemned works have since been reprinted for the benefit of curious scholars, without noticeable damage to public morals.

So far as can be judged from the type and paper of undated editions, which give a certain clue to the period of publication, the sinful works of Marlowe and Davies enjoyed a wholly unmerited popularity and continued to be published until about the time of Cromwell. They exist, at any rate, in six perfectly distinct editions, and one finds them to-day in the most unexpected surroundings. The Master of Emmanuel College, Cambridge, bought one edition, apparently as soon as it was published, bound it up with other versions of Ovid's other works, and later willed it to the College Library (which still has it), apparently out of pure scholarly interest. Not all purchasers were so high-minded. One of the Bodleian Library's most precious copies contains the scrawls of various illiterate owners, about whose interests there can be no doubt at all. One of them has composed a bawdy couplet of his own, and is so pleased with it that he copies it into his book twice and starts to copy it for a third time!

17.

Marlowe's Influence

"Stretcheth as farre as doth the minde of man."
Doctor Faustus

It is a curious fact that no writer is ever completely original. Each in his work betrays his borrowings from other men who have gone before, borrowings which are usually clearest in his earlier work and then gradually vanish, or else become so modified by his own mind in later works that their source is almost completely veiled. The youthful Chaucer imitates French and Italian masters, reaching his truest originality only when he has mastered all they have to teach and has emerged into the full and rich humanity of his "English period." The work of Keats, who never grew beyond his youth, is full of Milton and Shakespeare.

Marlowe himself stands at the beginning of an era and, having few models to copy, is more completely himself earlier in his career than any other English writer. Blank verse tragedy largely begins as his original creation; and so far as we can trace the working of his mind, he seems to have been singularly uninfluenced by other poets. So far as he had models at all, they seem to have been mainly classical. Vergil has been credited with helping to form the polished brilliance of the mighty line. The influence of Ovid is frequently apparent. Among English poets we can guess that Wyatt and Surrey helped Marlowe on his way; and we know that he borrowed from Spenser, often quoting lines entire, oftener still remodelling his original; but it is notable that most of these borrowings end with *Tamburlaine*, Marlowe's first important play. Thereafter he has found himself and he has found a métier all his own. It is significant that almost alone among Elizabethan dramatists he seems to have escaped the influence of the ten tragedies of Seneca—perhaps because that keen and critically rationalist mind scorned the ghosts and supernatural stage machinery with which the over-literary Roman loads his plays.

Though Marlowe had so few models of his own, it is doubtful whether any other English writer, except Shakespeare, has ever served as a model for so many of his fellows and successors; and no one, even among the Elizabethans, owed more to Marlowe than Shakespeare himself. In seven of his plays, Shakespeare is clearly, and probably consciously, copying Marlowe; and in eleven other plays there are faint traces and suggestions of Marlowe's influence, which grows slowly fainter and fainter as fashions change in the theatre; as the mighty line becomes only a memory; and as Shakespeare's own mind matures to the full mastery of his later manner.

More than a score of other poets and playwrights of the next half century show the Marlowe influence in one way or another—imitation, quotation, or allusion; and while their number includes many lesser figures who are to-day forgotten except by curious delvers in dusty piles of ancient books, it includes also most of the great figures of the period. Crusty, scornful old Ben Jonson, who averred that "Marlowe's mighty line was fitter for admiration than parallel"; envious Robert Greene; Dr. Thomas Lodge, whose *Rosalind* provided Shakespeare with the plot of *As You Like It;* Thomas Dekker, Philip Massinger, John Ford, John Marston, Beaumont and Fletcher, not to mention that host of forgotten playwrights whose work has survived their names—they all show by occasional allusions or adaptations how well they knew the plays of their great predecessor. Some of them have plundered his work shamelessly of whole scenes, the better part of a plot, the structure of a whole act or more.

The writers of lyric and narrative poems imitate *Hero and Leander* and *The Passionate Shepherd* with equal freedom. Among these are Michael Drayton; the mysterious Thomas Edwards, of whom almost nothing is known except his poems; the actor-poet, William Barksted; Dunstan Gale; Phineas Fletcher, cousin of Beaumont's famous partner; the obscure youngster, William Bosworth, who died too soon to prove his talent; Charles Cotton, who wrote a continuation of Walton's *Compleat Angler* and must have read *The Passionate Shepherd* quoted there; Sir Edward Sherburne, the same who told the antiquary John Aubrey the false tale[1] that Ben Jonson killed Marlowe; Richard Barnfield, who habitually borrowed from Marlowe in all his work; and later, greater poets like John Donne and Robert Herrick.

All of them borrowed, but few were so frank as the editor of young William Bosworth's *Arcadius and Sepha,* who says cheerfully enough: "The strength of his fancy and the shadowing of it in words, he taketh from Mr. Marlow in his *Hero and Leander,*" and who continues, with that absence of embarrassment about plagiarism which is a perpetual wonder as we moderns contemplate these early writers: "You shall find our Author everywhere in this imitation."[2]

Shakespeare's debt is chiefest and clearest and, to do the great man justice, would probably be the most frankly and admiringly acknowledged if the mighty dead could speak. The exact relationship of these two major figures is one of the chief puzzles of literary history. That it existed, that it was very far-reaching in its effects upon Shakespeare and through him upon all English letters ever after, there is no possible room for doubt. The purely literary evidence for an association of some kind is abundant enough; but what we want most of all to know is their personal relations.

Did Marlowe and Shakespeare know one another intimately? It is hard to doubt it; but it is equally impossible to prove. In 1589, Marlowe lodged in Norton Folgate, a few doors from Shoreditch, where Shakespeare lived. But alas! we do not know the date when Shakespeare lived in Shoreditch.

When and how did they meet? How long were they together? What—since they are known to have worked for rival companies of actors—were their personal and professional relations? On what terms did they work together? Did the great Christopher Marlowe, brilliant success of the day, merely give the young man from Stratford some elementary instruction in his art? Did they labour long and hard together through frantic nights, cooking up some swift success for the players? Or are plays like *The True Tragedy* and *The Contention*—parent plays of the second and third parts of *Henry VI,* in which both men's hands are clear enough—merely due to re-writing by Shakespeare of Marlowe's early work, long after Marlowe lay dead in the Deptford churchyard?

What did Shakespeare make of the brilliant, enigmatic figure of the impassioned, wicked, dashing Kit? And—most fascinating puzzle of all—what in the world did Marlowe think of that obscure young man from Stratford, who was always hanging around the playhouse?

The plainest and most famous of Shakespeare's innumerable allusions to Marlowe and his work has a regretful note that hints at personal acquaintance. It is Rosalind's speech alluding to Marlowe's *Passionate Shepherd* and quoting verbatim a whole line from *Hero and Leander:* [3]

> Dead shepherd, now I find thy saw of might,
> "Who ever loved that loved not at first sight?"

It has also been suspected that a casual allusion to "Ovid and the Goths," in the same act, is really a double reference, partly to the historical Ovid's banishment, and partly to the bishops' order to burn Marlowe's Ovid at about the time when Shakespeare was working on *As You Like It.* It was the kind of oblique topical allusion that always raises a laugh in its own generation and becomes meaningless a few years after.[4]

But in *As You Like It* there is another and more puzzling allusion—at least it seems to be an allusion—that hints at a quite different attitude on Shakespeare's part. If so, there was a harder and more callous side than we should expect to find in that tolerant, kindly, gently humorous humanity which his plays reveal. Marlowe had died in a quarrel over the reckoning in the little room of a Deptford tavern. One of his most famous lines is "infinite riches in a little room." Why, then, does Shakespeare write in *As You Like it:* "It strikes a man more dead than a great reckoning in a little room"? [5] Shakespeare wrote his play not many years after the Marlowe murder. Shall we recognize in this—as every one would have recognized in that day—an allusion to the tragedy? If so, its jesting tone is peculiarly heartless, wholly belying the note of sincere regret in the first allusion.

It is more charitable and more probable to suppose that we have here one of the innumerable quirks of the subconscious mind. Shakespeare was thinking about Marlowe while he was writing the third act of *As You Like It*—the quotation from *Hero and Leander* and the allusion to *The Passionate Shepherd* prove that up to the hilt. The comparison rose aptly from the sub-cellars of the mind and William Shakespeare wrote it down, never dreaming the sinister sense it might be made to bear, in years to come. After all, no one did make any comment on it until three hundred years had passed.[6]

Other similar reminiscences of Marlowe are so abundant in

Shakespeare that it is hardly possible to list them all. In *Two Gentlemen of Verona* he tells "how young Leander cross'd the Hellespont,"[7] and the play-acting clowns in *Midsummer Night's Dream*[8] allude to "Limander,"—a Malapropism that can refer only to Marlowe's Leander. *Much Ado About Nothing* has an allusion to "Leander the good swimmer."[9] Young Mortimer in *Edward the Second,* with his[10]

> . . . Weepe not for Mortimer,
> That scornes the world, and as a traueller,
> Goes to discouer countries yet vnknowne,

suggested to Shakespeare a passage in *Hamlet* that is too familiar even for quotation; and the method of murder which Marlowe's Lightborne suggests in the same play actually appears in *Hamlet:*[11]

> . . . To take a quill
> And blowe a little powder in his eares.

That, according to the ghost (who ought to know), is exactly how Hamlet's father died.

Doctor Faustus appears to have been Shakespeare's favourite among the Marlowe plays, for he quotes or alludes to it repeatedly. There is an allusion to "three German devils, three Doctor Faustuses,"[12] in *The Merry Wives of Windsor;* a reference to the frail heroine as[13]

> . . . a pearl,
> Whose price hath launch'd above a thousand ships

in *Troilus and Cressida;* and an obvious parody of the same passage in *Richard II:*[14]

> Is this the face which fac'd so many follies,
> That was at last outfac'd by Bolingbroke?

Shakespeare certainly borrows from Marlowe's Ovid the line,[15]

> The Moone sleepes with Endymion euery day,

and reproduces it in *The Merchant of Venice* as

> Peace, ho! the moon sleeps with Endymion.

One might suppose that Shakespeare had gone directly to Ovid's Latin, were it not for the fact that Marlowe happens to have translated this line rather badly; and the luckless Shakespeare reproduces it, mistakes and all, thus showing plainly where he got it. Ovid had written:

> Adspice, quot somnos iuveni donarit amato Luna.

In *The Merchant of Venice,* he writes another line that seems to come from Marlowe's Ovid. This is Shylock's question:[16]

> Hates any man the thing he would not kill?

which is very like Marlowe's

> Whom we feare, we wish to perish.

But this happens to be an accurate translation of Ovid's original

> Quem metuit quisque, perisse cupit.

This time Shakespeare may have gone directly to the Latin.

One of the most curious echoes of Marlowe is in *Julius Cæsar,* where the line

> Yet Cæsar shall go forth

is taken over from *The Massacre at Paris*. This was long supposed to be an indication that Marlowe had borrowed from Shakespeare. Such a line seemed clearly to have belonged originally to the play on Cæsar. A more careful study of the pamphlet literature of the French wars of religion, however, shows that the Catholic party habitually referred to their champion, the Duke of Guise, as "Cæsar," and one of their partisans even drew up a laborious comparison between the two heroes which occupies four printed pages.[17] Plainly, then, Marlowe wrote the line first. Shakespeare found it and tucked it neatly into a play of his own in which it fitted even better than in its original place. No wonder scholars were puzzled!

It is worth noting that whereas most of the Elizabethan writers admiringly imitated *Tamburlaine,* Shakespeare alludes to it only once. Shakespeare plainly thought the old play was more than a little ludicrous. He parodied it, just as in *Hamlet* he let his player king parody the style of *Dido*.

One might go on. Painstaking scholars have made out a host of other parallels, to show how carefully Shakespeare read his Marlowe. But Shakespeare went further than mere echoes.

He modelled many of his characters and even the structure of several earlier plays on Marlowe. It is curious to see how easy it is to pair off Marlowe's characters with some of Shakespeare's, and equally curious to see how many of these parallels are from the earlier Shakespeare. *Hamlet* and *King Lear* are the last plays to show even remote traces of Marlowe, and that usually only in faint reminiscences of a line or two or a minor character. Barabas and his daughter Abigail in *The Jew of Malta,* Shylock and his daughter Jessica in *The Merchant of Venice;* Edward II and Richard II in the plays named for them; Kent in *Edward the Second* and Kent in *King Lear;* Young Mortimer in *Edward the Second* and Hotspur in *Henry IV;* the Duke of Guise in *The Massacre at Paris* and Aaron in *Titus Andronicus;* the Duke of Guise, again, and Richard III; the murderers of the two little princes and the murderers of Edward II; the frail Queen Isabel in *Edward the Second* and the frail Queen Gertrude in *Hamlet,* are almost relatives by blood. Not all of their resemblances are due to the accidents of history or the common conventions of the Elizabethan stage. If Marlowe had never written of these folk, Shakespeare would have created characters quite other than he did.

He, who severely ignores contemporaries, is perpetually quoting or imitating Marlowe. Even the rival poet in the *Sonnets,* the only other contemporary writer to whom Shakespeare can possibly allude, may not have been George Chapman at all, as many scholars suppose, but only Marlowe once again. "The proud full sail of his great verse" in the eighty-sixth sonnet sounds very like Marlowe's mighty line, though it can also be interpreted as a reference to the seven-stressed line of Chapman's translation of Homer. Refusing to imitate other Elizabethans, Shakespeare lays under contribution every important work that Marlowe ever wrote—all of his plays, two of his poems, and one of his translations!

Marlowe's influence upon Shakespeare is of the first importance in *The Merchant of Venice,* which takes over the Shylock-Jessica-Lorenzo story almost entirely from *The Jew of Malta;* the second and third parts of *Henry VI,* which are mere re-writings of *The Contention* and *The True Tragedy,* old plays which certainly show traces of Marlowe's handicraft; *Richard II,* which takes its abdication scene bodily from *Edward the Second; Richard III* and *Titus Andronicus,* which have typical Marlowe villain-heroes; and *Julius Cæsar*. Faint traces of Marlowe appear in *Hamlet, Romeo and Juliet, Antony and Cleopatra, Henry IV, As You Like It, The Merry Wives of Windsor, Midsummer Night's Dream, Much Ado About Nothing, Troilus and Cressida,* and *King Lear*. Of the thirty-five plays ordinarily regarded as Shakespeare's, more than one half reveal some kind of indebtedness to Marlowe.

Other contemporary and later writers also imitated Marlowe—at first deliberately and then unconsciously, as the lessons he had taught became a part of that tradition of the language and literature to which every new writer, as he begins to write, submits without being very clearly aware which of his predecessors helped create it. The works which most influenced other writers were *Tamburlaine, Doctor Faustus, The Jew of Malta, Hero and Leander,* and *The Passionate Shepherd.*

It is possible, by making several large assumptions, to assert that the influence of *Tamburlaine* lasts down into the middle of the eighteenth century and appears even in Thomas Godfrey's *Prince of Parthia,* the first American play (1754) ever produced upon the professional stage. Godfrey was admittedly under the influence of Nicholas Rowe;[18] and Rowe had written a play on Tamburlaine which was quite probably more or less influenced by Marlowe.

But it is not necessary to strain the evidence in this fashion—however interesting the result may be—to show how profound was the influence of Marlowe's plays and poems. It may be too much to suppose that *Tamburlaine* reached out across two centuries and three thousand miles of sea, to link the London of Elizabeth with the embryonic literature beginning to spring up in a wild new world. But there is no doubt at all that the mighty line projects its influence clear through English literature, at least until Milton and even John Keats; and revives anew in the admiring Swinburne, who gloried in everything Elizabethan and above all Elizabethans in Marlowe, to whom he devoted his first published work as an undergraduate at Oxford; and with whom his last published work, left in manuscript at his death, still dealt, after a lifetime of eulogy and devotion.[19]

Tamburlaine was certainly an influence on succeeding plays at least until the closing of the theatres in 1642, and *Faustus* is remembered well into the eighteenth century, though toward the end it is degenerating into mere pantomine and its author is forgotten. *Hero and Leander* calls forth a flood of imitators who copy its exquisite versification as best they can and—with rather more success—its lush sensuality. This continues until the middle of the seventeenth century, when the fashion of parodying the classics was brought over from France and the old poem of Marlowe and Musæus became one of the most frequent victims. It became a popular subject for the tapestries woven at Mortlake by weavers brought to England from Flanders. The set of tapestries reproducing the story of Marlowe's immortal lovers was described by Sir Sackville Crow, who was in charge of the manufacture of tapestries in 1670, as the only one of the six designs in England "worth the making." Charles I purchased a set for £1,704 and another set was on the list of tapestries to be bought for Cromwell—a curious adornment for a Puritan palace.[20] *The Passionate Shepherd,* as we have seen, established a definitely new motif, which remained permanently in the English literary tradition, finding its most successful expression in poets like Donne and Herrick.

Marlowe's other works are practically without influence. No writers seem to have paid any attention to *Dido,* and there is no way of knowing whether John Webster's play of *Guise* was an imitation of Marlowe's *Massacre at Paris* or not. If so, it was the only one; and both plays soon dropped out of sight. The translations naturally were without influence.

The influence of *Tamburlaine* appears in one way or another in nearly thirty plays at least, and in various poems, beginning, immediately after it first appeared, with Robert Greene's flagrant imitation, and ending in 1702 with Nicholas Rowe's *Tamerlane the Great,* which was produced steadily until 1815.[21] The more literate among Marlowe's immediate successors were quite aware of his play's literary faults. Shakespeare was not alone in his derision. Joseph Hall in his satires poked fun at "Turkish Tamburlaine,"[22]

> Graced with huff-cap terms and thundring threats,
> That his poor hearers' hair quite upright sets.

Ben Jonson complained that such plays "fly from all humanity," and had "nothing in them but the scenicall strutting, and furious vociferation."[23] A satirical play—we should call it a *revue* to-day—*The Return from Parnassus* is plainly gibing at Marlowe in the guise of its character named "Furor Poeticus," who has "a very terrible roaring muse, nothing but squibs and fireworks" (there were plenty of both in *Doctor Faustus*); who is a "nimble swaggerer with a goosequill"; and who is made to describe his own works as "my high tiptoe strouting poesye." The fact that this was a Cambridge play shows that resentment against Marlowe still lingered at the University.

But these are the cooler, more detached opinions of later literary generations, who followed Marlowe by a decade or more, when critical standards had begun to develop, when the first startling thunder of the mighty line had grown dull in long-accustomed ears, and when the brilliance of Marlowe's original accomplishment was obscured by his bombastic faults, of which men grew increasingly aware. The first impulse among contemporary authors was to write plays as nearly like Marlowe's as possible. And the most impudent attempt at imitation was by Robert Greene, who was ready enough to sneer at his Cambridge coeval and quite as ready to steal his thunder, in one play after another. This is clearest in *Alphonsus King of Arragon,* in which Greene practically re-writes Marlowe's play scene by scene and episode by episode for two whole acts. From the third act on Greene finds energy enough to break away and write his own play, but the traces of *Tamburlaine* continue to the end.[24] All these resemblances are to the First Part of *Tamburlaine,* as if Greene had rushed his rival play on the boards as soon as he saw Marlowe's success—at the very moment when Marlowe was writing as hard as he could to finish the Second Part.

Greene often imitates *Tamburlaine* in other plays. His *Orlando Furioso* repeats the conquering hero play which Marlowe had made fashionable; employs the Marlowe trick of getting colour out of geographic names; and introduces a hero whose "glorious genius makes him coequal to the gods"—like Tamburlaine, "affecting thoughts coequal with the cloudes."[25] In still another play, *A Looking-Glass for London and England,* in which Greene is collaborating with Thomas Lodge, he imitates Tamburlaine's retinue of three tributary chieftains, lets his hero boast in the vein of Tamburlaine, and introduces a good many verbal echoes.

Other imitators of the same sort are George Peele, in his *Battle of Alcazar*, *Edward I*, and even occasionally his biblical play, *David and Bethsabe*. Lodge also imitates in his *Wounds of Civil War*, and so does the anonymous author of *The Wars of Cyrus*. Marlowe's erstwhile friend, Thomas Kydd, often sounds very much like Marlowe himself in such plays as *The Spanish Tragedie*, *Jeronimo*, and *Soliman and Perseda;* but as the two men were writing in the same room about the time these plays were produced, it is a little hard to tell who is borrower and who is lender. Only the abject terror in Kydd's tone, when he refers to his fiery companion, suggests pretty clearly who was likely to be the stronger character and the dominating influence.

Two highly theatrical "bits" in Marlowe's play made an enormous impression. One was the sensational entrance of Edward Alleyn as Tamburlaine, mounted in his chariot and whipping on his captive Turkish kings with the cry:[26]

> Holla, ye pampered jades of Asia:
> What, can ye draw but twenty miles a day?

The other was the humiliation of Bajazeth as a footstool for the conqueror.

Marlowe had lifted the chariot with the captive kings bodily from Gascoigne's *Jocasta*, but he made it so vivid that every one forgot about the older play. The Elizabethan audience did not know whether the episode was original with Marlowe and would not have cared a whit if they had known that it was borrowed. Marlowe's successors, knowing that the scene always "worked," were content with that. Even the famous line about the "pampered jades" is probably another borrowing—this time from the "pampered jades of Thrace" in Arthur Golding's translation of Ovid.

This scene is repeated through the next decade, on into the seventeenth century, and makes its last appearance in George Eliot's *Middlemarch*. A theatrical episode which can flourish in fiction no matter whether Elizabeth or Victoria is on the throne is no ordinary triumph. Four captives, usually Moors, draw the chariots of triumphant conquerors through one Elizabethan play after another. Indeed, remembering the frugal habits of the theatrical managers, as exemplified by old Philip Henslowe, there is the diverting probability that it was the same property chariot in all the plays.

Toward the end a derisive note slips into allusions to the famous speech. Shakespeare in *Henry IV* is using it as pure comedy. So are Beaumont and Fletcher with their "Weehee, my pampered jade of Asia," in *The Coxcomb;* John Ford and Thomas Dekker in *The Sun's Darling,* where it becomes, "I sweat like the pampered jade of Asia," or John Day and Henry Chettle in their *Blind Beggar of Bednall Greene,* which contains a threat to "murther your Tamberlayn and his Coatch-horses." The anonymous *Women Pleased* makes it, "Away, thou pampered jade of vanity"; and John Taylor, the water poet—an ordinary boatman of the Thames who took to literature—uses it twice as "pampered jades of Belgia."

Thomas Lodge, a serious soul who eventually abandoned the stage for the practice of "physic," uses the whole scene in all seriousness in his *Wounds of Civil War;* but his solemnity is scarcely greater than that of George Eliot, who reads an absurdly solemn and Victorian moral meaning into what was originally a bit of the purest Elizabethan stage hokum: "I take Tamburlaine in his chariot for the tremendous course of the world's physical history lashing on the harnessed dynasties." [27]

The deathless line—one begins at last to wish it were not quite so deathless—appears and re-appears, accurately quoted, in *Eastward Hoe,* by Ben Jonson and collaborators; in Edward Sharpham's *The Fleire* (1607); and R. Braithwaite's *Strappado for the Diuell* (1615). King James's subjects were as much interested in the famous scene as Queen Bess's. The writers of the period had never heard of Rudyard Kipling; but what they thought they might require, they went and took, the same as he.

The scene in which Tamburlaine uses the captive Turkish Emperor, Bajazeth, as his footstool is copied or alluded to almost as freely. The revisers of *Doctor Faustus* even drag this episode into their distortion of Marlowe's later play.[28] Philip Massinger, in *Believe as You List,* brings the chariot drawn by kings and the emperor used as a footstool together in a single passage: [29]

> Then by the senators, whom I'll use as horses,
> I will be drawn in a chariot. . . .
> Our enemy, led like a dog in a chain,

As I descend or reascend in state,
Shall serve for my footstool.

There are at least sixteen similar references by Marlowe's contemporaries or immediate successors.

There was at least one other Elizabethan play on Tamburlaine. This was called *Timur Khan*, now completely lost. It survives only in a playhouse "plotte," or outline of the play which the stage manager used to control properties, exits, entrances, and other business.[30] We know that it was distinct from Marlowe's play because the incidents outlined in the old manuscript "plotte" are not the same; and also because Ben Jonson sneers impartially at both "the Tamerlanes and Tamer-Chams of the late Age,"[31] as if they were different plays.

The anonymous author of *The Taming of a Shrew,* the source for Shakespeare's play, borrows both from *Tamburlaine* and from *Doctor Faustus;* but his style is so hopelessly pedestrian that the fifteen-odd purple patches that he has stitched in from Marlowe are instantly discernible. Shakespeare, who followed the older play carefully in his revision, is careful to cut out these passages from Marlowe as if he, too, were quite aware of their origin.

Other writers imitate *Doctor Faustus* and pilfer its best lines almost as freely as those of *Tamburlaine. Doctor Faustus* restored to favour on the stage a devil whose popularity had sadly waned since the days of the mystery, miracle, and morality plays. The Puritans regarded His Satanic Majesty as the chief ally of the sinful players. But until Marlowe's Mephastophilis appeared, the "abhominable presence" had been absent from the stage for some years. Thereafter, devils, accompanied by squibs, thunder produced by drums and rolling cannon balls, and other sensational stage devices—"tragical sport which pleased much the humors of the Vulgar"[32]—cavort steadily on the English stage almost without intermission except under the Commonwealth, when all stage plays were banned. Dekker is alluding to this interest in the diabolical when he gives its impudent title to his *If This Be Not A Good Play, the Divill Is In It.* Many other plays show how popular the foul fiend had become—such plays, for instance, as Ben Jonson's *The Divil Is an Asse* (1616), in which

Pug, the devil, is carried off to hell much like Faustus; *Grim, the Collier of Croydon,* whose author is unknown; *The Devil and His Dame,* attributed to William Haughton; *Belphegor, or the Marriage of the Devil*—all of which are in the fashion that Marlowe set going when he borrowed Faustus from Germany.

Robert Greene was again early in the field with an imitation of Marlowe's most recent success. Just as he had hastened to take advantage of the vogue of *Tamburlaine,* so now he is swift to produce *Friar Bacon and Friar Bungay,* a play about magicians in which he is clever enough to appeal to national pride by making an English and not a German magician his hero and by letting him triumph over foreign practitioners of the black art.

Thomas Dekker's *Old Fortunatus,* based on the story of the magic purse, is another obvious copy of *Doctor Faustus.* It has allegorical figures of virtue and vice; Doctor Faustus has good and evil angels. Fortunatus tricks the sultan; Faustus tricks the pope. Dekker's heroine Aggripina is won by magic; Marlowe's Helen is raised from the shades by magic. Fortunatus rejects wisdom for wealth; Faustus rejects wisdom for power. Both prosper by magic; both repent too late; both meet disaster through the magic power they have achieved. Fortunatus is carried off by satyrs; Faustus is carried off by fiends. It should have been a clear case for the copyright lawyers; but fortunately for Dekker there was no such thing in those days. It was quite safe for him to write a second imitation of *Faustus* in *The Witch of Edmonton.* This play takes over the story of the magic compact sealed in blood, which also reappears in *The Divil's Charter,* by Barnabe Barnes; *The Famous History of the Seven Champions of Christendom,* by Richard Johnson; *Amyntas,* by Thomas Randolph; and the anonymous *Merry Devil of Edmonton*—not to be confused with Dekker's play. Randolph even wrote: [33]

My blood congeales
Within my quill, and I can write no more.

Marlowe had written:

My bloude conieales, and I can write no more.

The anonymous *Two Merry Milkmaids* is a deliberate parody of Marlowe's play. A student dabbles in magic—exactly like the unfortunate Thomas Fineux of Corpus Christi College—and succeeds only in raising his tutor disguised as a spirit. Later the tutor raises a real spirit and performs some of the Faust miracles. Into the play creeps the telltale line:

> This is the Face that wud not let me rest.

James Shirley, John Fletcher, and the anonymous author of *The Contention* and *The True Tragedy* show occasional traces of *Doctor Faustus.*

John Milton seems at least once to be quoting Marlowe in *Paradise Lost,* when he writes of the fiend and [34]

> The Hell within him, for within him Hell
> He brings, and round about him, nor from Hell
> One step no more than from himself can fly,

and again makes Satan soliloquize:

> Which way shall I fly
> Infinite wrath, and infinite despair?
> Which way I fly is Hell; myself am Hell.

This is too much like Marlowe's

> Why this is hel, nor am I out of it

and his

> And where hell is, must we euer be

to be purely accidental.

Marlowe's influence on Goethe and Byron carries the effect of the old play down through the eighteenth and into the nineteenth century. It seems to have provided a model, at least in some degree, for Sir Henry Arthur Jones's *The Tempter* (1893), thus bringing Marlowe's direct literary influence down to the very threshold of the twentieth century. His dramatic life and death early attracted dramatists, poets, and novelists and since Johann Ludwig Tieck's *Dichterleben* in 1828 at least seventeen plays and novels have used Marlowe as a literary subject. Swinburne wrote six poems dealing either with Marlowe himself or with his characters. There were three plays and three poems about Marlowe in 1930, a play and a novel in 1936, another novel in 1937.

Thus the cobbler's son, whose short life gave him five or six years of active literary maturity at most, lives forever in his own work and in the work that he inspired in others.

18.

Marlowe and His Books

"About the borrowing of a booke or two."
The Jew of Malta

Tamburlaine was the only one of all Marlowe's works that their author lived to see in print. Two editions, each containing both parts of the play, were published in 1590 and 1592, and copies of each edition still exist though they are among the rarest books in the whole world. Early editions of *Hero and Leander, Edward the Second,* and the translation of Lucan were rushed to press two or three months after the murder, but all copies of these have entirely disappeared. Thirty-seven other editions of various plays and poems have survived to modern times, a flood which begins when the murder at Deptford stimulates public interest in the poet and his work. All of these, if they are dated at all, bear dates after the murder; and there is no reason to suppose that the undated plays and poems were published any earlier.

From the moment publication begins until the 1637 edition of *Hero and Leander,* Marlowe remains so popular that scarcely a year passes without a new edition of one or the other of his plays or poems. Then, as the troubles leading to civil war develop, people grow less interested in work which is by this time growing old-fashioned; and after the *Faustus* of 1663 there are no more new editions until the nineteenth century.

These little quartos and octavos, most of which are to-day worth a good deal more than their weight in gold, originally appeared as mere paper-covered pamphlets. Each title page bore the name of the play or poem, usually with the author's name in full or in initials or sometimes in abbreviation, an ornament of some kind, the name of the printer and publisher, the place where they were sold, and the date. Marlowe's name is frequently given merely as "Ch. Mar.," and in all editions of *Tamburlaine* is omitted entirely.

Except for a few of the earlier editions, *Doctor Faustus* is illustrated with a lurid wood-cut depicting the conjurer standing in his cabalistic circle, while a devil of fearsome aspect emerges through the trap door which was always built into Elizabethan stages for just such purposes. This lively stage picture evidently served its purpose of attracting buyers and served it well, for each successive publisher who brought out an edition of the play continued to use the wood-cut. As one wood block wore out, a new one—traceable by the minor variations that the new engraver introduced—was made to replace it.

Marlowe never rose to the dignity of a collection of his plays in folio, a fashion started by Ben Jonson long after Marlowe's death, and much ridiculed at the time as a piece of pretentious vanity by rare Ben's numerous enemies. The success of the four Shakespeare folios soon made play publication in folio respectable enough.

Our modern abomination of cheap wood-pulp paper was unknown in those happy days, and consequently the fugitive pamphlets in which Marlowe's plays and poems appeared, cheap as they were, had to be printed on good rag paper, which has endured the centuries unharmed. If cheaper paper had existed the early printers would undoubtedly have used it for little books like these, which were not in their own day regarded as especially valuable. Practically all of Elizabethan literature would then have crumbled into a fine yellow powder not later than the middle of the seventeenth century, the only exceptions being stray lyrics preserved in the manuscript commonplace books and the fortunate poets who, like Shakespeare, appeared in expensively printed folios. But even these would not have given complete and satisfactory texts of many plays and poems, for very often these cheap little quartos and octavos are nearer to what the author originally wrote than the gigantic folios. Without the good rag paper that went to make these queer old books, most of the great Elizabethan writers and all the lesser ones would have remained mere names. On such mechanical accidents do reputations in literature depend.

The Shakespeare First Folio, tradition says, was originally published at one pound a volume; but this was a large and important work, intended to form part of a permanent library, and may have been bound before being offered for sale. The little quarto and octavo pamphlets which have preserved Marlowe's writings to posterity were less seriously regarded. Most of them were sold in stationers' stalls around St. Paul's or at the city gates, much like the magazines heaped on similar stalls at modern railway stations. The 1600 and 1617 editions of *Hero and Leander*, say their title pages, "are to be ſolde in Paules Church-yard, at the ſigne of the Blacke-beare," and the 1606 *Tamburlaine* "neere the little North doore of Saint Paules Church at the Signe of the Gun." The old publishers seem always to visualize a pile of copies, for the title pages invariably say "are to be sold," never "is."

A fair average price was six-pence each—at least, one finds that sum noted on fly-leaves and title pages with amazing regularity. On one the price noted is as low as tuppence, but that is the British Museum's copy of *Lucan*, a very small and very dull book that might easily sell for less than the plays. Edward Alleyn paid five pence for his copy of the "Shaksper sonnetts," listed in his papers among the "Howshold stuff."[1] An early hand has marked "Price 0-3-0" and "Price 0-2-0" on two of the British Museum Marlowes; but such prices as two and three shillings must certainly include the cost of binding, or else were inserted by later buyers at a time when book-collecting was beginning and these little books were beginning to rise in value.

These early editions were usually either "quartos" or "octavos"—words which in modern publishing have lost their original meaning and have come to mean merely a rough indication of book sizes. To the Elizabethan printer, they meant exactly what they said. The normal printer's sheet of paper was, of course, hand-made. It could not be larger than the largest tray that a paper-maker could work by hand, and the sheets seem in practice to have been about 15 x 20 inches. If these sheets were folded to produce four leaves (that is, eight pages), the result was a quarto. If they were folded once more, to produce eight leaves (that is, sixteen pages), the result was an octavo. These folded sheets were gathered up and stitched together to make a book. The original sheets were labelled A, B, C, and so forth; and each leaf was also numbered. Thus the first sheet bore the signatures, "A1, A2, A3, A4," though the last was often omitted and the first was often given as simple "A." These lettered signatures were a guide to the hand-workers who gathered and stitched them, and after publication they served instead of page numbers.

Sometimes the workmen erred and then we have a confusion like that in the British Museum's copy of the priceless 1598 *Hero and Leander*, in which signature H and signature D have been transposed, to the amazing damage of the sense; whereas the only other copy of this edition, in the Huntington Library, has the signatures in the correct order. Or there are other mistakes like that in the 1612 edition of *Edward the Second*, in which one page appears in its proper place in Signature I4, and then suddenly reappears a little further on—identically the same—as Signature K2. In the British Museum copy this blunder has been corrected. Some printer must have seen the error and corrected it; but as if to plague him, practically none of the corrected copies have survived the years, whereas there are several of the other kind.

Edward the Second never fared very well with printers. The next edition (1622) exists in copies with different title pages. The first state has the usual line, "As it was sundrie times publiquely acted in the right honourable citie of London, by the right honourable the Earle of Pembrooke his seruants." Then some one about the printshop seems to have remembered that there had been a more recent performance. As a result, about half the surviving copies substitute the line, "As it was publikely Acted by the late Queenes Maiesties Seruants at the Red Bull in S. Iohns streete."

The Elizabethan printers who turned out these little books originally gave them pages almost as big as those of modern novels, but they left exaggeratedly wide margins. If the sharp scythe of time and the still sharper and far crueller edge of the book-binder's knife had been kinder, the great Elizabethan collections of to-day would contain more books like the Levy-Bandler *Jew of Malta*, probably the tallest Elizabethan quarto in the world, whose pages are 21.5 cm. high by 15.1 cm. wide, and whose margins are 6.35 cm.—roughly two and a half inches—wide, while the bottom margin is 4.5 cm.

As can be seen from these measurements, the type mass on these large pages was proportionately much smaller than a modern publisher would use for pages of similar size. But the little books were not especially valuable in the eyes of their original purchasers and their edges have rotted away or have been ruthlessly cut and trimmed through the centuries, so that to-day some early books of Marlowe's have no margin at all but have been trimmed even into the type itself.

The contempt in which the play pamphlets were held by the severer school of Elizabethan thought is illustrated in the views of Sir Thomas Bodley, who described them as "riffe raffe" and sternly forbade the Keeper of the great Oxford library, which he had just founded, to admit anything of the sort. The Stationers' Company early began providing free copies of all books that the university libraries asked for; and had the Bodleian's founder been a little less stubborn, his library would to-day possess nearly all the Elizabethan plays ever published.

But, said Sir Thomas sternly: [2] "I can see no good reason to alter my opinion, for excluding suche bookes, as almanackes, plaies, & an infinit number, that are daily printed, of very vnworthy maters & handling, suche as, me thinkes, both the keeper & vnderkeeper should disdaine to seeke out, to deliuer vnto any man. Happely some plaies may be worthy the keeping: but hardly one in fortie. . . . Were it so againe, that some little profit might be reaped (which God knowes is very litle) out of some of our play bookes, the benefit thereof will nothing neare counteruaile, the harme that the scandal will bring vnto the Librairie, when it shalbe giuen out, that we stuffe it full of baggage bookes."

Since no one thought very highly of these little books, most readers took slight trouble to preserve them; but there were a few far-sighted book collectors, even in those early days. Sir Thomas Egerton was buying and preserving these plays and poems as early as 1600; and since he was fortunate in descendants who shared his tastes, his collection has reached the twentieth century unharmed. At Barham, near Marlowe's own Canterbury, Henry Oxinden's library was built up half a century later, including several of Marlowe's plays and poems. Sir Thomas Isham, of Lamport Hall in Northamptonshire, was also buying at about the same time the precious quartos which in the early eighteenth century were stored in his lumber-room and conveniently forgotten for one hundred and fifty years, emerging after their long oblivion as fresh and clean as new books even to this day.

Many of the early collectors made a practice of gathering up several plays or poems at once and handing them over to a binder to be put together in a single volume. Marlowe's translation of Ovid's *Elegies* often appears to-day in little books made up a couple centuries ago from the various seventeenth century translations. The British Museum has a fairly complete volume of Marlowe's works made up in this way, which comes from the library of George III, but was probably put together long before his time. The Bodleian has a similar collection made by the eighteenth century collector, Edmund Malone, and the library of Charles II contained a somewhat less complete collection, formerly in the Huth Library. Many of the other surviving Marlowe plays are still parts of miscellaneous dramatic volumes, made up for the libraries of English country gentry, centuries ago.[3]

Later generations of book-collectors have bought these volumes of old plays and broken them up to get at the more valuable works for separate binding. Still later collectors, as Elizabethan books grew in value, took off these bindings to put on new ones of greater splendour. Each re-binding meant a further re-trimming of pages whose edges had often already had to be trimmed because of damage by mice, water, or weather, centuries before. It is really no wonder that wide margins are precious in collectors' eyes; for down the centuries most of these old books have been bound and re-bound again and again. Practically no Elizabethan quarto or octavo has reached the twentieth century with its margins wholly uncut. Some have been so badly trimmed that only the text remains and sometimes even that has been partly slashed away. Usually, however, the "headlines" or "running heads" at the top of each page and the signatures and catch-words at the bottom have been the first to suffer.

In many cases the old books have obviously lain for a long time unregarded in attics or cellars or as unimportant parts of the stock-in-trade of second-hand book dealers, exposed to air, damp, and mice, until interest in the Elizabethans began to revive at the end of the eighteenth century. To-day dexterous patches, made by fraying the edges of torn or gnawed surfaces and then uniting the fibres with those of a new piece of paper, somewhat improve the appearance of injured pages.

From the time of his death until the last *Hero and Leander* in 1637, Marlowe's better works were being constantly reprinted. After that there was but a single edition, the 1663 *Doctor Faustus;* and then until well on in the nineteenth century he is completely out of print. Of the thirty-nine extant editions of these early books, there are two hundred and ten known copies which can be definitely located; several have dropped out of sight in the last twenty years; while at least a score of other copies almost certainly still lie in unknown hands and others are probably yet to be discovered.* The known copies are widely scattered about Great Britain, Europe, and America, the chief collections being those of the British Museum and the Victoria and Albert Museum, London; the Folger Shakespeare Library in Washington; the Huntington Library at San Marino, California; and the Bodleian Library, Oxford. Cambridge University and Corpus Christi College, Cambridge, sad to say, do not own a single early edition of any of the works of their famous son, though a few copies are scattered in other Cambridge libraries. The Pierpont Morgan Library, Harvard, Yale, Wellesley, and various Oxford colleges own a few; and one of the two known copies of the 1628 *Doctor Faustus* is in the Kungliga Biblioteket (Royal Library) in Stockholm.

The Jew of Malta, in its single edition of 1633, is the most abundant of all Marlowe's plays, forty-two copies being known. Ten editions of other plays and poems exist only in single surviving copies. Four editions appear in the Stationers' Register but are represented by no surviving copies and there is some reason to believe that still a fifth edition has vanished, leaving no trace even in the Register. This is the supposed second edition of *Dido*, said to have been seen by two scholars in the eighteenth century but since unknown.

The values of these early Marlowes range from the £15,000 which the late Henry E. Huntington paid for the volume containing his unique copy of Marlowe's Ovid and Shakespeare's Sonnets down to about £5, which is a depression price for a rather bad *Jew of Malta*. The late H. C. Folger paid $12,900 for one of the three known copies of *Dido*. The late Dr. Bernard Bandler paid $7,600 for the Levy-Bandler *Jew of Malta*, but in that case the value was due not to the rarity of this very common play, but to the extraordinarily fine condition in which this particular copy has been preserved. Doubtless the lowest price ever paid for a Marlowe edition was the tuppence which some subject of Queen Bess gave for Marlowe's translation of Lucan—a price carefully

* For a checklist of these editions, see Appendix B.

noted on what is now the British Museum copy. Some years ago, another collector found a Marlowe Ovid "in an old clothes shop for 4d." It turned out to be the finest copy of that edition in private hands and is to-day valued at £42.

It was not until the end of the eighteenth century that book-collectors began to realize the value of Elizabethan plays and poems. Men like Richard Heber, who maintained several houses to receive his libraries, and who liked to say that every man should own three copies of every book he owned at all—one to read, one to show, and one to lend to his friends; early editors of Shakespeare like Edward Capell, Isaac Reed, George Steevens, and Edmund Malone; actors like David Garrick and John Philip Kemble all searched the old book shops and haunted the auction rooms. King George III was likewise a notable collector and many of the nobility either added to the old libraries which they had inherited, or at least preserved them intact.

So keen were the rivalries for old books that friendships did not always remain intact. It is doubtful whether Steevens ever forgave Malone for bidding £17/17 for Dr. Richard Wright's copy of *Dido*. Steevens himself stopped bidding at £16. The book which destroyed their friendship is now preserved among Malone's other books at the Bodleian, to which they were given by his brother after James Boswell, son of the biographer, had finished using them in preparing his edition of Shakespeare.

Isaac Reed consoled Steevens by presenting him with his own copy, which he had bought from "a man in Canterbury" for a shilling. This book, now in the Folger Shakespeare Library in Washington, is probably the very copy once owned by Henry Oxinden, whose two commonplace books and whose 1629 *Hero and Leander* give one of the early accounts of Marlowe's death. Most of Oxinden's books remained in his family until 1807, when his great-grandson left the library to the parish of Elham, Kent. Here the parishioners were allowed to borrow as they pleased. Many rare and valuable books were taken, forgotten, and later sold by people who had no idea that these were the parish's books. The *Dido*, however, seems to have escaped from Oxinden's library before this general disaster overtook the collection. At least it is said that the actor John Henderson (1745-1785) bought it from the dealer Yardley for four pence.[4]

Steevens was overwhelmed by Reed's gift and wrote in the book: "This copy was given me by Mr Reed. Such liberality in a collector of Old Plays is at least as rare as the rarest of our dramatic pieces." When Steevens died, his book went to John, Duke of Roxburghe, and at his death it was bought by Sir Egerton Brydges for £17. From his library it went to Richard Heber and then to the Duke of Devonshire, who paid £39. When Henry E. Huntington bought the Devonshire plays en masse he became the owner of two of the three known copies of *Dido*. One was the Reed-Steevens copy. The other was the Bridgewater copy, which had passed down until 1917 among the descendants of Sir Thomas Egerton (1540?-1617) who must have bought it as a new copy on publication. This entire library was also sold to Huntington.

While the books were together in the Huntington Collection, some one removed the Reed-Steevens inscription and placed it in the Bridgewater copy, which is still in the Huntington Library. The Reed-Steevens copy was then sold in 1923 to Herschel V. Jones, at whose sale it was bought by H. C. Folger. There is no doubt that the Folger copy is the Reed-Steevens copy, since it still bears the Steevens stamp and the Roxburghe arms.

Since the eighteenth century there have been rumours of a fourth copy of *Dido*, which is supposed to contain an elegy on Marlowe written by his friend and collaborator, Thomas Nashe. If this book could be found, great would be the excitement among bibliophiles, first because nothing whatever is known of the elegy, which probably contains new biographical facts; second, because this lost copy may represent an entirely unknown edition.

There seems to be no doubt that this edition once actually existed. Bishop Thomas Tanner (1674-1735) and Thomas Warton (1728-1790) both allude to a copy of the play containing the elegy, which is not in any of the three known copies. Edmund Malone, in a note affixed to his copy of *Dido*, now at the Bodleian, says that when he inquired of Warton,

> He informed me by letter, that a copy of this play was in Osborne's catalogue in the year 1754; that he then saw it in his shop (together with several of Mr. [William] Oldys's books that Osborne had purchased), & that the elegy in question "on Marlowe's untimely death" was inserted immediately after

> the title page. . . . Unluckily he did not purchase this rare piece, & it is now God knows where.

As Professor Tucker Brooke once pathetically observed, it is "still God knows where." And "God knows where" is probably some dusty attic in America. A fourth copy was sold in New York City in 1860—for twenty-five cents! This was one of several Marlowes, all of which brought ridiculous prices, in the library of William E. Burton, an English actor who had had his greatest successes in America.[5] Several catalogues of his sale exist and many of them are annotated with prices; but none gives the name of the purchaser, so that there is no hope of tracing its fate. This priceless book may long since have been destroyed; yet on the other hand, it may still be ensconced upon some forgotten shelf waiting its fortunate discoverer.

Burton's *Dido* has been missing for less than a century. Marlowe quartos have been lost for longer periods than this and yet have been recovered in perfect condition. The most romantic episode of this sort was the discovery of two copies of an entirely unknown edition of *Hero and Leander*, found together in the lumber-room of Lamport Hall, Northamptonshire, the seat of the Isham family. In 1867, Sir Charles Isham requested Charles Edmonds, Librarian of Birmingham, to examine the main library at Lamport Hall, which was known to contain some rare and valuable books. Not content to stop here, the bibliographer pushed his investigations further and at length burst into an ancient "back lumber-room, covered with dust and exposed to the depredations of mice, which had already digested the contents of some of the books." Here, amid hundreds of worthless volumes, he discovered a small collection, "the very sight of which would be sufficient to warm the heart of the most cold-blooded bibliomaniac. In this same place they had remained uncared for and unexamined for a period exceeding 'the memory of the oldest inhabitant.'"[6]

No one knows exactly how or why they got there; but one can reconstruct a fairly plausible tale by examining the history of Lamport Hall. The books seem to have been bought by Sir Thomas Isham, the third baronet, who succeeded to the estate in 1595, dying in 1605. He is described as "a man of considerable literary acquirements, as well as an enlightened bibliomaniac." His grandfather, Nicholas Barker, may have been one of the family of Queen's Printers. The Isham books were therefore probably bought as soon as they were published, and were then bound in the Elizabethan vellum which they still wear.

The fifth baronet, Sir Justinian Isham, made extensive alterations at Lamport Hall in the time of George I; and these books are supposed to have been removed to the lumber-room while the alterations were in progress. The library was crowded with other books; Elizabethan writers were very much out of fashion at the time—and there the old books lay until the inquisitive Edmonds arrived more than a century and a half later.

The seventh baronet seems to have been the last who knew where the books were. He did not like to have the main library used; and always kept the key to the lumber-room in his own hands. When he became too infirm to walk upstairs, only the butler was allowed to use it. Afterwards, the books were completely forgotten. Being bound in old-fashioned Elizabethan vellum without labels or lettering, they looked particularly uninviting to the average spectator.

Their long oblivion served the old books well. The English Civil War came and went. Many a manor house was raided or burnt and its books destroyed, but Lamport Hall was undisturbed. The great fire swept over London destroying every book in its path. About half a century after the fire, the books were put into the lumber-room, where they lay through the reigns of all the Georges and halfway through Victoria's reign. India was subdued, the colonies revolted, Napoleon was crushed, baronets were born and died. Surviving quartos in other manor houses were slowly read or thumbed out of existence.

But while all this was happening the Northamptonshire dust merely settled a little thicker in the locked and silent lumber-room at Lamport Hall. The mice which scurried over the silent floors gnawed occasionally, but there were hundreds of old books and by some miracle these literary rodents spared the chief treasures.

When Edmonds stepped across the threshold, he found a totally unknown Shakespeare, the 1599 *Venus and Adonis;* the second known copy of *The Passionate Pilgrim;* two copies of a second and unknown 1598 edition of *Hero and Leander;* and a totally unknown edition of Marlowe's *Ovid.* It was for this that Henry E. Huntington paid the £15,000 said to have been the highest price ever paid for any English book except the First Folio, but a large part of its value was the Shakespeare bound with it. Edmonds was positive "that the books had remained in the house from a very remote period, and that no additions of any moment have been made to the library for the last 150 years"—which would take the books back to 1717.

One *Hero and Leander* was bought for the British Museum, where it still remains, its pages looking almost as fresh and new as the day they came from the printers. The other, together with the *Ovid*, eventually found its way to the Huntington Library; and from the day of the discovery to this, no other copy of either edition has ever been traced.

The 1594 *Edward the Second* and the 1628 *Doctor Faustus* also slumbered unknown for a long time. The first copy of this edition of *Edward the Second* was found in the Landesbibliothek at Kassel, Germany, in 1876. It was unbound but wrapped up in the pages of an early English translation of the Bible. It probably reached Kassel soon after publication, for English actors visited the court in 1594 and may have brought the book with them. It may also have been taken to Germany by Prince Otto of Hesse, who was in London in 1611, or by the Landgraf Moritz der Gelehrte, who was much interested in English plays and who bought a good many early editions which are still in the Landesbibliothek. In the Zentralbibliothek at Zurich there is another copy of the same edition, which once belonged to Johann Jakob Bodmer, Swiss critic, disciple of Addison, and translator of *Paradise Lost*.

These sole survivors of the disaster which has overtaken the rest of the edition escaped because they were allowed to lie unread after the enthusiasts who had taken them to the Continent had died. The two surviving copies of the 1628 edition of *Doctor Faustus* remain for the same reason. The bare existence of the edition itself was unknown until the Lincoln College copy was found some time between 1910 and 1920 after centuries of oblivion. Later, another copy turned up in the Kungliga Biblioteket at Stockholm. This, together with a *Jew of Malta*, had been part of the library of Major-General J. A. Hamilton (1734-1795), a Scotch soldier who became Master of the Royal Household of Sweden. The Swedish branch of the Hamilton family retained the books until they passed to the Kungliga Biblioteket as a gift from the present Baron Hamilton of Boo in the province of Närke. The unique copy of *Titus Andronicus* now in the Folger Shakespeare Library probably reached Scandinavia in much the same fashion.

One of the most valuable early copies of Marlowe has been lost. This is the Prideaux copy of the 1629 *Hero and Leander*. It is infuriating to reflect that the history of this book—which contains Oxinden's annotations on the life of Marlowe and a copy of the Manwood epitaph—can be traced from about the time of its publication to 1917, when it vanishes from the hands of a well-known London dealer who cannot now remember to whom he sold it. Since these annotations, as published during the nineteenth century, correspond almost word-for-word with the two Oxinden Commonplace Books, and since Oxinden habitually repeated himself, it is safe to assume that this copy of *Hero and Leander* was part of his library. It probably shared the fate of his other books at the hands of the parishioners of Elham. It appears in 1834 at the sale of Richard Heber's library [7] when it went to an unnamed collector for ten shillings. It was later owned by John Payne Collier and passed to his son-in-law, F. Ouvry. Colonel W. F. Prideaux purchased it soon after Ouvry's death, and when his books were sold in 1917, this one went to the London firm of Dobell, who sold it to the mysterious unknown.

Modern collectors are more than making amends for the early neglect of these rare old books. Their more precious volumes have gradually, by will or by gift, come into the hands of the world's great libraries where they can cease from their adventures and find permanent homes. Other great collectors, like the first J. P. Morgan, H. C. Folger, and H. E. Huntington, have turned their private collections into semi-public libraries, available to qualified scholars. At the same time, all the great libraries have for at least a century or more been buying really valuable early editions, including Marlowe's, whenever the funds were available. Thus gradually the more important copies have come into the possession of great institutions where all can use them who have any right to do so, and where they can receive the careful, expert handling that even the best made book begins to require after the first few centuries of its existence.

The 1619 *Doctor Faustus* is now the only unique Marlowe

item in private hands. All three copies of *Dido* and both copies of the 1628 *Faustus* have long been in libraries, and so have two of the three copies of the 1620 edition. Even a very common play like *The Jew of Malta* is represented by twenty-six copies in university and other libraries as against sixteen in private hands.

Neglect in the past, no doubt, has deprived us forever of much of the best work of Marlowe and the other Elizabethans; but what has managed to survive to our own day is now preserved and protected for as long as our own order of society can hold itself together.

Appendices

Bibliography

Notes

Appendix A

The Buttery Book, Corpus Christi College

The Buttery Books of Corpus Christi College are long, slender volumes, varying from 31 to 55 cmm. in height and from 22 to 10 cmm. in width. The three books in which Marlowe's name appears vary from 45 to 40.5 cmm. in height and from 16 to 8 cmm. in width. Since their discovery in April, 1935, they have been cased in modern bindings. Their bearing on Marlowe's life was discovered by the present writer in August, 1936, and the Marlowe entries were transcribed by him for the first time immediately after discovery.

For their period, the books are remarkably clear. The old rag paper is still almost perfect and the accounts would be entirely legible were it not for a few periods of confusion in the record, a certain difficulty with some of the totals, and the extremely crabbèd hand in which most entries are made.

The purchases are recorded weekly. The old Bursar wrote down the roll of the entire college, beginning with the Master and Fellows, following with masters, bachelors, undergraduates, and servants in residence, in the order of their rank, ending with the "coquus" and "subcoquus." Opposite each man's name his purchases were entered in Roman numerals. In the twelfth or thirteenth week, just before the end of term, a list of totals was made up. When each man paid his bill, the Bursar or the steward marked these "*fol*" for "solutum," adding a big double cross and his initials. Sometimes he placed these marks on each side of the entry. In many cases Marlowe's accounts stand unpaid; but for some reason these amounts are never added to the totals of the following term.

In the original, the dates are indicated at the top of each page. In this transcript, the varying forms of these dates are transcribed verbatim; but in order to save space they are placed opposite the charge against Marlowe, all intervening names being omitted. In the original, Marlowe begins well down the list and moves slowly upward as he gains higher academic rank.

The dates are indicated only by the Church calendar. The accounts start regularly with the annual audit on the Feast of the Annunciation, the beginning of the Elizabethan new year, usually known as Lady Day, which fell on March 25. The succeeding weeks are then numbered "Septimana prima post Annunciationem," "Septimana secunda post Annunciationem," and so on. The second, or summer term, is dated from the Feast of St. John Baptist, June 24. Sometimes, however, the Bursar dates from Trinity Sunday or even from Easter. Sometimes he uses two systems of dating at once. The October term is dated from the Feast of St. Michael and All Angels, which is usually called "Michaelmas." The last term is dated from Christmas Day, which the Bursar usually calls "Nativitas."

Marlowe's name is usually spelled "Marlin" or "Marlen," but many other spellings are used. Fortunately, there is never any doubt about his identity. He remains in approximately the same relative place on the list; he is frequently associated with Lewgar, another of Archbishop Parker's scholars; and at about the proper time, when from other records we know that he is approaching his bachelor's degree, the usual honorific "ds.," for "Dominus," is prefixed to his name.

The Bursar is almost always accurate in his totals—a matter of some importance as it enables the transcriber to make sure of his own accuracy. Occasionally there is a variation of a half-penny and in one or two places there is a confusion in the accounts which cannot be satisfactorily explained. The initials, "R.C." and "S.S.," signed when the term bill is paid, are those of Richard Chever and his successor in the bursary, Sophynam Smyth, Fellows of Corpus Christi.

The more important abbreviations are "co" for "commons," "nõ co" for "no commons," usually when Marlowe is absent, "ob." for "obolus" or half-penny, "se co" for "senior commons." The abbreviations written above the entries are obscure. "Coq" is undoubtedly "coquus," or cook. The letter "b" probably stands for beer. There is no clue to the others. The entries are as follows:

*f*eptimana 10a po*f*t Michael [*]. nõ co Marlen — i d
[11a] Marlen. xij d. iij d. j d. ob. ob. iij d. i d ob. i d. — xv d.
    [Totals] Marlen. — iij^{s}. ii d. ob
*f*ep 12 a po*f*t Mich. Marlen vj d ob. v d — ij^{b}d — xv d.
Sept. Nativitatis. marlen. vij d. v d. — ij d. — xj d.
    [With this Christmas entry, Marlowe's name suddenly moves to the middle of the left-hand page.]
*f*eptimana la po*f*t Nativitats. marlin. — vj d ob. iiij d ob. —
    ij d ob. xiiij d.
2a po*f*t Nat. marlinge iiij d. i d ob. — xvj d. v d.
3a po*f*t Nat. marlinge. iiij d ob. j d ob. — ij d ob — iiij d. j $\overset{oo}{d}$.
4a po*f*t Nat. marlinge. vj d ob. ij d. — ij d ob — v d.
5a po*f*t Nat. marlen iiij d ob. iiij d. ij d.^{b} — vij^{d}. j d ob^{co}
[6a] marlen v d ob. iij d. — iij d ob. iij d.

* "Nativita" has been crossed out at this point.

[7a] marlinge. vij d. iiij d ob. ij d^{b} ob – ij d
[8a] Marlen. viij d ob. j d ob. $\overset{d}{\text{iij}}$ d. j^{b}d. v^{b}d. j d.
[9a] Marlyn – vj d
[10a] Marlyn. – ob. j d ob. j d. ob. – v d.
[11a] Marlin – $\overset{\text{promi}}{\text{iiij}^{d}}$. vj d.
[Totals] *fol*: R:C: Marlen – xix s. v d.
*f*ept. 12a po*f*t Nat. marlen. ob. – j d – iij d
*f*ept. 1a. pa*f*chalis. Marlinge – iij d
*f*ept. 2a po*f*t pa*f*ch. Marlin – iij d Coid. xv d [*]
*f*ept 3 a pa*f*ch. marlen – vj d
*f*ept. 4a pa*f*ch. marlen. ob $\overset{g}{\text{j}}$ d – vj d
Coid xvij d [†]
*f*ept: 5a pa*f*chi marlen v d
*f*ept: 6a pa*f*chi marlen – iij d
*f*ept: 7a pa*f*chi. marlen – iiij d
*f*ept. Penteco*f*ti marlen – iiij d
*f*ept. 9a pasch: marlen – j d – iiij d.
*f*ept. 10a pa*f*ch: marlen – j d – iiij d
*f*ept: 11a pa*f*ch: marlen – ij d. j d. j d. j d ob. ob – iij d
[12a] marlen. – v d
[Totals] *fol*: R C. # Marlin – v s [?] iiij d
[Francis Kett's name appears in the totals for the last time.]
[No date] Marlen – ix d. ob. – j d. v d. j d
1 Sept. Joh. Bapti*f*t. marlin. ix d ob. vj d.
being ab*f*ent
he left peters in co͞mons
2 Sept. Co͞mit. Marlen. vj d ob iiij d xvj d
3 1a po*f*t marlin viij d ob. v d
4 2a po*f*t Marlyn ix d ob. $\overset{1}{\text{j}}$ d iiij d – vij s j d ob j d
*f*eptimana tertia ij s xj d ob [‡]
po*f*t Joha͞ne͂ Bapti*f*ta
5 3a po*f*t Marlen viij d $\overset{b}{\text{j}}$ d ij d xvj d for putting
Septimana 4a
po*f*t Jo͂em Baptista Ds grenewood in co͞mens [§]
6 4a po Septimana. Marlen vij d – $\overset{gg}{\text{j}}$ d $\overset{\text{coq}}{\text{ob}}$ – iiij d
5a po*f*t Joa͞em Bp.
7. 6a po*f*t J. Bapti*f*t. Marlen. vij d ob $\overset{gg}{\text{j}}$ $\overset{1}{\text{d}}$ $\overset{\text{coq}}{\text{ob}}$ – iiij d
8 7a hebd. Bapt: Marlen vj d ob – iiij d

---

* Probably unrelated. The "C" is not the usual Elizabethan letter and may be a mere parenthesis.

† Probably not related to Marlowe's account.

‡ Final entries opposite all names are unusually large this week.

§ At bottom of next page, facing this: "Ds Grenewood–xvj d." Kett's name appears here for the last time, marked "no͂ co." He has made no purchases at the buttery during this term.

9. 8a hebd. Bapt. nõ co marlen. vj d. xij d^{d}

10. 9 hebd nõ co Marlen – ob^{co}
11 Marlen vij d. j d. j d ob. ob. iiij d
[12] marlen. xj d ob. – iij d
[13] marlen. ob^{co} – ix d ob – iij d
[Totals] # marlyn – xvij s. v d. ob. *f*ol: R:C.
Septi: mihailis 1581 marlyn j d ob – iij d – iij d
Septi: *f*ecunda marlen – vj d ob – ij d – v d
Sept: 3a marlen. vj d – iiij d – j^{co} d
Sep: 4a. Marlen xj d ob – v j d. iiij d
Sep: 5 a. marlyn. x d – iiij^{b} d ob – v d – ij d ob^{co}
Sept: 6a marlen xiij d j d^{b} – vij d – j d ob^{co}
Sept: 7a Marlen xij d ob. jd ob iiij^{R} d – iiij d
Sept. 8a Marlin v d. ij d – j^{co} d iiij d
9a Marlin jd – ob^{co}. iiij d
10 a marlen ob. – iij d ob – ij d – v d
11a Marlin. v d ob. iij^{d} d. j.d.^{c} j$^{[?]}$ d^{b} – ob^{co} – vj d
12a marlen xij d j d.ob. j d ob. – vj d j^{b} d. – ob^{co} – iiijd

13a [Totals] *f*ol: R:C # Marlin. iij d iij d – j d^{d} iiij d – xxj s xj d

[Correct total for this quarter is 15s. 10½d. The Bursar's total of 21s. 11d. is probably due in part to a confusion of "x" and "v." The figures preceding total are probably last-minute purchases by Marlowe.]

Septimana Nativit marlin. vj d – vij d – j d
2a Sept. 1a po*f*t nativitatem. marlin–– v d – j^{b}d – xij d
3a Sept: 2a po*f*t Nativit. marlin vjd – vij d – ob^{co}
4a marlin – vj d–– iij d – j d^{co}. vd
5a marlin. viij d. j^{d}d – ob^{b} iiij^{d}
6a marlen. j d. vj d ob. ij^{d}d. j^{gg} d iiij^{d}
7a Marlin – vj d. xij d – jd^{co}
8a marlen ij d. viij d ob – iiij d – vj d
9a marlin. j d. viij d. iij^{d} d. v d
10a Marlin vij d – ij d – j d^{co}ob
11a marlen – j d. j d ob. ob. – viij d – iiij d
Sept: 12 a Marlin ix d ob. – ij^{ob} d. j^{g} d – ij d
Sept: 13a Marlin – iiij d iij d
[Totals] # Marlen – xv s. xj d ob. *f*ol: R:C

Sept: Annunciat: 1582 Marlin – viij d. iij d
Sept: 1a poft Annunciat: marlin – viij d – ij d
co
Sept: 2a poft Anũciat Marlin – viij d ob – ij d. viij d
Septimana Pafchalis 1582. Marlin – viij d. x d
co
Sept. 4a poft Anũciat: Marlin – viij d ob – jd. iiij d
co[?]
Sept: 5a poft Anũciat: Marlin – viij d ob – iiij d. –j d
Sept: 6a poft Anũciat: marlin viij d. – iiij d
Sept: 7a poft Anũciat. Marlin – viij d ob – v d
R
Septimana 8a poft Anũciat. Marlin – viij d – iiij d – iij d
gg
Septimana 9a poft Anũciats. marlin – viij d – j d iij d
Septimana 10a poft Anũciats. Marlin. viij d. viij d
gg
Septimana. 11a poft Annunciatis. marlin – vj d ob – ij d – iij d
Septimana. 12 poft Anunc. Marlin – viij d iiij d ob – j d ob. p d. ob
[Totals] # Marlin – xv s. fol: R:C.
co
Septimana Johan. Baptist. Marlin – viij d – j d ob iij d
Sept. 1a poft Joh. Baptift: Marlin – viij d. vj d
Sept. 2a poft Jo: baptift: nõ co marlin [blank]
Sept: 3a poft Jo: baptift. nõ co Marlin [blank]
Septim: 4a Jo: baptift: nõ co Marlin [blank]
Septima 5a Jo. baptift. nõ co Marlin [blank]
Septim: 6a nõ co Marlin [blank]
Septimana 7a poft Joañ Baptift. no co Marlin [blank]
Septimana 8a poft Jon. Baptift. no co Marline [blank]
Sept: 9a Marlin xj d – v d
Septimana 10a poft Johannẽ Baptift. Marlin. viij d. – v d
Septimana 11a poft Johannẽ Baptift. Marlin vij d ob – jd –vj d
Septimana 12a poft Johañ Marlin – v d. ij d
co
Septimana poft Johannẽ Baptift. 13a Marlin – j d. j d ob. ob – ix d – iiij – ob
[Totals] # Marlin – vij s viij d ob j d fol: R:C:
co
Septimana Michaelis 1582 Marlin – viij d. j d ob vij d j d. j d
Septimana. 1a. poft Michaelis fefta Marlin viij d – iiij d
Septimana 2a poft Michaelem: Marlin – xv d ob iiij d
Septimana 3a poft Michaelem: Marlin – xij d ob v d
Septimana quarta poft michaelem. marlin xiiij d ob vj d

Septimana quinta: poſt Marlin xiij d ob. $^{\text{[Illegible note]}}$ — vij d j^{g}d. ij d. iiij di. ij^{co} d michaelem.

Septimana. 6a. poſt michaelē̃: marlin — vij d — j d. ij d. ob

Septimana Septima Poſt marlin — iiij d j d. iij d iiij d ob^{co} michaelē̃

Septimana. 8a Poſt Michaelem marlin — vj d. ij^{d} d. iij d

Septimana nona Poſt michaelem marlin — vj^{d} d — iiij^{g} d. iiij d

Septimana decima. marlin — viij d. jd iiij d ob^{co}. vjd iiij d

Septimana vndecima marlin x d — j d. j d ob. ob. ij^{co} d. ij d

[Totals] # marlin — xvij s ij d ſol: R:C:

Septim: michaelis 1582. marlin xij d ob. xiiij d [Last page of this volume.]

[On the very last page of the "Buttery Book 1581-82" appears the entry above. This is repeated on the first page of the following volume, "Buttery Book 1582-86," but it is here marked "Solut." Thus:]

Septim: Michaelis: 1582 ſolut, marlin — xij d ob. xiiij d ſolut. S.S.

[This is the first appearance in the records of the new bursar, Sophonyam Smyth.]

Septim Circuſionis Dñi. 1582. marlin. xviij d. ob. xvj d

Septimana tertia. Sept epiphan. marlin. viij d j s j d

Septimana 1a poſt epiph. marlin. vj d iiij d

Septimana 2a poſt epiph. marlin viij ob vj — iiij d

3a poſt epiph. marlin vij d — iij d

[4a] marlin. x d. j^{l}d. j^{g}d j^{b}d xij d iiij d

Prima poſt purificatione marlin. — xj d. ii s j^{b}d. ob. ob — vj d

Secunda Poſt: Marlin xi d ob. j^{l} d

3a poſt purificatione marlin xi d iij d. j^{b}d

[4a] marlin. viij d ob. j^{l}d. ij^{g} d. — j^{co} d ob

[5a] marlin. xij d. j^{l}d iij^{d} d. iiij^{g} d. j d ob

[6a] marlin xiij d. j d. j d ob. ob. ſolut. ſoph. ſmith

[7a] marlyne [blank, like most names this week.]

[At this point there is a gap in the record, after which the hand changes.]

Martij. 22° 1583 Marlyne — vj d. ob. j d ob

Septimana Anũtiationis

Septimana Paſchal. Marlye — iij d ob. ix d. ob

Septimana poſt paſchal 2a Marlye. — iiij d. ob^{b} v d

Septimana post Paſcha Marlin — iiij d. ob. iiij d ob

Sept. Post Paſcha 3a. Marline. — ij d ob. j^{d}d. j^{b}d. xij^{Beadle} d. iiij d

Septimana Post Paſcha. 4a. Nõ co: Marly [blank]

Septimana Post **Pafcha.** 5a.	Nõ co: Marlye [blank]
Sept. Post Pafcha. **6a.**	Nõ co: Marlyn [blank]
[7a]	Nõ co: Marlin [blank]
[8a]	Nõ co: Marlin [blank]
[9a]	Nõ co: Marline [blank]
Post pafcha. **10a.**	Nõ co Marlin – j d^{co} ob
[11a]	Marly – xj d. iiij d. j d. j d ob. ob
[12a]	Marlin vj s viij d.
Septimana Johan. Baptist 1583 prima	Marlyne – xiiij d. ob iiij d.

[In the week of John Baptist the book returns to its earlier hand.]

Septimana post Baptist. 1a.	Marlin – xix d. j$^{\overset{r}{m}}$d. ij d
Sept. post. Joh. Baptist. 2a.	Marlin – vij d. iij^{b} d. vj^{d} d. iiij d
Sept. post Bapt. 3a.	Marlin – vj d. iij^{b} d. ob. j d^{b}. ij^{g}d ob viij d iiij d. ob
Sept. post Bapt. 4a.	Marlin – xxij d ob v^{b}d. ij^{g} d. ij d
Sept. post Bapt. 5a.	Marlin – viij d. iij^{b} d. vj^{b} d. j^{g} d. iiij d.
Sept. 6a.	Marlin – viij d iiij d. vij^{d} d j^{g}d. iiij d
Sept. 7a.	Marlin – xv. iiij^{b} d ob. vj^{d} d j^{g}d iiij d
Sept. post Bapt. 8a.	Marlin – vij d iij^{b} d. iij^{d} d. v d
Sept. post bapt. 9a.	Marlin – viij d. iiij d
Septimã: post Bap. 10a.	Marlin – xv d. iiij^{d} d iiij d
Septimã. post Bap. 11a.	Marlin – x d. iij d ij d. ob^{co}. iiij d
Septimã. Post Bap. 12a.	Marlin – ix d. ij^{b} d. iij d
Septimã. Post Bap. 13a.	Marlin – xij d ob. ij^{b}d ob. iij^{d} d iij d j d j d ob ob

[Totals] *fol. fo. f.* Marlin – xxv s. iiij d # Sol. Soph. S.

[These totals are obviously for the quarter only. The incomplete entries immediately preceding the quarter seem never to have been totalled at all.]

Septimana Michaelis. 1583. Prima	Marlin – xxij d ij^{b} d ob iiij d
Septimana post Michaelẽ. 1a. ,	Marlin – xij d ij^{b} d j d^{co} v d
Septimana post Michaelẽ. 2a.	Marlin – xxiij d. v d
Septimana post Michaelẽ. 3a.	Marlin – xiiij d. iiij d
Septimana post Michaelẽ. 4a.	Marlin – xx d. ob^{b}. ij^{g} d iij d

Septimana post Michaelem. 5a.	Marlin – iij d. $\overset{b}{\text{iiij}}$ d. j^{g}d. v d
Septimana post Michael. 6a.	Marlin – vij d. $\overset{g}{\text{j}}$ d vj d
Sep: post Micha. 7a.	Marlin – iiij d. $\overset{b}{\text{ij}}$ d $\overset{l}{\text{ij}}$ d j $\overset{co}{\text{d}}$ ob v d
Sept post Mich. 8a. 1583	Marlin – vj d $\overset{b}{\text{ij}}$ d $\overset{co}{\text{ob}}$ vj d
Sept post Micha. 9a. 1583	Marlin – iij d $\overset{b}{\text{iiij}}$ d j^{g}d iiij d
Sept. post Micha. 10a. 1583	Marlin – vj d $\overset{b}{\text{ij}}$ d iiij d ob.
Sept post Mich 11a 1583	Marlin – v d. $\overset{b}{\text{iij}}$ d iiij d j d j d ob ob
[Totals]	Marlin – xvijs xj d ob – x s– iij d

[The correct total for the quarter is 17s. 11½d. The amounts following this in the total are evidently later purchases.]

Sept. Nat. Dñi. 1583	Marlin – vj d $\overset{b}{\text{ij}}$ d xij d
Septimana poſt Nat. Dñj. 1a. 1583	Marlin – viij d xix d
Sept. poſt Nat. Dñj. 2a 1583	Marlin – viij d xv d
1583 Sept. poſt Nat. Dj̃. 3a.	Marlin – viij d v d
1583 Sept. poſt Nat. Dñj. 4a	Marlin – viij d $\overset{co}{\text{xvj}}$ d v d
1583. Sept. post Nat. Dnj. 5a	Marlin – v d $\overset{b}{\text{iij}}$ d vd
Sept. post Nat. dj̃. 6a	Marlin – v d. $\overset{b}{\text{iij}}$ d viij d
Sept. post Nat. Dnj. 7a.	Ds. Marlin – v d $\overset{b}{\text{iij}}$ d v d
Sept. post Nat. Dñj. 8a.	Ds. Marlin – vj d $\overset{b}{\text{ij}}$ d iiij d ob
Sept. post Nat. Dñj 9a	Ds. Marlin – v d $\overset{b}{\text{ij}}$ d $\overset{b}{\text{j}}$ d iiij d
Sept. post Nat. Dñj. 10a.	Ds. Marlyne – xiij d iiij d iiij d

1583 Sept. post Nat Dñj. 11a. Ds. Marlin – ob

Sept: post Nat: Dñj: 12a.	Ds. Marlin – ix d $\overset{b}{\text{ij}}$ d j d j d ob ob. iij d
[Totals] *f*ol. Soph. #	Ds Marlin – xviijs j d # Smyth
1584. Sept Anuntiationis	Ds. Marlin – viij d

1584. Sept. post Anũtiat. 1a. Ds Marlin. – viij d ij s vj d

Sept. post Anũt. 2a.	Ds. Marlin – iiij d $\overset{b}{\text{iiij}}$ d
1584. Sept. post Anũt 3a	Ds Marlin – v d $\overset{b}{\text{iij}}$ d v s. Mr Read.

1584. Sept. pa*f*ch Ds. Marlin – vj d ij[b] d ix d

Sept. post pa*f*ch. 1a. Ds. Marlin – v d ob ij[b] d ob v d

post Anũt. 5a.

1584 Sept. post Anut. 6a Ds. Marlin – viij d j d vj d

1584. Sept. post Anut. 7a Ds Marlin – viij d vj d

1584. Sept. post Anuntiat: 8a. Ds. Marlin – viij d vj d

1584. Sept. post Anũt. 9a Ds. Marlin – viij d ij d

A*f*centionis: sept

1584. Sept. post Anũtiat. 10a Ds. Marlin – iiij d iiij d viij d

1584. Septi. post Anutiat. 11a Solut Soph. # Ds. Marlyn – viij d.
iiij[rm] d.

Penticostes ij[d] s. vj d x d #

[A few others pay what appears to be a total this week. The rest pay the following week. Marlowe pays twice, thus:]

1584. Sept. post Anuntiat. 12a. Sol. Soph. S. # Ds. Marlin – ij d j d j d j d ob iij d # v d

Sept. Johan: Baptist: 1584. Ds. Marlin – viij d vd

Sept. post Johan: Bapt. 2a Ds Marlin – viij d iiij d

Sept: post Bap: 2a Ds. Marlin – viij d ij d

Commitior Sept:

Sept. post baptist. 3a. Ds Marlin – x d iij d

Sep. post Bap: 4a. Ds Marline – v d vij d vj d

Sep. post Bap: 5a. Ds Marline – xj d iiij[dean] d vj d

Sept. post: Bapt. 6a Ds Marlin – vj d. ij[d] d vj d

Sept. post Joh: Bapt. 7a Ds Marlin – iij d j[l] d iiij[d] d v d

Sept. post Joh. Bapt. 8a. 1584. Ds. Marlin – viij d v d

Sept. post. Joh. Bapt. 9a. 1584. Ds. Marlin – iiij d iiij[d] d vj d

Sept. post Joh. Bapt. 10a. 1584. *f*e co: Ds. Marlin – x d ij d ob

Sept. post Joh. Bapt. 11a. 1584 nõ co Ds. Marlin [blank]

Sept. post Joh: Bapt: 12a. 1584 nõ co: Ds. Marlin [blank]

Sept. post Johannẽ Bapt: 13a 1584 *f*ol. Soph. #. Ds. Marlin – iij d iij d vij d j d j d ob iij d S. Smyth #

[The records seem to be in confusion at this point. The next two pages have a list of names with practically no charges. The payments listed above are obviously too small to be totals. The Bursar's failure to collect may be due to Marlowe's prolonged absence.]

Sept: Michaelis 1584 nõ co: Ds. Marlye [blank]

M[r]. Harris Stewarde

Sept post Mich. 1a 1584 nõ co: Ds Marlin [blank]

Sept. post Mich. 2a 1584 *f*e co: Ds. Marlin vij d iij d

Sept. post Micha: 3a 1584 Ds. Marle vij d ob. vj d ob.

Sept. post Mich. 4a 1584. *f*e co: Ds. Marlin iij d

Sept post Mich. 5a 1584. nõ co: Ds. Marlin [blank]

Sept: post. Michelẽ. 6a. 1584. nõ co: Ds. Marlin [blank]

Sept: post Mich: 7a 1584. nõ co: Ds. Marlin $\overset{b}{ij}$ s
Sept: post Mich. 8a. 1584. nõ co: Ds. Marlin [blank]
Sept. post Mich. 9a. 1584. nõ co: Ds. Marlin [blank]
Sept. post Micha. 10a 1584 nõ co: Ds. Marlin – iij d
Sept: post Mich: 11a. nõ co: Ds. Marlin – j d j d ob iij d
vj d [erased]
[12a. Totals?] Ds. Marlin – iiij s xi d ob
Sept: Nat: Chrĩ. 1584 nõ co Ds. Marlin [blank]
Sept. Circucifionis./ nõ co Ds. Marlin – iiij d
post. Nat. dnĩ. 1a. 1584
Sept. Epiphaniae. post Nat. nõ co: Ds. Marlin [blank]
dnĩ. 2a 1584
Sept. post Nat. Dnĩ. 3a. 1584. nõ co: Ds. Marlye [blank]
Sept post Nat dnĩ. 4a. 1584. nõ co: Ds. Marlin [blank]
Sept. post N. Dominj. 5a. 1584. Ds. Marlye – viij d viij d
Sept. post Nat. dnĩ. 6a. Ds. Marlyne – viij d x d
1584. purificatio Mariae
Sept. post Nat. Dnj. 7a Ds. Marlin – x d viij d
1584
Sept: post Nat: Dnĩ. 8a. 1584. *f*e co Ds. Marlin – $\overset{b}{iiij}$ d $\overset{d}{iiij}$ d iij d
ob
Sept: post Nat. Dnĩ. 9a. 1584 Ds. Marlin – ix d. $\overset{b}{j}$ d viij d
Sept: Comitior: 11.
Sept. post Nat: Dnĩ. 10a. Ds. Marlin – vj d $\overset{b}{iiij}$ d $\overset{b}{ij}$ d – xviij d vj d
1584
Sept. post Nat: Dnĩ. 11a. 1584 Ds. Marlin – vj d $\overset{b}{ij}$ d vj d
Sept: post Nat. Dnj. 12a. 1584. Ds. Marlin – viij d. j d j d ob iij d
iiij d. v d
[Totals] Ds. Marlye – xiij s ij d
Sept. Anuntiationis 1585 Ds. marly – xiij d iiij d
[The Elizabethan New Year]
Sept. post Anuntiationem. 1a Ds. Marlyne – xiij d v d.
1585
Sept post Anunt: 2a. Ds. marly – xij d iij d
1585
Sept: post Anũt. 3a 1585. nõ co Ds. marly – ij d
Sept. Pa*f*ch.
Sept: post Anunt: 4a. 1585 nõ co: Ds. Marlye [blank]
Sept. post Anunt: 5a. 1585. nõ co: Ds. Marlye [blank]
Sept. post Anunt. 6a 1585. nõ co: Ds. Marlye [blank]
Sept: post Anuntiat: 7a nõ co: Ds. Marlye [blank]
1585
Sept: post Anuntiat: 8a nõ co: Ds. Marlye [blank]
1585

Sept. Afcentjonis.
Sept. post Anutiat. 9a 1585 nõ co: Ds. Marlye [blank]
Sept. post Anunt. 10a. nõ co: Ds. Marlye [blank]
1585. Sept. Penticoft.
Sept post Anutiat. 11a. 1585 nõ co: Ds Marlye [blank]

[Beginning with the fourth week after Annunciation and continuing until the twelfth the Buttery Book contains a great many blanks as if few members of the College were in attendance. Toward the end of the period these gradually increase, and in the twelfth week there is a sudden resumption of normal charges.]

Sept. post Anũt. 12a 1585. nõ co: Ds. marlye – iiijd j d j d ob iij d
[Totals] Ds. Marlye – vs j d ob
Sept. Joh. Bapt. 1585. Ds. Marlye – x d v d
Sept. post Bapt. 1a 1585. Ds. Marlye – ij d ob vj d
Sept. post. Joh: Bapt. 2a 1585 Ds. Marlye – viij d vd j d iiij d ob
Sept post Joh Bapt 3a 1585 fe co Ds. Marlye viij d iiij d
Sept. post Joh. Bapt: 4a. 1585 nõ co Ds. Marly [blank]

[Lewgar, another of Archbishop Parker's scholars and presumably one of Marlowe's room-mates is absent from this date until Marlowe's return in the thirteenth week after St. John Baptist. Tilman, another student, is absent from the fourth to ninth weeks, inclusive.]

Sept. post Joh. Bapt. 5a 1585. nõ co: Ds Marly [blank]
Sept: post. Joh Bap: 6a 1585. nõ co: Ds. Marly [blank]
Sept post Joh. Bapt. 7a. 1585. nõ co: Ds. Marly [blank]
Sept. post Joh. Bapt. 8a. 1585 nõ co: Ds. Marly [blank]
Sept post Joh Bapt. 9a. 1585 nõ co: Ds. Marly [blank]
Sept. post Joh. Bapt.10a. 1585. nõ co: Ds. Marlye [blank]
Sept. post Joh. Bapt. 11a. nõ co: Ds. Marlye [blank]
1585. Sept. Nat. Doĩae
Sept post Johan. Bapt. 12a 1585 nõ co: Ds. Marlye [blank]
Sept: post Joannẽ: Bapt. 13a. 1585 Ds. Marlye – viij d iiij d j d j d ob iij d iij d ob
[Totals] Ds. Marly vj s iij d

Septimana Michaelis. 1585 Ds. Marly iiij d iiij d ob
Sept. post Mich: 1a. 1585. Ds. Marlye – xvj d vj d
Sept. post Mich 2a. 1585 Ds. Marly – xix d v d ob
Sept. post Mich. 3a. 1585 Ds. Marly – xiiij d v d
Sept. post Mich. 4a. 1585. Ds. Marlye – xxj d v d
Sept post Micha. 5a. 1585. Ds. marly – xv d ix d
Sept. post Mich – 6a. nõ co: Ds. Marly [blank]
Sept post Mich. 7a. 1585 nõ co: Ds. Marlye [blank]
Sept. post Mich. 8a. 1585. Ds. marlyn xj d vj d ob
Sept: post Mich. 9a. 1585 Ds. Marlye xiiij d iiij d ob
Sept. post Mich 10a. Ds. Marlye x d v d – ij s
Sept. 11a poft Mich. 1585. Ds. Marlyn – xv d v d
[12a] Ds. marlye – xij d v d j d j d ob iij d iiij d iiij d
[Totals] Ds. Marly – xx s ix d ob
Sept. Nat. Dnĩ. 1585 Ds Marlye – xiiij d xix d
Sept. Epiphaniae 1585 Ds marly – xviij d xix d
Sept. post. Nat. Dnĩ. 2. 1585 Ds. Marlyn – xv d ob vj d vij d

Sept. post Nat. Dnj. 3a. 1585. Ds. marlye — xviij d v d
Sept. post Nat. Dnj. 4a. 1585. D. marly — xvj d ob v d
Sept. post Nat. 5a. Ds. marlyn — ij s viij d ix d
Sept. post Nat. 6a Ds. marly — xiij d v d
Sept. post Nat. Dnj. 7a Ds. marlyn — ix d ix d ob
Sept post Nat. Dnj 8 1585. Ds. marlyn — xiij d ob v d j d iiij d ob
Sept. post Nat. Dnj 9a. 1585. nõ co: Ds. marlyn [blank]
Sept. post Nat. Dnj 10a. 1585. Ds. marlyne [blank]
Sept. post Nat. Dnĩ 11a. nõ co: Ds. marlyn — j d j d ob iij d iiij d

[Totals] Ds. marly — xxj s ij d

Sept Anuntiationis. 1586. nõ co. Ds. marlye [blank]
Sept. post Anutiat: 1a. 1586. nõ co. Ds. marlye [blank]
Sept. post Anutiat: 2a nõ co Ds. marlyn — iiij d
Sept. Paſch: 1586
Sept. post Anutiat. 3a. 1586 nõ co Ds marlyn [blank]
Sept post Anutiat 4a nõ co: Ds. marly [blank]
Sept post Anutiat. 5a 1586 Ds. marly [blank]
Sept post Anutiat. 6a. 1586 Ds. marly [blank]
Sept post Anutiat. 7a 1586. nõ co: Ds. marly [blank]
Sept. post. Anutiat/.8a. 1586 nõ co: Ds. marly [blank]
Sept. Penteco*ſ*t Sept. post Anut. 9a. no co: Ds. marly [blank]
Sept. post Anutiat. 10a nõ co Ds marly — x [erased]
Sept post Ant. 11a nõ co Ds. marly
Sept post Anut. 12a 1586. nõ co: Ds marly j d j d ob iij d

[Totals] Ds. marly ix d ob

[Lewgar is again absent at the same dates and he has the same charges as Marlowe.]

Septimana Johĩs Baptist: 1586 Ds marly — x d v d
Sept. post Joh: Bapt. 1a. 1586 Ds marlye — xvjd vij d iiij d (d over vij)
Sept. post John: Bapt: 2a. 1586 Ds. Marlye — xiij d iij d ob
Septi post John. Bapt: 3a. 1586. Ds. Marlye — xj d. ob vj d ob
In pane / In potn } xvj^s vij d
Septi. post Johã Bapt. 4a Ds Marly — xv d vj d In { pane- / potn- } xj^s xj d ob
In { pane / potue } xiij^s iiij d
Septima. post Joh. Baptist. 5a Ds Marly — xx d ob vj d vj d ob (d over first vj)
Septima. po*ſ*t Joh. Bapti*ſ*t. 6a. Ds Marlye — xiiij d viij d ob
Septima post Joh. Baptist. 7a. Ds Marly — xvij d vj d
Septimana post Joh. Baptist. 8a Ds Marlye xj d vij d viij d (b over vij)
Sept post John Bapt. 9a Ds Marlie — xxj d vj d x d (b over vj)
Sept post Johñ Baptist. 10a Ds Marley — xxj d iiij d viij d ix d (b over iiij, d over viij)

Sept. post Johñ. Bapt. 11a — Ds Marlye – j d ob ix d

Sept. post Johñ. Baptist. 12a — Ds Marly – xx d $\overset{b}{\text{iij}}$ d x d

Sept. post Johñ. Bapt. 13a — Ds Marly – xiiij d x d j d j d ob iij d

[Total] Ds. Marlye – xxix^{s} vj d

Sept. Michael. 1586 — Ds Marly xviij d $\overset{b}{\text{iiij}}$ d

Sept – post mich la — Ds Marly – xiij d $\overset{b}{\text{j}}$ d

2a post — Ds Marly – xvj d

[The Buttery Book for the rest of Marlowe's sojourn in Cambridge is lost.]

Appendix B

CHECK LIST OF EXTANT EARLY EDITIONS

Tamburlaine

1590. Black letter octavo. Parts I. and II. [STC 17425].—2 copies known: Bodleian; Huntington, the latter also possessing two leaves of a third copy.

1592. Black letter octavo. Parts I. and II. [STC 17426].—Unique copy at the British Museum. Sometimes erroneously described as a 1593 copy. No such edition exists.

1597. Black letter octavo. Parts I. and II. [STC 17427].—Unique copy in Huntington.

1605. Black letter quarto. Part I. only. [STC 17428].—10 copies known: British Museum, 2 copies; Bodleian; Dyce; Huntington, 2 copies; Boston Public Library; Barnet J. Beyer, New York; Rosenbach (White copy), New York; Magdalene College, Cambridge.

1606. Black letter quarto. Part II. only. [STC 17428a].—8 copies known: British Museum, 2 copies; Bodleian; Dyce; Huntington; Rosenbach (2 copies, White and Clawson); Worcester College, Oxford.

Doctor Faustus

1604. Black letter quarto. [STC 17429].—Unique copy at Bodleian.

1609. Black letter quarto. [STC 17430].—2 copies: Hamburg; Huntington.

1611. Black letter quarto. [STC 17431].—Unique copy at Huntington.

1616. Black letter quarto. [STC 17432].—Unique copy at British Museum.

1619. Black letter quarto. [STC 17433].—Unique copy: Robert Garrett, Baltimore.

1620. Black letter quarto. [STC 17434].—3 copies: British Museum; Worcester College, Oxford; A. Edward Newton.

1624. Black letter quarto. [STC 17435].—Unique copy: British Museum.

1628. Black letter quarto. [Unknown to STC].—2 copies: Lincoln College, Oxford; Kungliga Biblioteket, Stockholm.

1631. Black letter quarto. [STC 17436].—8 copies: British Museum; Bodleian, 2 copies; National Library of Scotland;

Huntington; Harvard; Yale; Barnet J. Beyer, New York (Clawson copy).
1663. Quarto. [Not listed in STC, being later than 1640].—8 copies: British Museum, 2 copies; Dyce; Huntington; Harvard; Yale; Carl H. Pforzheimer, New York; Worcester College, Oxford.

Jew of Malta
1633. Quarto. [STC 17412].—42 copies known.

Edward the Second
1594. Quarto. [STC 17437].—2 copies: Landesbibliothek, Kassel; Zentralbibliothek, Zurich.
1598. Quarto. [STC 17438].—7 copies: British Museum, 2 copies; Bodleian; National Library of Scotland; Huntington, 2 copies; Folger.
1612. Quarto. [STC 17439].—6 copies: British Museum; Dyce; Huntington, 2 copies; Harvard; John E. Hannigan, Boston.
1622. Quarto [STC 17440 and 17440a].—12 copies: British Museum, 2 copies; Bodleian; Dyce; Yale; Harvard; Boston; Owen D. Young, New York; Rosenbach; Nationalbibliothek, Vienna; Huntington; Worcester College, Oxford.

Dido
1594. Quarto. [STC 17441].—3 copies: Bodleian; Huntington; Folger.

Massacre at Paris
(No date). Octavo. [STC 17423].—11 copies: British Museum; Bodleian; Dyce; Magdalene College, Cambridge; Huntington; Williams College; Folger; Charles W. Clark, New York; Rosenbach; Library of Congress; P. J. Dobell, Tunbridge Wells.

Hero and Leander
1598A. Quarto. [STC 17413].—Unique copy at Folger.
1598B. Quarto. [STC 17414].—2 copies: British Museum; Huntington (Lamport copies).
1600. Quarto. [STC 17415].—3 copies: British Museum; Huntington; Rosenbach.
1606. Quarto. [STC 17416].—4 copies: British Museum; Bodleian; Morgan; Wellesley (Rowfant copy).
1609. Quarto. [STC 17417].—3 copies: Dyce; Folger; Rosenbach (W. A. White copy).
1613. Quarto. [STC 17418].—2 copies: British Museum; Huntington.
1616. GHOST EDITION. No copies known; probably never existed, though many books refer to it.

1617. Quarto. [STC 17419].—4 copies: Huntington, 2 copies; Rylands Library, Manchester; Worcester College, Oxford.
1622. Quarto. [STC 17420].—3 copies: Huntington; Yale; Estate of F. B. Bemis, Boston.
1629. Quarto. [STC 17421].—10 copies: British Museum; Dyce; Bodleian; Trinity College, Cambridge; Library of Congress; Huntington; Folger; Williams College; John E. Hannigan, Boston; Prideaux copy (in hands of unknown owner since 1917).
1637. Quarto. [STC 17422].—14 copies: British Museum, 2 copies; Dyce; National Library of Scotland; Trinity College, Cambridge, 2 copies; Rylands Library, Manchester; Huntington; Folger; Harvard; Morgan; University of Texas; Williams College; Carl H. Pforzheimer, New York.

Lucan

1600. Octavo. [STC 17415].—5 copies: British Museum; Bodleian; Huntington; Folger; Rosenbach.

The translations of Ovid exist in six separate editions. Having been surreptitiously printed without printer's name or date, the editions can be distinguished only by choosing a check-copy of each edition and naming the whole edition for it. The ornaments on the title pages are different on each edition and these are given in parenthesis in the list below:

1. Check-copy: Mason AA 207 (Bodleian). 6 asterisks in two rows of 3 each, the whole in brackets. Octavo.—3 copies: Bodleian; Dyce; Huntington.

2. Check-copy: Douce 0 31 (Bodleian). Ornamental band at top of page; lower on page a long band made up of 2 dolphins, 2 birds, and a head. Octavo. Unique copy at Bodleian.

3. Check-copy: Isham copy found at Lamport Hall. Quarto. 2 lace designs. Unique copy at Huntington.

4. Check-copy: Bindley copy (C 34.a.28) British Museum. Quarto. One lace ornament.—2 copies: British Museum; Carl H. Pforzheimer, New York.

5. Check-copy; Malone 368 (Bodleian). 3 leaves above 2 hands. Octavo.—11 copies: Bodleian; British Museum; Dyce; Huntington; Morgan; Wellesley; Yale; Carl H. Pforzheimer, New York; John Bakeless, New York; Quaritch; Myers, London.

6. Check-copy: Malone 133 (Bodleian). Square formed of four smaller squares, that in the upper left corner being turned the wrong way. Octavo.—8 copies: British Museum, 2 copies; Bodleian; Huntington; Folger; Harvard; Emmanuel College, Cambridge; George Arents, Jr., New York.

Bibliography

Manuscripts

[*This list contains all MSS. directly relating to Marlowe and his family, together with some of the more important MSS. relating to his friends or associates.*]

Will of Richard Marley, 1521. Consistory Registry, Canterbury, Vol. XIII, f. 61. [Transcribed by C. F. Tucker Brooke.] Public Record Office, Canterbury.

Will of Christopher Marley, 1539/40. Archdeaconry Registry, Canterbury, Vol. XXI, ff. 258 ff. [Transcribed by Brooke.] Public Record Office, Canterbury.

Will of John Hobbes [Father-in-law of Christopher Marley], 1545/6. Archdeaconry Register, Vol. XXIV, f. 62. [Transcribed by Brooke.] Public Record Office, Canterbury.

Will Nuncupative of Dorothy Arthur [Aunt of the dramatist], 1597. Archdeaconry Register, Vol. L, f. 361. [Transcribed by Brooke.] Public Record Office, Canterbury.

Will of John Marlowe [Father of the dramatist], 1604/5. Archdeaconry Register, Vol. LII, f. 373. [Transcribed by Brooke.] Public Record Office, Canterbury.

Will of Katherine Marlowe [Mother of the dramatist], 1605/6. Archdeaconry Register, Vol. LIV, f. 267. [Transcribed by Brooke.] Public Record Office, Canterbury.

Treasurer's Accounts, King's School, Canterbury. In the Cathedral Library.

Register Book of St. George the Martyr, Canterbury. In the custody of the Rector.

Chamberlain's Accounts, City of Canterbury. [These form the basis for J. M. Meadows's lists of Freemen and Intrantes.] Royal Museum and Public Library (Beaney Institute), Canterbury.

Register of St. Andrew's, Canterbury. Now in custody of the Rector of St. Margaret's, Canterbury.

Register of St. Mary Bredman, Canterbury. Now in the care of the Rector of St. Margaret's, Canterbury.

Matriculation Book, University Registry, Cambridge University, Cambridge.

Supplicats for B.A. and M.A. University Registry, Cambridge University, Cambridge.

Grace Book Delta, 1542-1589. University Registry, Cambridge University, Cambridge. [Transcribed by John Venn.]

C.C.C.C. Chapter Book, 1569-1626. Strong Room of the Estates Bursary, Corpus Christi College, Cambridge. This contains, following p. 292, the *Registrum Parvum,* which has two entries relating to Marlowe's admission. The Chapter Book itself contains much interesting information relative to the life of the College.

"Statuta & c. & c." Spencer Room, Corpus Christi College, Cambridge. Contains many of the indentures relating to the Norwich and Canterbury scholarships and official forms of college oaths.

Buttery Books. Strong Room of the Estates Bursary, Corpus Christi College, Cambridge. These documents lay unbound and unknown in the Estates Bursary until April, 1935, when they were found. Their relation to Marlowe was discovered by the present writer in August, 1936.

Audit Books. Strong Room of the Estates Bursary, Corpus Christi College, Cambridge. [Transcribed by G. C. Moore-Smith and John H. Ingram.] The annual audits include quarterly accounts of scholarship payments. The audit for 1585/6 is lacking, but fortunately this gap is covered by the Buttery Book, which itself breaks off in 1586/7 as the Audit Book resumes. We thus have a complete record of Marlowe's attendance.

"The names of all the Readers and Auditors of eueri of the Lectures in cambrige anõ dñi 1581." Lansdowne MS. 33, ff. 84-85, British Museum. [Discovered by G. C. Moore-Smith.]

Petition of William Bradley, Queen's Bench Controlment Rolls, K.B. 29/226, Membrane 119 verso. [Discovered by J. L. Hotson and transcribed by Mark Eccles.] Public Record Office, London.

Coroner's Inquest on William Bradley. Chancery Miscellanea, Bundle 68, File 12, No. 362. [Discovered and transcribed by Mark Eccles.] Public Record Office, London.

Pardon of Thomas Watson, Patent Rolls, 32 Elizabeth, Part 4. Also in Originalia, E. 371/540, No. lxxi. [Discovered and transcribed by Mark Eccles.] Public Record Office, London.

Watson and Marlowe at Newgate Prison. Middlesex Sessions Roll, 284, No. 12. [Discovered and transcribed by Mark Eccles.] Middlesex Guildhall, London.

Marlowe's Recognizance, Middlesex Sessions Roll 284, No. 1.

Gaol Delivery Roll, October 3, 31st Elizabeth. Nos. 1 and 2. [Discovered and transcribed by Mark Eccles.] Middlesex Guildhall, London.

Constables' Appeal to the court for protection against Marlowe. Middlesex Sessions Roll, 309, No. 13. [Discovered and transcribed by Mark Eccles.] Middlesex Guildhall, London.

Bills of the Keepers of the Gatehouse Prison, Westminster. Additional MSS. 41257, No. 30, British Museum. Contains the name of "Christopher Marlowe" used as a Jesuit's alias. Formerly owned by P. J. and A. E. Dobell.

Thomas Kydd's two letters to Sir John Puckering. Harleian MS. 6848, f. 154; Harleian MS. 6849, f. 218. The first discovered and transcribed by F. S. Boas, the second by Ford K. Brown. At least one, however, had previously been known to William Oldys and is referred to in his annotated Langbaine, now in the British Museum.

Baines Libel. Harleian MS. 6848, ff. 185-186; Harleian MS. 6853, ff. 188-189 (folios formerly numbered 170-171, 307-308).

Philip Henslowe's Diary, Dulwich College, Dulwich.

Henslowe Papers, Dulwich College, Dulwich.

Heretical Papers found among the effects of Thomas Kydd. Harleian MS. 6848, ff. 187-189, British Museum (folios formerly numbered 172-174). Transcribed by F. S. Boas: *Works of Kydd,* pp. cx-cxiii; Samuel A. Tannenbaum: *Book of Sir Thomas More,* pp. 103-104; W. D. Briggs: SP, 20:153-159 (1923); F.-C. Danchin, *Revue Germanique* 9:567-570, N-D 1913.

Notations in the Prideaux copy of the 1629 *Hero and Leander,* now lost.

Commonplace Book of Henry Oxinden, Folger Shakespeare Library, Washington.

"Oxinden Amici." MS. in Folger Shakespeare Library.

Another Commonplace Book of Henry Oxinden. Additional MS. 28012, ff. 514-v-515-r. British Museum. There are also Marlowe quotations on ff. 492, 495, 496. The two Commonplace Books and the notations in the Prideaux copy of *Hero and Leander* are the same.

"Remembrances of wordes and matters against Ric[hard] Cholmeley." Harleian MS. 6848, f. 190 (formerly numbered 175). British Museum.

Another spy's report. Harleian MS. 6848, f. 191. British Museum.

Investigation of Raleigh's religious beliefs. Harleian MS. 7042, ff. 401 ff. British Museum. [Printed by G. B. Harrison in his edition of *Willobie His Avisa* and by F. C. Danchin in *Revue Germanique* 10:578-581 (1914).]

Atheist's Tragedy. [Forgery.] Additional MS. 32380, ff. 16-v-12-v. Bought by the British Museum at J. P. Collier's sale, August 7, 1884, Lot 214. The forged poems are copied on the blank verso of the leaves of a genuine MS. copy of the *Eikon Basilike,* probably made from the first printed edition of 1648/9. They run from the back to the front of the book. See *Catalogue of Additions to the Manuscripts of the British Museum* (1889), p. 110. Collier printed part of the Marlowe forgery in *New Particulars* (1836), p. 47-n.

Burial Register of the Church of St. Nicholas, Deptford.

Original MS. Calendar of Patent Rolls for 35 Elizabeth. Public Record Office, London.

Coroner's Inquest on Marlowe. Chancery Miscellanea, Bundle 64,

File 8, No. 241 b. [Discovered and transcribed by J. L. Hotson. Now on display in the Public Record Office Museum.] Public Record Office, London.

Writ of Certiorari. Chancery Miscellanea, Bundle 64, File 8, No. 241 a. [Discovered and transcribed by J. L. Hotson.] Public Record Office, London.

Pardon of Ingram Frizer. Patent Rolls of Chancery, 1401. 35 Elizabeth. [Discovered and transcribed by J. L. Hotson.] Public Record Office, London.

"Will" of Ingram Frizer. 99 Skynner. Somerset House, London. [Discovered by the present author.] "99 Skynner" indicates that it is the 99th will in the book beginning with the will of a certain Skynner. Actually, it is not a will but a court's "sentence" disposing of the estate.

Will of Robert Poley. 97 Hele. Somerset House, London. [Discovered by the present author.]

Woodleff vs. Frizer. Chancery Proceedings, Elizabeth, Bundle W. 25, No. 43. [Discovered by J. L. Hotson.] Public Record Office, London.

Acts of the Privy Council, Vol. VI, June 29, 1587. Order to Cambridge authorities to award Marlowe's degree. Vol. XI, May 18, 20, 1593. Marlowe's appearance before Privy Council. Transcribed by Dasent, XV. 141, XXIV. 244. Public Record Office, London.

"Collier Leaf." A scene from *The Massacre at Paris* in Elizabethan handwriting. Folger Shakespeare Library, Washington.

Aubrey MS. 6, f. 108 (formerly folio 77). Bodleian Library. Records an erroneous story of Marlowe's death at the hands of Ben Jonson.

Version of "The Passionate Shepherd" in the Commonplace Book of John Thornborough. Folger Shakespeare Library, Washington.

Version of "The Passionate Shepherd" in Ashmolean MS. 1486, ii (Ash), f. 6-v. Bodleian Library.

Version of "The Passionate Shepherd" in a Commonplace Book of unknown origin, in the possession of Dr. A. S. W. Rosenbach, ff. 298-v-299.

Manuscript notes of Edmund Malone, notably in his copy of Langbaine and in his volume of original editions of Marlowe (Arch. G. d. 48). Bodleian Library. Various annotated Langbaines in the British Museum are of rather less importance.

Hunter's Chorus Vatum. Additional MS. 24488, ff. 372-380. British Museum. Complete photostatic copies in New York Public Library and Newberry Public Library, Chicago. Photostatic copy of the Marlowe section in the author's personal collection.

Three letters by Algernon Charles Swinburne to Sir Sidney Lee (1888), dealing with the Marlowe Memorial at Canterbury. Bodleian Library.

William Smith's "Particular Description of England." (1588.) Sloane MS. 2596. British Museum. Valuable for its watercolor pictures of Canterbury and Cambridge during Marlowe's life.

Collected Editions

UNDATED. Edmund Malone made a collected edition of Marlowe for his own private use by binding together early editions and manuscript copies. This book (originally numbered Malone 133, now re-numbered Arch. G. d. 48) is now at the Bodleian. One of the three known copies of *Dido* is in this book.

The British Museum has a similar collection from the library of King George III. The library of Charles II contained a volume of three Marlowe plays, bound together. This passed to the Earl of Charlemont, then to the Huth Library (Part IX, Addenda, No. 8258, p. 2275) and then disappeared. It was probably broken up by a dealer.

1818-1820. *Dramatic works of Christopher Marlowe, with prefatory remarks, notes, critical and explanatory.* By W. Oxberry, comedian. London: W. Simpkin and R. Marshall. [No date on title, but the individual plays, which were also issued separately, bear dates from 1818 to 1820.]

1826. *Works of Christopher Marlowe.* 3 vols. London: William Pickering. [Often called "Pickering's edition" or "Wreath edition." No editor's name appears but the editor is identified as E. G. Robinson, or George Robinson, in N&Q, 4th ser. 11:295 5 Ap 1873. Cf. John H. Ingram: *Christopher Marlowe and His Associates,* p. 280. For an early review, see *Gentleman's Magazine,* (OS) 169 (NS) 15:45-48 Ja 1841. The British Museum copy has MS. notes supposed to be J. Broughton's.

1850. *Works of Christopher Marlowe, with notes and some account of his life and writings by the Rev. Alexander Dyce.* 3 vols. London: William Pickering. Reprinted 1858. Revised edition in one volume 1865, 1870, and ca. 1885. For an early review, see *Fraser's Magazine,* 47:221-234 F 1853. The British Museum copy has MS. notes supposed to be J. P. Collier's.

1856. Poems of Greene, Marlowe, and Jonson. [Edited by Robert Bell.] London: J. W. Parker & Sons, 1856. Reprinted, London: G. Bell & Sons, 1889; New York: Hurst, nd. [Bell's annotated edition of the English poets.] Contains a memoir of Marlowe and the second edition prints the portrait of Lord Herbert of Cherbury which reappears in Cunningham's edition as a [false] portrait of Marlowe.

1860. *Shakespeare's Zeitgenossen und ihre werke.* Berlin: R. Decker. III. 153-173. Partial translation by Friedrich Martin Bodenstedt based on Dyce's text. Introduction, pp. 155-172.

1870. *Works of Christopher Marlowe.* Edited with notes and introduction. London: Crocker Brothers. Later editions 1871, 1872, 1897, 1902.

1870. *Works of Marlowe. Including his translations.* Edited with notes and introduction, by Lt. Col. Francis Cunningham. London: John Camden Hotten, nd. Reprinted from same plates but with minor alterations at intervals until 1912, when Chatto & Windus brought out a reprint.

1884-1885. *Works of Christopher Marlowe edited by A. H. Bullen, M.A., in three volumes.* London: Nimmo, 1884-1885; Boston: Houghton Mifflin, 1885. English edition limited to 400 copies, American edition to 350 copies.

1885. *Dramatic works of Christopher Marlowe.* Selected and edited by Percy E. Pinkerton, with a prefatory notice biographical and critical. London: W. Scott; New York: J. Pott & Co. [Canterbury Poets.] There is also an 1889 edition.

1885-1889. *Marlowe's werke historisch-kritische ausgabe von Hermann Breymann . . . und Albrecht Wagner.* Heilbronn: Gebr. Henninger. [Englische sprach- und literaturdenkmale.] This edition was never completed.

1887. *Best plays of Christopher Marlowe.* Edited by Havelock Ellis. With an introduction by J. A. Symonds. [Also in *Shakespeare's Predecessors*, q.v.] Mermaid edition. First edition unexpurgated. Slight changes in editions of 1903 and 1905, also more recent reprints. This edition, originally brought out by Vizetelly in London, was taken over by Unwin in England and Scribner in America and is kept constantly in print. The circumstances of its expurgation are described in Houston Peterson: *Havelock Ellis,* p. 177. There is a review in *The Dial*, 8:97-100 S 1887.

1889. *Théâtre. Traduction de Félix Rabbe avec une préface par J. Richepin.* 2 tom. Paris: A. Savine.

1902. *Passages from the works of Marlowe. Selected and edited for young students by J. Le Gay Brereton, B.A.* Sydney, Australia: Kealy & Philip, nd. [Australian tutorial series.]

1905. *Plays & poems of Christopher Marlowe.* London: George Newnes; New York: Scribner's. From same plates as the 1930 Simpkin Marshall edition, q.v.

1906. *Christopher Marlowe. Dramatic works.* London: Routledge. [Muses' Library.]

1905-1907. *Dramatic works of Christopher Marlowe.* London: Routledge; New York: Dutton. [New University Library.]

1909. *Plays of Christopher Marlowe.* Introduction by Edward Thomas. London: Dent; New York: Dutton. [Everyman Library.] A reissue in 1914.

1910. *Works of Christopher Marlowe edited by C. F. Tucker Brooke*, Oxford: Clarendon Press. Standard text on which all subsequent work has been based.

1912. *Christopher Marlowe with an introduction by William Lyon Phelps.* New York: American Book Company. [Masterpieces of the English Drama.] The introduction reprinted in *Essays on Books.*

1917. *Doctor Faustus, Edward the Second, The Jew of Malta,* Leipzig: Tauchnitz; Paris: Librairie Henri Gaulon. [Collection of British and American Authors.] Text based on Dyce.

1930. *Works and life of Christopher Marlowe.* General editor: R. H. Case. London: Methuen; New York: Dial Press. *The Life and Dido,* by C. F. Tucker Brooke (1930); *Tamburlaine,* by U. M. Ellis-Fermor (1930); *Jew of Malta* and *Massacre at Paris,* by H. S. Bennett (1931); *Poems,* by L. C. Martin (1931); *Doctor Faustus,* by F. S. Boas (1932); *Edward II,* by H. B. Charlton and R. D. Waller (1933).

1930. *Plays and Poems of Christopher Marlowe.* London: Simpkin Marshall Hamilton Kent & Co., Ltd.; New York: Scribner's. Identical with Newnes edition of 1905, q.v.

1932. De luxe edition of the *Works.* London: Golden Hours Press (in progress).

Marlowe as a Literary Subject

1828. Johann Ludwig Tieck. *Das Fest zu Kenelworth.* Berlin: Reimer. Reprinted in Tieck's *Gesammelte Werke* as *Dichterleben,* Berlin: Reimer, 1852-54. Translated as *The Life of Poets,* Leipsic: Fischer, 1830. This introduces Peele, Greene, Marlowe, and Shakespeare as characters. Marlowe is slain by the footman, "Ingeram."

1837. R[ichard] H[enry, later changed to Hengist] Horne. *Death of Marlowe.* London: Thomas Hailes Tracy, 1870. This ran through several editions and appears as Vol. 89 in Lacy's acting edition of plays. It is reprinted by Bullen, III. 315-353. The play was attacked by Swinburne but praised by Bullen [III. 315] as a "noble and pathetic tragedy." It was also praised by Leigh Hunt, to whom it was dedicated, and by Elizabeth Barrett Browning, with whom the author had at one time collaborated.

1878 and later. Algernon Charles Swinburne. *Poems and Ballads,* 2nd series. Stanzas 8-40 of "In the Bay" are supposed to refer to Marlowe.

Channel Passage and other poems
"Prologue to Doctor Faustus"
"Afterglow of Shakespeare"
"Prologue to Arden of Feversham"
"Prologue to The Broken Heart"

Sonnets on the Elizabethan Dramatists
1884. Ernst von Wildenbruch. *Christoph Marlow. Trauerspiel in vier akten. Gesammelte Werke,* VIII. Berlin: Grote, 1911-1924. More influenced by Tieck's story than by history. See discussion in TLS, No. 1176, p. 477, 31 Jy 1924.
1890. W. L. Courtney. "Death of Christopher Marlowe." *Universal Review,* 6:356-371 15 Mr 1890. Produced by Arthur Bourchier at the Shaftesbury Theatre, London, July 4, 1890; revived at St. James's Theatre, 1892.
1894. Ernest Rhys. "Marlowe" (poem). *London Rose,* New York: Dodd, Mead; London: Elkin Matthews and John Lane, p. 91.
1896. James Dryden Hosken. *Christopher Marlowe, a tragedy.* London: Henry and Company.
1899. E. A. V. Valentine. "To Christopher Marlowe" (poem). *Critic,* 35:888-889 O.
1901. Josephine Preston Peabody. *Marlowe, a drama in five acts.* Boston: Houghton Mifflin. First produced at Radcliffe College, Cambridge, Mass., June 19, 20, 1905.
1905. Sarah Hawks Sterling. *Shakespeare's Sweetheart.* Philadelphia: G. W. Jacobs & Co. Based on the story of Anne Hathaway. Marlowe is introduced as an actor in the rôle of Tybalt.
1913. Alfred Noyes. *Tales of the Mermaid Tavern.* New York: Frederick A. Stokes Co.
i. A Coiner of Angels, pp. 17-41
ii. The Sign of the Golden Shoe, pp. 71-96

1922. Clemence Dane [Pseudonym of Winifred Ashton]. *Will Shakespeare. An invention in four acts.* London: Heinemann. Shakespeare accidentally kills Marlowe.
1923. J. Lindsay. "Death of Marlowe" (one act playlet). *Vision,* 1:23-26 Ag.
1924. Ernest Milton. *Christopher Marlowe.* With a prologue by Walter de la Mare. London: Constable. Reissued in 1929.
1925. D. Ainslie. "Christopher Marlowe" (poem). *English Review,* 41:578 O.
1929. Charles Williams. *A Myth of Shakespeare.* Oxford University Press. Excerpts in *The Periodical,* 14:80-81 Je 1914.
1929. Charles Norman. "Exequy on the Death of Marlowe" (poem). In *Poems,* New York: Knopf.
1930. Charles Edward Lawrence. *"The Reckoning. Telling possibly the truth of the death of Marlowe."* Play in one act. *Cornhill Magazine,* 69:10-28 Jy.
1930. Charles Norman. "Faustus" (poem). *Theatre Arts Magazine,* 14:309-312 Ap.
1930. Charles Norman. "A Poem to Commemorate the Birthday of Christopher Marlowe." *Bookman,* 71:265-269 Je.
1930. W. R. Leigh. *Clipt Wings: A drama in 5 acts.* New York: Thornton W. Allen Co.

1930. Austin Melford. *Kit Marlowe; a play in one act.* London: S. French. [French's acting editions, No. 762.]
1930. Clinton Scollard. "Of Kit Marlowe" (poem). *Sewanee Review,* 38:132 Ap.
1936. Maria M. Coxe. *Kit Marlowe.* Produced by Hedgerow Players, Rose Valley, Philadelphia, Pa.
1936. Elizabeth Jenkins. *The Phoenix Nest.* London: Gollancz; Toronto: Ryerson.
1937. George W. Cronyn. *Mermaid Tavern. Kit Marlowe's Story.* New York: Knight Publications.

Notes

[The following abbreviations are used: CHEL—*Cambridge History of English Literature;* Jahrb.—*Jahrbuch,* German Shakespeare Society; MLN—*Modern Language Notes;* MLR—*Modern Language Review;* N&Q—*Notes and Queries;* PMLA—*Publications of the Modern Language Association;* RES—*Review of English Studies;* SP—*Studies in Philology;* TLS—*Times Literary Supplement.*]

1: The Mind of Marlowe

1. *Doctor Faustus,* 118; Harleian MS. 6848, f. 185 and Harleian MS. 6853, f. 188.
2. Kydd's letter to Sir John Puckering, Harleian MS. 6849, f. 218 and 6848, f. 154.
3. Harleian MS. 6848, f. 185 and 6853, f. 188.
4. Thomas Nashe: *Have with You to Saffron Walden,* McKerrow's Nashe, III. 85.
5. Brooke's edition, pp. 491, 647; *Hero and Leander,* III. 183.
6. II. *Tamb.* 4434-4435.
7. I. *Tamb.* 1942.
8. I. *Tamb.* 1925.
9. *Jew of Malta,* 14-15.
10. *Doctor Faustus,* 1342.
11. I. *Tamb.* 621.
12. II. *Tamb.* 3878.
13. *Hero and Leander,* I. 361.
14. I. *Tamb.* 876.
15. Caroline F. Spurgeon: *Shakespeare's Imagery,* pp. 12, 15, and Charts I and II.
16. *Doctor Faustus,* 560.

2: A Shoemaker's Son

1. On William Morle, see J. M. Cowper: *Roll of the Freemen of Canterbury,* col. 288; MSS. *Accounts 1393-1445,* Vol. I, fol. E xii. The Canterbury accounts are preserved in the Royal Museum and Public Library (Beaney Institute). On Thomas Morle, see Cowper, *op. cit.,* col. 288; MSS. *Accounts 1445-1506,* Vol. II, fol.

E ix. On Simon Morle, see Cowper, *op. cit.*, col. 288; MSS. *Accounts 1393-1445,* Vol. I, fol. E xxxix. The folio numbers in these MSS. do not run through consistently and are at best rough guides.

2. On the first John Marle, or Marley, see Cowper, *op. cit.;* MSS. *Accounts 1445-1506,* Vol. II, fol. Ciiij. On Richard Marley, tanner, see Cowper, *op. cit.*, col. 57; MSS. *Accounts 1512-1520.* His will is in *Consistory Court Register,* Public Record Office, Canterbury, Vol. XIII, fol. 61 and is transcribed by Tucker Brooke, *Life,* p. 83 ff.

3. Christopher Marley's will is in *Archdeaconry Register,* Public Record Office, Canterbury, Vol. XXI, fol. 258 ff.

4. This story was told to Mrs. Dorothy Gardiner by old inhabitants of Canterbury.

5. Cf. Conversations of Henry Oxinden with Simon Aldrich, Folger Library, Oxinden Commonplace Book; British Museum, Additional MS. 28012.

6. II *Tamb.* 4220-4234. References are to line numbers in the Oxford (1910) edition of Marlowe's *Works,* edited by Tucker Brooke.

7. The original *Register Booke of St. George the Martyr,* now in the care of the Rector, is actually a copy made in 1599, when many of the local registers were re-copied. Unfortunately, as the copyists say, "finding the saide records (some of theim) Vnperfectly Wrotten, and confuzedlye bound together, they could not so orderly proceade as they desired." The entire work has been transcribed by the late J. M. Cowper and carefully indexed, so that all references here given may be easily located.

8. Cowper: *Roll of the Freemen,* p. xi.

9. "Burghmote Orders 1469 &c.," Bunce MSS. II. 328. Original said to be "at the end of the large book of H6." The Bunce MSS. are preserved at the Royal Museum and Public Library (Beaney Institute). Cf. Cowper: *loc. cit.*

10. Bunce MSS. II. 192; "Rights and Privileges. New Transcribed," Bunce Minutes, No. XXIV; Bunce MSS. I. 108.

11. On Canterbury incomes and other statistics for 1522, see Bunce Minutes, No. XVI. The data as to John Marlowe's apprentices are in the municipal archives, MSS. *Accounts 1558-1568,* Vol. 12; *Accounts 1568-1577,* Vol. 13; *Accounts 1577-1587,* Vol. 14; *Accounts 1592-1602,* Vol. 16, ff. 10-r, 11-r. Cf. J. M. Cowper: *Roll of the Freemen,* cols. 200, 213, and John Bakeless, TLS 36:12 2 Ja 1937.

12. All the Marlowe wills are in the Public Record Office, Canterbury. John Marlowe's is in *Archdeaconry Register,* Vol. 52, fol. 373.

13. Will of Dorothy Arthur, *Archdeaconry Register,* Vol. 50, fol. 361.

14. Will of Katherine Marlowe, *Archdeaconry Register,* Vol. 54, fol. 267.

3: The King's Scholar

1. Bunce Minutes, No. XVI give a total of 893 residents in 1522.

2. *Jew of Malta,* 1861.

3. John Tucker Murray: *English Dramatic Companies.* See Index under "Canterbury." Bunce MSS. I. 49; Bunce Minutes, No. V.

4. Bunce MSS. II. 27.

5. *Acta Capituli,* Vol. I, fol. 20; *Publica Exercita Loveioii* [i.e., Lovejoy's] Scholarium, formerly MS. E-41 in the Cathedral Library, now in the care of the Headmaster, King's School. Cf. King's School Catalogue (1936), p. 10; *Cambridge History of English Literature,* V. 155; Dorothy Gardiner: *Canterbury,* pp. 69-76; Woodruff and Cape: *Schola Regia,* p. 89.

6. Bunce MSS. II. 359; Bunce Minutes, No. XXII.

7. John Brent: *Canterbury in the Olden Time* (2nd ed., 1879), p. 184; Bunce MSS. I. 138; II. 194-195.

8. I. *Tamb.* 758-759, 1552.

9. *Cal. State Papers, Venetian,* XV. 258; J. Q. Adams: *Shakespearean Playhouses,* pp. 130-131; W. B. Rye: *England as Seen by Foreigners,* pp. 3-53.

10. John H. Ingram: *Christopher Marlowe and His Associates,* p. 24 and note; John Brent: *Canterbury in the Olden Time* (1st ed.), p. 40; Bunce MSS. I. 49.

11. Bunce MSS. I. 196 (1576).

12. Bunce MSS. I. 182 (1557).

13. Bunce MSS. I. 187.

14. John Brent: *Canterbury in the Olden Time* (2nd ed., 1879), pp. 218-219; Bunce Minutes, No. V; MSS. *Accounts 1530-1538,* Vol. 8.

15. *Historians' History of the World,* XIX. 251.

16. Bunce MSS. I. 47.

17. MSS. *Accounts, 1539-1545,* Vol. IX; Bunce MSS. I. 49.

18. Bunce MSS. I. 126, 188; II. 196-197, 198, 201; Bunce Minutes, Nos. V, VI, VII.

19. II. *Henry IV,* V. i. 42-43.

20. *Passionate Shepherd,* 7-8; *Jew of Malta,* 1809, 1813. Cf. Dorothy Gardiner: *Literary Tradition of Canterbury,* 17-20.

21. *Jew of Malta,* 1382.

22. *Jew of Malta,* 973-974.

23. *Doctor Faustus,* 1342.

24. *Jew of Malta,* 1166.

25. *Jew of Malta,* 2091-2092.

26. Bunce MSS. I. 171; Bunce Minutes, No. V. There are refer-

ences to "the Fyle" in MSS. *Accounts 1530-1538,* fol. 15, for the year 1534/5.

27. *Plays Confuted in Five Actions.* Reprinted by W. C. Hazlitt: in *English Drama and Stage,* p. 161.

4: "Learning's Golden Gifts"

1. Indenture of April 2, 1580, preserved in an old MS. book labelled "Statuta &c &c," in the Spencer Room of Corpus Christi College. See especially ff. 56-58. Discovery of this indenture by the present author confirms the deductions of Mr. G. C. Moore Smith from the college accounts. Cf. MLR, 4:167-177 Ja 1909.

2. British Museum, Lansdowne MS. 33, f. 86; Lansdowne MS. 51, f. 144; Cooper: *Annals,* II. 435; II. 403; CHEL, V. 404.

3. John Josselin: *Historiola Collegii Corporis Christi,* par. 2.

4. *Ibid.,* par. 4.

5. Paul Hentzner: *Journey into England* (Ed. 1807), pp. 29-30; Cooper: *Annals,* II. 330.

6. On Kett's resignation, see the "Chapter Book, 1569-1626," p. 84. Fineux's academic career is recorded in the accounts of Corpus Christi, the University Matriculation Book, and the two Oxinden Commonplace Books, one in the Folger Shakespeare Library and the other in the British Museum, Addit. MS. 28012, ff. 514-v-515-r.

7. John Venn: *Grace Book Delta,* pp. vii-viii.

8. John Willis Clark: *Letters Patent of Elizabeth and James I Addressed to the University of Cambridge,* p. 23. Cf. Thomas Dinham Atkinson: *Cambridge Described and Illustrated,* p. 485.

9. British Museum, Harleian MSS. 6849, f. 218.

10. Corpus Christi Library, Parker MS. No. 49. 2, ff. 3, 7-10. Cf. Catalogue by M. R. James, II. 444. The Buttery Book sometimes lists more than twenty "magistri," but these were probably not all fellows but other masters of arts who for one reason or another remained in residence.

11. Cooper: *Annals,* II. 329; George Braun or Bruin: *De Praecipuis Totius Universi Urbibus,* Lib. II, Cap. I; *Gentleman's Magazine,* 46:201 My 1776.

12. Cooper: *Annals,* II. 455 (1588); 448 (1587).

13. Cooper: *Annals,* II. 455 (1588).

14. J. B. Mullinger: *University of Cambridge,* II. 389; *Documents Relating to the University and Colleges of Cambridge,* I. 482-483.

15. *Historical Register,* p. 190; Cooper: *Annals,* II. 161-163, quoting Cole MS. 42, fol. 290; Hartshorne: *Book Rarities in the University of Cambridge,* p. 446-n.

16. *Doctor Faustus,* 118-119.

17. I *Tamb.* 2306.

18. John H. Ingram: "New View of Marlowe," *Universal Review*, 4:380-399 (1889).
19. Cooper: *Annals*, I. 398-399.
20. Cooper: *Annals*, I. 398, 352 (1540/41, 1577); Atkinson: *op. cit.*, p. 260.
21. *Returne from Pernassus*, I. i.
22. British Museum, Lansdowne MS. 33; ff. 84-86. Marlowe's name appears on f. 85-v, col. 3.
23. Cap. VI. "De Ratione Studiorum." Stat. Univ. Cantab. In *Documents Relating to the University and Colleges*, I. 459.
24. *Doctor Faustus*, 34.
25. *Doctor Faustus*, 40, 17, 31.
26. *Doctor Faustus*, 84, 672, 645-690.
27. British Museum, Addit. MS. 6786, f. 491. The reference may, however, be to Captain Edmund Marlowe, who is mentioned in the same collection of Harriot's notes, Addit. MS. 6788, f. 39.
28. Cooper: *Annals*, II. 396 (1593); *Stat. Acad. Cantab.* in *Documents*, I. 462; John Venn: *Grace Book Delta*, p. 404, fol. 150-v of the original; E. G. Duff: *English Provincial Printers*, p. 126; E. J. L. Scott: *Letter-Book of Gabriel Harvey*, pp. 59, 61, 74.
29. Cooper: *Annals*, II. 389-390 (1582).
30. Cooper: *Annals*, II. 389 (1581/82); *Stat. Acad. Cantab.* in *Documents*, I. 357; C. Sayles: *Annals of the Cambridge University Library*, p. 53.
31. See the *Catalogus Librorum MS* (*Donors' Book*), p. 21 ff., now in the University Library; C. Sayle: *Annals of the Cambridge University Library*, pp. 49, 52, 53; *Rough List of the Parker Books* (MS.), Nos. 47, 298 in the Library of Corpus Christi College.
32. C. Sayle: *Annals of the Cambridge University Library*, p. 53.

5: Archbishop's Bounty

1. Royal Historical Society, *Transactions* (NS) 6:34-35 (1892).
2. British Museum, Lansdowne MS. 73, No. 29, 7 Calend. Maij 1581. Cooper: *Annals*, II. 383 (1581); II. 382 (1580); *Stat. Acad. Cantab.*, p. 461; J. J. Smith: *Cambridge Portfolio*, I. 102.
3. Royal Historical Society, *Transactions*, (NS) 6:34-35 (1892).
4. *Have with You to Saffron Walden*, McKerrow's Nashe, III. 117; Cf. E. H. Sugden: *Topographical Dictionary*, p. 93. The author is supposed to have been that very Thomas Beard who later wrote the best known account of Marlowe's death.
5. *Apology for Smectymnuus*, *Works*, 1851, III. 267; G. C. Moore Smith: *College Plays Performed in the University of Cambridge*, pp. 48, 62, 63.
6. Cooper: *Annals*, II. 400 (1584); John Strype: *Life and Acts of Archbishop Parker*, II. 195-197, Book IV, Chap. XVIII.
7. J. B. Black: *Reign of Queen Elizabeth*, pp. 192-193.

8. Cooper: *Annals*, II. 405-406 (1584-1585); William Oldys: *Life of Raleigh* (Oxford, 1829), I. 60-63; Edward Edwards: *Life and Letters of Sir Walter Raleigh*, I. 63; II. 24-25.

9. Cooper: *Annals*, II. 440-441 (1587).

10. G. C. Moore Smith, MLR, 4:169 Ja 1909; Robert Masters, *History of CCC*, p. 85; John Josselin: *Historiola* (Ed. J. W. Clark, 1880), pp. 42-43; G. C. Moore Smith, *loc. cit.*

11. James Heywood and T. Wright: *University Transactions*, pp. 221-223.

12. *Doctor Faustus*, 196-197. Cf. John Venn: *Grace Book Delta*, pp. 373, 375; original MS. *Grace Book*, fols. 142-v, 143-r.

13. *Doctor Faustus*, 34-35.

14. The original is, of course, in Latin. It is No. 199 among the Supplicats 1583/4, University Registry, Cambridge.

15. The statement, sometimes made, that Greene left Cambridge permanently in 1579 is erroneous and is disproved by the University Archives. See the B.A. Supplicats, 1579/80, No. 115; M.A. Supplicats, 1592/3, No. 29; *Grace Book Delta*, ff. 284 and 140-r.; Venn's transcript, pp. 326, 329, 360.

16. B.A. Supplicats, 1583/4; MS. *Grace Book Delta*, fol. 142-v.; Venn's transcript, p. 396.

17. Harleian MSS. 6848, ff. 185-r., 305-v. (formerly numbered 170 and 320).

6: "His Faithful Dealing"

1. Brooke's edition, pp. 550, 552.

2. Acts of the Privy Council, June 29, 1587. Dasent's edition, XXIV. 244. The original is in Volume VI, Public Record Office.

3. London Guildhall, Letterbook Z, ff. 115 ff. 3 January 23 Eliz.

4. *Cal. State Papers, Domestic Elizabeth, 1601-1603*, p. 23. The original is in Vol. CCLXXIX, SP 12/279, Public Record Office.

5. Patent Rolls, 1401; Chancery Miscellanea, Bundle 64, File 8, No. 241 b, both in Public Record Office. Cf. J. L. Hotson: *Death of Marlowe*, pp. 29, 32.

6. Lansdowne MS. 49, No. 25, f. 63, British Museum. Various other manuscript versions of this letter are extant.

7. Harleian MS. 6848, f. 185; Harleian MS. 6853, f. 307; Tucker Brooke: *Life*, p. 99.

8. II. *Tamb.* 3252-3269; *Practise of Fortification*, Ch. II, pp. 2 and 3; F. C. Danchin: "Etudes Critiques sur Christophe Marlowe," *Revue Germanique*, 8:23-33 Ja-F 1912; U. M. Ellis-Fermor: *Tamburlaine*, pp. 45, 224-226. Ive appears in the Declared Accounts at the Public Record Office, E 351/542, July 9, 15, 1587, f. 96-v; August 23, 1587, f. 96; E 351/543, August 18, 1600, f. 59-v.

9. C. H. Cooper: *Annals of Cambridge*, II. 430, 329; *Stat. Acad. Cantab.*, p. 467.

10. A. K. Gray, PMLA, 43:682-700 S 1928; *Cal. State Papers Domestic,* 1581-90, CLXX, No. 44; Conyers Read: *Sir Francis Walsingham,* II. 323-n; Ethel Seaton, RES, 5:273-267 Jy 1929; Anthony Munday: *English Romayne Life* (Ed. G. B. Harrison, Bodley Head Quartos), pp. 2, 6.

11. *Cal. State Papers, Domestic, Elizabeth, Additional 1580-1625,* XXX. No. 43, October 2, 1587.

7: London and Fame

1. William Smith: *Particular Description of England* (1588), British Museum, Sloane MS. 2596. Cf. W. B. Rye: *England as Seen by Foreigners,* p. 185; Diary of Lupold von Wedel in *Transactions of the Royal Historical Society,* (NS) 9:228-229 (1895).

2. Mark Eccles: *Christopher Marlowe in London,* pp. 104-107; Middlesex Sessions Roll, 309, No. 13, Middlesex Guildhall, Westminster, London.

3. Thomas Heywood: *Rape of Lucrece* (Mermaid ed.), pp. 424-425.

4. Rye, *op. cit.*

5. *Lupold von Wedel's Diary, loc. cit.,* pp. 228 ff.; Rye, *op. cit.,* p. 183.

6. Rye, *op. cit.*

7. *Lupold von Wedel's Diary, loc. cit.,* p. 253.

8. John Norden: *Speculum Britanniae* (1593), p. 35.

9. Norden, *loc. cit.*

10. J. Q. Adams: *Shakespearean Playhouses, passim.*

11. London Ordinance of 6 December 1574; W. C. Hazlitt: *English Drama and Stage;* J. Q. Adams: *Shakespearean Playhouses,* p. 24.

12. Thomas Middleton: *The Black Book.* See Bullen's Middleton, VIII. 13.

13. C. W. Wallace: *First London Theatre,* pp. 121 ff.; J. Q. Adams: *Shakespearean Playhouses,* pp. 56 ff.

14. Adams, *loc. cit.*

15. Adams, *op. cit.,* p. 140.

16. Adams, *op. cit.,* p. 145.

17. Henslowe's Diary, fol. 7; Greg's ed., I. 13.

18. Stow's *Survey of London* (1598), p. 371 (Ed. Henry Morley, 1890).

19. *Holy State,* I. 338 (Ed. 1841).

20. I. *Henry VI,* I. iii; *Troilus and Cressida,* V. x. 55; cf. E. H. Sugden: *Topographical Dictionary,* p. 69.

21. *Bartholomew Fair* (Mermaid ed.), V. iii.

22. Stow, *op. cit.,* p. 371.

8: A Young Career

1. *Massacre at Paris,* 97-106.
2. I. *Tamb.* 44-45.
3. I. *Tamb.* 1372-1378.
4. I. *Tamb.* 1559-1566.
5. Pius II: *Asiae Europaeque Elegantissima Descriptio* (1531), in the Parker Bequest, Corpus Christi, Cambridge.
6. I. *Tamb.* 1897-1899, 1916-1956 and the following scenes.
7. For provincial productions, see *Pleasant Notes upon Don Quixot,* Ed. 1654, p. 271. The passage is omitted in the edition of 1768. The book is sometimes referred to as *Festivous Notes upon Don Quixot.* Cf. II. *Henry IV.* II. iv. 178-179.
8. II. *Tamb.* 2896-2921.
9. II. *Tamb.* 2969-3001.
10. II. *Tamb.* 3980-3982.
11. *Middlemarch,* Chapter XXII. Beaumont and Fletcher: *Coxcomb,* II. i; *Women Pleased,* IV. i; Ford and Dekker: *Sun's Darling,* III. ii; John Taylor: *Works,* Ed. 1630, Sigs. L-13 and Rob-2; Day and Chettle: *Blind Beggar of Bednall-Green,* Ed. Bang, line 1660; Ben Jonson: *Eastward Hoe,* II; R. Braithwaite: *Strappado for the Diuell,* Ed. 1878, p. 159; Edward Sharpham: *The Fleire,* Ed. Nibbe, p. 22; Thomas Lodge: *Wounds of Ciuill War* (III).
12. Baptista Ignatius: *De Origine Turcorum* (1556), p. 185; Andrew Cambine: *Turkish Affaires,* f. 6-r.; Paulus Jovius: *Shorte Treatise upon the Turkes' Chronicles* (1546), Chapter V, f. xiii; Philip Lonicer: *Chronicorum Turcorum* (1578), Book I, Tom. I, f. 16-r; Pope Pius: *Asiae Europaeque Elegantissima Descriptio* (1531), p. 86; II. *Tamb.* 3111.
13. I. *Tamb.* 317; Baptista Fulgotius: *Exemplorum Libri IX,* p. 379 of the Corpus Christi College copy, which is No. 47 in the Parker List. It is also called *De Dictis Factisque Memorabilibus.* The passage is in Book III, Chapter IV of the 1509 edition, which has no page numbers, and on p. 104 of the 1578 edition. It is copied almost word for word in Philip Lonicer, *op. cit.,* f. 15-r, Book I, Tom. I.
14. *Bondage and Travels of Johann Schiltberger,* edited by Karl Friedrich Neumann and translated into English by Commander J. Buchan Telfer, R.N.
15. Heinrich von Effenham: *XIII Homiliae* (1571), f. 72-k, Book II, Chapter I. (Copy in Harvard College Library.)
16. Mir Khwand (the elder): *Rauzat-us-Safa* (Teheran edition, 1854), Vol. VI, ff. 15 and 15-v; Ali-i-Yazdi: *Zafarnameh* (Bibliotheca Indica, Calcutta), Vol. I. pp. 356-357, Vol. II, pp. 1-5.
17. Silvestre de Sacy: "Mémoire sur une correspondance inédite de Tamerlane avec Charles VI." *Mém. de l'Acad. des Inscrip-*

tions, 6:470-482 (1822); *Narrative of the Embassy of Ruy Gonzales de Clavijo to the Court of Timur*, translated by Clements R. Markham. There is a later (1928) translation by Guy M. Strange.

9: "The Watch Strikes"

1. *Doctor Faustus*, 102-103. The earlier quotations are from the opening soliloquy.

2. Oxinden Commonplace Books, Folger Shakespeare Library, Washington, D.C., and British Museum, Additional MS. 28012, ff. 514-v-515-r; "Oxinden Amici," Folger Shakespeare Library; Annual Audits, Corpus Christi College; Matriculation Book, Cambridge University.

3. *Doctor Faustus*, 312-318; II. *Tamb*. 2909-2910.

4. *Doctor Faustus*, 294, 338-339, 559-560.

5. *Doctor Faustus*, 1328-1347.

6. *The Knave of Clubs* (1609) in *Works of S. Rowlands*, Vol. II. p. 29 (Hunterian Club, 1880). Cf. Alexander Tille: *Faustsplitter*, pp. 65ff.

7. *English Faust Book*, Chapter 45; *Iliad*, Gamma, 156; opening lines of *Iphigenia; Aeneid*, II. 197-198.

8. II. *Tamb*. 3055-3056; *Dido*, 1610-1612, 1162, 1329.

9. *Doctor Faustus*, 1359-1360.

10. Josephine Preston Peabody: *Marlowe*, I. i.

11. *The Black Book*, attributed to Thomas Middleton. Bullen's Middleton, VIII. 13.

12. CHEL, III. 198. The lines are in Stanza 22 of the Haslewood (1815) edition of the *Mirror*, II. 466.

13. Tucker Brooke, PMLA, 37:384 (1922); Boas's edition, p. 8.

14. See p. 84 and note.

15. Cf. Wilhelm Scherer's (1884) reprint of the *Faustbuch*, pp. 102-103; *English Faust Book*, Chapter XX; *Doctor Faustus*, 839-843, 844-845.

16. *English Faust Book*, Chapter XXII; *Doctor Faustus*, 805.

17. *Acts*, XIX. xix.

18. Heidelberg University Archives, I. 3, No. 50, f. 36-r.

19. *Explicationum Melanchthoniarum* in *Evangelia Dominica*, Parts II and IV; Alexander Tille: *Faustsplitter*, Nos. 9 and 10; Ward's edition of *Doctor Faustus* (1910), p. lxv and note.

20. *Doctor Faustus*, 967-984; Mermaid edition, p. 210 and note; Bullen's edition, I. 258 and note; Percy Simpson, *Essays and Studies*, VII. 154.

21. *Henslowe's Diary*, f. 108-v; Greg's edition, I. 172.

22. *The Black Book*, attributed to Thomas Middleton. Bullen's Middleton, VIII. 13; John Melton: *The Astrologaster* (1620), p. 31. There is a copy of this book in the Harvard College Library. Cf. Brooke: *Trans. Conn. Acad.* 25:375 (1921-1922).

23. *Histrio-Mastix* (1633 ed.), Part I, f. 557-r, 556-r; *Gentleman's Magazine,* 2nd ser. 34:234 S 1850; Chambers: *Elizabethan Stage,* III. 424; J. Q. Adams: *Life of Shakespeare,* p. 126; John Aubrey: *Natural History and Antiquities of Surrey* (1718-19), I. 190.

24. On Continental productions, see Johannes Meissner: *Die Englischen Comoedianten zur Zeit Shakespeares in Oesterreich,* p. 90. Pope's Allusion is in *The Dunciad,* Book III, lines 229-236 and notes.

25. *Merry Wives of Windsor,* IV. v. 70-71; *Richard II,* IV. i. 281-286; *Troilus and Cressida,* II. iii. 6; II. iii. 80-81. Cf. *Doctor Faustus,* 1327-1329 and McKerrow's Nashe, III. 185.

26. *Doctor Faustus,* 195, *Faust* 481, *Faust Fragment* 128, *Urfaust,* 128; *Doctor Faustus,* 699, *Faust* 482, *Faust Fragment* 129, *Urfaust* 130. Cf. Otto Heller: *Faust and Faustus,* p. 51 ff. and James Taft Hatfield, JEGP, 24:450 Jy 1925.

27. Henry Crabbe Robinson's Diary (Macmillan, 1869), August 2, 1829, II. 434. Cf. Eckermann's *Goethe Gespräche,* August 2, 1829, VII. 108 and Goethe's *Tagebücher, Goethes Werke* (Weimar, 1894), III Abth., Band 6, p. 215.

10: Bloody, Bold, and Resolute

1. Mark Eccles: *Christopher Marlowe in London,* p. 57. The original document is in the Public Record Office, London, K. B. 29/226, fol. 119. It was originally discovered by Dr. J. L. Hotson. All the other episodes relating to the duel are, however, the discoveries of Mr. Eccles.

2. J. L. Hotson: *Shakespeare versus Shallow,* p. 9.

3. Eccles, *op. cit.,* pp. 48, 57.

4. City Guildhall (London) *Letter Book &c,* f. 329. The book which is oddly numbered "&c" follows the one numbered "Z."

5. "To the Gentlemen Students," prefixed to Robert Greene's *Menaphon,* Grosart's Greene, VI. 23. The relation of this passage to the duel has not previously been noted.

6. Originalia, E. 371/549. lxxj; Eccles, *op. cit.,* p. 26.

7. John Cordy Jeaffreson: *Middlesex County Records,* I. xliii.

8. Middlesex Sessions Roll, Middlesex Guildhall, No. 248; Eccles, *op. cit.,* p. 34.

9. St. Andrews Parish Register; Eccles, *op. cit.,* p. 46.

10. Middlesex Sessions Roll, 284, No. 1, printed in Jeaffreson's *Middlesex Sessions Records,* I. 189, as an abstract. Cf. Brooke: *Life,* pp. 96-97; Sir Sidney Lee, *Athenæum,* No. 3486: 235-236 18 Ag 1894; H. F. Westlake in London *Times,* June 24, 1936, p. 17-d; J. L. Hotson in *Atlantic Monthly,* 138:40 Jy 1926.

11. *Bibliotheca Monastica-Fletewodiana,* No. 1351, p. 76. Priced copy in the Bodleian. This curious fact has not been previously noted.

12. Letter to the Lord Mayor, first noted by Eccles, *op. cit.*, p. 91. Cf. Remembrancia, I. Nos. 505, 516 (ff. 256, 262); W. H. and H. C. Overall: *Analytical Index to the Series of Records Known as the Remembrancia* (1878), p. 154; J. L. Hotson, *Atlantic Monthly*, 138: 37-44 Jy 1926; Eccles, *op. cit.*, p. 69.

13. This bond has been known since Sir Sidney Lee printed it in the *Athenæum* (see note 10); but no one had any idea what it signified, until Mr. Mark Eccles revealed the Bradley-Watson duel and documents. The date is often erroneously given as 1588. This is because the documents are dated merely "31 Elizabeth," the regnal year being dated from the day the Queen ascended the throne, namely, November 17, 1558. Thus "1 Elizabeth" ends November 16, 1559.

14. John Cordy Jeaffreson: *Middlesex Records*, I. 258.

15. Mark Eccles: *Christopher Marlowe in London*, p. 35.

16. Middlesex Sessions Roll, 309, No. 13.

17. British Museum, Harleian MSS. 6848, f. 154 and 6849, f. 218.

18. Harleian MS. 6848, ff. 187-189. The leaves have been arranged in reverse order and must be read backwards.

19. Harriot Papers, British Museum, Additional MSS. 6782-6789.

11: A Great Play Botched

1. *Jew of Malta*, 72; CHEL, III. 366; *Sad Shepherd*, I. i. 13; Chapman: *Ovid's Banquet of Sence* (Parrott's ed.); *As You Like It*, III. iii. 15-16.

2. Thomas Heywood: "To the Reader," prefixed to *The English Traveller*. Quotations from *The Jew of Malta* are from lines 2370, 386, 940 ff.

3. Lewis Perry in the Williams College acting version (1909), pp. xvi, xviii.

4. J. R. Green: *Short History of the English People* (1888), Part II. 205.

5. Public Record Office, London, SP 12/82, f. 7; N&Q, 2nd ser. 8:448 3 D 1859; Sidney Lee: *Trans. New Shaks. Soc.* 1887-1892, p. 158.

6. Walsingham's Diary (Camden Soc. Misc.), Vol. VI, p. 12, Nov. 21, 1571.

7. Godfrey Goodman: *Court of King James the First*, I. 152-153. (Ed. John S. Brewer.)

8. Sidney Lee: "Original of Shylock," *Gentleman's Magazine* (OS) 246 (NS) 24:185-200 F 1880; "Elizabethan England and the Jews," *Trans. New Shaks. Soc.*, 1st ser. Vols. 11-14: 143-166 (1887-1892); Camden's *Annales* (3rd ed., 1635), pp. 430-431; William Murdin: *Collection of State Papers Left by William Cecil, Lord Burghley*, p. 669.

9. *Doctor Faustus,* 1149-1150.

10. William Rowley: *Search for Money* (1609). Percy Society Reprint (1890), p. 19. This author must not be confused with the dramatist. Cf. *Jew of Malta,* 1229.

11. E. E. Stoll: "Shylock," JEGP, 10:236 Ap 1911; W. Creizenach: *Geschichte d. neueren dramas* (1909), IV. 514; J. P. Collier: *Memoirs of the Principal Actors in the Plays of Shakespeare,* pp. 52 ff.; Karl Elze: *Jahrb.* 6:161 N 1871.

12. English (1608) edition, Sigs. Aij, verso; ij, recto.

13. Chester Louis Reiss: *Christopher Marlowe and Atheism,* New York University Master's Thesis (MS), 1932.

14. Albert Croll Baugh's edition of *Englishmen for My Money,* Pennsylvania Diss., 1917; Arthur Bivens Stonex: "Usurer in Elizabethan Drama," PMLA, 31:190-210 (1916); Walter Reinecke: *Der Wucherer in alteren englishen drama,* Halle Diss., 1907.

15. H. Graetz: *History of the Jews,* IV. 595.

16. Lonicer: *Chronicorum Turcorum Tomi Duo,* pp. 273, 296. Cf. Ethel Seaton, "Fresh Sources for Marlowe," RES, 5:390-393 O 1929; Belleforest: *Cosmographie Universelle,* II. 580.

17. *Jew of Malta,* 2090-2092; Nicholay, Book I, Chapter xix; Villegagnon, pp. 61-62; cf. pp. 63, 109.

18. Villegagnon, p. 98.

12: Maturity Achieved

1. John Tucker Murray: *English Dramatic Companies,* I. 59.

2. *Edward the Second,* 51-53.

3. Charles Lamb: "Characters of Dramatic Writers," *Works* (1876), IV, 215.

4. *Edward the Second,* 1274, 1361, 1745, 1881-1882, 2465; Holinshed (Ed. 1586) III. 321, III. 325, III. 339, III. 341. Holinshed (Ed. 1807) II. 551, II. 559, II. 583, II. 587.

5. E. K. Chambers: *Elizabethan Stage,* II. 447, 420; Mark Eccles: *Christopher Marlowe in London,* pp. 163-169.

13: Friends and Foes

1. Bodleian Library, Aubrey MS. 6, fol. 77-v; John Aubrey: *Brief Lives* (Oxford, 1898), II. 192.

2. Thomas Fuller: *Worthies of England* (Ed. 1811), I. 287.

3. Aubrey MS. 6, f. 75-v; Aubrey, *op. cit.,* II. 182.

4. Aubrey MS. 6, f. 77; Aubrey, *op. cit.,* II. 188.

5. Aubrey MS. 6, f. 77; this indecorous episode is omitted by the Oxford edition, but is printed by John Collier: *Life and Credulities of John Aubrey,* p. 35; Aubrey: *Brief Lives* (Oxford, 1898), II. 183.

6. Aubrey MS. 6, f. 76; Aubrey, *op. cit.*, II. 191.
7. Aubrey MS. 6, f. 75-76-v; Aubrey, *op. cit.*, II. 182, 186.
8. Aubrey MS. 6, f. 76; Aubrey, *op. cit.*, II. 186.
9. Harleian MS. 6848, f. 185. The other copy (Harleian MS. 6853, f. 307) omits this phrase.
10. The parallel first detected by Miss M. C. Bradbrook: *School of Night*, pp. 17-18; Raleigh, *Works*, VIII. 554; Harleian MS. 6848, f. 186; Harleian MS. 6853, f. 308.
11. Harleian MS. 6849, f. 218; Tucker Brooke: *Life*, p. 105.
12. Aubrey MS. 6, f. 77; Aubrey, *op. cit.*, II. 185.
13. Harriot's papers are at the British Museum, Additional MSS. 6782-6789 and Harleian MSS. See p. 58 and note.
14. F. S. Boas: *Marlowe and His Circle*, p. 70.
15. Harleian MS. 6848, f. 185; Harleian MS. 6853, f. 187.
16. Preface to the translation of Homer; J. E. Spingarn: *Critical Essays of the Seventeenth Century*, I. 69-70.
17. Harleian MS. 6849, ff. 184-190. For transcript, see G. B. Harrison's edition of *Willobie His Avisa*, pp. 255-271; cf. J. M. Stone: "Atheism under Elizabeth and James I," *The Month*, 81:174-187 Ja 1894.
18. The dialogue is verbatim from the official report referred to in the preceding note.
19. Ibid.
20. McKerrow's Nashe, II. 180; III. 195, 198.
21. *Perimedes the Blacksmith.*
22. McKerrow's Nashe, III. 85.
23. The passage appears only in the Huntington Library's copy of *A Quip for an Upstart Courtier*. Cf. *Papers of the Bibliographical Society of America*, XIV. 7-8, Part I.
24. Harleian MS. 6849, f. 218; Brooke: *Life*, p. 104.
25. J. R. Dasent: *Acts of the Privy Council*, XIX. 153-154, May 24, 1590.
26. The "sentence" on Frizer's estate is preserved at Somerset House, London (99 Skynner). On his career, see J. L. Hotson: *Death of Christopher Marlowe*, pp. 41-51; F. S. Boas: *Marlowe and His Circle*, pp. 109-111; J. L. Hotson, *Atlantic Monthly*, 138:39 Jy 1926; Eugenie de Kalb, TLS, 24:351 21 My 1925; J. W. Kirby, TLS, 29:592 17 Jy 1930.
27. J. A. Venn: *Alumni Cantabrigienses*, III. 380.
28. First noted by Sir E. K. Chambers, MLR, 21:84-85 Ja 1926. Cf. F. S. Boas: *Marlowe and His Circle*, p. 32; State Papers, Dom. Eliz., CCXXII, Nos. 13 and 14. P 12/122. Nos. 13 and 14.
29. Bodleian Library, Ashmolean MS. 830, f. 4r; British Museum, Cottonian MS. Calig. B. V. art. 22, f. 170 r; Calig. C. IX. art. 154-157, especially f. 303, formerly 240. Cf. *Calendar of State Papers*, Scotland, Elizabeth. 1589-1603, II. 972; State Papers, Vol. XVI, No. 7.
30. *Calendar of State Papers.* Foreign Ser. 1586-1588 Part I (General), p. 229. Feb.? 1587. The original in the Public Record

Office is in the volume labelled "France, XVII." No. 26 bis. It was placed there in 1925 and bears Poley's signature.

31. Poley's will is at Somerset House (97 Hele).

32. Lansdowne MS. 44, No. 38, f. 118. First noted by Sir E. K. Chambers, TLS, 24:352 21 My 1925. Cf. Boas, *op. cit.*, pp. 96-97, and T. Wright: *Queen Elizabeth and Her Times,* II. 248. See also *Acts of the Privy Council,* XXXII. 130; *Calendar of Scottish Papers,* VIII. 564. The Original is in Mary Queen of Scots Papers, XIX. 2 in the Public Record Office.

14: "Stabd with a Dagger"

1. Harleian MS. 6848, f. 154.

2. Harleian MS. 6849, f. 218.

3. J. R. Dasent: *Acts of the Privy Council,* XXIV. 244. The original manuscript is in the Public Record Office, London, this passage being in Vol. XI. Cf. Brooke: *Life,* p. 58; Ingram: *Christopher Marlowe and His Associates* gives a wrong reference.

4. Bunce MS. I. 127. Royal Museum and Public Library (Beaney Institute), Canterbury.

5. See Note 3 above. This entry occurs on the same page of the original manuscript.

6. J. R. Dasent, *op. cit.,* XXIV. 118. Cf. pp. 128, 137, 144, 277, and Note 3.

7. Anthony Marlowe frequently appears in the records. See W. W. Greg: *Henslowe Papers,* p. 51; *Cal. State Papers, Foreign,* XIX. 132; Joseph Lemuel Chester: *London Marriage Licenses, 1521-1869,* p. 887.

8. J. L. Hotson: *Death of Christopher Marlowe,* pp. 31-32, translating the original Latin of the pardon, Chancery Miscellanea Bundle 64, File 8, No. 241b, Public Record Office, London.

9. On Poley's comings and goings, see Declared Accounts of the Lord Treasurer of the Chamber (E 351/542) and of the Master of the Posts (E 351/543) in Public Record Office, London. Also Ethel Seaton: "Marlowe, Robert Poley, and the Tippings," RES, 5:1-15 Jy 1929; "Robert Poley's Ciphers," RES, 7:1-14 Ap 1931. Miss Seaton has discovered Poley's ciphers in State Papers, 106, Vol. II, Nos. 105, 105A, 105B, Public Record Office.

10. William Vaughan: *Golden Grove,* ed. 1600, Sig. C4v; ed. 1608, Sig. C5.

11. Vaughan, *loc. cit.*

12. Harleian MSS. 6868, f. 154 and 6849, f. 218.

13. Hotson, *op. cit.*, p. 33.

14. J. C. Jeaffreson: *Middlesex Records,* I. xlv-xlvii. The originals are preserved in the Middlesex Guildhall, London.

15. Samuel A. Tannenbaum, M.D.: *Assassination of Christopher Marlowe,* passim, and especially the medical opinions appended.

16. Patent Rolls of Chancery 1401, Public Record Office.
17. McKerrow's Nashe, V. 80-81.
18. Harleian MS. 6849, f. 218.
19. DNB, II. 15; Benjamin Brook: *Lives of the Puritans,* II. 396; Carlyle's Cromwell (*Works,* New York, 1897), VII. 67; Hunter's *Chorus Vatum,* British Museum.
20. *Theatre of Gods Judgments,* slightly modernized.
21. One of the Oxinden manuscripts is in the Folger Shakespeare Library, Washington, D.C. It is known as the "Oxinden Commonplace Book." The other is in the British Museum, Additional MS. 28012, ff. 514-v-515-r. There were similar notations in the Prideaux copy of the 1629 *Hero and Leander,* now lost.
22. A folio manuscript, apparently prepared as the basis of a fifth edition, appears in P. J. and A. E. Dobell's Catalogue No. 22, Item No. 193.
23. *Thunderbolt of God's Wrath,* Ch. XXII, p. 29.
24. Vaughan, *loc. cit.*
25. *Returne from Pernassus,* I, ii.
26. Reprinted in G. Gregory Smith: *Elizabethan Critical Essays,* II. 324.
27. Anthony à Wood: *Athenae Oxonienses* (Ed. 1815), II. 7.
28. F. Paul in *American Catholic Quarterly Review,* 42:588 O 1917.
29. Three are reprinted by W. W. Greg: *List of Masques, Pageants, &c.*; and there is another in the series "Old English Drama, Students Facsimile Edition."
30. Chetwode, p. 8; Baker, ed. 1764, Sig. X2r; Ed. 1782, I. 301; *Encyclopaedia Britannica,* 3rd ed. (1797), X. 576; *Nouvelle Biographie Générale,* XXXIII. 860-863; Taine: *Hist. Eng. Lit.* (Edinburgh, 1872), I. 238; Iwan Bloch: *Englische Sittengeschichte,* II. 10. Kemble's book is now in the Folger Shakespeare Library.
31. *Death of Marlowe.*
32. *British Stage and Literary Cabinet,* 5:22 Je 1821. The signature there given, "Dangle, Jr.," is believed to conceal Broughton himself. Cf. Hotson, *op. cit.,* p. 17; Brooke: *Life,* p. 77; *Gentleman's Magazine* (OS) 100 (NS) 23:6 Ja 1830.
33. James Cordy Jeaffreson, *op. cit.,* I. xxxviii-xlvii, 249; "C.C.C.C. Chapter Book. 1569-1626" (MS), f. 37, now in Estates Bursary, Corpus Christi.

15: Poetic Interludes

1. *Biographica Dramatica* (1812), Pt. II. p. 493.
2. British Museum, Lansdowne MS. 807.
3. Steevens and Reed: *Shakespeare* (1803), II. 371-372; Frederick Thornhill: "Old Dramas in Mr. Warburton's Collection," *Gentleman's Magazine* (OS) 118 (NS) 85:217-222 S 1815; Wil-

liam Prideaux Courtney: Article, "Warburton, John," DNB, XX. 755; W. W. Greg: "Bakings of Betsy," *Library*, 3rd ser. 2:225-259 Jy 1911; Egerton Brydges: *Censura Literaria* (1807), V. 273.

4. *Massacre at Paris*, 257; II. *Henry VI*, First Folio, p. 134; Second, p. 470; Third, p. 134; Fourth, p. 145.

5. E. Sawyer: *Memorials of Affairs of State . . . Collected (Chiefly) from the Original Papers of the Right Honorable Sir Ralph Winwood* (1725), I. 425.

6. Cazamian and Legouis: *Hist. Eng. Lit.* I. 284; CHEL, VI. 166-167; John Bakeless: "Christopher Marlowe and the News-books," *Journalism Quarterly*, 14:18-22 Mr 1837.

7. Arber's reprint, ?? 265.

8. Jean de Serres: *First Booke of the historie of the last troubles of France*, p. 202 (wrongly numbered 184). Bound with *Historical Collection*. Copy in the New York Public Library.

9. *A true and plaine report of the Furious outrages of France*, quoted in Matthias A. Shaaber: *Some Forerunners of the Newspaper*, pp. 179-n, 237.

10. *Correspondance diplomatique de Bertrand Salignac de la Mothe Fénelon*, VII. 402.

11. *Doctor Faustus*, 1328, 1330, 1329, 1472, 1428; *Dido*, 1612, 1329, 1162, 1269, 26.

12. *Hero and Leander*, I. 382; *Dido*, 526.

13. Cf. *Dido*, 481; *Edward II*, 2030; II. *Tamb.*, 2945, 3529. For "blubbered cheeks," cf. *Dido*, 1541; I. *Tamb.* 1802; for "lawles spoyle," cf. *Dido*, 260; I. *Tamb.* 548. There are scores of similar parallels.

14. Thomas Matthews Pearce: *Marlowe's "Tragedie of Dido" in Relation to Its Latin Source*. University of Pittsburgh Diss. (MS) 1930.

15. *Hamlet*, II. ii. Cf. Edward Capell: *Notes and Various Readings to Shakespeare* (1783), I. 134-135; *Dido*, 548-549; *Hamlet*, II. ii. 494-495; *Troilus and Cressida*, V. iii. 40-41.

16: "Marlowe's Mighty Line"

1. *Notes and Queries*, 1st ser. 1:469-450 18 May 1850.

2. *Hero and Leander*, III. 183-198.

3. Ibid., VI. 276-280.

4. The only known copy is in the Bodleian Library. It was reprinted by Léonce Chabalier in his *Héro et Léandre, Poème de Christopher Marlowe et George Chapman*. Dyce's edition reprints a few passages. Cf. DNB, XV. 975-976; Warton: *Hist. Eng. Poetry* (1781), III. 434-n; E. H. Sugden: *Topographical Dictionary*, pp. 31-32; STC, 19803-19808.

5. British Museum, Roxburghe Ballads, I. 250.

6. Ashmolean MS. 1486, ii. f. 6 verso.

7. Quaritch Catalogue 525 (1936), No. 48, p. 11; Sotheby Catalogue, June 8-9, 1936, Nos. 459-460, pp. 65-66; E. V. Lucas: *Life of Charles Lamb* (1920 ed.), II. 745-746.

8. *Jew of Malta*, 1809-1816.

9. I. *Tamb.* 278-302; PMLA, 40:692-742 (1925).

10. R. S. Forsythe: "Passionate Shepherd and English Poetry." PMLA, 40:692-742 (1925).

11. *Aeneid*, II. 326-339; *Dido*, 475-485.

12. Matthew Arnold: "To a Friend" (Oxford ed., 1913), p. 40; John Keats: "Ode to a Nightingale," Stanza 7.

13. *Odyssey*, m. 185.

14. I. *Tamb.*, 1951; *Jew of Malta*, 81; II. *Tamb.*, 2529-2530; II. *Tamb.*, 2702, 2717.

15. I. *Tamb.*, 30-31; 73-74; 262-263; 339-340. Cf. Ruth Janet Barber: *Certain Elements in the Structure of pre-Shakespearean Dramatic Blank Verse*. Stanford University, Master's Thesis, 1923, p. 10; C. F. Tucker Brooke: SP, 19:195 Ap 1922.

16. *Edward the Second*, 1751-1755. Tucker Brooke: "Marlowe's Versification and Style," SP, 19:189 2 Ap 1922.

17. Janet Spens: *Faerie Queene*, Chap. I; M. C. Bradbrook: *School of Night*, p. 5; Charles Crawford: *Collectanea*, I. 66 ff.; Georg Schoeneich: *Der litterarische Einfluss Spensers auf Marlowe* (1907); II. *Tamb.*, 4049-4103; *Faerie Queene*, I. vii. 32.

18. Henry Bradley: "Shakespeare's English" in *Shakespeare's England* [Ed. Sidney Lee, 1916], II. 542.

19. I. *Tamb.* 1431; *Edward the Second*, 1700.

20. Mark Eccles: "Marlowe in Kentish Tradition," *Notes and Queries*, 169:39-40 20 Jy 1935.

21. William A. Jackson: *Catalogue of the Carl H. Pforzheimer Library*, No. 413.

17: Marlowe's Influence

1. Bodleian Library, Aubrey MS. 6, fol. 108.

2. George Saintsbury (Ed.): *Minor Poets of the Caroline Period*, II. 527; Douglas Bush: *Mythology and the Renaissance Tradition*, pp. 193-195; DNB, II. 904.

3. III. v. 81-82; *Hero and Leander*, I. 176. The passage is also quoted by Thomas Heywood in *The Captives* (II. ii. 139-141) and with slight changes by George Chapman in *The Blind Beggar of Alexandria* (Ed. 1873, I. 47): "None euer lou'd but at first sight they lou'd."

4. III. iii. 9-10.

5. III. iii. 15-16.

6. Oliver W. F. Lodge in TLS, 24:335 14 My 1925.

7. *Two Gentlemen of Verona*, I. i. 22-27.

8. *Midsummer Night's Dream*, V. i. 199-200.

9. *Much Ado About Nothing,* V. ii. 30-31.
10. *Edward the Second,* 2632-2634; *Hamlet,* III. i. 79-80.
11. *Edward the Second,* 2366-2367; *Hamlet,* I. v. 63.
12. *Merry Wives of Windsor,* III. i. 15-27; IV. v. 70-71.
13. *Troilus and Cressida,* II. iii. 80-81; *Doctor Faustus,* 1328; Cf. McKerrow's Nashe, III. 185.
14. *Richard II,* IV. i. 281-286; *Doctor Faustus,* 1328 ff.
15. *Elegies,* II. xiii. 43; *Amores,* I. xiii; *Merchant of Venice,* V. i. 109.
16. *Elegies,* I. ii. 10; *Amores,* II. ii. 10; *Merchant of Venice,* IV. i. 67.
17. *Massacre at Paris,* 1005, 1027; *Julius Caesar,* II. ii. 10, 28; *Fourth Booke of the Commentaries,* p. 207. (Bound with J. de Serres: Historical Collection, New York Public Library.)
18. Thomas Clark Pollock: "Rowe's Tamerlane and The Prince of Parthia." *American Literature,* 6:150-162 My 1934.
19. "Early English Dramatists," in *Undergraduate Papers,* 1:7-15 1 D 1857. There are copies of this short-lived periodical in the Bodleian Library and British Museum. Cf. "Christopher Marlowe in Relation to Greene, Peele, and Lodge," *Fortnightly Review* (OS) 105 (NS) 99:764-769 My 1916; *North American Review,* 203:742-748 My 1916. Also published in an edition of 20 copies by T. J. Wise (1914), a copy of which is in the University Library, Cambridge. Reprinted in the Bonchurch edition of Swinburne, XII (Prose Works, II). 127-135.
20. William George Thomson: *Tapestry Weaving in England,* pp. 82, 124, 148; George Leland Hunter: *Decorative Textiles,* II. 305.
21. Gibbon: *Decline and Fall,* Chap. LXV, ii; Prescott: *Conquest of Mexico* (1855), II. 152-n.
22. Hall's Satires, Book I, Satire III (Vergidemiarium).
23. *Discoveries* (Ed. G. B. Harrison, Bodley Head Quartos), p. 33.
24. Adapted from E. Hübener: *Einfluss von Marlowe's Tamburlaine* (Halle Diss., 1901). Cf. Nikolai Il'ich Storozhenko: *Grin, yevo zhizn* (Life of Green), translated in Grosart's Greene, Vol. I.
25. *Huth Library,* XIII. 128; I. *Tamb.* 261. Cf. E. H. Wright: *Influence of Christopher Marlowe,* p. 4 (Columbia University Master's Thesis [MS.]); E. Hübener, *op. cit.;* Adolf Geissler: *Einfluss der Tamburlaine-Rolle,* Ch. VII. (Berlin Diss., 1925.)
26. II. *Tamb.* 3980-3981. Cf. George Gascoigne: *Complete Works* (Ed. J. Cunliffe, 1907), I. 246.
27. *Coxcomb,* II. i; *Sun's Darling,* III. ii; *Women Pleased,* IV. i; *Blind Beggar* (Ed. Bang), line 1680; *Eastward Hoe,* II.; *The Fleire* (Ed. Nibbe), p. 22; *Strappado for the Diuell* (Ed. 1878), p. 159; *Middlemarch,* Chapter XXII; *Wounds of Civil War,* III.
28. *Doctor Faustus,* 889-892, p. 203 of Brooke's edition.
29. III. iii, p. 424 of the Mermaid edition.

30. Reprinted in James Boswell's revised edition of Malone's *Shakespeare* (1821), III. 356-357, from originals in Malone's collection. Cf. W. W. Greg: *Elizabethan Playhouse Documents.*

31. *Discoveries* (Ed. G. B. Harrison, Bodley Head Quartos), p. 33.

32. William Winstanley: *Lives of the English Poets,* p. 134.

33. Edition of 1638, IV. vi; *Doctor Faustus,* 494.

34. I owe the parallels with Milton to F. C. Owlett, Esq., of London. Cf. *Paradise Lost,* IV. 18-22; 73-75; *Doctor Faustus,* 312, 555.

18: Marlowe and His Books

1. Dulwich College MSS. No. II. 12. Transcribed in *Alleyn Papers,* II. 44.

2. Bodleian Library, MS. Bodley 699, Nos. 220-221 (1612). G. W. Wheeler: *Letters of Sir Thomas Bodley to Thomas James, First Keeper of the Bodleian Library,* Nos. 220, p. 220; No. 221, pp. 221-222.

3. Lowndes (ed. 1861), Vol. III. Pt. 2, p. 1479; European Magazine, 2:457 (1787); Gentleman's Magazine, 100:314 Ap 1830.

4. Tucker Brooke: *Dido,* pp. 119-120.

5. *Bibliotheca Dramatica. Catalogue of . . . William E. Burton,* No. 1291, p. 95. None of the annotated copies give the name of the purchaser. Cf. Boston Public Library, Barton MSS., p. 30 v, List of Shakespeariana dated January 7, 1864.

6. Charles Edmonds: *Isham Reprints,* p. vi; London *Times* October 4, 1886, p. 8-f; Léonce Chabalier: *Héro et Léandre* (Paris Thèse, 1911), p. 167; Brooke's (1910) edition, p. 486; Bullen's edition, I. xlix; Charles Edmonds: *A Lamport Garland;* R. E. Graves: "The Isham Books," *Bibliographica,* III. 418-429 (1897).

7. *Heber Catalogue,* Part IV, No. 1415, p. 183; *Notes & Queries,* 1st ser. 1:302 9 Mr 1850; 6th ser. 11:305-306 18 Ap 1885; 6th ser. 12:15 4 Jy 1885; F. Ouvry Sale Catalogue, Lot. 1031 (1882); Prideaux Sale (Sotheby's), Lot. 2521 (1917); Ingram: *Christopher Marlowe and His Associates,* p. 274 and Note 19. The most recent and thorough discussion is Mark Eccles: "Marlowe in Kentish Tradition," *Notes & Queries,* 169:60-61 27 Jy 1935. Cf. also the MS. Catalogue of the books of Lee Warly (1760) now among the books belonging to Elham Parish, Kent, preserved in the Howley Library, Canterbury Cathedral (folio 34).

Index

Aaron, 241
Abigail, 29, 140, 241
Abydos, 214
Accounts, 11, 18, 22, 33, 36, 54, 55, 57ff.
Actors, 22, 59, 76-77, 114, 117, 151, 202, 262
Acts, Apocryphal, 112
Acts, Book of, 112
Adam, 164
Addison, Joseph, 262
Admiral, Lord, 76, 157, 173
Aeneas, 108, 208, 219
Aeneid, 4, 107, 155, 208, 222
Aggripina, 248
Alarum for London, 198
Alcazar, battle of, 301
Aldrich, Simon, 190-91
Alexandrian period, 214
Alexandrines, 214
Algebra, 163
Ali-i-Yazdi, 101
Allen, Thomas, 166
Alleyn, Edward, 49, 79, 80, 94, 96, 226; as Barabas, 146, 147; as Faustus, 107, 109, 118, 119, 125; as Tamburlaine, 91, 94, 245; family, 81; founds Dulwich, 119; reader of Shakespeare, 253; star, 80, 157
Alleyn, John, 80, 125
Alphonsus of Arragon, 169, 244
America, discovery of, 205
Amintae Gaudia, 157, 230
"Amor Constans," 157, 230
Amores, 232-34
Amyntas, 248
Analytics, 44, 58
Anchises, 208
Angel Inn, 175
Anglo-Saxon, 10
Anne, Queen, 157
Anti-Machiavel, 148
Antioch, 112, 122, 123
Antony and Cleopatra, 97, 242
Apocryphal Gospels, 112
Apostles, Epistles of the, 112
Apprentices, 9, 12, 15, 18, 22
Arabia, King of, 91
Arcadia, 82
Arcadius and Sepha, 236
Archbishop of Canterbury, 13, 84, 233
"Archer, Francis," 195
Archilaus, Duke, 216
Arden, Mary, *see* Shakespeare, Mary
Arden of Feversham, 198, 199, 205
Aretino, Pietro, 173
Ariosto, 98
Aristotle, 3, 44, 45, 58, 103, 167, 226
Armada, 19, 41, 63, 68, 69, 72
Arnold, Matthew, 224
"Arrian," 136
Arte of English Poesie, 221
Arthur, Dorothy, 19, 181
Arthur, Rev. Christopher, 12
Arthur, Thomas, 181
Artillery, 175
Artillery Garden, 215
Artillery Lane, 215
Ascanius, 219
Ashmolean Collection, 218
Asiae Europaeque Elegantissima Descriptio, 100
Astarte, 122
Astronomy, 7, 31, 45, 46, 163
As You Like It, 134, 139, 236, 238, 242

Atheism, 65-66, 164, 165, 170-71, 180, 183, 187ff., 191, 192
Atheist's Tragedy, 77
Athenae Oxonienses, 192-93
Aubrey, John, 133, 159-60, 161, 164, 236
Avon, River, 21, 28

Babington, Anthony, 64, 176, 178
Babylon, 96
Backgammon, 184
Backs, The, 50
Bacon, Francis, 71, 195
Bacon, Friar, *see* Friar Bacon
Bacon-Shakespeare Theory, 195
Bajazeth, 88, 89, 91, 92, 99, 100, 245, 246
Baker, David Erskine, 199
Ballard, Father, 177
Bandler, Dr. Bernard, 257
Bankside, 71, 81-82
Banquet of Sence, 139
Barabas, 3, 27, 81, 88, 139ff., 146, 148, 149, 150, 241
Barham, 255
Barker, Granville, 157
Barker, Nicholas, 260-61
Barksted, William, 236
Barnes, Barnabe, 248
Barnfield, Richard, 236
Barton, Mrs. Salomon, 19
Barton, Salomon, 19
Basingstoke, 175
Bathing, 50-51
Battle of Alcazar, 145
Bear-baiting, 25, 50, 81
Beard, Thomas, 189-90, 191, 192
Beaumont, Francis, 59, 72, 87, 96, 137, 229, 236, 246
Beeston, William, 133
Belgium, 69
Believe as You List, 203, 246
Bellamira, 218
Belleforest, François de, 149
Bell, Harry, 30
Bell Inn, 77
Bell Savage Inn, 77, 117
Belphagor, 248
Benefit of Clergy, 26, 131, 132
Benet Hall, *see* Corpus Christi, Cambridge
Bentham, 33
Berkeley Castle, 153
Berlioz, Hector, 103
Bethsabe, David and, 245
Betsy, Warburton's cook, 200
Bible, 24, 44, 131, 144, 162, 164, 166, 167
Binders, *see* Bookbinders
Bindings, 256
Biographie Générale, Nouvelle, 194
Birde, William, 115, 116, 117
Birkbeck College, 157
Bishop of London, 232, 233
Blackfriars, *see* Theatres
Black Guard, 23
Blackwood's, 122
Blank verse, 86, 87, 171, 226-27, 235
Blind Beggar of Bednall Green, 246
Bloch, Iwan, 194
Blount, Edward, 2, 231
Boar's Head Inn, 77
Bodleian Library, 85, 218, 231, 234, 256, 257, 258, 259-60
Bodley, Thomas, 255
Bodmer, Johann Jakob, 262
Boiling to death, 27, 141
Bondsmen, 17-18
Boniface IX, 99
Bonne, William, 202
Boo, Baron Hamilton of, 263
Book trade, 40-41, 46-47
Bookbinders, 254, 255-56
Book prices, *see* Prices
Boswell, James, 258
Bosworth, William, 236, 237
Bottom 4, 28
Bowling, 50
Boyle, John, 34

Boyle, Richard, 34
Bradley, Richard, 126
Bradley, William, 2, 124-31, 138, 167, 179, 187, 230, 231
Braithwaite, R., 236
Branding, 35, 132-33
Brandon, Edward, 149
Brewer, Mistress, 166
Bristow, 156
British Museum, 77, 164, 191, 200, 253, 254, 256, 257, 258, 262
British Theatre, 194
Brooke, Tucker, 227, 259
Brothels, 81-82, 194
Broughton, James, 195
Browning, John, 52
Brownists, 233
Brydges, Sir Egerton, 259
Buckinghamshire, 10
Bull, Eleanor, 183, 184, 190, 194, 212
Bull Inn, 77
Bull-baiting, 24, 51, 81
Bull-days, 24, 81
Burbage, Cuthbert, 79-80, 125
Burbage, James, 78, 79-80, 105, 125
Burbage, Mrs. James, 79, 80, 125
Burbage, Richard, 72, 78, 79, 80, 91, 105, 125
Burghley, Lord, *see* Cecil, William
Burghmote, 22, 25
Burned books, 168, 233-34
Burton, William E., 260
Buttery Book, *see* Corpus Christi, Cambridge
Byron, Lord, 120, 121, 122, 249

Cade, Jack, 3
Cadiz, 162
Caesar, Julius, 21, 111, 198, 231, 240
Caesura, 227
Calderón, 120, 122, 123
Calepinus, 100
Callapine, 150, 219
Calvin, John, 63
Cambine, Andrew, 99, 100
Cambridge, city of, 38, 53
Cambridge, mayor of, 53
Cambridge University, 1, 7, 22, 31, 48, 49, 67, 68, 71, 82, 88, 92, 93, 104, 124, 133, 142, 147, 158, 167, 168, 174, 179, 204, 206, 236; arrival of Marlowe, 56; curriculum 45-46; dress, 40 ff.; German influence, 113-14; government, 39, 40, 42, 44, 46, 47; Hebrew, study of, 144; library, 46-48, 99, 155, 214, 257; plays, 51-52, 75, 155, 192, 244; seal, 46; Statutes, *see* government; traces in the plays, 35, 43, 45, 58, 108-9, 148, 155, 170
Cambridgeshire, 53
Cam, River, 50, 61
Canterbury, 12, 16, 18, 21, 22-25, 27, 28-30, 51, 71, 82, 133; actors, 22-3; Burghmote, 22, 25; Cathedral, 9, 14, 29, 31, 32, 33, 35; freemen, 15ff., 25, 31; Huguenots, 204; life in, 26, 28-31; plague in, 181; traces in the plays, 27, 28, 30, 31, 35, 96, 140; walls, 14; wealth, 23
Canterbury, Archbishop of, *see* Archbishop
Capell, Edward, 258
Captives, The, 143
Caput, 40
Carthage, *see Dido*
Catchwords, 260
Cathedral, 9, 30, 31, 32, 33, 35, 54
Catholics, 2, 9, 38, 63, 64, 67, 68, 176, 177, 179, 189, 205, 206, 240
Catiline, 98
Cecil, Robert, 68

Cecil, William, 39, 41-42, 49, 50, 63, 68, 118, 130, 202
Celebinus, 100
Central Criminal Court, 130
Chamberlain, Lord, 76
Chancellor of Cambridge, 39, 40, 41, 46, 63, 67
Chancery, 188
Channel, 21
Channel Islands, 149
Chapman, George, 2, 72, 139, 162, 165, 178, 203, 212-14, 241
Chappell, reprint, 121
Charles I, 76, 142, 143, 243
Charles II, 119, 142-43, 198, 256
Charles V, 211
Charles IX, 205
Chaucer, Geoffrey, 21, 84, 220, 235
Chettle, Henry, 170, 246
Chetwode, William Rufus, 194
Chislehurst, 124, 172, 173, 181, 182, 183
Christ Church, Oxford, 157
Christ's College, 51
Christ's Teares Over Jerusalem, 168
Chronicle, see Holinshed's *Chronicle*
Chronicorum Turcicorum Libri, 99, 100
Chronik, Schedel's, 114
Churchyard, Thomas, 110
Cicero, 98
Cinque Ports, 76
Circulation of the blood, 35
Civil War, 261
Clare College, Cambridge, 175
Clarence, Duke of, 22
Clark, Samuel, 191-92
Classics, 31, 45, 46
Clavijo, Ruy Gonzalez de, 102
Clifford, Henry, 155
Clifford's Inn, 130
Clink, Liberty of the, 80, 82
Clink Prison, 82
Clowns, 114, 116
Cock-fighting, 24
Cockpit, *see* Theatres
Coligny, Admiral, 201, 204
Collected works, 251-53
College of God's Gift, *see* Dulwich College
Collier, John Payne, 76-77, 191, 230, 263
Colyer, Stephen, 25
Commoners, 54
Commonplace books, 211-12, 217, 218, 230, 263
Companion to the Playhouse, 199
Compleat Angler, 217, 236
Comus, 198
Conquest of Granada, 101
Constables, 2, 72, 128, 129, 134, 149, 179, 237, 241, 249
Contention, The, 134, 149, 237, 241, 249
Conversations with Goethe, 121
Convictus Secundus, 54
Copernicus, 46
Corinna, 110
Cork, Bishop of (Richard Boyle), 34
Cork, Earl of (John Boyle), 34
Coroners, 127ff., 185ff.
Corpus Christi, Cambridge, 6, 24, 32, 35, 66, 70, 106, 109, 167, 195, 232, 249; accounts, 54, 55, 57, 61-62; Admissions Book, 56; buildings, 37-38; Bursar, 57; Buttery Book, 26, 33, 37, 39, 54, 55, 56-57, 61-62, 184, 267-79; Fellows, 26, 38, 40; government, 40; history, 37-38, library, 35, 46, 47-48, 90, 99, 100, 150, 155, 257; Master, 38, 40; plays, 51; records, 195; scholarships, 33, 36-37, 38, 53ff., 60, 62, 101, 204
Corpus Christi, Guild of, 37
Corpus Christi, Oxford, 182
Cosmographie Universelle, 149

Costume, 41-43, 58, 76, 92, 117, 159, 201-2
Cotswold Hills, 21
Cotton, Charles, 236
Court Hall, 30
Courtiers, 19, 22-23, 67, 72, 96, 144, 160, 187, 204
Covent Garden, 119
Coventry, Bishop of, 152
Coxcomb, The, 246
Cranmer, Archbishop, 31-32, 136
Crete, 149
Creusa, 209
Cripplegate, 126
Criticism, textual, 113, 115-16
Crofts, 68
Cromwell, Oliver, 144, 189, 234, 243
Cross Keys Inn, 77
Crow, Sir Sackville, 243
Curtain, *see* Theatres
Curtain Road, 78
Cyprian, 112, 122, 123
Cyprus, 149
Cyrano de Bergerac, 122, 123
Czech production, 156

Damascus, 90
Danby, William, 187, 188
Dark Entry, 29
David and Bethsabe, 245
Davies, John, 233-34
Day, John, 133, 199, 200, 246
De Anima, 167
Death of Zoroas, 221-22
Defoe, Daniel, 118
De Globis, 163
Degrees, 36, 45, 55, 57, 58, 61, 62, 66-67, 106, 169-70, 171
Dekker, Thomas, 28, 236, 246, 247, 248
De Origine Turcarum Libellum, 47
Deptford, 8, 18, 111, 158, 183, 187, 190, 195, 196, 237, 238, 251
Descartes, René, 163
Description of England, 139
Devereux, Robert, Earl of Essex, 43-44, 71, 145, 161, 178
Devil and His Dame, 248
Devils on stage, 116-17
Devonshire dialect, 161, 166
Devonshire, Duke of, 259
Dialectics, 44
Dialogue in Verse, 48
Dialogues of the Dead, 107
Dichterleben, 249
Dictionary of National Biography, 195
Dido, Queen of Carthage, 123-27, 218; collaboration with Nashe, 5, 59, 88, 168, 199-200, 208, 209; date, 206-7; degeneracy, 154; editions, 143, 257, 258, 259, 260, 264; famous phrases in, 207-8, 218; influence, 208, 243, 246, 247; production, 209; sources, 155-56, 207, 221; technique, 207-8; translation, 122; versification, 222-23
Didot brothers, 194
Discours de la Guerre de Malte, 150
Divil is an Asse, 247
Divil's Charter, 248
Dobell, P. J., 191, 263
Doctor Faustus, 2, 3, 21, 32, 35, 42-43, 44, 45, 46, 55, 58, 81, 87, 88, 93, 103ff., 138, 208, 209, 219, 226, 247; Cambridge traces, 35, 43, 45, 58, 107-8, 109; date, 110-11; editions, 116, 119-23, 142-43, 146, 251-52, 256, 257, 258, 259, 262, 263-64; influence, 147, 169, 239, 240, 242, 246-49; production, 78, 115-19; revision, 246; sources, 106-8, 111-15, 148, 155-56, 195ff.;

Doctor Faustus (Continued)
success, 117, 202; technique, 8, 109-10, 226; thousand ships, 8, 107-8, 116, 122, 140, 207, 210, 216, 242
Dogberry, 4, 28, 72, 128, 134
Donne, John, 213, 236, 243
Doubtful documents, 47. *See also* Collier, John Payne
Doubt, religious, 38-39
Dover, 21, 75
Drake, Sir Francis, 72, 163, 208
Drayton, Michael, 236
Dryden, John, 101, 226
Dudley, Robert, Lord Burghley, 22, 145
Duels, 126ff., 132-33, 179, 180, 185, 186, 230, 231
Dulwich College, 48, 119
Dunciad, 119
Dutch, 21

Earle, John, 179
East Smithfield, 130
Eastward Hoe, 246
Eccles, Goodman, 181
Eccles, Mark, 231
Eckerman, J., 121
Edinburgh Review, 122
Edmonds, Charles, 260, 261, 262
Edward I, 144, 245
Edward II, 152 ff., 241
Edward the Second, 3, 5, 8, 29, 30, 35, 47, 88, 110, 138, 148, 151ff., 207, 210, 211, 230, 241; date, 151; echoes *Dido* 207; editions, 142, 151, 156, 251, 254, 262; influence, 239; production, 156-57; sources, 155-56, technique, 138, 152-55, 227
Edward III, 153, 198
Edward IV, 21
Edwards, Thomas, 236
Egerton, Sir Thomas, 255, 259
Egnatius, Baptista, 47, 99, 100
Egypt, Soldan of, 89-92
Elegies, 232-34, 256. *See also* Ovid
Elham, Kent, 175, 258, 262, 263
Eliot, George, 96, 245, 246
Elizabethan Stage Society, 157
Elizabeth, Queen, 19, 20, 23, 25, 39, 41, 51, 52, 72, 73, 74, 117, 143-44, 145, 153, 158-59, 160, 172, 173-74, 176, 187, 193, 196, 202-3, 218, 223, 242, 245, 246
Ely, 54
Emmanuel College, 234, 262
Emption, 16
Encyclopedia Britannica, 115, 194
England, 201
England's Helicon, 216-17, 218
England's Parnassus, 219-20
English Channel, *see* Channel
Enjambement, 226
d'Epernon, duc, 204
Ephesus, 113
Epitaph, *see* Manwood, Roger
Erdgeist, 120
Essex, Earl of, *see* Devereux, Robert
Euphues, 83
Examinations, 58-59
Exchequer, 71
Executions, 14, 26-28, 63, 74-75, 146
Exeter, 119

Faerie Queene, 111, 162, 228
Fal of the Late Arrian, 136
Famous History of the Seven Champions, 248
Farewell to Folly, 170
Faust Books, 110, 111-14, 155
Faust, Dr. John, 103, 110, 113-14, 123
Faust (Goethe's), 120-21
Faustus, see Doctor Faustus

Feake, James, 186
Fellow-commoners, 38, 54, 55
Fineux, 39, 66, 105, 249
Finsbury Fields, 98, 125, 162
First Folio, 252, 262
Fitziames, John, 167
Flanders, 242
Fleetwood, William, 130, 313, 178
Fleire, The, 246
Flemings, 180, 243
Fletcher, John, 59, 72, 87, 96, 137, 229, 236, 246, 249
Folger, H. C., 257, 259, 263
Folger Shakespeare Library, 48, 191, 218, 230, 257, 258, 263
Foot-ball, 50
Ford, John, 149, 236, 246
Foreste, The, 98
Forgery, 77-78
Forsythe, R. S., 219
Fortescue, Thomas, 98
Fortunatus, 248
Fortune, *see* Theatres
Fowler, William, 68
Fox's *Book of Martyrs*, 26
France, 149, 201, 202, 205, 242
Francesco's Fortunes, 198
Frankfurt, 113
Freeman, 10, 11, 12, 15-16, 18, 22
Free verse, 223. *See also* Blank verse
French Wars, 204-5
Freudian psychology, 231
Friar Bacon and Friar Bungay, 119, 169, 248
Frisius, Gemma, 45, 163
Frizer, "Francis," 195
Frizer, Ingram, 71, 127, 168, 174-78, 183ff., 193, 194-96
Frogge, Henry, 47, 48
Fulgotius, Baptista, 99, 100
Fuller, Bishop, 82
Funeral, The, 201
Furor Poeticus, 244
Fust, Johann, *see* Faust, Dr. John
Fyle, The, 30, 32

Gale, Dunstan, 236
Galileo, 163
Game at Chesse, 203
Games, 50
Gammer Gurton's Needle, 51
Garrick, David, 258
Gascoigne, George, 96, 245
Gast, John, 113
Gaveston, Piers, 149, 152ff., 156
Genesis, 164
Gentillet, Innocent, 147-48
Geometry, 15
George I, 261
George III, 256, 258
Germany, 103, 113ff., 119, 121, 149
Gertrude, Queen, 241
Ghosts, 235
Gibbons, Orlando, 74
Globe, *see* Theatres
Gobbo, Launcelot, 4
Godfrey, Thomas, 242
Gods, heathen, 194
Goethe, Johann Wolfgang, 103, 119-23, 249
Golden Grove, 68, 192
Golding, Arthur, 96, 245
Golding-lane, 118
Goldsborough, Nicholas, 35
Goldsmith, Oliver, 27
Gondomar, 203
Gonville and Caius College, 172
Gorboduc, 85, 86, 227
Gospels, Apocryphal, 112
Gosson, Stephen, 34
Goths, 236
Gounod, Charles Francois, 103
Grace Book, 45, 55, 58-59
Graetz, 119
Grand jury, 25
Granta, River, 61

Gray's Elegy, 232
Greek, 45, 58, 75, 214, 226
Greene, J. R., 144
Greene, Robert, 84, 168-71; attitude toward Marlowe, 49, 59, 67, 71, 84, 124, 137, 167ff., 235; death, 171, 172, 188; education, 59, 66; *Francesco's Fortunes*, 198; imitates Marlowe, 168, 172, 248; plays, 119-20, 169, 244
Greenwich, 190
Grim, the Collier of Croydon, 248
Grimald, Nicholas, 221-22
Groatworth of Wit, 171
Guiana, 162
Guilds, 21
Guise, Cardinal of, 202, 206
Guise, Duchess of, 202
Guise, Duke of, 3, 87, 88, 138, 148, 200, 201, 203, 204, 205, 206, 240, 241
Gutenberg, 113
"Gwisse," 201
Gynaikeion, 143

Hague, 184
Hall, Joseph, 243
Hamilton, Baron, of Boo, 263
Hamilton, J. A., 262
Hamlet, 71, 78, 98, 105, 116, 209, 239, 240, 241, 242
Hammond, William, 53
Hampden, Walter, 122
Handbooks, theatrical, 193
Hardy, Thomas, 3
Harriot, Thomas, 30, 45, 46, 82, 136, 161, 162-65, 178
Harrison, William, 139
Harvard College Library, 257
Harvey, Gabriel, 72, 171-73; hatred of Marlowe, 124, 167, 170, 182, 188, 189, 233; hatred of Nashe, 84, 233-34; poetic theories, 221; suppression of his books, 233
Harvey, Richard, 48, 124, 167, 171-73, 182, 183
Hasted's *History of Kent*, 195
Haughton, William, 248
Hawkins, John, 72
Hazlitt, William, 197
Headlines, 256
Heber, Richard, 258, 259, 263
Hebrew, 144
Heidelberg University, 113
Helen of Troy, 4, 7, 106-7, 210, 248
Hellespont, 214, 237
Helliott, Nicholas, 134
Henderson, John, 258
Henri III, 200
Henry II, 81
Henry IV, *see* Henry of Navarre
Henry IV, 92, 96, 201, 202, 203, 241, 242, 246
Henry V, 79
Henry VI, 122, 198, 237, 241
Henry VIII, 27, 30, 31, 37, 44, 63, 82, 144
Henry of Navarre, 5, 201, 202, 203
Henslowe, Philip, 71, 80, 81, 91, 92, 106, 115, 117, 138, 143, 146, 156, 157, 200, 202, 212, 245
Hentzner, Paul, 38
Heretics, 25-26, 38-39, 135-36
Hero and Leander, 5, 7, 8, 32, 48, 71, 82, 121, 139, 154, 162, 174, 181, 191, 210, 214-16, 230; completion, 212; echoes in *Dido*, 207; editions, 215, 231, 251, 253, 254, 256, 258, 260, 261, 263; influence, 236, 237, 238, 242-43; sources, 47, 168, 214, 216, 242; versification, 225
Herrick, Robert, 224, 236, 243
Hertford, Lord, 22
Hesse, Prince Otto of, 262
Hewes, William, 18

Heywood, Thomas, 58, 59, 73, 115, 142-43
High Street, 22
Hirelings, 117-18
Histoire Angloise, 202
Histrio-Mastix, 118
"Hobbinol," 172
Hog Lane, 125, 126, 127, 133
Hogs, 53
Holborn, 129
Holinshed's *Chronicle*, 48, 98, 152, 155, 156
Holland, 78
Holland's Leaguer, 82
Holy Cross, Church of the, 17
Homer, 162, 212, 221, 224, 241
Homunculus, 120
Hooker, Brian, 122, 123
Hopton, Sir Owen, 128-29, 134
Horace, 84
Horsey, Sir Raulfe, 166ff.
Hotson, John Leslie, 194, 195, 196
Hotspur, 241
Howard, Henry, 211, 221, 222, 235
Howard, Lord, 72
Howe, Anthony, 181
Hudson, Thomas, 20
Hues, Robert, 162, 163, 164
Huguenots, 148, 204
Huntington, Henry E., 257, 259, 262, 263
Huntington Library, 172, 254, 257, 262
Huth Library, 256

Iago, 154
Iarbas, 208
If This Be Not a Good Play, 247
Ignatius, Baptista, *see* Egnatius
Iliad, 212
Ilium, 212
Incomes, Canterbury, 18
India, 260
Indians, 165
Inns, 76, 77, 78
Intrantes, 11, 16
Iodelle, *see* Jodelle
Iphigenia in Tauris, 107
Ironside, Rev. Ralph, 166ff.
Isabel, Queen, 3, 152, 153, 154, 241
Isham books, 260, 261
Isham, Charles, 260
Isham, Justinian, 261
Isham, Thomas, 255, 260
Isleworth, 163
Isola, Emma, 218
Italian comedians, 202
Italy, 220
Ithamore, 29, 140, 150, 218
Iulus, 209
Ive, Paul, 66, 111
"I walkt along a streame," 218-19, 225

James I, 20, 51, 68, 71, 156, 161, 162, 203, 246
James IV, 169
Jeronimo, 245
Jessica, 241
Jesuits, 63, 64, 75, 164, 165
Jesus College, Cambridge, 53
Jew, The, 144
Jew of Malta, The, 115, 138ff., 151, 210, 218; Canterbury traces in, 27-28, 29, 35; date, 138-39; echoes in, 218; editions, 141, 254, 257, 262, 263; influence, 138-39, 147-49, 201, 241, 242; "pollicie," 87; production, 8, 81, 119, 143, 146-47; sources, 59, 114, 142; technique, 6, 100, 141-43, 148-50
Jews, 143-47
Jocasta, 96, 245
Jodelle, 192
Johnes, Mr., 44
Johnson, Richard, 248
Johnson, Samuel, 27, 67

John, Troublesome Reign of King, 198
Jones, Henry Arthur, 249
Jones, Herschel V., 259
Jones, Richard, 115
Jones, William, 151
Jonson, Ben, 18, 28, 67, 68, 71, 82, 98, 115, 131, 132, 139, 206, 235, 236, 243, 246, 247, 251
Jordan, Thomas, 147
Josselyn, John, 37-38
Journalism, 84, 205-6
Jovius, Paulus, 47, 48, 99, 100
Julian the Apostate, 173
Julius Caesar, 240, 242. *See also* Caesar.
Juries, 16. *See also* Coroners

Kassel Landesbibliothek, 262
Kean, Edmund, 146
Keats, John, 8, 108, 214, 219, 224, 235, 242
Keeper, Lord, *see* Puckering, John
Kemble, J. P., 194, 258
Kent, 241
Kepler, Johannes, 163
Kett, Francis, 26, 38-39, 66
Kew, 187
Keymer, a vintner, 53
King John, see John
King Lear, see Lear
King's College, Cambridge, 175
King's School, 4, 22, 29, 30, 31, 33, 37, 38, 51, 54, 55, 57; accounts, 32-33, 54, 56; history, 30-34, 54; life at, 32-33; plays at, 22, 51
Kipling, R., 246
Kungliga Biblioteket, 257, 262
Kydd, Thomas, 189; arrest, 135-36, 185, 187; attitude toward Marlowe, 2, 126, 151, 173, 179, 184, 185, 187; patron of, 4, 158; possible author of early *Hamlet*, 71; shares room with Marlowe, 86, 135, 138, 162, 167, 180, 245; *Spanish Tragedy*, and other plays, 86, 245
Kytchine, Richard, 130

Lady Day, 11n.
Lamb, Charles, 154-55, 197, 210, 218
Lamb of God, 48, 172
Lamport Hall, 255, 360, 361
Landesbibliothek, *see* Kassel Landesbibliothek
Latin, 40, 44, 58, 59, 75, 85, 128-29, 156, 166, 206, 226, 230, 240
Laurence, Friar, 8
Lavallette, 150
Leander, *see Hero and Leander*
Lear, 71, 241, 242
Lee, Sir Sidney, 195
Legge, Thomas, 51
Leicester, Earl of, *see* Dudley, Robert
Levy-Bandler *Jew of Malta*, 254, 257
Lewes, 33
Lewgar, 108
Lexicon of Suidas, 48, 214
Libels, 180, 181, 187
Liberties, 77, 78, 81, 122
Life of Tamerlane, 191
Lightborne, 239
Lincoln College, Oxford, 262
Locrine, 198
Lodge, Thomas, 84, 236, 244, 246
Loggats, 50
Logic, 44
London, 17, 21, 42, 62, 70ff., 73, 83, 84, 88, 89, 104, 122, 123, 131, 133, 181, 193, 257
London, Bishop of, *see* Bishop
London Bridge, 27, 74, 75, 133
London, Great Fire of, 261

London Street, 189, 190
London University, 156
Lonicer, Philip, 99, 100, 149
Looking-Glasse both for Saints and Sinners, 191-92
Looking-Glass for London, 244
Lopez, Rodrigo, 53, 144-46
Lord Mayor, 74, 78
Lord Rich's Players, 51
Lorenzo, 139, 242
Lost works, 197, 198, 210, 211
Love's Labour's Lost, 85
Low Countries, 22, 41, 68
Lucan, 210, 231, 251, 257-58
Lucian, 107, 113
Lucrece, 58, 73
Lust's Dominion, 197
Luther, Martin, 63, 113
Lycidas, 232
Lycophron, 192
Lyly family, 33
Lyly, John, 83, 85
Lyric, untitled, 219-20

Macbeth, 48, 71, 153
Machiavelli, 3, 4, 5, 87, 147-48, 201
Magdalene College, Cambridge, 67
Magic, 106, 112-13
Magico Prodigioso, 122
Magus, *see* Simon Magus
Maiden's Holiday, 133, 199, 200
Maid of Kent, 29
Maitland, Henry, 122
Malone, Edmund, 256, 258, 259-60
Malta, 138, 148, 150
Manfred, 121-22
Manwood, Sir Roger, 174, 212, 230, 263
Marble Arch, 133
Marguerite, 103, 120
Marle, John, lockyer, 10
Marley, Joan, 11
Marley, John, tanner, 11, 15, 16, 17
Marley, Richard, 11, 12, 16, 17
Marlowe, play, 109
Marlowe, An, 15, 35
Marlowe, Anthony, 183
Marlowe, Christopher (the first), 11, 12, 16-17
Marlowe, Christopher (the poet), 171, 173; absent from Corpus, 37, 55, 57, 62, 84; actor, 77, 78; admission to Corpus, 47, 50, 54ff., 57; ancestry, 13, *see also* Marley; assassination plot, 182; birth, 12, 15; boyhood, 56; character, 1ff., 40, 104, 109, 128, 133-37, 142, 160, 203-4; death, 8, 18, 19, 57, 71, 127, 144, 163, 166, 167, 172, 174, 185ff., 212, 236-37; degrees, 42, 45, 54, 57-60, 67; doubtful works, 197-200, 231-34; education, 23, 31ff.; finances, 67; home life, 12-18, 19-20; humour, 7-8, 114, 116; influence, 32, 96, 119-20, 138ff., 147-49, 152, 154, 159, 207-9, 216-19, 235ff., 246; Latin, knowledge of, 210, 211, 231ff.; legal troubles, 125ff., 134-35, 137, 171; lost works, 197-98, 210-11, 212; matriculation, 54; models, 235-36; name, spelling of, 9-10, 12, 56, 170, 252; plays at Corpus, 51; plays, *see* individual titles; power theme, 87-88, 147-49; Privy Council, 63-68, 181-83; rant, 60, 86; reading, 47-49, 89, 91, 97ff., 109-10; religion, 38-39, 59-60, 66, 106ff., 134-36, 161ff., 180-81, 188ff.; secret service, *see* Spies; technique, dramatic, 2-3, 107-8, 138, 140-41, 152-55, 206-8, 210; versification, 1-2, 8, 88-89, 108, 154, 171, 220-21

Marlowe, Christopher, Jesuit alias, 75
Marlowe, Christopher, others of the same name, 181
Marlowe Dramatic Society, 155
Marlowe, Dorothy, 15, 35
Marlowe, Edmund, 163
Marlowe house, 12-13, 181
Marlowe, John, 15, 35
Marlowe, John, father of the poet, 9-10, 11-18, 22, 31, 41, 53, 73, 181, 191
Marlowe, Katherine, 9, 12, 14, 18-20, 22, 30
Marlowe, Margaret, 15, 35
Marlowe, Mary, 14-15
Marlowe, Thomas, 15
Marlowe village, 10
Marlowe, William, 26
Marston, John, 236
Martial, 84
Martire des Deux Frères, 206
Martyn, Elias, 35
Martyr's Green, 26
Mary, Bloody, 31, 72
Mary, Queen of Scots, 64, 176
Mary, William and, 193
Massacre at Paris, 5, 6, 35, 48, 87, 151, 199-206; Cambridge traces in, 35, 304; Canterbury traces in, 35; date, 138, 147, 150; editions, 143; influence, 240, 241, 243; production, 202-3; sources, 5-6, 148, 204-6; technique, 138
Massacre of St. Bartholomew's, 148, 199, 200, 203, 205
Massinger, Philip, 203, 236, 246
Mastiffs, 25
Matriculation, 54
Maunder, Henry, 180, 181, 182, 183
Maye, Mary, 20
Medici, Catherine de', 148, 201
Medici, Margaret de', 201
Melancthon, 113
Meleager, 51
Menaphon, 171
Mephastophilis, 7, 46, 105, 106, 111, 219, 247
Merchant of Venice, 139, 239-40, 241
Mercutio, 127
Mere, John, 54
Meres, Francis, 192-93, 194
Merlin, 170
Merry Devil of Edmonton, 248
Merry Wives of Windsor, 239, 242
Mexia, Pedro, 6, 98-99, 100
Micro-Cosmographie, 179
Middle Ages, 14
Middleburg, 233
Middlemarch, 245
Middlesex, 74, 130
Middleton, Thomas, 203
Midsummer Night's Dream, 239, 242
"Mighty line," 86-87, 210ff., 244
Milton, John, 46, 51, 198, 220, 235, 242, 249
Miques, João, *see* Nassi, David
Miracle plays, 75
Miracles, 113
Mir Khwand, 101
Mirrour for Magistrates, 110
Misers, 138, 149
Misfortunes of Arthur, 86
Monopolies, 52-53, 159
Moodie, Richard, 47, 48
Morality plays, 8, 75
Morgan, J. P., 263
Morgan Library, *see* Pierpont Morgan Library
Morgan, Thomas, 177
Moritz der Gelehrte, 262
Morle, Simon, 10
Morle, Thomas, 10
Morle, William, 10
Morley, Laurence, 10
Morley, Lord, 22
Morley, Mr., 68
Morrice, Goodwife Sarai, 20
Mortimers, 3, 110, 152, 153, 156, 239, 241
Mortlake, 243

Mortymer, 156
Moses, 164, 166
Mucedorus, 198
Much Ado About Nothing, 28, 72, 239, 242
Müller, Wilhelm, 121
Mugeroun, 202
Mulfuzat Timury, 61
Munday, Anthony, 67
Musaeus, 214, 215, 216, 243
Muscovy Company, 183
Mychell, Thomas, 18
Mystery plays, 75, 76

Narke, province of, 263
Nashe, Thomas, 72, 84, 126, 164, 171, 207-8, 259; collaborates with Marlowe, 59, 199, 208; education, 51, 167, 169; hatred of Gabriel Harvey, 84, 168, 173, 233
Nassi, Joseph, 149
Nature of a Woman, 231
Navarre, Henry of, *see* Henry of Navarre
Navarre, Queen of, 201
Navigations, peregrinations and voyages, 150
Naxos, 149
Near East, 149
"Neck verse," 131
Nerissa, 139
Newe Letter, 188
Newgate Prison, 129, 130
Newington Butts, *see* Theatres
Newsbooks, 205-6
News plays, 206
New Testament, 163
Nicholay, Nicholas, 150
Nicholls, Allen, 134
Nocera, Bishop of, *see* Jovius, Paulus
Norgate, Robert, 60, 62, 64, 66
Northamptonshire, 255, 260
Northumberland, Earl of, 162-63, 173
Norton Folgate, 77, 122, 125, 126, 129, 133, 160, 229, 237
Norwich, 26
Nouvelle Biographie Générale, 194
Nymph's Reply, 162, 218

Octavos, 252, 254, 256
Odyssey, 224
Old Bailey, 131
Old Court, 36, 48, 62, 101, 109
Old Fish Street, 81
Old Fortunatus, 248
Old Testament, 144, 164, 166
Oldys, William, 259
Opponencies, 58, 59
Optics, 163
Orchanes, 99, 100
Ordo Senioritatis, 60
Organon, 44
Oriental sources, 94, 98, 101-2
Orlando Furioso, 98, 244
Ortelius, 6, 47, 89, 94, 97, 98, 225
Osborne, Thomas, 259
Othello, 71, 154
Otto, Prince of Hesse, 262
Ouvry, F., 264
Ovid, 44, 96, 109, 110, 192, 210, 218, 232-34, 235, 238-40, 245, 256, 257, 258, 261, 262
Oxberry, W., 121
Oxford University, 31, 37, 52, 64, 156, 160, 171, 192, 230, 242, 257
Oxinden, Henry, 190-91, 212, 230, 255, 258, 263

Page of Plymouth, 206
Palmier, Matthew, 99
"Pampered jades," 96, 245
Paper, 257
Paradise Lost, 249, 262
Pardons, 130

Paris, 187, 204, 205
Parker, Archibishop Matthew, 36-37, 38, 45, 46, 47, 53-55, 195
Parker, John, 36, 54
Parker Library, 21, 32, 35, 45, 46, 100, 155
Parker scholarships, *see* Scholarships
Parma, Duke of, 41, 68, 72
Parthia, *see Prince of Parthia*
Pashley, Christopher, 54, 57, 108
Passi, David, 149
Passionate Pilgrim, 216, 218, 261
Passionate Shepherd, 5, 35, 61, 162, 210, 212; echoes in other works, 236; influence, 238, 242, 243; versification, 225
Payne, Abel, 181
Peabody, Josephine Preston, 109
Pedantius, 51
Peele, George, 72, 84, 245
Pembroke, Countess of, 82, 157, 173
Pembroke, Earl of, 151, 156, 157, 158, 173, 254
Pensioners, 54, 158, 169
Pepys, Samuel, 119
Perez, Antonio, 145
Perkes, Clement, 28
Perkins, Richard, 146
Perondinus, Petrus, 98-99, 100, 101
Perseda, Soliman and, 245
Persia, 48
Perspective, 45
Peterhouse, 59
Petowe, Henry, 96, 215-16
Pharsalia, 219, 231
Philip II, 41, 197, 211
Philocassander and Elanira, 215
Philosophy, 44, 45
Phoenix Society, 147, 157
Physicians, College of, 144
Piccolomini, Aeneas Sylvius, 47, 90, 99, 100
Pierce Pennilesse, 164
Pierpont Morgan Library, 257
Pistol, Ancient, 49, 96
Pius, Pope, *see* Piccolomini, Aeneas Sylvius
Plague, 77, 163, 172, 181ff.
Plantina, 99
Playfair, 34
Pliny, 83
Poel, William, 157
Poetics, 226
Poisoning, 113
Poley, Robert, 65, 68, 133, 167, 174-78, 183ff.
Police, *see* Constables
"Pollicie," 4, 5, 147, 201
Pompey, 231
Pope, Alexander, 119
Porter, Henry, 133
Portia, 139
Portugal, 144
Postgate, J. R., 116
Practice of Fortification, 66, 111
Prague, 156
Prices, book, 253, 257-58, 262
Prideaux, W. F., 230, 263
Prince of Parthia, 242
Printers, 45, 114, 205, 231-32, 252, 253, 254
Prior Analytics, see Analytics
Privy Council, 4, 54, 57, 62, 63, 66, 67, 68, 158, 174, 179, 180, 182, 184
Proctors, 58, 171
Propaganda, 205-6
Properties, stage, 116-17, 201, 243, 246
Prospero, 8
Prostitutes, 25, 81
Protestants, 10, 63, 64, 180, 198, 201, 205
Prynne, William, 118
Ptolemy, 45
Public Record Office, 195, 196
Publishers, 40, 46-48, 84, 114, 151, 161, 188, 210-11, 212, 231-33, 251

Puckering, 136, 137, 162
Puppet shows, 119, 120
Puritans, 60, 62, 63, 65, 72, 77, 78, 119, 188, 189, 193, 230, 233, 247
Pyramids, 111
Pyrrhus, 209

Quadrantarii, 55, 169
Quadrennium, 57
Quaestio, 58
Quartos, 251, 255, 256, 260
Queen's College, 51
Queen's Players, 51, 156
Quip for an Upstart Courtier, 172

Radford, the little tailor, 202
Raleigh, Carewe, 165-67
Raleigh, Sir Walter, 4, 6, 30, 52-53, 72, 74, 82, 85, 132, 158-68, 173, 178, 187, 204, 208, 210, 211, 212, 218, 228
Ramus, Peter, 44, 45, 201, 204, 206
Randolph, Thomas, 248
Red Bull, *see* Theatres
Redemption, 16
Reed, Isaac, 258, 259
Regent Theatre, 157
Registry, Cambridge University, 58, 62
Religion, 38-39, 92-93
Renaissance, 1, 4, 64, 122
Repetitions, 206, 218-19
Responsions, 58, 59
Return from Parnassus, 44, 192, 244
Reve, Katherine, 20
Rheims, 63, 64, 65, 66
Rhetoric, 44
Richard II, 71, 153, 155, 239, 241
Richard III, 149, 241, 242
Richardus Tertius, 51
Rich, Lord, his players, 51
Rimes, 223, 226-29
Riots, 52, 53, 180
Robin, 4
Robinson, Henry Crabbe, 120
Rolles, Anne, 182
Romans, 12, 78
Rome, 63, 232
Romeo and Juliet, 127, 242
Rosalind, Lodge's, 236
Rose, *see* Theatres
Rosenbach, A. S. W., 218
Rostand, Edmond, 122
Rowe, Nicholas, 242, 243
Rowland, Humphrey, 130, 131
Rowley, Samuel, 115, 116, 117
Roxburghe, John, Duke of, 259
Royden, Matthew, 68, 162
Royston, 67
Rudierd, Edmund, 191
"Run-on" lines, *see* Enjambement
Rychardsson, Garrard, 12

Sad Shepherd, 139
Saffron Walden, 171
St. Andrew's, Holborn, 129
St. Angelo, Castle, 111
St. Augustine's Abbey, 23, 29
St. Bartholomew's, *see* Massacre of St. Bartholomew's *and Massacre at Paris*
St. Benet's Church, 54
St. Botolph, 130
St. Clement, 112
St. George's Lane, 12-13, 22-23
St. George the Martyr, Church of, 13, 14-15, 23
St. Giles, Cripplegate, 126
St. John's College, 43, 51, 52, 124, 167
St. John's Street, 254
St. Martin, 125
St. Mary Bredman, 13, 31
St. Mary, Guild, 37
St. Mary le Bow, 170

St. Nicholas, Church of, 187, 195
St. Paul, 112, 113, 122, 167
St. Paul's Cathedral, 71, 72, 84, 132, 189, 210, 231, 253
St. Peter, 112
St. Peter's Church, 12
St. Sepulchre's Nunnery, 29
St. Stephen's, 230
St. Thomas, pageant, 22
Sanitation, 15, 72
San Marino, 257
Scadbury, 173, 181
Scanderbage, George, 244
Scandinavia, 262
Schedel, 113
Schiller, Charlotte von, 121
Schiltberger, Johan, 101
Scholarships, 32-33, 36, 37, 38, 53ff., 56, 57, 59, 62
School of Abuse, 34
School of Night, 6, 85, 180
Schools, the, 58
Scots, 152
Scrooge, 149
Scudamour, Lord, 164
Seager, a painter, 211
Secret service, *see* Spies
Selimus, 198
Seneca, 198, 235
Sermon and clerum, 57
Sermones conviviales, 113
Sestos, 212, 214, 216
Seven Deadly Sins, 121
Shakespeare, Joan, 15
Shakespeare, John, 9, 28
Shakespeare, Mary, 9
Shakespeare, William, 2, 7-8, 9, 28, 29, 30, 32, 48, 55, 58, 67, 70-71, 72, 79, 80, 83, 85, 91, 97, 125, 128, 170, 171, 188, 192, 201; acquaintance with Marlowe, 133-34; apocryphal plays, 198, 199; boyhood, 21, 56, 75; editions, 258, 261; Folios, 84, 252, 261; influenced by Marlowe, 32, 48, 92, 96, 121, 126, 134, 138-39, 144, 149, 153, 154, 155, 198, 209, 216, 236, 237, 246-47; plays, *see* individual titles; poems, 211, 216, 220, 224, 231, 241-42, 251; residence, 77, 97, 98; Sonnets, 241, 257; sources, 117, 246; versification, 86-87, 96, 226
Shallow, Justice, 28
Sharpham, Edward, 246
Sheepeardes Calender, 172
Shelley family, 33
Sherburne, Sir Edward, 236
Shirley, James, 249
Shoe-Maker's Holiday, 28
Shopping list, 163
Shoreditch, 73, 78, 128, 133, 134, 151, 179, 237
Shore's Wife, 110
Shylock, 147, 241
Sidney, Sir Philip, 22, 71, 82, 177, 204, 220
Sigismund of Hungary, 93
Silva da Varia Leccon, 98
Simmern, 113
Simon Magus, 112, 123
Sion House, 163
Sizars, 54-55, 169
Skeptic, The, 162
Skeres, Nicholas, 175, 178, 184ff.
Smithfield, East, 130
Snout, 28
Soliman and Perseda, 245
Solomon, 166
Soone, William, 38
Sources, *see* Individual plays
Southwark, 72, 80
Spain, 19, 68, 72
Spanish Tragedie, 86, 115, 135, 245
Spectator, 119
Spencer, Gabriel, 131, 186, 195
Spencers, The (play), 156
Spenser, Edmund, 71, 98, 111, 162, 172, 220, 228, 235

Spies, 64, 68, 92, 93, 158, 162, 164, 174ff.
Stage setting, 106, 116, 201, 252
Stanneries, 159
Stationers' Company, 233-34, 255
Stationers' Register, 115, 151, 199, 205, 231, 257
Statutes, 31
Steele, Richard, 201
Steevens, George, 258, 259
Stenography, 114
Stettin-Pomerania, Duke of, 50
Stews, 81-82
Stockholm, 257, 262
Stone, Friar, 27, 28, 140, 141
Stour, River, 28, 29, 30
Stow, John, 133-34
Strange, Lord, 22, 81, 173
Strappado for the Diuell, 246
Stratford, 9, 15, 28, 71, 72, 188, 223, 257
Stratford Grammar School, 8, 30, 33
Street-cries, 58, 73
Strychnine, 113
Sturbridge, 46
Suidas, 47, 214
Sun's Darling, 246
Sunspots, 163
Supplicat, 55, 58, 59
Surrey, Earl of, *see* Howard, Henry
Surrey Side, 75, 80
Swans, 73-74
Swinburne, Algernon Charles, 199, 242, 249
Swyft, Hugh, 125
Sydney, 37
Symcock, Thomas, 216
Syracuse, 112

"Tables," 184
Taine, Hippolyte, 194
Tamburlaine, 3, 4, 6, 7, 21, 23, 32, 35, 47, 48, 84, 86, 87, 88, 106, 107, 110, 114, 115, 130, 134, 171, 188-89, 199, 204; Cambridge traces, 7, 13, 22, 43; Canterbury traces, 14, 35, 97; date, 86; death scene, 94-95, 97; echoes *Dido*, 207, 219; editions, 142, 251, 253ff.; importance, 86-92; influence, 92, 147, 169, 219, 240, 242, 243-45, 247; printer of, 115; production, 78, 92-93, 146; sources, 9, 12, 47-48, 50, 66, 88, 94, 96-102, 148, 150, 205, 228, 235; success, 87-89, 93, 117, 170, 202; technique, 86, 87, 153-54, 225, 226
Tamerlane, Life of, 191
Tamerlane the Great, 92-93, 243
Taming of a Shrew, 117, 247
Taming of the Shrew, 117
Tanner, Thomas, 259
Tanners, 17
Tapestry, 242-43
Taylor, John, 92, 246
Techelles, 153, 225
Tempter, The, 249
Tents, 91
Terminus et Non Terminus, 51
Textual criticism, 114, 126
Thames, 73, 74, 75, 87
Theatres, 71; Blackfriars, 78; Cockpit, 143; Curtain, 78, 86, 126, 133; Fortune, 79, 86, 117; Globe, 79, 80, 209; Newington Butts, 80; Red Bull, 92, 156; Rose, 80-81; The Theatre, 78, 79, 80, 86, 87, 91, 105, 109, 124, 126, 133
Theatre of God's Judgment, 189
Theatrical handbooks, 193
Theatrical Intelligencer, 194
Theatrum Orbis Terrarum, 47
Theodore, Archbishop, 31
Theophilus, 112, 123
Theridamas, 88, 153, 219
Thompson, Paul, 211

Thornborough, John, 218
Thorpe, Thomas, 2, 231
"Thousand ships," 8, 107, 108, 116, 139, 206, 216, 242
Three Partes of Commentaries, 206
Throckmorton, Elizabeth, 160, 162
Thunderbolt of God's Wrath, 191
Tieck, Ludwig, 249
Timur Khan, 247
Timur Lenk, 88, 101-2
Tin mines, 159
Titus Andronicus, 241, 263
Tobacco, 166
Tocsain contre les Massacreurs, 206
Tottel's Miscellany, 212, 221
Tower of London, 74, 75, 128, 152, 160, 162, 163, 177, 215
Tragedy of Charles Duke of Biron, 203
Translations, *see* Lucan, Ovid
Trencharde, Sir George, 167
Trier, 111-12
Trig-Stirs, 82
Trinity College, Cambridge, 51, 52
Trinity Hall, Cambridge, 171
Tripoli, siege of, 150
Troilus and Cressida, 209, 239, 242
Troublesome Reign of King John, 198
Troy, *see* Helen
True History of George Scanderbage, 198
True Tragedy, 134, 149, 237, 241, 249
"Tumbling ending," 228-29
Turks, 47, 88, 93-94, 139, 150, 218, 245-46
Twelfth Night, 71
Two Gentlemen of Verona, 239
Two Merry Milkmaids, 248
Tybalt, 127
Tyburn, 132, 144-45

Umbarffeld, Richard, 18
University Wits, 84-85
Usumcasane, 153, 225
Usurers, *see* Misers
Utrecht, 68

Vaughan, William, 68, 192, 195, 196
Venetian diplomats, 149
Venus, 219
Venus and Adonis, 71, 261
Verges, 28
Vergil, 208, 221, 222, 236
Vergil, Polydor, 156
Verse-paragraphs, 227
Versification, 8, 85-86, 93, 109, 154, 171, 207, 220-31
Vice-Chancellor, 39, 40, 46, 53, 58, 59, 62, 66
Victoria and Albert Museum, 257
Victoria, Queen, 245, 261
Vienna, 119
Villain-hero, 140, 201, 242
Villegagnon, Nicholas de, 150
Virgin Mary, 112
Visor, William, 28
Vita Magni Tamerlanis, 98ff.
Voltaire, 188
Vowels, 224-25

Waldegrave, Robert, 233
Walsingham, Francis, 64, 65, 66, 67, 68, 69, 82, 145, 174, 176
Walsingham, Thomas, 4, 64, 65, 68, 82, 124, 158, 173-74, 175, 178, 180, 181, 184
Walter the Iester, 23
Walton, Izaak, 217, 218, 236
Warburton, John, 200
Warden, Lord, his players, 22, 76
Warner, Walter, 162, 163, 164

Warning for Fair Women, 205-6
Wars of Cyrus, 245
Warton, Thomas, 259
Warwickshire, 28
Washington, D.C., 257
Watch, *see* Constables
Watermen, 71, 73, 74, 92
Watling Street, 21
Watson, Thomas, 68, 72, 83, 124-33, 157, 174, 187, 221, 230, 231
Wayte, William, 125
Weavers, 242
Webster, John, 149, 243
Wedel, Leopold von, 73-74
Wellesley College Library, 257
Welsh, James, 67-68
Westgate, 14, 29
Westminster, 72
Whetcomb, Mistress, 166
Whistler, James McNeill, 84
Whitehall, 74, 142
Wilde, Oscar, 84
William and Mary, 193
Wills, 16-20
Winchester, Bishop of, 81
Winwood, Sir Ralph, 202-3
Witch of Edmonton, 248
Wits Treasury, 192
Wittemburg, University of, 58, 103, 192
Wolf, John, 215
Women Pleased, 246
Wood, Anthony à, 164, 192, 193
"Wormall," 77
Wortels, *see* Ortelius
Wounds of Civil War, 245, 246
Wren, Sir Christopher, 72
Wright, Richard, 258
Wyatt, Thomas, 220, 235
Wyck, Mr., 23
Wyld, Stephen, 129

Yale University Library, 257
Yardley, book dealer, 258
Yeomans, Joan, 176
Yeomans, William, 176
Ylderim Bajazeth, *see* Bajazeth
York, Duke of, 119
Yorkshire Tragedy, 206

Zabina, 89, 90
Zenocrate, 4, 88, 89, 90, 91-92, 94-96, 97, 99, 101, 153,
Zoroas, Death of, 221-22
Zurich Zentralbibliothek, 262

WASHINGTON SQUARE PRESS CLASSICS

A new and growing series presenting distinguished literary works in an inexpensive, well-designed format

Anthologies of Short Stories, Poetry and Essays Now in Washington Square Press Editions

CHAUCER, GEOFFREY, *The Canterbury Tales.* Translated by R. M. Lumiansky, Preface by Mark Van Doren. Illustrated. W 567 (60¢)

CRANE, STEPHEN, *Maggie and Other Stories.* Selected and with an Introduction by Austin McC. Fox. W 133 (45¢)

FROST, ROBERT, *New Enlarged Anthology of Poems.* Edited by Louis Untermeyer. Illustrated. W 556 (60¢)

HAWTHORNE, NATHANIEL, *Twice-Told Tales and Other Short Stories.* Introduction by Quentin Anderson. W 580 (60¢)

MILLAY, EDNA ST. VINCENT, *Collected Lyrics.* Introduction by Norma Millay. W 550 (60¢)

MILLAY, EDNA ST. VINCENT, *Collected Sonnets.* Introduction by Norma Millay. W 551 (60¢)

PETERSON, HOUSTON, ed., *Great Essays.* W 598 (60¢)

POE, EDGAR ALLAN, *Great Tales and Poems.* W 246 (45¢)

SHAKESPEARE, WILLIAM, *The Complete Sonnets, Songs and Poems.* Edited by Henry W. Simon. W 131 (45¢)

SPEARE, M. EDMUND, ed., *A Pocket Book of Short Stories.* W 255 (45¢)

SPEARE, M. EDMUND, ed., *The Pocket Book of Verse.* W 241 (45¢)

WILLIAMS, OSCAR, ed., *Immortal Poems of the English Language.* W 553 (60¢)

WILLIAMS, OSCAR, ed., *The Pocket Book of Modern Verse.* W 554 (60¢)

If your bookseller does not have the titles you want, you may order them by sending retail price, plus 10¢ per book for postage and handling, to: Mail Service Department, Washington Square Press, Inc., 1 West 39th Street, New York 18, N.Y. Please enclose check or money order—not responsible for orders containing cash.

WSP-1 (B)

928.2
M349b